NEW MEXICO STORIES

NEW MEXICO STORIES
*Truths, Tales and Mysteries
Along the Río Grande*

A Memoir

DAVID ROYBAL

SANTA FE

<>
<>
<>

© 2019 by David Roybal
All Rights Reserved

No part of this book may be reproduced in any form or by any electronic or mechanical means including information storage and retrieval systems without permission in writing from the publisher, except by a reviewer who may quote brief passages in a review.

Sunstone books may be purchased for educational, business, or sales promotional use. For information please write: Special Markets Department, Sunstone Press, P.O. Box 2321, Santa Fe, New Mexico 87504-2321.

Book design › R. Ahl
Printed on acid-free paper

Library of Congress Cataloging-in-Publication Data

Names: Roybal, David, 1952- author.
Title: New Mexico stories : truths, tales and mysteries from along the Rio Grande : a memoir / by David Roybal.
Description: Santa Fe, New Mexico : Sunstone Press, [2019] | Includes bibliographical references. | Some sections appeared in author's previous books or newspaper columns in The Santa Fe New Mexican or Albuquerque Journal.
Identifiers: LCCN 2019019652 | ISBN 9781632932679 (pbk. : alk. paper)
Subjects: LCSH: New Mexico--Biography--Anecdotes. | New Mexico--History--Anecdotes. | Roybal, David, 1952- | Journalists--New Mexico--Biography.
Classification: LCC CT250 .R69 2019 | DDC 978.9--dc23
LC record available at https://lccn.loc.gov/2019019652

WWW.SUNSTONEPRESS.COM
SUNSTONE PRESS / POST OFFICE BOX 2321 / SANTA FE, NM 87504-2321 /USA
(505) 988-4418 / ORDERS ONLY (800) 243-5644 / FAX (505) 988-1025

Dedication

For Jim

Jim Maldonado would have spent a full career reporting aggressively, passionately on the scourges of our times had he, himself, not fallen victim to their grip.

Contents

Preface / 9

1 / Scorned Ancestors in a Coveted Territory / 12

2 / Americanizing Hispanics of Far-Flung Communities / 31

3 / On the Medals of War and the Stories of Life / 51

4 / Mysteries and Other Influences on Youths / 75

5 / A Career Launched on 25 Cents per Inch and a Quest for Equal Opportunity / 88

6 / The "King Tiger" Springs into Futile Battle for Land Grants / 105

7 / New Mexicans Persevere Amid Poverty's Relentless Grip / 126

8 / Fugitives in the Night and Secrets of a Federal Government / 148

9 / Spirits in the Hills / 166

10 / The Political Reign of Emilio Naranjo / 170

11 / Changing Santa Fé / 193

12 / When Talk of Diversity Moves Beyond Tourism Campaigns / 220

13 / A Fuller Meaning of National Security / 235

14 / A Stench at the Back Door / 256

15 / The Irritant of Ethics Reform / 269

16 / The Treacherous Trail of DWI / 287

17 / Love and Despair Among New Mexico's Young / 295

18 / The King Who Would be Governor / 314

19 / They All Had Plans Yet Here We Are / 346

20 / New Mexicans and Our Neighbors to the South / 379

21 / Back Home in Cundiyó / 389

Bibliography and Newspaper Articles / 392

Preface

New Mexico stories sometimes can have their origins in surprising places.

I began developing a wonderful friendship a decade ago with a *hotelero* in the small Mexican village of Rincón de Guayabitos along the Pacific Coast about an hour north of Puerto Vallarta.

Francisco Javier Alonzo Sánchez pulled me aside one day after seeing me walk across his hotel's garden *patio*.

"*Mi* David, I have something for you," he told me in Spanish.

He handed me a large silver coin, one of a handful just like it that one of his employees recently gave to him.

The employee's husband, said Javier, was among laborers who had been working for months on a new, major highway intended to speed traffic along the coast near Guayabitos.

Excavating the packed, rocky ground not far from old railroad tracks was a major part of the project. It was in that digging that the hotel employee's husband came upon a small bundle of silver-colored coins.

They were Chinese coins buried in the Mexican dirt about 800 miles from the U.S. border and 7,000 miles from the nearest village on the Chinese map.

"They're probably not worth anything, and that's why they were given to me," Sánchez said. "Still, I'd like you to have one, something so that you might remember us. And who knows? Perhaps you'll discover later that here, today, you became a very rich man," he said playfully, alluding to the coin's possible antique value.

I looked closely at the coin later. Chinese characters are on one side; English lettering on the flip side. The denomination was listed on the English side: one tael. Origin: Shensi Province. A dragon occupies most of the surface on the English side of the coin.

Taels generally are more than 100 years old. Apparently, only a few Chinese provinces minted taels after 1900. Today's common value of a tael is about one U.S. dollar. But old, genuine taels can be extremely valuable, according to internet searches.

Therein is the catch.

Those same internet searches tell that counterfeiting of taels was rampant in China during the late 1800s into the 1900s. Counterfeit or not, how did taels wind up buried in the Mexican ground alongside old railroad tracks?

Well, the Southern Pacific Railroad of Mexico relied heavily on Chinese laborers during intense railroad construction in Mexico's northwestern states between 1880 and 1910. One of those laborers must have stashed a pocket full of taels to be retrieved later only to be denied the recovery by injury, death, flight or some other unexpected twist of fate. They wound up a century or so later in hands of a Mexican laborer who knew not what to do with them so he apparently allowed his wife to give them away.

Once back in New Mexico, I was determined to learn whether my tael was the real thing or a so-called fantasy coin. Who might know? Ah, the China Kitchen!

Chinese-Americans for years have operated the China Kitchen on Riverside Drive in my former hometown of Española, which I still visit multiple times a week. I didn't know the proprietors well, but their restaurant in northern New Mexico seemed like a logical first stop in my pursuit of information about a Chinese coin unexpectedly unearthed from Mexican soil.

The coin was passed among several people inside the restaurant who alternately focused on the coin's side with Chinese characters. They concluded the coin might be quite valuable, indeed, because characters referred to a leader long gone from China.

My research continued and eventually a very simple test led to an anticlimactic ending: A magnet would not stick to a real silver coin. If the magnet stuck, the coin was likely made of brass—counterfeit.

The small magnet I dislodged from my refrigerator door stuck.

But the coin's value was not all gone. My dear friend, Javier, must have concluded that I would mine some kind of story from his gift to me; it's how I would remember him and his Mexican compatriots. He and his beloved seaside village would fit in someplace among New Mexico stories. He was right. I've taken his story with me to multiple engagements.

I've had stories, like Javier's, simply dropped onto my lap over the years. I've pursued others into dark corners where I was not supposed to be. I've been invited onto well-tended Mexican *patios* in the shadows of the *Sierra Madres* and into small, unassuming homes along foothills of the southern Rockies.

My grandfather's own four-room adobe home in northern New Mexico, the one without flush toilets or running water of any sort, in time would connect telephonically to the White House and other points in Washington, DC, for stories to be collected and constructed for delivery across the globe.

Two U.S. presidents, one Spanish king, governors, congressmen and countless people just trying to get by are among those who have responded—kindly and otherwise—to my visits and queries.

In fact, early into this project it became clear that this would not be a traditional memoir. The book wouldn't be about me. It would be about so many of the people and situations that I came upon during more than fifty years of "hitting the bricks," as one superior liked to put it. Another man prone to softer terminology professed that "taking the pulse of the community" was a big part of any good day's work.

Under those definitions, I've had more than a few decent days. Much of the time was spent as a newspaperman. But there were other responsibilities beginning at an early age that had me out among the people. It is with considerable joy that I share in these following pages some of what I collected along the way.

I end some chapters of this book with entries that I've titled "From the Roybal Files," which are segments from my previous books or newspaper columns that appeared in *The Santa Fe New Mexican* or *Albuquerque Journal* that track with surrounding text.

Unless otherwise noted, I took most of photographs and others are from family collections.

—David Roybal

1
SCORNED ANCESTORS IN A COVETED TERRITORY

Growing up my grandmother, Juanita Tafoya, likely never knew what many people in high places of the country's populated East thought about her, her family and their fellow inhabitants of the recently acquired New Mexico Territory. If she had, it might have made her crawl into a hole outside her home below the majestic Truchas Peaks and forget entirely about contributing to the world around her.

The United States took possession of the territory in the 1840s in the midst of a two-year war with Mexico. Spanish and then Mexican flags had flown over the territory since 1598. It was part of Mexico's northern half until the U.S. war against Mexico. U.S. President James K. Polk and other

José Albino and Juanita Tafoya Roybal helped define the early profile of northern New Mexico.

General Stephen Watts Kearny in 1846 led his Army of the West into Las Vegas, New Mexico, to claim the territory for the United States. Kearny delivered his remarks just a few steps from this central section of the community's Old Town.

expansionists considered it to be our country's manifest destiny to possess the territory and other land extending to the Pacific Ocean. California was coveted most among lands extending from the edge of the Great Plains to the blue Pacific.

General Stephen Watts Kearny in August 1846 said he came with good intentions while leading his Army of the West into Las Vegas, New Mexico, to take possession of the territory for the United States. Good intentions aside, he warned the populace that opponents of the U.S. occupation would be hung.

With the New Mexico Territory, of course, came its people, and that displeased many. A large part of the Anglo-American influx in and around the New Mexico Territory during the mid 1800s was middle class, wrote journalist and historian Carey McWilliams. What they found as they moved into the territory, he wrote, were almost entirely Mexican lower classes, seven-eighths of whom were illiterate. From the beginning, Anglo-Americans of a predominantly Protestant nation developed extremely negative opinions, McWilliams wrote.

To be sure, the New Mexico Territory through the 1800s did not resemble images of America that were portrayed during the period by Thomas Moran and other Hudson River School painters of the East.

Historian Rubén Sálaz Márquez tells of an 1847 report about the territory in the *Missouri Republican* that read: "A country with but few exceptions is inhabited by ignorant, dishonest, treacherous men..." Virtue among women was said to be scarce. Are these people "worthy of protection from the Indians?" the newspaper asked.

General William Tecumseh Sherman concluded that natives of the New Mexico Territory were of an inferior race lacking "cultivation." Sherman, by some accounts, suggested in Washington, DC, that the United States declare a second war against Mexico and force it to take back all of New Mexico.

Juanita Tafoya's parents, Juan de Dios Tafoya and Rafaelita López, entered the world while New Mexico was still in its early transition as a U.S. territory.

Their generation and that of their parents, more than daughter Juanita, would have been the target of rampant scorn coming from the East, where Anglo-Saxon standards dominated. But disdain was still thick when Grandma Juanita became a part of New Mexico families in 1884.

The Atchison, Topeka and Santa Fé Railroad had arrived in New Mexico just five years earlier. Las Vegas, on the western edge of the Great Plains, was the first town it encountered. Las Vegas was dominated by *Hispanos* so the railroad decided to organize development of a new adjacent community. The *Las Vegas Optic* sprung from the new town and quickly proclaimed that East Las Vegas was an American town to be governed only by Americans, meaning people who came from the East.

"It was absolutely set out that way and nobody made any bones about it," said Jesús López, a Las Vegas lawyer and historian who more than a century later spoke of the times with distaste.

Grandma Juanita was born in the tiny mountain community of Truchas at the feet of the southern Rockies and little more than 100 miles north of Las Vegas. Family accounts say she was born into a family that was relatively rich in land and sheep and blessed with pretty daughters.

Truchas was one of the outlying communities that developed to the east of Santa Cruz de la Cañada, which in 1695 followed Santa Fé as an officially designated Spanish villa in the territory. Lesley Poling-Kempes tells how the capital of Santa Fé, 25 miles to the south of Santa Cruz along the Río Grande, was reserved for ranking Spanish officials and military dignitaries along with their families. Santa Cruz was designated for soldiers and settlers. As crowding mounted in Santa Cruz, Tafoyas were among Hispanic families that settled in new communities further east along foothills of the Rockies' Sangre de Cristo range.

Tiny Truchas in 1837, incredibly, became a base for rebels in New Mexico's Río Arriba district amid internal fighting over ruling authority and tax impositions. This was during the final decade of the territory's

Cipriano Romero and Marcelo Romero waited for rain in Truchas to break the summer drought of 1993.

Mexican period. Instability characterized Mexican government since the country's independence from Spain in 1821, and people of the New Mexico Territory were among those who suffered from what at best was Mexico City's inattentiveness, abandonment at worst.

By the time of the U.S. war with Mexico beginning in 1846, people in the New Mexico Territory must have thought that life couldn't get much worse under a new government. Few could have anticipated that it would take well more than half a century for them to be taken in as full citizens of a country that coveted their land and resources.

Refuge On a Storybook Farm

Juanita Tafoya emerged from it all as the grandmother I never knew. She gave birth to my Father, Amos, in 1923. He was her last surviving child and they, themselves, barely got to know one another. My Dad's Father, José Albino Roybal, and Mother, Juanita, both grew up in the Truchas area. Grandpa Albino died in 1949 three years before I was born.

My closest ties to my Father's ancestors developed amid a work-driven environment that enveloped Grandma Juanita's elder sister, Trinidad, and her

Henry Romero of Truchas irrigated fields in 1993, relying on a small irrigation ditch fed by water brought down from the high mountains by *La Acequia de La Sierra*. Spanish settlers used picks and shovels to carve *la acequia* through granite and other obstacles of the lower Rockies about 250 years ago.

husband, Ramos Barela, barely half a mile from where I was raised in San Pedro. San Pedro is little more than a large neighborhood of mostly middle-and low-income homes situated along a narrow two-lane state road near the eastern banks of the Río Grande. Only parts of it are within Española city limits. It is a couple of miles from Santa Cruz and less than 20 miles from Truchas.

Trinidad Tafoya Barela and husband, Ramos, lived on one of the last large farms to be found in the Española Valley. It was storybook in character, but not large in the same sense as farms 300 miles down river in Las Cruces and the Mesilla Valley. The Barela farm was not agribusiness. It was a family enterprise with essentially a husband and wife plus their children at its core. It relied on one tractor, hoes and shovels, pruners, wheel barrows, buckets, canvass bags plus human hands and backs that were well-accustomed to tiring by day's end.

Two large cottonwood trees just inside the farm's fence provided immense shade for parked vehicles and workers during the growing seasons. Within that shade were sheds filled with food, grain for livestock, tools, supplies and pesticides. Cats ran around at will. The house with its pitched roof of corrugated tin stood to one side of the trees. Wooden pens for several milk cows and sheep were at the opposite side.

A huge field of grass and alfalfa reached well beyond the corrals as if aiming to reach moist ground extending from the Río Grande. A garden of lilacs, hollyhocks, dahlias, gladiolas and poppies encircled much of the stuccoed house. Just beyond the kitchen and back entrance to the home was a substantial vegetable garden, furrowed for irrigation from an *acequia* fed by water diverted from the small Río Santa Cruz, a tributary of the Río Grande. An orchard of apples, peaches and other fruit ran the length of the vegetable garden further away from the large adobe home.

Trinidad Tafoya Barela was my Father's aunt. Much as she served as a sort of surrogate grandmother for me, she was the closest thing to a mother that my Father ever knew. Respectfully, I referred to her and her husband as *tía* and *tío* as my parents did.

Tía Trinidad, no stranger to work outdoors, had an even-greater presence in the kitchen of her home. Protected by a simple apron, she seemed to be forever standing at her large wood-burning stove or at the wooden table that so often was covered with freshly baked bread or large pans and buckets filled with fresh milk strained through cloth of emptied flour sacks. One or two cats frequently rested in the warmth and comfort under the stove.

The aroma of coffee was often in the air, coffee that was served in cups crafted of thick brown ceramic, looking utilitarian, not decorative. They reflected evidence of long use and all but asserted that they had been made specifically for that home, for that family of workers and its occasional guests.

If *Tía* Trinidad was content to move through her daily responsibilities quietly for the most part, *Tío* Ramos was far more overt, prone to joking, riddles, laughter, and not at all shy about calling attention to his ventures big and small. His assertions, to be believed, routinely had to be cut in half. He was still alive beyond middle age and able to tend to the farm's work, he told me once with a straight face, only because of a button on his shirt that kept a bullet from piercing his chest years earlier.

Tío Ramos, too, was a grass-roots politician. In 1937 he secured for daughter, Gabriela, the position of deputy county clerk for Río Arriba after successfully supporting the Democratic Party candidate for county clerk. That story is recounted in the memoirs of a cousin, retired university professor Arturo Madrid (*In the Country of Empty Crosses*, Trinity University Press, San Antonio, Texas, 2012). Arturo is one of Gabriela's sons and spent formative years around the courthouse in Tierra Amarilla following his mother's appointment to the clerk's office.

Tío Ramos for years worked as an official justice of the peace and easily mixed stories about the laws with those of his farm. He was a longtime *mayordomo*, or irrigation boss, of the *acequia* that was relied upon to carry waters diverted from the Río Santa Cruz not only to his substantial farm but to the rest of Lower San Pedro as well.

He wore his shirts buttoned to the neck. Elastic bands above the elbows were used to control movement of the shirts' long sleeves. If the bands drew a little added attention to his presence, then so be it.

I don't know if it was the politician in my *tío* that made him a good salesman or if it was the other way around. Either way, he had the gift of gab. He could convince you that you needed something even if you started that day thinking you were perfectly content with what you had.

Lessons While Riding On Firestones

More than once I accompanied my *Tío* Ramos on seasonal trips that he made up the Río Chama Valley to sell fruits and vegetables as they ripened on his farm. He found ready takers all along the way, buyers whom he cultivated over the years with savory talk about how he grew some of the best food in New Mexico. Good food it was, to be sure. If it wasn't some of the best in New Mexico, there was no one around to prove *Tío* Ramos wrong so sales were usually brisk in communities up and down the valley reaching to just below the Colorado border.

Word of *tío's* presence in the community would spread as if in a breeze that reached into every home, roadside bar and even the county courthouse where years earlier his daughter, deputy county clerk Gabriela, upset her boss in an election to become Río Arriba's first woman county clerk.

Screen doors would swing open as women in aprons stepped out holding small buckets, pans or paper bags in which to carry away purchases that they made along the back of *tío's* truck. Men clasping shovels—or cans of beer—would step up to the truck to barter.

Proper greetings started most of the encounters. But easy conversation, arguably bordering at times on harmless flirtation, was not uncommon as business unfolded between *tío* and women outside his truck. Joking and *cuentos* told with flair colored the business among men. My uncle, in most ways that mattered, was among his people and all were at ease.

As *tío* secured the sales, he would direct me in a firm voice to fill some of the orders while I stooped at the back of the truck and moved amid containers of fragrant apples, peaches, pears, plums, cucumbers, melons, chiles, corn, carrots and anything else that my uncle was able to tie down before leaving San Pedro.

Tío Ramos had become a familiar site amid steeply pitched tin roofs in Ensenada, Tierra Amarilla and Chama. Prior to heading north on his trips, he would rise hours before sunup at his farmhouse and step into the dark morning to make one final inspection of his tightly packed cargo. He checked the snugness of tarps that he draped the previous day over produce that rose in small mounds over buckets, bushels and boxes of varying sizes.

Tío would make his way around the truck while frogs croaked loudly throughout his farm and in swamps along the Río Grande just beyond. As he worked outdoors, dim yellow light beamed from the kitchen at the other end of the farmhouse where *Tía* Trinidad stood over the wood-burning stove, tending to coffee and breakfast to be consumed prior to the trip.

I remember climbing into *tío's* white three-quarter ton flatbed Ford on a cool, dark morning moments before Firestone tires began rolling for one such trip. I couldn't have been more than ten, and it must have been my first time at my uncle's side as he steered his truck northward because I recall being dismayed by his unusually slow driving.

I had fallen asleep, probably before the truck crept past the old Bond and Willard store on Española's west side approaching the outskirts of town. It was still dark when I awoke. A few lights could be seen in the distance. *"Es Tierra Amarilla?"* I asked my uncle, employing the little Spanish that I knew.

"No, *mi hijo*," he replied. "*Este es Abiquiú*."

We had traveled little more than 20 miles. We had another 45 to go before seeing Tierra Amarilla.

Having sold out of produce at the end of one of our trips, *Tío* Ramos pulled into a small restaurant in Chama so we could grab a meal before returning home. As I chewed on a hamburger and fries, a white cap hanging on a horizontal rack of hooks caught my attention. My uncle visited with others around the wooden counter while he ate.

As he did, my admiration of the white cap grew. It wasn't a regular cap of those days crafted of unformed cotton. A thin layer of foam had been sewn into the front of the cap so that its form remained unbothered as it hung on the hook. The visor was curved slightly and evenly. The cap was not only white, it was clean, seemingly free of perspiration from where I sat.

When the time came to leave, I made it a point of walking a couple of steps behind my uncle. That was probably his first clue. Kids, back then for sure, were expected to walk in front of supervising eyes on such occasions. It not only guarded against mischief, it ensured that nobody was left behind.

Once outdoors, my uncle made as if he were checking on his tarps and empty containers at the back of the truck before climbing inside the cab. There he must have seen on my lap the white cap that I had lifted off its hook on my way out of the café.

Tío Ramos didn't say a word, but he stepped back out of the truck, shut his door and walked back into the café. I saw him through the window talking to no one in particular inside and pointing briefly to the rack where the white cap had hung. He then walked up to one of the men who had been listening, reached for his wallet and handed the man some money.

I saw my uncle pay for our food before we walked out of the café so I knew he wasn't repeating that obligation. He didn't say a word about the cap when he got back into the truck; not a word about it on the long drive home. I concluded that he went back into the café to disclose that his young nephew had swiped somebody's white cap. If the owner wanted it back, my uncle likely offered, he would retrieve it from the truck and return it. But if the owner was willing to part with it, *Tío* Ramos probably said he was prepared to pay a fair price.

I got to keep the cap but was left to guess about what was said inside the café. More importantly, I was left to sit in my own guilt on the 85-

mile drive back home. If the drive north two days earlier seemed long, the return trip appeared endless. Left to stew in one's own guilt was a common teaching tool within my aunt's and uncle's adopted religion, I would come to learn.

CATHOLICS AND LIQUOR GOT SIMILAR TREATMENT

Tío Ramos and *Tía* Trinidad together left Catholicism for the Presbyterian faith in 1921. My aunt embraced her new church with considerably more enthusiasm than my uncle, by all accounts. Her change of faiths was important because it apparently influenced similar conversions later by my grandmother Juanita and grandfather José Albino. My Father, Amos, was born to the couple in 1923, the same year that his parents became Presbyterians.

Cousin Arturo Madrid says there are different stories about what sparked the conversions. He wrote in his memoirs that *Tía* Trinidad, who loved to sing, long enjoyed listening to the protestants move from hymn to hymn during their evening and Sunday services. *Tía* Trinidad told Arturo that her family lived near the mission of *protestantes* in Truchas and that she had been encouraged to sing at the mission school. Her mother, who came from the López family of Catholic *santeros* in nearby Córdova, feared losing my aunt to the *protestantes* and would not permit thoughts of conversion.

"Grandpa tells a different story," Arturo wrote. "He says they left the Catholic Church because of a falling out with their priest. As my mother remembers it, the break came when her brother George died shortly after being born and Grampa asked the priest to toll the bell. The priest refused and berated my grandparents for sending their children to the mission school.

"Uncle Ray gives a different twist. According to him, the priest demanded twenty-five dollars to say Mass, an exorbitant sum at the time."

Yet another story was shared by a relative from *Tío* Ramos' side of the family. "In *Tía* Leonardita's version, it was Grandma's brother Pula Tafoya who had died, and the priest's refusal to say Mass had to do with the fact that Pula had married outside the church," wrote Arturo.

Indeed, there was an intense rivalry between the Catholic and protestant churches in rural northern New Mexico beginning in the mid-1800s when Presbyterians established churches, schools and clinics in the region. Historians tell of a shortage of Catholic priests during the period. Presbyterians stepped in to fill the void.

Tía Trinidad, the convert, became a bit of a fanatic. She was known to assert that Catholics were nothing short of the enemy.

Arturo Madrid tells this story in his memoirs about one of Ramos Barela's brothers: "Only one other of Grandfather's brothers visited the farm, though he was not, I sensed, a welcome guest. *Tío* Epifanio was received in the small *portal* that sheltered the entrances to the two formal rooms of the farmhouse. On the rare visits, Grandma pulled two chairs out of the kitchen and into the *portal*, one for *Tío* Epifanio and one for Grandpa. She then retreated into the house, emerging only when Grandpa called out that Epifanio was leaving. I came to understand that Grandma associated Catholics with liquor and preferred that neither enter her home."

Another member of the family suggested that Epifanio was kept out of the San Pedro farmhouse because he had stolen a relative's wife and left him to raise the couple's baby on his own. Surely, my aunt would have concluded that no self-respecting *protestante* could condone such things.

On Courtships and Marriage

Serving as a sort of surrogate for the paternal grandmother that I never knew, *Tía* Trinidad from her San Pedro farm offered glimpses of what Grandma Juanita might have been like. But it almost didn't turn out that way. There might never have been a Barela farm. And if there had been, I never would have come to know of it because *Tía* Trinidad would not have been a part of it. Fate nearly took my aunt to El Valle, a mountain village miles north of Truchas, far enough from San Pedro that I very likely would have seen very little of her, if at all.

Arturo Madrid tells this story about his great-uncle, Pedro Romero: "(He) left home at an early age to roam the world, *a corer mundo*, as the *ancianos* say. *Tío* Pedro returned to his village of El Valle some years later, ready to take up his responsibilities, which included getting married and having a family. When he first saw my grandmother Trinidad or where he met her is lost to us, but not the fact that he was smitten enough to send his parents to Las Truchas to ask for her hand in marriage. Whether his parents didn't know whose hand they were requesting or were dealt a Tafoya-Lopez sleight of hand, *Tío* Pedro ended up marrying Trinidad's oldest sister, Senovia. Later in life, and probably out of *Tía* Senovia's earshot, he was heard to say, *"Fui por Trinidad, y me quedé con Senovia."* He asked for Trinidad but ended up with Senovia."

My money says it was a sleight of hand that led to the eventual pairing. My great-grandparents likely concluded that it was best to push their eldest daughter along, recognizing that Trinidad had more time on her side for courtship and marriage.

Courtship in time came for another one of the Tafoya-López sisters in Truchas. Juanita, soon after statehood in 1912, married José Albino Roybal. The couple had ten children: Adela, Aurora, José Arquín, Rafaleita, Victoriano, Inez, Porfirio, Ricardo, Lucano and Amos.

"Gentlemen Soldiers" and a Pauper's Grave

Roybals in New Mexico can be traced back to the period of the 1680 Pueblo Indian revolt against Spanish colonizers. Captain Ignacio Roybal was among soldiers who arrived from Spain to join Don Diego de Vargas near El Paso del Norte and participate in the reclaiming of New Mexico in 1692. He was among the so-called Hundred Gentlemen Soldiers From Spain. (I'll not ask any of my Indian friends how gentlemanly those soldiers truly were.)

Ignacio Roybal was born around 1673 in Galicia in the northwestern region of Spain. The origin of the Roybal name is said to be in the municipality of Moraña, Galicia.

With New Mexico back in Spanish hands, Governor Pedro Rodríguez Cubero granted Ignacio Roybal land near current-day Sena Plaza just east of Santa Fé's central Plaza. Roybal within a few years also acquired land about 15 miles to the northwest in what today is known as Jacona near banks of the Río Grande.

Spanish Captain Ignacio Roybal was granted acreage near the Río Grande north of Santa Fé after joining Don Diego DeVargas to reclaim lands following the 1680 Pueblo Revolt. His old home makes up part of what is now Rancho Jacona, a guest ranch off State Road 502.

Ignacio Roybal is said to have been one of New Mexico's leading citizens during the first half of the 18th Century, having held various municipal offices and reportedly serving as High Sheriff of the Spanish Inquisition. Land granted to Roybal near the Río Grande was later determined to belong to Pueblo Indians but Jacona for years was known as Los Roybales.

Three centuries after Ignacio Roybal began making his mark in New Mexico I engaged in small talk with former New Mexico state historian, Stan Hordes, while having lunch at Felipe's Tacos in Santa Fé.

"Do you have any relatives around Jacona," Hordes wanted to know.

"No, none that I'm aware of," I replied.

Hordes then assured me that all Roybals in New Mexico could trace their ancestry to Jacona and the Pojoaque Valley.

Roybals had settled in Río Arriba County near Santa Cruz by the early 1800s and soon became a part of the familial mix in Chimayó among Trujillos, Ortegas, Medinas, Vigils and others. The 1904 wedding of Eulogia Roybal and Encarnación Trujillo "was an extravaganza for its time," wrote Patricia Trujillo-Oviedo of Chimayó

José Albino Roybal's marriage to Juanita Tafoya about a decade later apparently occurred amid a considerably quieter celebration.

My paternal grandparents promptly began raising a family in Truchas. Hard times were unshakable companions in Truchas and other outlying communities. Men had to leave for months at a time every year to work mines or herd sheep in Colorado, Utah, Wyoming or Montana. Women stayed behind to give birth to children, tending to the newborns and others until husbands returned to the inescapable work inside and outside their homes. Dreaded ailments, like whooping cough, could claim multiple members of the same family before finishing its sweep through a community.

Hard times claimed more than one member of my paternal grandparents' family. By the time I came into the world in 1952, only my Father and four of his siblings were alive: Adela, Inez, Victoriano and Lucano.

Adela lived with her own family in a frame house overlooking the railroad tracks and the Colorado River in Glenwood Springs, Colorado. Inez ran a tiny store out of the front room of her family's small home just off State Road 76 winding through Chimayó. Victoriano repaired timepieces out of his Owl grocery and liquor store on St. Francis Drive in Santa Fé. He and his family had a modern home not far from the Governor's Mansion in the city's northern foothills. Lucano, a divorcee, had soured on most women, coughed many times each day as a result of too much time spent working in coal mines and lived alone in the dark basement of a modest house in Helper, Utah.

Grandmother Juanita must have known that she couldn't shield her children from all hardships but she undoubtedly hoped that they could be spared ostracism and other cruel injustices that she herself experienced after her mother, Rafaelita, died in 1919.

Juan de Dios Tafoya took a second wife following the death of his first. According to family lore, wrote Arturo Madrid, Juanita, Trinidad and other siblings did not get along with the new wife, Pula Mondragón. "Matters became even more complicated when (their father) died," Arturo wrote. "The widowed stepmother inherited all the properties and then frittered them away."

Juanita, Trinidad and their siblings ended up dispossessed, as the story goes.

Grandma Juanita had no way of knowing that cruelties very similar to hers—and even worse—were about to strike within her own household.

My Father, Amos, did not talk much about his childhood in Truchas. In his later years, though, he'd allow discussions to explore times that he spent harvesting firewood and *vigas* with my Grandpa Albino from the countryside around their home. He'd tell of riding out in a horse-drawn wagon and then returning to block the wood with a long two-man saw that he and his father worked together. "We had some good times," is as far as my Father would go.

Dad shared no recollections of time spent with his Mother. He had none. He was just two months past his third birthday when his Mother died.

Grandpa Albino was working in coal mines of Leadville, Colorado, in the late autumn of 1926. Grandma Juanita was with him as winter approached. It's not clear whether my Father was with his parents at the time or if he had been left temporarily with elder siblings or other relatives in Truchas.

There is no record of the illness that grasped Grandma Juanita while in Leadville. Whatever the ailment, its grip was fatal. Born into a proud and accomplished family in New Mexico, she was treated like a transient in Leadville and buried in a pauper's grave. My Father never knew where.

Memories Best Left Alone

Grandpa Albino in time married another woman and what followed for my Father in Truchas, from all indications, was misery. Again, my Father said very little about those times, but as he grew enough to record memories, he must have yearned for the childhood that had escaped him. He was punished severely by his stepmother and apparently was forced to wear dresses as punishment. He was fed poorly, made to feel unwelcome in his own home and eventually was pushed out to live with relatives, according to stories that I was able to piece together from him and others in Truchas.

As my four siblings and I grew through adolescence and our teens, Truchas and its surrounding hills were often the destination for picnics or harvesting firewood. Truchas seemed like the natural pick. It had been Dad's home. It was the environment that Dad knew best.

Each time that we drove through the village, we inevitably passed the flat-roof adobe house where my Father spent his first years. It was unoccupied just off the two-lane road, separated from traffic by neglected strands of barbed wire. Not once during our trips through Truchas did my Father offer to park his pickup and walk us up to the house, to peer through the windows or jiggle the screen door. We had no idea what was inside.

Decades later, I pointedly asked around Truchas about the house and its owners of the time. David Romero, who lives across the road from grandpa's old house, said it was owned by a couple from out of state. They come in for a couple of weeks every summer, otherwise the house is left alone, he said.

I gave Romero my phone numbers and asked that he call me the next time the couple returned to the house. I hurried up the hill when the call came months later and was graciously given a tour of the small Truchas house. It was nothing like what I expected. It was mostly unfurnished. Plaster over adobe walls was crumbling. Floors were unattended. A back room showed evidence where livestock apparently had been able to come in. The warmth and understated comfort that embraces people in many homes of northern New Mexico's rural communities was nowhere to be found.

Owners kindly agreed to let me bring my Father up from San Pedro so that he could take a look inside the house. I told them it likely would be just a day or two before I returned.

I carried the news happily to San Pedro but to my surprise, Dad had no interest in going to the house. In turning down the offer, he didn't suggest that he would sleep on the idea or that, perhaps, we might go on another day when he had less to do. He said clearly that he had no desire to step inside the Truchas house again. He did not elaborate.

Still, I learned that day just how painful my Father's memories of his early years must have been.

Tía Trinidad had moved on to the next life by the time I was allowed to set foot in the house that her sister Juanita shared with Grandpa Albino. My aunt, who battled with epilepsy throughout her life, fell while working on a ladder at her farm and never recovered. It was suspected that a seizure led to the fall.

The beautiful farm and home that *Tía* Trinidad and *Tío* Ramos brought to life over a period of many years was condemned in the late 1970s by the City of Española, which wanted the property for its own use. Both my aunt and uncle had died by then. Arturo Madrid's parents assumed responsibility for the property and moved into the farmhouse.

But the City of Española needed a site for a new, bigger sewage treatment plant. At least one study concluded that the Barela property was best suited for the new facility that would treat the municipality's waste water. Gabriela and her husband waged an intense but futile battle to save the family home. Española's expansive treatment ponds today sprawl over land where corrals once held milk cows and alfalfa swayed in the breeze. The farmhouse and sheds were razed to be replaced by the city's animal shelter.

My good fortune was to have experienced so much of what likely characterized Grandma Juanita's view of the world and her own approach to life before it was all swept away as if it were history that need not be remembered.

From the Roybal Files...
The Santa Fe New Mexican, October 19, 2003
Commentary: A Ghost Story for Halloween

I was leaving Las Vegas just after nightfall the other day, taking the mountain route home, which waited about a hundred miles away on the other side of the Sangre de Cristos. The night was especially still as I approached Storrie Lake on the eastern outskirts of Las Vegas.

A receding moon reflected off still water of the lake, which drought had left at one of its lowest levels in years. The lake was in my rearview mirror when I saw what appeared to be the image of a horseman on a large white stallion walking knee-deep in the water. I slammed on the brakes and watched out of my window for several minutes before shifting into reverse and slowly, quietly rolling the car closer to the horse and its rider, now advancing in my direction.

I stood outside my car just a few feet from the lake and watched silently as the horseman came into clearer view. A small coyote had been drinking water at the lake's edge and darted out of sight as the horseman drew closer.

A disabling chill ran across my shoulders and down my spine. The man who had moved along in the moon's glow wore an old military uniform, everything in place—everything except his boots, for the rider had no feet. His horse stepped out of the water close enough to me that I could feel his warm breath. It was immediately evident that the animal's legs, too, ended at the ankles.

"You're the first one, you know," the man said, looking at me from atop his horse, "The first one to notice me here, or, at least the first one brave enough to come for a closer look."

Bravery had nothing to do with it. I couldn't describe the force that pulled me down to the lake's dry ringed edge.

"My name is Kearny, Stephen Watts Kearny. But I'm still partial to being called General," the man said.

Anyone familiar with New Mexico history has heard of the name, Kearny; of the man, too. Making every effort to be discreet, I glanced again at the man's legs and at those of his horse.

"I know of you, General. But you're a bit out of place, aren't you?" I said, hoping to draw out enough information that would tell me more about the figure before me, someone who claimed to have sprung from the 1800s.

"Not at all," the man replied. "Your question suggests that you know your history. But how close have you come to the spiritual world? The spiritual world has its own rules; its own way of dealing with you and the record you made for yourself as a mortal."

Spirits. I almost expected to hear the word because of what I was seeing.

"I know you as a prominent general of the Mexican War," I said, playing along but still not certain about whom I was really talking to or how I had gotten into this situation. "I know you as the man who made lofty promises and pretty serious threats on the Plaza in Las Vegas on your way to stripping Mexico of its claims to this territory."

"You said you wanted people of these parts to feel secure; you promised you would disturb not even a pepper while claiming the area for the United States."

The man atop the horse smiled. "Not a pepper nor an onion, is what I said. A poor choice of words in today's light, perhaps. Didn't seem to be back then. This used to be rough territory. Feelings weren't hurt so easily."

I was becoming convinced that I was truly talking to the brigadier general who commanded the U.S. western armies that conquered New Mexico and California during the Mexican War more than 150 years earlier.

The man broke out in laughter that poured out from deep within his chest.

"Rough territory, indeed," he said. "I'll never forget William Sherman's disdain for what he found. Old Tecumseh went back to Washington and all but insisted that we go to war with Mexico all over again so that we could force the Mexicans to take back every inch of this territory."

"Why, it was barely fit for human habitation," said the horseman. "A lot of whiskey, lot of shooting; lot of killing, too. Indians seemed to jump out from behind every rock. They stole women and children almost at will back then. I told the Mexicans who were here when I came that I'd protect them from all that; told them we wouldn't disturb a thing while we were here."

Talk there at the cool water's edge had turned increasingly to sensitive terrain. "What you told them in no uncertain terms was that you were here to take possession of what Mexico had secured for itself and extend over them the law of the United States," I said. "To my knowledge, the populace hadn't invited you, but you said you came as friends, not as enemies; as protectors, not as conquerors. You said you didn't expect the people here to take arms against their own, but you threatened to hang anyone who took arms against you."

The man tugged firmly on the reins in his hands as his horse stirred restlessly. "It was war, son," the horseman said. "For reasons of their own, our leaders in Washington wanted this land and it was my job to get it for them. You say a lot of things when you're fighting a war. You say it with authority and a straight face, even if you know that you're stomping on the truth. Separating people from their country and imposing your own authority is tough business."

"I did my part and now I must suffer my fate. My fate for eternity is to reappear in the old haunts of that Mexican War every time the U.S. of A. gets into new combat on other people's soil. I've never been clear about the purpose. I must admit, though, I cringe at some of the things I hear our leaders say these days about why they're creating battlefields on foreign soils."

Again, I found my eyes aiming in the direction of the man's legs, too scared to actually ask what was on my mind. I didn't have to.

"I lost my feet during the first Gulf War. My horse and I both did," the horseman said. "We were out one night amid the crumbling chimneys of nearby Fort Union when I heard President Bush—the daddy—say he was going to kick Saddam's butt. That man, Bush, was not a fighter and I said so right there amid the darkness around that old fort. If Saddam's butt gets kicked, I said, it'll be by men braver than Bush. Next thing I knew my feet were gone. My horse was punished, too. There's just no challenging the Commander in Chief, I guess; not even in the afterlife. I suppose I should have known that in my line of work."

I heard a coyote cry in the junipers just beyond the lake and took it as my signal to leave. Incredulous as ever, I began walking back toward my car parked alongside the road. But after only a few steps, I stopped and turned around for one last look. The horseman already had his back to me and once again was in the shallow lake astride his horse, leaning from side to side and peering into the ripples below. Without ever looking at me, he knew that I had turned around.

"It's got to be in here somewhere," he said. "With the water so low, now's the time to find it."

I knew immediately what he was searching for. Word is that descendants of the people who heard Kearny's threats and promises on the Plaza in Las Vegas more than a century and a half ago grew angry one day at the sight of the bronze plaque posted within the square to commemorate the U.S. general's proclamation. They supposedly ripped lose the plaque in the dead of night, drove with it for miles and tossed it deep into waters of Storrie Lake.

"Once I find it," the man said still loud enough for me to hear even from a distance, "I'm going to pay a surprise visit to the vandals, wherever they might be. Then I'm going to introduce them to the fear that comes when you violate an angry old general."

2
"Americanizing" Hispanics of Far-Flung Communities

Spain's *Duque de Veragua* in October 1991 got a glimpse of a tiny, tranquil northern New Mexico village named Cundiyó during a goodwill visit of territory that for centuries had been claimed but largely neglected by his country.

The slender man of soft features and easy manner is also known as Christopher Columbus XX. His renowned ancestor of the 15th Century thought he had come upon a New World when he set foot in the Americas.

The *Duque de Veragua* saw villages that resembled old Spain as he

Christopher Columbus XX (fourth from left) visited northern New Mexico communities in 1991 as Spain sought to cultivate goodwill on lands that once were part of a Spanish empire.

moved through Cundiyó, Córdova, Truchas and Las Trampas en route to meeting with Native-American artist R.C. Gorman and others in Taos.

Chimayó, Córdova and Truchas were far flung in the New Mexico Territory that had been governed by Spain and Mexico. But residents of Cundiyó nestled in piñon-studded hills between Chimayó and the Pojoaque Valley were isolated like few others. Chimayó, Córdova and Truchas at least were lined up in succession along a course leading higher into foothills of the Sangre de Cristos. Cundiyó sat alone as if intentionally isolated from that course along a little-used path of its own.

The Santo Domingo de Cundiyó Land Grant was approved in the mid-1700s. Settler Joseph Isidro de Mendoza was joined by several others in petitioning for the land. Like other Spanish grants approved during the period, the government's intent was to promote settlement and protect claims of the Spanish government amid raids of various Indian tribes who were fighting among themselves as well as against the increasing number of what they considered to be foreign interlopers and menacing threats.

"The real settlers of New Mexico were the villagers, whose descendants still inhabit such fabulous mountain villages as Cundiyó, Córdova, Truchas, Trampas, Chamisal, and Peñasco," wrote historian Carey McWilliams. "Most of these villages were established as part of a series of outer defenses against the Indians. Here, the soldier-settler was given a small (land) grant in payment for his services in manning a lonely outpost against the Indians."

Cundiyó, some 180 years after it was first settled, came to be home of my Mother, Stella Vigil. She was born in April 1925 into a family that would include 12 daughters: Rosiña, Rebecca, Carmelita, Susie, Emelinda, Floy, Stella, Benina, Elvira, Juanita Floy, Florencia "Lencha" and Bertha "Brita". There also were two sons: Roberto and Carlos.

Three of the girls—Floy, Elvira and Emelinda—died before adulthood.

Their Father, Pedro Vigil, was born in 1886. He built the family home out of *adobe* bricks before any of his children came into the world. When finished, the home's interior space measured 26-feet-by 28-feet and included four rooms of comparable size. Double rows of *adobes* form all exterior walls that are nearly two feet thick. Only one of the interior walls is half the bulk. Grandpa completed the basic structure of the four-room home in 1907, five years before New Mexico was granted statehood. Still before statehood, Pedro Vigil installed a pitched roof on his square home in 1911.

I unexpectedly came upon long-forgotten evidence of the construction's time frame nearly 80 years later.

San Antonio Mayor Henry Cisneros (left) welcomed Spanish King Juan Carlos I to the Texas city in September 1987 before the king left for Houston and then Santa Fé as part of his tour through the U.S. Southwest to cultivate relations.

The family home is just a few fenced meadows up from where two clear mountain streams—the Río Medio and Río Frijoles—converge about a mile before flowing into Santa Cruz Lake, which is contained behind a dam built in the late 1920s.

Petronila Vigil, born in 1896, gave birth to each of the children within the adobe walls of the house built by Grandpa Pedro. Some arrived while my grandfather was laboring in distant lands. Very often Grandma Petronila tended to the children while grandpa was away for months at a time tending to other people's sheep in Wyoming. For him and many other men of the area, it was the most reliable way—if not the least-imposing way—to earn money needed to support their families.

My Father's home of Truchas, with a population that never has reached much more than 1,500, always has been several times larger than Cundiyó. Cundiyó is a village where until recently, people routinely swept

The southern entrance to Cundiyó has long been a familiar site to artists and photographers on the original High Road to Taos.

their yards, not just their floors, and were equally attentive to keeping clean family reputations. It was also known for having a sort of unwritten zoning code easily expressed in one sentence: You had to be named Vigil to live there.

A Visitor Named Oppenheimer

Arguably, the Vigil zoing code existed for generations in the community of little more than 35 households at least in part to keep Anglos out. Don't cringe. Carefully worded and much-disguised zoning requirements in parts of communities throughout the country are driven largely by desires to restrict who comes in. In such cases, minorities and the poor usually are the ones locked out.

Vigils probably remembered how Anglos coming into the New Mexico Territory from the East often looked down on Hispanics and sought to keep them at a distance.

In Cundiyó, an independent spirit named McGuire was among the first to break the Vigil code long applied to residency. Artist Frank McGuire, who had worked as a staffer for former New Mexico Governor Jack Campbell and former Navajo Nation President Peter McDonald, arrived in Cundiyó in 1969 in pursuit of a slower pace that might allow him to work on his stone carvings and other artwork.

Pedro and Petronila Vigil were proud members of a community that tended faithfully to their homes and their reputations.

The four-room home of Pedro and Petronila Vigil in Cundiyó was built before New Mexico statehood. The first addition to the home, pictured here, was an indoor bathroom built 70 years after the home's original construction.

Even before McGuire, there was Oppenheimer, the American physicist whose name would become known throughout the world. The father of the atomic bomb did not live in Cundiyó, to be sure. But on more than one Christmas Eve, Robert Oppenheimer quietly traveled beyond the storied gates that isolated Los Álamos in the Jemez Mountains and was driven east across the Río Grande Valley to penetrate Cundiyó's own isolation. In the tiny village and within adobe walls that cradled wood-fired heat, Oppenheimer visited for hours with the community's longtime patriarch, Noberto Vigil, before retiring for the night in what became known as the Christmas room on a bed reserved for his visits.

The home was the most-prominent one in the mountain village not only because of the patriarch who lived there. Along with the living quarters, it housed a store that was stocked with basic food supplies, candies, sodas and other sweets. It also was home to the community post office with its cabinet of narrow compartments and tiny doors that concealed envelopes and parcels inside. The community's only telephone was in the building. The phone belonged to the U.S. Forest Service, which had a substantial presence in the mountainous area but it was kept in the Noberto Vigil home because of the daily activity that unfolded within those particular adobe walls. It's where people from the outside called when they wanted messages delivered to village residents. My Mother remembered that as a child she was sent perhaps once or twice a month to cross the village into the Noberto Vigil home to use the phone for communications that required prompt attention.

One of the busy home's occupants remembered the times and the extraordinary holiday visits from the prominent Los Álamos scientist decades later. "Very few people know that at the beginning, when Los Álamos was still a very secret community, Oppenheimer would come into Cundiyó and sleep in our house. The next morning someone would come in from Los Álamos to pick him up," said Adelina Vigil, one of the family's daughters. "Oppenheimer and my Dad spent many a night talking. I don't think they talked about science or anything like that. I think they talked about the mountains and northern New Mexico. But I really don't know for sure because the rest of us had to go to bed while they stayed up talking till eleven."

Long-time New Mexico State Historian Myra Ellen Jenkins was well aware of the unofficial Vigil zoning code in Cundiyó. Still, she confided as we discussed histories of land grant communities in the 1970s that Cundiyó, despite the self-imposed segregation, was her favorite among northern New Mexico's mountain villages.

A Spanish Priest and His Tiny Chapel

Cundiyó was also special to the Rev. Casimiro Roca, who in the 1950s was a young fiery Spanish priest assigned by his Catholic Church to serve the mountain villages and small farming communities of northern New Mexico. In time, the church gave him assignments elsewhere but none of them stuck. In his mind, the region around Cundiyó had gotten him as close to his native Spain as he could without setting foot on the *Meseta* or listening to the splashing waters of the Mediterranean.

"Cundiyó is almost home," he told me as we made small talk outside the village's little adobe chapel decades after I first began developing an impression of him while inside that same chapel. The chapel, according to parish records, was built around 1850 by José Antonio Vigil and his sons.

I recall attending church services in the chapel with a narrow, pitched bell tower as a very young boy in the 1950s. The diminutive *Padre* Roca was unbending in his beliefs and railed against everything from speeding drivers to promiscuity, undeterred from making such topics dominant themes of his sermons, even at funerals, weddings and baptisms.

At many of the services, some men of the village visited outside in the sunshine, leaning against a wall that rises three feet and encircles

Santo Domingo chapel in Cundiyó was built by José Antonio Vigil and his sons around 1850 soon after the United States claimed the New Mexico Territory.

the churchyard while listening to gurgling water in a nearby *acequia* and clutching wooden handles of shovels as if they were inseparable elements of life. Inside the church, heads of every woman were topped with appropriate hats or veils to reflect a kind of reverence that seemingly escaped the men outdoors as *Padre* Roca moved through his lectures.

My imagination thrust the small but imposing curate into my favorite childhood story. It was a story about my Mother, her sisters and cousins walking daily down the hill from their homes to the public grade school about a mile away near the tiny Catholic chapel. As the noisy band of kids approached the bottom of the canyon where clear waters of the Río Medio and Río Frijoles converge, chatter turned to a hush and steps of the children fell softly, silently onto the road of packed earth.

The kids prepared to climb the course rising beyond the bridge and toward the one-room schoolhouse while peering carefully up the red granite cliff that overlooks the water and trail below. They were convinced that their caution was a matter of survival, or at least one that could determine whether they went through life with all their body parts intact.

As the story goes, a wild goat lived up in the rocky cliff and took its joy from life by charging down every day to scatter the school-bound children just as they reached the bottom of the canyon. The frightened

Surely a scowl from the Rev. Casimiro Roca would have kept the feared hilltop goat away from children of Cundiyó. (Photograph by Steve Northup)

kids, depending on how far along they had gotten, would either race madly up the trail to school or turn around and scamper back toward their homes, where doors would swing open in succession just long enough for the children to escape horns of the charging goat.

That's the point in the story where *Padre* Roca entered my mind every time I listened at my mother's side. Having to face a charging goat every day on the way to school must have been scary. But, surely, this man with friends in High Places and such deeply rooted beliefs against all things wrong would have saved my Mother and her companions from the fierce beast, I thought. Heck, it might well have been a large part of why he had been assigned to minister to the community. It mattered nothing to my imagination that *Padre* Roca was still fighting his own battles in Spain, which were rooted in the Spanish civil war, during my Mother's childhood.

Hispanic Kids and Presbyterian Schools

With or without *Padre* Roca, Cundiyó has been a predominantly Catholic community. Presbyterian outreach begun in the mid-1800s did not reach directly into my Mother's village. Separate cemeteries are provided side by side at the high southern end of the village overlooking the valley of *vegas, lomitas* and sloping tin roofs. More than 50 grave markers in the Catholic cemetery encroach its northern boundary. Eight markers rise out of the adjacent cemetery for *protestantes*, all showing evidence of at least occasional attention yet stand unmistakably isolated.

My Mother says Grandpa Pedro worked as a handyman at nearby Presbyterian mission outposts, presumably the two closest ones in Truchas and Chimayó. "He'd look for work all over," Mom said, as if to imply that my grandfather put the ever-pressing need to support his family above his personal religious beliefs.

Mom thinks that it was during his work at the region's small mission schools that Grandpa Pedro learned of the bigger Presbyterian Menaul School in Albuquerque some 85 miles from Cundiyó. Rev. James A. Menaul opened the school in 1896 with the intent of serving Hispanic boys from New Mexico. Soon boys began arriving at the boarding school from southern Colorado, too.

Very few Hispanics of the region were successfully completing courses at public schools during the period. A formal education wasn't often assigned high priority. Besides, young people were needed to contribute to the support of family homes and farms. Educators at Menaul aimed to help change conditions. They promoted use of the English language while otherwise "Americanizing" Hispanics and teaching "the niceties of being middle class," according to one researcher. Good behavior and good posture were among basic expectations.

Menaul became co-educational in 1934, retaining its original objectives while teaching its largely Hispanic student body how to become perfect ladies and gentlemen, at least by Presbyterian standards.

Mom's elder brother, Roberto, benefited from Grandpa Pedro's work at mission schools. Roberto was enrolled at Menaul, joining other Catholics there who at first had to adapt to objectives and routines that were as foreign to them as polished silver and three-piece suits. In time, though, *Tío* Bobby reflected traits around which Menaul's curriculum and discipline were developed. He sang the school's praises on visits home to Cundiyó, fueling imaginations of his siblings who knew little of the world beyond the hills around them.

Tía Rosiña, one of Mom's elder sisters, heard enough from her brother to be convinced that Menaul would become her own ticket to advancement. She envisioned herself at the Albuquerque school and eventually thought she was winning her parents' support for her dreams, Mom said.

Amos and Stella Vigil Roybal were brought together at Presbyterian boarding schools.

But her dreams were dashed. Just before the start of the school year that was to have seen *Tía* Rosiña in Albuquerque, she was told she could not leave. "My parents told her she was needed at home to weave and otherwise help support the family," my Mother said. "My poor sister cried for weeks."

Weaving had produced marketable rugs and blankets in the region since before 1920. Within 20 years, products were marketed successfully in Santa Fé and beyond, according to Chimayó historian, Patricia Trujillo-Oviedo. Residents of Cundiyó and other northern mountain villages were paid to produce in their

Rosiña and Stella of the Vigil household: Rosiña as a teen was relied upon to help support the family with her weaving; Stella preferred gathering firewood and tending to other outdoor chores.

Roberto Vigil brought to Cundiyó stories about opportunities beyond the village.

Carlos Vigil was the youngest of 14 children born to Pedro and Petronila Vigil of Cundiyó.

homes much of what was marketed out of Chimayó. My aunts Rosiña, Rebecca and Carmelita were among those weavers who worked under agreements with Chimayo's entrepreneurial Ortega and Trujillo families.

Beyond the weaving, *Tía* Rosiña's responsibilities that deprived her entry into Menaul School included caring for my Mother and other siblings in the home that had no running water or other utilities. Water for drinking, cooking, washing and bathing was taken from a narrow *acequia* that runs barely more than 50 feet from the house. Regular maintenance of the *adobe* house was required. Livestock needed attention. Grass had to be cut and stored; butchered meat tended to; an orchard and garden irrigated; fruit and vegetables harvested; firewood collected, chopped and stacked.

Mom was never included among weaving sisters. She preferred the work of outdoors and apparently convinced her parents that she was more useful if left to gather firewood from hills around the family home. "I just didn't have the patience for weaving. I couldn't sit still inside," she said.

Mom had a reliable companion who was equally restless indoors. Her cousin, Corina, lived several *vegas* away and, as much as Mom, enjoyed the feel of grass and dirt on bare feet. "We'd run and play all over the *vegas* and *laderas* without a care in the world. Always in bare feet," Mom said. "In those days, there was nothing for us to worry about in terms of dangers as we ran between houses. Yes, there were coyotes, bears and mountain lions in the hills. But we weren't concerned about any of that and, I guess, we didn't have to be."

The *chivato* on the cliff: That's what children of the village had to worry about.

Money in the Petticoat

Among other memories, my Mother recalls being sent periodically to the upper end of the village near the Noberto Vigil home to keep her widowed Grandma Nieves company. Nieves Vigil was Mom's maternal grandmother. Stories about her left me perplexed because she was nothing like her daughter, Petronila.

My Grandma Petronila stood thin and erect. Her person and her house were both clean, well tended to. In my dominant recollections, I see my grandmother cooking at her kitchen's wood-burning stove or stooped over slightly as she moved purposefully along a tiled floor of green and white squares, sweeping dust, dirt and food crumbs with her *escobita*, a broom made of dried grass about three feet long and tied tightly at its trimmed end with a strip of cloth. I believe I inherited my grandmother's penchant for sweeping floors and have kept an *escobita* of my own over the years by which to remember her.

Grandma Petronila had a small, kind face, barely wrinkled and particularly attractive when revealing one of her frequent smiles. Her smiles concealed pain that few knew about until years later.

I've long wondered how Grandma Petronila and Great-Grandmother Nieves could have been cut from the same fabric. Mom describes her Grandma Nieves as a big woman, heavy set and not preoccupied with her appearance or that of her house. "I used to dread being sent to spend nights over there because when you lit a lamp in a room at night you could see bugs crawling up the walls," Mom said.

Between those overnight visits, Mom was sent daily to collect her family's mail at the post office. The post office was a little more than a mile away from Grandpa Pedro's house and right across the village's narrow road from where Great Grandma Nieves lived. "I was expected to stop and visit my Grandma Nieves every day as part of my walk to the post office," Mom said. "And if I didn't stop, the next time that I went in Grandma Nieves would almost accuse me of neglecting her and she'd want to know why."

Mom said her Grandma Nieves had a son, Timoteo, who received a government check monthly following military service. Her grandmother served as caretaker of the money. "She wore long dresses that hid layers of petticoats that had pockets sewn into them," Mom said. "She'd wrap the money with pieces of old bed sheets and keep the money in those pockets under her dress. Every month she would take me to a back room, lift up her dress and take out the money. 'Come on,' she would tell me. 'Count it and tell me how much there is.'"

Great Grandma Nieves had a suitor of convenience who lived in Santa Fé and apparently knew when the government checks arrived. "We knew that the man would show up every month after Grandma Nieves had the check cashed," my Mother said. "So my parents would send me to stay with Grandma Nieves all day until the man left. 'Don't you leave her side for even a minute as long as he is there,' my Mom would tell me. So there I was, pretending to play games in the kitchen all day."

"Sometimes the man would tell me, 'Why don't you go play outside for a while? Your grandma and I have things we need to talk about.' But I pretended that I wasn't paying attention and I wouldn't leave the two alone."

Alone is how Great Grandma Nieves spent most of her days.

"I remember that most of the time she'd just sit at her window that faced the road, looking out to see who went by. And back then not many people did," my Mother said.

Great Grandma Nieves was married to a man who, if family lore is to be believed, could be both bold and furtive or, maybe, just vexatious depending on your point of view. Eulogio Vigil is said to have ambushed the chief of a small Indian settlement just outside of Cundiyó, killing the man and burying him amid the brush never to be found. "I don't know how true it is but supposedly it happened, and we were told that it's what led those Indians to leave the area," Mom said.

Indians of the abandoned pueblo likely were responsible for giving Cundiyó its name, which is a corruption of the Tewa word, *kudijo*. Tewa Indians in nearby Nambé refer to it as "round hill of the little bells." A distinctive round hill rises in the south over the village near the site of the abandoned pueblo. Small wild flowers resembling light purple bells bloom in the village every summer.

Great Grandpa Eulogio must have met his own untimely fate along the way because he was nowhere to be seen by the time my mother was sent as an adolescent to spend time with her Grandma Nieves.

A Romance Buds in Missionary Schools

My Mother in time would be increasingly entrusted with shaping her own young life even as her parents were fully aware that lessons ahead would not always track with the lives of her elders. The nation's Great Depression was taking root far away from Cundiyó's isolation when my mother left her village and its Catholicism to begin junior high school at the Allison-James School in Santa Fé. The Presbyterian-sponsored school had its origins in (1884) when Matilda Allison took in ten girls and created what was first called the Santa Fe Industrial and Boarding School for Mexican Girls.

The drive among Presbyterians to import their brand of education to the upper Río Grande region apparently was driven at least in part by the same negative perceptions others had of the local population. "I want above all else to see my church come into this area of degradation and ignorance," Jennie St. John Mitchell wrote to Presbyterian leaders in Philadelphia in 1866. Jennie Mitchell was the wife of General Robert B. Mitchell, New Mexico territorial governor from 1866–1869.

Allison's school grew and in 1908 it was merged with the Mary James Missionary Boarding School for Boys. By 1934 the Allison-James School was accredited to serve students in grades seven, eight and nine along Santa Fé's northern-most boundary.

Mom arrived at the school just a few years later. English, vocational education, home economics and farming were central elements of the structure that was provided. So, too, was discipline.

The steady dose of discipline at the school caused problems for more than one student. Amos Roybal was among them. Dad was enrolled at Allison-James after getting his first taste of a mission school in Truchas.

He would be expelled back to Truchas, where he completed the ninth grade in the mountain community's small public school.

"I don't know exactly why he was sent back to Truchas. Repeated misbehavior," my Mother said. "I ran away from him when I'd see him."

Dad must have looked at his expulsion from Allison-James as a necessary part of the learning process. If he held ill feelings toward the school, they apparently didn't last into adulthood. As they raised and educated their own children, Mom and Dad both spoke regularly of the Allison-James School with reverence. They referred to it simply as The Allison, as if it were a venerable title that would be recognized anywhere it was spoken, much like The White House, The Kremlin or The North Pole.

As teens, Mom and Dad were reunited as boarding students at Menaul, where the Presbyterian philosophy was more deeply ingrained in them. Conveyors of the philosophy had their own elevated stations in life, as far as Mom and Dad were concerned. Miss Buck and Mr. Donaldson (surnames were so imposing that first names seemed entirely unnecessary) figured prominently in our family's incessant lessons about right and wrong. I heard of these people so often while growing up that I thought they might have been members of our household.

Dad's youthful penchant for misbehavior must have been kept relatively in check at Menaul or he wouldn't have been allowed to stay. Evidence that it hadn't been left behind entirely, though, was revealed one day when Dad fired a taunt aimed at getting Mom's attention.

"The science teacher, Miss Hart, asked me to take a walk with her one day toward the cemetery near the school," Mom said. "I don't know why she asked me to walk with her but there we were minding our own business when Dad goes by in his bicycle and he says, *"Estelita la palita."*

In an ill-considered attempt to flirt, Dad accused Mom of cozying up to the science teacher, and he did it loud enough for both teacher and student to hear. It drew an immediate rebuke from Miss Hart.

Mom didn't know how Dad in his poverty and near abandonment came upon the bicycle but it probably was something he was able to buy with money that he earned from his part-time job as a dishwasher at one of downtown Albuquerque's restaurants. Dad in later years talked occasionally about that job, usually while telling of sacrifices and commitments that had to be kept to get ahead.

He'd tell of watching other students at Menaul get ready on weekends for dances or parties while he prepared for evenings characterized by dirty dishes, food scraps and soapy water in the back of a hot kitchen. Sometimes, he'd say, he had just settled into bed at school, tired from his night's work, when he'd hear others returning to the dormitory laughing and boasting of their evening's exploits.

Dad more than once would end those stories with an assertion that he would make throughout his adult life while talking about effort required to get ahead. "Work never killed anybody," he'd insist.

Making grand pronouncements, after all, is what self-assured men did. Or, at least, it might have been easy for my Father to reach that conclusion. FDR had looked bold and unstoppable while proclaiming during the depths of the Great Depression that the nation had nothing to fear but fear itself. True or not, people believed it. President Harry Truman pronounced boldly in 1950 that the globe was closer to peace than it had been since the end of World War II five years earlier. The Korean War broke out weeks after Truman's boast.

If anything, Truman's declaration signaled that a man's pronouncements didn't necessarily have to be true. What mattered in my Dad's mind—and in the minds of so many like him during his times—was that a man look like he had the experience or the crucial inside information needed to make pronouncements and that he appear confident while making them. If he did, then inspiration would surely follow.

Between his classes at Menaul and his restaurant job, Dad apparently found time to convince my Mother that he had matured enough that she could move beyond apprehensions that she carried at The Allison. He wanted her to stop feeling as if she had to flee whenever she saw him.

It was in Dad's best interest to mature for more reasons than one. He needed to stay in school not only to secure the education that he was increasingly convinced might put his cruel desperation behind him. Being at Menaul was also critical if he were to continue his romantic overtures and, perhaps equally important, remain in a position from which he could report to his dishwashing job that for the first time in his life enabled him to jingle money in his pockets on a regular basis

Surely it must have been a tightrope that Dad had to walk because Menaul's disciplinary standards were legendary. Even as I was growing up, I'd hear adults threaten to send their rebellious teens to Menaul if they didn't fall into line.

Long after my parents graduated from the Presbyterian school, they got a phone call at home from a Menaul administrator 90 miles away. My elder sister, Elsa, had been sent to Menaul as a sort of pre-emptive measure. My parents didn't want Elsa victimized by the distractions and temptations that tug at most teenage girls. Menaul, they concluded, would keep her on the straight and narrow.

It did for the most part.

"I remember Daddy drove all the way to Albuquerque after getting that call from the office at Menaul," Elsa recalled. "They called him at home to tell him that I had broken off a flower—one flower—from the faculty's garden. I guess Dad thought he had to go to Menaul to assure them that he and Mamma didn't approve of what I did and that it wouldn't happen again."

Brother Tim Carved Through Dogma

The whole protestant business eventually got to be too much for the first-born of my siblings. Tim wasn't much into any organized religion but he had taken up woodcarving as he neared middle age, and much of his work soon was devoted to creating religious crosses. In time, he was asked to build new *bancos* to replace decades-old benches used for seating in the famed Santuario de Chimayó.

Tim joined a small group of artists known as *La Escuelita*, and the men spent hours together every month, creating crosses, *bultos*, *retablos* and other works commonly associated with Catholicism.

Creations also reflected elements of our region's dominant Hispanic culture. So, too, did conversation that flowed during *La Escuelita's* work sessions. Talking mostly in Spanish, the artists told stories of Hispanic values, customs, music, hardships and celebrations. Tim's appreciation for *la cultura Hispana* eventually consumed him. The "Americanizing" of

Hispanic youths that was at the core of Presbyterian teachings embraced by our parents ran counter to much of what Tim came to believe.

Dad more than once told his children that The Allison and Menaul saved his life. He was certain of it. But Tim, amid our frank brotherly conversations, shared with me his own heartfelt conclusion: "The Presbyterians really messed with Mom and Dad."

Tim's fondness for *la cultura* and his dismissal of what he considered protestant elitism could not be equated with unfettered devotion to Catholic teachings. Even as Tim crafted furniture and crosses for the altar of Abiquiú's Santo Tomás Catholic Church, he openly questioned central beliefs of Catholicism during conversations with Abiquiú's young parish priest.

Those conversations at times grew spirited as Tim challenged issues like the church's requirement of an unmarried clergy. Tim eventually found himself talking to receptive ears. "Father left the church and then he got married," Tim's wife, Anna, said of the handsome Abiquiú priest, a northern New Mexico native known for wearing jeans and scuffed cowboy boots under his robe.

A successor priest in time was called upon to give an anniversary Mass for Tim a year after he died in 1998 at the age of 50, taking his beliefs and disillusionment with him. The seemingly

Tim Roybal carved crosses and furniture for multiple northern New Mexico churches. (Photograph by Kitty Leaken)

uninspired priest had to pause for several uncomfortable moments and clumsily refer to his notes when the time came to mention Tim as the parishioner who was being remembered that day. At least some who knew of Tim's disillusionment felt my brother stir in his tomb.

Raising a family was very much on Dad's mind as he courted Mom through their junior year at Menaul. His own experiences told him it probably wouldn't be easy. Sure, there would be joy. But there also would be disillusionment and sometimes worse. Nothing in Presbyterian or Catholic churches was likely to change that. It had become clear to Dad that the world was bigger than any single faith.

And the world came knocking just as Dad prepared to begin his senior year at Menaul amid the school's assurances that hard work, honesty, perseverance and devotion to the America that was first defined by East Coast Pilgrims paved the way for good to triumph over evil.

From the Roybal Files...
Nerve of a Patriot, Global Trails of Leveo V. Sánchez, 2015
Excerpts, Chapter 2—Barriers Built Around Blood and Religion

The large adobe house of Sylvester and Josefa Davis in Galisteo became a meeting place for intellectuals, politicians, writers and travelers. "Whenever Bishop Lamy came to officiate at weddings, baptisms or funerals, he stayed at my grandparents' home," wrote Victoria D. de Sánchez.

It was into this family of established prominence and influence that Leveo M. Sánchez reached when his time came to court the woman whom he would make his bride. His own family of five boys and five girls was of far-more humble origins. Leveo was the seventh-born child of Atilano and Marcelina Sánchez.

Much of what is known about that Sánchez family today is shared by Atilano's and Marcelina's grandson, Leveo V. Sánchez, who was named after the father whom he never knew. "My father and his family were Presbyterians who came to Galisteo from Dixon to the north in Río Arriba County," he said. "Their roots ran deep in Dixon. I think they were a spinoff of a Sephardic group that came from Mexico. They had strong traits of Judaism."

Whatever their distant ties, the Sánchezes were Catholics before becoming devout Presbyterians. They were not the only residents in and around Río Arriba County who made the conversion in the late 1800s and into the next century.

Presbyterians offered increased access to education but it might have been something far less lofty than education that helped set the religious course for Atilano Sánchez and his family. "I don't know what, if any, role this played in their conversion but an aunt told me that my grandmother became quite ill in Dixon," said Leveo V. Sánchez. "It was a very cold winter day. My grandfather went to the priest, probably to ask that he come to pray or, maybe, give last rites. The priest refused. As grandfather left, the screen door slammed on my grandfather's hand. I don't know if the priest slammed it on the hand but it might have put the finishing touch on the conversion."

Leveo M. Sánchez became a part of his family's religious conversion and was a Presbyterian when he began courting the young Victoria Davis of the influential Davis household in Galisteo. Her newfound suitor's religion did not deter Victoria even while well aware of her grandmother Josefa's firm embrace of Catholicism. It was the grandmother whom Victoria so admired and loved.

"We dated for a full year before I told grandmother (Josefa) that Leveo and I wanted to get married," Victoria wrote. "She became very upset at the news. She had wanted me to marry a mature, wealthy Catholic—or at least a potentially successful one. My arguments that Leveo did not drink liquor, smoke or gamble like so many other young men of the times fell on deaf ears. Neither she nor I was able to convince the other to budge. Even so, I moved forward with the wedding plans."

As the wedding day drew closer, Leveo M. Sánchez took a major step to please his bride to be, something that he must have hoped also would have eased tensions in the Davis family: He converted to Catholicism.

The Sánchez family was not informed of the conversion and apparently never learned of it. Indeed, Leveo M. Sánchez, who died during the first year of his marriage to Victoria, was buried in a Presbyterian cemetery.

3

ON THE MEDALS OF WAR AND THE STORIES OF LIFE

Adolf Hitler had no use for Americans or their ways when his German troops invaded Poland on September 1, 1939, igniting World War II. Europe quickly became enmeshed in war and most Americans, while opposing Hitler and the Axis alliance, seemed willing to let combatants destroy one another so long as threats that fueled fighting didn't cross the oceans.

Amos Roybal left Menaul School in Albuquerque
to serve in the U.S. Army during World War II.

Amos Roybal stood with his "tall buddy" from Pennsylvania in January 1945, just days before being shot in the left knee during the Battle of Luzon.

It was too much to ask. The Japanese attack on Pearl Harbor in Hawaii on December 7, 1941, pressed the United States to activate and fortify its own war machine. Young men were called into uniform. Two and a-half years passed before my Father became part of the U.S. Army and began training to join in the fight.

Dad was just days away from starting his senior year at Menaul. He and Mom were classmates even though Dad was 19 months older. His fits and starts with school meant he was a month shy of 20 when he was inducted as a private in Company F of the 1st Infantry in August 1943.

"One of the teachers at Menaul drove him to the Albuquerque train station. I wasn't invited so we said our goodbyes at the school," said Mom.

The U.S. and its allies were engaged in fierce fighting to stop Japanese expansion in the Central and South Pacific when Dad was dispatched to the war's Pacific Theater in March 1944. He was stationed on the island of New Guinea, which Japan invaded in 1942, threatening Australia to the south. The island was home to important battlefields in the Southwest Pacific Theater. About 216,000 Japanese, Austrailian and U.S. combatants are said to have died during the New Guinea campaign. From New Guinea, Dad was among U.S. forces sent more than 1,000 miles north to the Philippines to liberate those islands from the Japanese.

In the European Theater, the United States and Allied forces had reclaimed Rome and were pushing Germans toward eventual defeat in northern Italy. Allied victories were also being secured in other parts of Europe when the largest U.S. campaign in the Pacific Theater began unfolding in the Battle of Luzon within the northern Philippines in January 1945.

Dad's left knee was shattered in the Battle of Luzon on January 25th.

He was one of 36,550 U.S. Army and Army Air Force members wounded during the months-long battle on the Philippine's largest and most-populated island; 10,640 U.S. fighters were killed.

The Philippine capital of Manila on the island of Luzon was taken by the Allies in March and in the end, the Battle of Luzon was considered a decisive Allied victory.

Dad never talked much about time he spent at war. But I do remember him saying once or twice, "I killed the Jap who shot me."

Others must have fallen at his hands in battle because later in his life I recall him talking about a situation where he thought someone was putting one of my siblings at risk. Dad warned the man to stay away.

"I told him that I've killed men for less," Dad said, recalling his warning. Dad wasn't the killing type so his warning undoubtedly alluded to his time at war and, possibly, reflected remorse for the deadly exchanges among young soldiers of opposing sides who come to learn that they must kill simply to avoid being killed.

Dad spent most of his time recovering from his war injury at Northington General Hospital in Tuscaloosa, Alabama. He was released from the hospital on November 29, 1945, six months after Germany surrendered to end fighting in Europe and three months after Japan's surrender in the Pacific.

Dad was awarded the American Campaign Medal, the Asiatic Pacific Campaign Medal, the Philippine Liberation Medal, the Good Conduct Medal and the Purple Heart. I was aware of the Purple Heart but didn't learn about the other medals until reading Dad's military discharge papers well after I had entered middle age. From the age of 21, Dad walked through life with a stiff left leg and a large oval scar that covered what used to be his knee.

He was different in more ways than one from the man who left the train station in Albuquerque only 27 months earlier. Mom was waiting for him and embraced him, changes and all.

Mom Takes First Job Then Marries

Mom graduated from Menaul in 1944 and promptly enrolled at the University of Albuquerque, studying to become a teacher. She was at U of A for two years then a job offer prompted her to continue studies during summers at New Mexico Highlands University in Las Vegas. The job had her teaching in the same small building in Cundiyó where she studied as a child. Her charges ranged from kindergarten to the sixth grade and they all sat in the same room.

During the mid-1940s, only about half of all public school teachers

Stella Vigil: graduate of Menaul School

in New Mexico had completed high school and fewer than six percent had a college degree.

Mom faced extraordinary challenges while teaching a classroom full of relatives, some of whom had known her as she grew up only a few years apart from them in Cundiyó. One of them, Manuel, recounted how he and a couple of other sixth-graders concurred that their best chance for getting through the class was to follow the lead of the most assertive and rambunctious student in the class.

"Not all of us were good students and since Félix pretended to know everything, we thought we would do what he did," said Manuel. "Estelita was strict as a teacher but we thought that since we all knew one another, everything would be ok in the end. When the time came for a big test, Félix had written answers for every question. I copied from him and the others copied from me. When the grades came back, we all got "Fs."

For Mom, it was simply a matter of fulfilling her responsibilities. She had been taught about responsibilities at home, at The Allison and at Menaul. Her lessons at home continued even as she assumed new roles associated with young adulthood.

"I was living with my parents while I taught in Cundiyó," said Mom. "Amos went back to Truchas when he returned from the military in November 1945. We continued dating and soon after he got back from the Army, he made his first trip to Cundiyó to meet my family."

"Elizardo 'Nicky' Lucero from Truchas had been at Menaul all the time that I was there. He was a good friend of mine and Amos. He gave Amos a ride to Cundiyó that day but he had to ask one of the neighbors for directions ahead of time. So people knew that he and Amos were coming, and they had a big audience when they drove into Cundiyó.

"Amos got out of the car with his cane. He met my Mom and the others who were there. But my Dad hadn't gotten home from work in Los Álamos so 'Nicky,' Amos and I decided to go to Española until Dad got back from work. When we got to Española, 'Nicky' parked his car off the dirt road not far from where *Tío* Ramos and *Tía* Trinidad lived. He wanted to give us time alone so he walked to *Tío* Ramos' house and visited inside for a while.

"We went back to Cundiyó when we knew that my Dad would have gotten home from work. Amos met Dad. We talked for a little while. It was kind of tense. When it was over, Amos left with his tail between his legs."

Grandpa Pedro usually had a serious look and didn't waste words even in comfortable settings. But if my Father was intimidated in his first meeting with grandpa, it didn't last long.

"Amos enrolled at Highlands University that first winter after he got back from the Army," Mom said. "He took classes and tests to complete high school requirements while also beginning studies to get a degree in education. We continued seeing one another. In April, he proposed and we were married in that August of 1946, August 21st."

Path Home Includes Fire, Other Obstacles

Mom and Dad were married in the First Presbyterian Church near the Allison-James School that they both attended in Santa Fé's north side. The Santa Fé County clerk was paid $2.50 to register the marriage license.

Still a Catholic, Mom had no immediate plans to change religions as husband and wife moved together to Las Vegas where Dad continued his studies at Highlands University.

Mom's studies got put aside as she stepped into motherhood. My brother, Tim, was born in November 1947. My sister, Elsa, came a year later. The four soon moved into housing that became available for military veterans after World War II at Camp Luna, north of Las Vegas.

An Army installation, Camp Luna had drawn a lot of activity to the Las Vegas area during the war. National Guard members who later suffered at the hands of the Japanese in the Philippines' Bataan Death March trained at Camp Luna.

Barracks were remodeled at the camp following the war and were more than accommodating for Dad and his young family. "Our rent was twenty-one dollars a month for a one-bedroom apartment, and that included utilities." Mom said. "When we asked for two-bedrooms, our rent rose to twenty-seven dollars."

The family's comfort didn't last long, though. A massive fire swept through the camp, destroying living quarters and the limited possessions that struggling families relied upon.

Dad was in classes on the Highlands campus when the fire broke out.

"Amos had one suit," Mom said. "It had belonged to his brother, Victor. Dad was going to graduate in that suit but it was lost in the fire. Timmy's and Elsa's clothes and toys were lost.

"We had bought a used sewing machine from one of Dad's aunt's in Truchas. She used it for years before going blind. She sewed Daddy's shirts on that machine, and she made clothes for other people in Truchas, too. We lost that sewing machine in the fire. We lost everything except the little bit that I could carry and put into our green Chevy before driving away."

After the fire, Mom and Dad rented in East Las Vegas for much of the time that Dad worked toward a bachelor's in education.

Dad graduated with a bachelor's from Highlands in 1949 and promptly took a job teaching woodwork and, later, mechanical drawing at tiny Santa Cruz High School near the Catholic church and unpretentious plaza that had anchored early settlement in the region.

Whatever discomfort Dad might have felt while meeting Mom's family in Cundiyó had been overcome entirely. There was a vacant strip of just over one acre adjacent to the property where Mom grew up. The strip's upper quarter rose above an *acequia* and would have made an ideal site for a home. The rest of the property had access to irrigation from clear water running through the ditch and sloped gently to the Río Medio with beautiful views of *vegas* on the other side of the stream. It was the scenery of picture books.

Dad liked everything about the site. He and Mom thought of raising their family there while remaining close to her parents, each household capable of benefiting from the other. But Dad quickly came to learn that he faced far more than a sale price and barbed wire fencing to get onto the land.

Cundiyó's patriarch, Noberto Vigil, told Dad that he would not be permitted to buy the property. In that community of Vigils, Dad might have married a Vigil, said Noberto, but Dad himself was not a Vigil. As Roybals, Dad, Mom and their two children would have to live elsewhere. To this day, that strip of property remains unoccupied.

Amos Roybal: graduate of New Mexico Highlands University

One or two small families of Anglos apparently lived temporarily in Cundiyó during the late 1930s as part of a work project in the area. But it was Mom's cousin and childhood companion, Corina, who apparently made one of the first real dents in Cundiyó's Vigil residency code. Corina in 1962 married Harold Pool of Lubbock, Texas, and the two settled on property along the Río Frijoles long owned by Corina's Father, Marcos, and his father before him.

In Mom's eyes, Corina was the appropriate person to have busted the Vigil code.

Corina and Harold Pool were raising a toddler, Tina, before artist Frank McGuire made his move into Cundiyó in 1969.

Blocked by the informal residency code 13 years prior to the Pool's union, Dad took his young family downstream along the Río Santa Cruz and settled into small rental quarters that were part of an *adobe hacienda*-like estate owned by Emily Underwood about a mile northeast of the Santa Cruz Plaza.

"Mrs. Underwood had some beautiful horses. She might have entered them into shows but I don't think she raced them or anything like that. Dad used to feed them and clean their stalls to help pay the rent," Mom said. "Mrs. Underwood was very good to us."

The move to Santa Cruz was accompanied by another milestone.

Stella Vigil Roybal and her first three children—Tim, David and Elsa—enjoy a watermelon break.

Mom unceremoniously converted from Catholicism to Presbyterian.

"We were a family," Mom replied simply when she was asked about the conversion years later.

Dad was part of a generation whose men often thought that where husbands went, wives would follow; a period when wives frequently were expected to think, vote and worship as their husbands did. Too, Mom's years at The Allison and Menaul surely figured into her decision to convert.

Mom and Dad through their visits to the Barela farm over the years had become familiar with the San Pedro area. They began paying on a six-room house on about half an acre in Lower San Pedro not quite a mile from the Barelas by the time I was born in February 1952.

Mom mentioned to Dad before long that she would like even just a tiny patch of additional land behind the house where she could plant a few radishes. Dad wound up buying another acre or so, where radishes, *chile*, corn, cucumbers, tomatoes, berries and assorted fruit trees took root. The front yard in time became consumed with dahlias, roses, gladiolas and other flowers. Mom grew as faithful to her gardening as she was to any religion.

Rooms were added to the San Pedro house to accommodate a growing family.

Brothers Manuel and José Ramón Vigil used a horse into the 1990s to work the ground behind their family home in Cundiyó.

Pedro Vigil and son, Carlos, prepare a young Tim Roybal for a horse ride.

Three or Four Shifts at Sunday Table

If San Pedro seemed to approach perfection, Cundiyó's profound allure retained its hold on our young family. Often I'd spend a week or more at my grandparents' home during summers when I was able to soak in the sights, sounds and fragrances of a mountain village that was defined in large part by its pitched roofs of corrugated tin, green meadows sloping down juniper and piñon-studded hills, fruit trees, patches of melons and pumpkins and, of course, the two clear streams that moved slowly down separate valleys originating in high peaks of the Sangre de Cristos.

During those visits, I'd live among people in Cundiyó who seemed unbothered that their manner and attitudes did not reflect those of a modernizing world just a few miles beyond. I came to learn what made these mountain people smile and what made them sad. I learned that to be appreciated or valued things need not be big or sparkly. Their value often was measured by how they were able to help one get through the day. Items weren't used then discarded. They were used one, two, three, four times or until they couldn't be used anymore.

Every Sunday no matter the season members of my grandparents' family drove from their own homes to Cundiyó to share in a meal and conversations that went on through the afternoons. Meals were simple: fried potatoes mixed with some kind of meat, often *carne seca* from beef or wild game that was ground nearly to a powder; pinto beans; *chile*; *tortillas*; fruit, apple butter or, maybe, *sopa (capirotada)* for dessert.

The extended family was so large that it took three or four shifts at the kitchen table to feed everyone. Even then, some would take their plates into a small screen porch adjacent to the kitchen or even outdoors where they would eat while leaning up against vehicles parked under a large cottonwood tree that my grandparents planted in the yard as a sapling to commemorate my Mother's birth midway through April in 1925.

Water for drinking or washing hands was carried in from the nearby *acequia* in silver tin buckets that were kept atop a white cabinet beneath the kitchen's horizontal window and its sill nearly two feet across on which potted geraniums rested. A tin dipper was used to scoop water out of the buckets and into glasses or a washbasin resting on a narrow stand at the entrance to the kitchen.

An outhouse made of pine boards waited for use as needed down the sloping yard beyond the *acequia*. Old Sears or Montgomery Ward catalogues inside the small wooden quarters served multiple purposes.

Surviving siblings of the Vigil household assembled for an informal reunion during the 1990s.

Dry willow sticks lay atop the bench to stir around the seat openings and collect cobwebs from around the rims and scatter spiders or other critters positioned below the edges.

No matter the number of visitors, the four-room Cundiyó house on Sundays in effect became a two-room house: the kitchen and an adjacent bedroom that doubled as a sitting room. A more-formal living room was rarely used. My grandparents' bedroom was entirely off limits.

My Mother and her siblings marveled periodically after the visits at how so many children were squeezed into that house while the Cundiyó family grew from year to year.

Conversations during those Sunday visits to Cundiyó seemingly had no bounds other than decency. Well, stories were framed within boundaries of propriety by all, perhaps, except *Tío* Ramón, the Nambé laborer who married one of Mom's elder sisters, Susie, herself soft spoken and mostly withdrawn. *Tío* Ramón never got lost in the family crowd on those Sundays. Anyone looking for this smartly dressed, slightly rotund man and his sharp wit simply had to move toward the laughter. Even *Tía* Susie allowed herself to join in the laughter all the while looking at least half embarrassed by her husband's jokes and tales.

For the most part, though, stories were about unspectacular events in the lives of people who had been taught to respect elders, value culture and traditions, and to tend faithfully to their families and their lands. Oh, mischief couldn't escape from figuring occasionally into recollections. It had to with so many young lives having sprouted from the property.

Milestones Along the *Cuesta*

For our family and several others, the weekly visits to Cundiyó meant climbing a winding, narrow stretch of unpaved road carved along the side of a hill just south of tiny Río Chiquito and about three miles from my grandparents' house. The drop from the road approaches 200 feet at its highest point. Climbing the hill at the beginning of the day meant that it had to be descended at the end of the visits.

Drivers would routinely honk their vehicles' horns as they approached tight, blind curves to alert possible oncoming traffic. The road was mostly without barriers to separate it from deep drops at its edge. Large cottonwoods growing at the bottom of the cliff looked like mere bushes from the road. The road's packed clay surface got muddy in the rains, snow-packed and icy during winters. It was treacherous even in the best of conditions and was the subject of some of the most-colorful stories told during Sunday visits.

One of my favorites told how *Tío* Bobby late one afternoon took his young wife, Pulita, and my *Tía* Benina up that *cuesta* in an old Dodge pickup, driving in reverse the entire way after learning that forward gears inexplicably lacked necessary power.

Mom experienced one of life's major milestones on that same *cuesta*. My Father taught Mom how to drive on

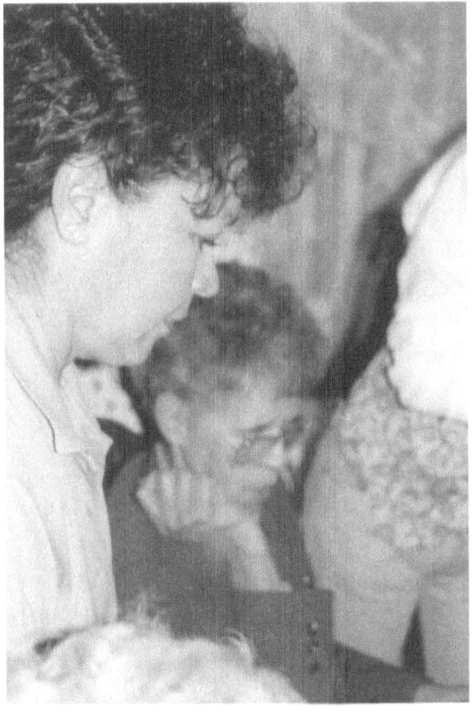

Elsa Roybal Trujillo visited with Aunt Benina Vigil Trujillo at the Cundiyó home.

the winding, dipping stretch of road between Cundiyó and Río Chiquito, which included the dreaded *cuesta*. "We were in Amos' 1938 Ford V-8 and I guess he thought it would give me confidence once I saw that I had made it through the *cuesta*," Mom said.

Dad, relying on the same car and the same route, also taught one of Mom's younger sisters how to drive. "He took me down the *cuesta* and when we were at the bottom he turned the car around and said, 'If you really want to learn, you'll drive us up.' I did it but I almost went rumble, rumble down one of those sharp turns," *Tía* Benina recalled decades later.

Tío Bobby, *Tía* Pulita and their two daughters, Gloria and Virginia, were among families that approached Cundiyó through Río Chiquito and the *cuesta* for Sunday visits. *Tía* Pulita, was a grade school teacher in Chimayó, and her family of farmers had considerable land holdings in the community. We learned in conversations about the hundreds of fruit trees that *Tío* Bobby planted in Chimayó while starting his family after returning from Menaul and World War II.

Sleepy Bears, German Browns and Cursed Elms

It was *Tío* Bobby who planted three young Siberian Elms on my grandparents' Cundiyó property along the fence line between the four-room *adobe* house and the two-lane road that already was being used as a popular, scenic route to Taos. The plantings were made with the best of intentions during the era when Clyde Tingley, an Albuquerque commissioner and New Mexico governor during the 1930s, reportedly bought 2,000 elms for $20 and gave them away to anyone who would plant them. It was at a time when additional greenery and shade were considered to be important elements of the state's development.

Favored for their tolerance of drought and cold, Siberian Elms worked their way into New Mexico through the Great Plains, having been used as belts of shelter following the devastation associated with the Dust Bowl era. Tingley's efforts helped popularize elms of multiple varieties but Chinese and Siberian elms eventually came to be scorned in much of the state after it was learned they would proliferate beyond control, coming to be recognized more as a nuisance than as providers of shady comfort.

"*Los Chineses*, is how my *Tía* Rebecca, one of the elder and more-vocal of the Vigil sisters, referred to the elms with considerable disdain no matter their variety. To her and other like-minded elders, "*Los Chineses* surely would come to have their own special corner in hell.

A cousin of mine who stayed often with my grandparents might agree. Sunday stories in Cundiyó turned occasionally to how Grandpa Pedro used one of his elms to hang the occasionally unruly boy by his feet and whip him with a strap when occasions demanded serious discipline.

Also on Sundays we learned how some men of Cundiyó hunted bears in the hills as long winters drew to an end. Hunters sought out caves thought to hold bears still groggy as they awakened from hibernation. Rags soaked in kerosene or other dirty fuel would be tied to ends of long poles or branches for one man to poke into entrances of the caves before withdrawing the smoky torch and standing back. Other men waited and any bear that stepped out would immediately be fired on.

The somewhat greasy *carne seca* made of bear was relied upon as a food source in some Cundiyó homes, including that of my grandparents, to supplement beef or pork garnered from traditional *matanzas*.

Fish, too, were eaten with regularity. Fat German Brown trout a foot long and even bigger swam clear waters of the Río Medio at the edge of my grandparents' property. *Tío* Carlos and Harry Drake, who married *Tía* Juanita and grew up fishing the Colorado River near his childhood home in Glenwood Springs, always seemed ready for the short walk to the Río Medio that invariably ended with food for somebody's table.

The two men sometimes took a small saddle rifle with them along with fishing rods to deal with fish that refused to take a hook.

"Kiss Her and Let's Go Home"

Tío Carlos and I became the subject of a story that my uncle's wife, Lydia, was fond of sharing when conversations turned to romance or courtships. Little more than six, I was spending summer days with my grandparents and wound up one night in a car with *Tío* Carlos. We must have been on an errand of some sort and on our way back to Cundiyó when my uncle pulled into the Chimayó home where Lydia lived with her parents and brother. My uncle and Lydia visited outside the car as dusk fell. I stirred restlessly inside as the couple visited amid smiles and harmless petting just beyond the car's hood. The wait seemed like hours. Each time the story was recalled *Tía* Lydia ended it with laughter and what became a familiar line: "Finally, David stuck his head out the window and told Carlos, 'Oh, hurry up and kiss her so we can go home.'"

Long before *Tío* Carlos started dating, he and his rambunctious cousin, Félix, pursued joy wherever they could find it. They found it one day atop a neighbor's flat roof, where melons, pumpkins and other squashes were stored temporarily. Félix, said *Tío* Carlos, took a tire iron to the squashes and left most of them ruined.

Both boys were sent running home to escape threatened thrashings.

"Carlos, Félix and Corina's brother, Manuel, were always into mischief," Mom said. "And they got pretty good at deflecting blame."

Weddings, Kidnappings and Rendezvous

Changing times, including the escalation of kids' misbehavior, were on *Tía* Rebecca's mind during Sunday visits. So, too, were everyday attitudes and expectations. Her stories told of weddings in years past when gifts might have consisted of no more than two spoons and two forks, or two plates wrapped in paper. The moral: Nobody expected the moon, and people were grateful for whatever came their way.

Tía Rebecca shared a saying that she grew up hearing among well-worked ladies at the end of busy days: *"Hoy trabajé como una india."* The saying referred to Indian women who had been kidnapped and taken to Hispanic villages to work long and hard as servants. Indian communities might well have had corresponding comments to tell of Hispanic women who were forcibly taken to work among the tribes.

Tía Rebecca's husband, Emiliano, favored hunting stories. He was the storyteller who spoke of bear hunts that relied on both rifles and torches at cave openings as winters drew to their end. Coyotes, who were constant threats to livestock and family pets, he said, were shot on sight no matter the season. But a special superstition accompanied coyotes, to hear *Tío* Emiliano tell it. He was among those who refused to directly touch a dead coyote. Special care was taken while discarding a carcass to ensure that it didn't brush up against skin or clothing, he said.

Tía Benina liked to tell how she and her sister, Juanita, would sneakily follow older sisters into the hills just north of Cundiyó for previously arranged meetings with boys from neighboring Córdova. The older teens supposedly did nothing more than talk but *Tía* Benina and *Tía* Juanita confronted their sisters after several of those meetings and successfully blackmailed them for whatever pocket change was at their disposal. "We told them that if they didn't pay up, we were going to tell Daddy," said *Tía* Benina. "Boy, they would have been in deep trouble."

One of the older sisters eventually wised up and told the young blackmailers that they better stop their games or they would be turned in for leaving home without permission. Enough said.

Milestones Recorded Between Sundays

And, of course, there were milestones—good and bad—between the Sunday meetings at my grandparents' home.

I was the ring boy at the June 1959 wedding of *Tía* "Lencha" (Florencia) and Alex Archuleta of Truchas. I remember watching my aunt prepare for her dates, tending carefully to her hair and attire. If modesty had underlined what she had been taught while growing up in Cundiyó, she came upon more-boisterous behavior while meeting with Alex. Alex was full of stories, exaggerations, laughter. He liked loud music and fast cars. *Tía* "Lencha" liked him plenty, and I also came to enjoy being around him.

The wedding was in the Truchas Catholic church. Father Roca presided and true to the reputation that was already developing around him, he warned against untoward behavior and other forms of fast living.

The reception was at the hall of the often-busy Line Camp bar in Pojoaque between Cundiyó and Santa Fé. If the site didn't track with the priest's message, it didn't seem at all out of character for the new groom.

It all seemed fine to me except that I probably hadn't ever spent as much time in a white shirt, bow tie and snug-fitting three-button coat without being allowed to complain.

Florencia "Lencha" Vigil and Alex Archuleta celebrated their wedding day in Truchas. It marked the first time that this book's author, serving as ring boy, wore a bow tie and a three-button coat.

The wedding came just six months after a tragedy robbed one of my Mom's other sisters of expectations for her own nuptial and other joys that fill minds of teenage girls.

It was Christmas Eve 1958. We had only recently acquired our first phone in our San Pedro home. Party lines were the norm so calls didn't always get through even if nobody in the house was on the phone. The call made to our home late on the night before Christmas 1958 got through and carried a message never to be forgotten.

I remember the ringing that moved through the darkness. It was soon accompanied by gasps and cries of disbelief. More needed to be learned. But this much was known: Nineteen-year-old "Brita" (Bertha), the youngest of my grandparents' children, had been in a terrible car accident in Chimayó on the way home from a dance in nearby La Puebla. It didn't look good.

The car in which *Tía* "Brita" and several of her young companions had been riding crashed into a utility pole just off the road. My aunt was thrown through the windshield, her head striking the pole. DWI, apparently, had made its first claim on our extended family. The deadly late-night turn of events occurred only three miles from the dance hall and perhaps another five from where Tia "Brita's" bed waited in Cundiyó.

"I had been in Cundiyó that day and 'Brita' asked me if Cornelio and I were going to the dance, recalled *Tía* Benina. "I told her our kids were too small; we had to stay with them."

It was *Tío* Carlos who ended up driving "Brita" to the dance.

"She went with me and Lydia," said Tío Carlos. "I think 'Lencha' and Alex were there, too. When it was time to come home, 'Brita' asked me if she could ride back with some people who she knew from nearby. There by the post office in Chimayó, the car they were in went off the road and hit a pole.

"Part of 'Brita's' face was taken off in the wreck. My Dad and I were the only ones who saw her looking like that. The others all said they didn't want to remember her like that; they wanted to remember her the way she was before the wreck." *Tío* Carlos said.

Tía "Brita's" head was wrapped in white cloth and covered with a satin pillow in the casket. "My Mother wanted to see before the head was covered with the pillow," said *Tía* Benina. "I went with her so that she wouldn't fall in case she got real shaken up. I went blind temporarily when we got close. I don't think God wanted me to see my sister like that. I didn't see anything again until my Mother and I had already walked away from the casket."

Tía "Brita's" wake was in the small house where she grew up. Her casket was placed against one of the thick *adobe* walls in my grandparents' bedroom. The wood-burning kitchen stove that she liked to stand behind while listening to conversations during family gatherings helped keep the house warm as mourners filed through.

On the day of her funeral, my aunt's casket was placed on the bed of my *Tío* Emiliano's black Ford pickup, which carried the young body off the community's main road and onto a narrow, bouncy course between small juniper and piñon trees to the cemetery on the crest of a rocky hill overlooking the village.

Tía "Brita's" passing was not easily forgotten for more reasons than one. We had watched my aunt graduate from high school in Pojoaque only months earlier. Barely more than ten years older than my parents' first-born child, she and my Father had developed an especially close bond. I, too, had grown close to her. As part of our family's mourning, the television in our home was unplugged for a year.

The years went by. My younger sister, Sylvia, barely got to know Grandma Petronila before grandma succumbed to a long and painful battle with stomach cancer in the spring of 1962. Younger brother, Tomás, was born days before grandma's death.

Grandpa Pedro fought Parkinson's for years. His children took turns caring for him at their homes when he no longer could stay in Cundiyó alone. Seven years passed before he followed grandma to the grave. His happiness had been gone for a while.

Tía Benina revealed well into her life that for years her family in Chimayó was visited at Christmas time by a man who lived just a couple of miles away in the same community. He'd come bearing home-cooked goods or frozen meats. "We'd see the man around during the year," said *Tía* Benina. "He was even related to my sister, Rosiña, through marriage. But we never knew why he came to our house every Christmas. It was much later that I found out that he was in the same car with 'Brita' on the night that she died in that wreck."

STORIES TOOK FLIGHT FROM SPANISH

Times surrounding life and death in Cundiyó were often explained, celebrated or mourned in the language of our ancestors who had walked the region when it was governed alternately by Spain and Mexico. I realized at an early age that I would need to learn Spanish not only to understand but to truly appreciate much of what occurred around me. Limited to English, I was missing out on a lot.

My Spanish was self-taught so for years it crippled along, increasingly understandable to others, yet vulnerable to criticism and receptive to coaching.

Tío Emiliano was among those who didn't hesitate to try to get me beyond my errors. His coaching often was accompanied by genial laughter as if to suggest that progress would come and that the world would not end just because I spoke of *un culebra* or *los muchachas*.

Tío Emiliano was, after all, a kind and patient man. He had big hands and a warm smile. He was fond of hot coffee and sweet fruit pies. He so liked living in a clean, well-kept house that more than one of *Tía* Rebecca's sisters were known to imagine that my uncle was looking for dust on light fixtures or cobwebs in the ceilings as he scanned their homes amid conversations during visits.

Using *adobes* that he made on the site, *Tío* Emiliano built his own family home within view of my grandparents' property. In fact, he told me that he used the house and his work on it to help win *Tía* Rebecca's affections.

Sisters Rebecca Vigil and Susie Vigil Herrera shared stories at the Cundiyó home.

My aunt's affections for her husband probably waned little, if at all, over the years. I might have heard her speak critically of my uncle only twice. Oh, I'm sure there were other times. People don't stay married for more than 60 years without testing nerves at least occasionally.

Once, I heard *Tía* Rebecca criticize *Tío* Emiliano for leaving her to be the disciplinarian of their family. He had no problem letting her be the enforcer, she said. My uncle smiled amid the critique.

Another time my aunt spoke of what she knew would be her unfulfilled dream of riding on a large cruise ship to visit distant lands. She had heard at least two of her sisters tell of making such voyages. *Tía* Rebecca, into her late sixties and seventies, came to dream of it as a once-in-a-lifetime experience. But she knew that *Tío* Emiliano would no sooner board a cruise ship for a ride across the seas than he would pack his belongings and move to New York City's Park Avenue.

Hearing the scold as he sat near a crackling fire in his kitchen's wood-burning stove, my uncle flashed his familiar smile. "On the ocean, there are no embankments to hold onto during times of trouble," he said in Spanish.

Tío Emiliano walked through life much more slowly after colon cancer claimed *Tía* Rebecca in 2001 at the age of 87. Doctors kept telling her that she

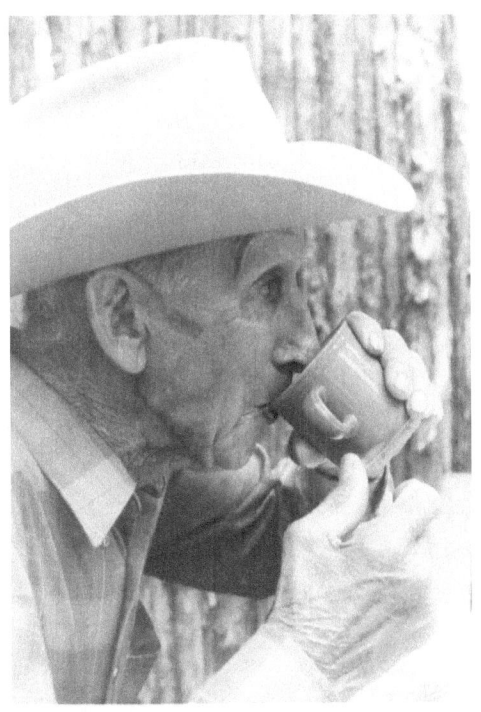

Emiliano T. Vigil enjoyed hot coffee, sweet pies and a good story.

was well until one day when she refused to leave the examining room. "If I'm well, then why do I feel so sick?" she asked. It was too late by the time her cancer was found.

One day, nearly three years after my aunt's death, *Tío* Emiliano and I visited in his kitchen. Nearly ten years older than *Tía* Rebecca, his body at last was shutting down. He ached everywhere. His exercise mounted to little more than walking slowly to a dry block of a tree stump outside his kitchen window, where he soaked in sunshine like the familiar geraniums positioned alongside the glass. Therapists came to my uncle's home periodically to gently massage his body and ease him toward the inevitable.

During our visit, *Tío* Emiliano kept rubbing his right side along the ribs and complained about a sharp pain that wouldn't go away.

"*¿Qué será, tío?*" I asked.

His reply reminded me why I had considered it so important to learn Spanish from him and others decades earlier. It was a gem of a story, filled with love, longing and subtle humor.

"The therapists come in to try to help me. They rub me here and they rub me there," he said, slowly moving both his hands against several parts of his torso. Then he lifted his hands directly over his heart before moving them gently to the other side of his chest. "My heart has been hurting ever since your *tía* died," he said. "I'm beginning to think that the therapists, with all their rubbing, moved my heart all the way from where it used to be way over to this other side where the pain seems to get worse and worse."

He struggled to smile.

Four months before his 100th birthday, *Tío* Emiliano was buried alongside his loving wife in the Cundiyó cemetery. Two of their children, claimed one right after another by whooping cough that swept through the village in 1940, were in their own plots nearby.

Cundiyó would continue playing a major role in shaping my life to an extent that I could not have envisioned even in my dreams.

From the Roybal Files...
The Santa Fe New Mexican, December 29, 2002
Time Has its Own Pace in Villages of Northern New Mexico

Emiliano T. Vigil of Cundiyó has seen 98 New Years. He's shooting for 100. Number 99 has seemed slow in arriving.

"Are you sure I'm not a hundred?" he asked recently in Spanish with at least a hint of impatience in his voice. "Time all of a sudden seems to have slowed down."

He sounds as if he has concluded that hitting 100 is his last goal in life, and he's ready to get it done.

Emiliano is my uncle and neighbor, the oldest living resident of Cundiyó, a tiny mountain community 25 miles north of Santa Fé. Here cattle are still driven down the main road that runs alongside about 35 *adobe* homes, including one to which J. Robert Oppenheimer used to steal away decades ago for food, drink and conversation with an old friend.

My Tío Emiliano's interests for most of his long life have been in the mountains of our blessed region, but not in the Jemez Mountains to the west, where Oppenheimer helped give birth to atomic weaponry. Emiliano's affections to this day are in the Sangre de Cristos that rise to the east of the home he built with *adobes* of his own making.

The simple home went up right next to one that housed 12 sisters, one of whom he courted until he made her his wife.

My uncle is rich with stories of bear hunts and fishing trips that were taken into the Rockies and their foothills for far more than sport. People of the community relied on the mountains for food. Catch and release had no meaning to them.

Families were big, with members young and old. Young or old, everybody ate.

Even if to a lesser extent today, food remains one of my uncle's lingering loves. Beans, *chile*, *menudo*, coffee, pastries of all kinds. He'd sit at the kitchen table next to the wood-burning stove and savor every bite of the food put in front of him. Concerned about the latest news regarding fat and cholesterol, my aunt some years back put aside the ever-present blue and white box of Morrell lard and began frying potatoes in vegetable oil. It didn't last long.

"I don't know what's going on, but you need to stop cooking potatoes in that oil that looks like the one we use for the truck," he instructed Rebecca, the love of his life.

This will be Emiliano's second New Year without his wife, and time sure moves slowly now.

The Rev. Casimiro Roca has ministered the people of Cundiyó almost since he first arrived in the United States from Spain in 1951. "Cundiyó is like my home," he has said many times. He speaks fondly and, occasionally, with melancholy of his adopted home that is remarkably isolated from much of what unfolds in communities just a few miles down the road but still reflects change from one New Year to the next.

"One day, I'm going to sell these first few rows of benches," he teased in Spanish and smiled as he gave the homily recently in Cundiyó's tiny adobe chapel. "Fewer and fewer people come to church, and those of you who do come insist on sitting in the back."

In a later service, after re-enacting Las Posadas leading up to Christmas this year, the Rev. Roca spoke specifically of the young people who stay away from church, seemingly more and more with time.

Maybe it's because they're all getting cars at such an early age, he opined. Parents apparently have been convinced that they're supposed to give cars to their kids upon graduation—even graduation from the eighth grade, he exaggerated to make his point. The cars then take kids everywhere but to church, he said.

Joe E. Gonzales of the Pojoaque Valley might have related easily to the Rev. Roca's stories about cars and kids. Gonzales, 84, was one of eight teens who made up the first graduating class of Pojoaque High School, whose student body soon included more than a few from Cundiyó.

A car for graduation? Huh! Not in those days, said Gonzales. Before Santa Fé County created the Pojoaque schools, Gonzales attended the private school in Santa Cruz, where he was taught by nuns. He vividly recalls the rides to and from school each day.

"We used to go in what was called 'the chicken coop,'" Gonzales said. "It was a little house made of wood on the back of a 1931 Chevy truck owned by one of my neighbors. It had little benches inside. For us, there was no such thing as a school bus."

"There was a lot of poverty in my days. We didn't go hungry. No, no, no. Everybody in the valley planted something. And people had sheep and cattle galore."

Just not a lot of money. And no cars for graduation.

Changes have been staggering for some. It could help explain why my *Tío* Emiliano has been in such a hurry to hit a hundred. He'd like to move on.

4
Mysteries and Other Influences on Youths

The importance of education was not lost on me as I learned how my Mother's parents sacrificed to get even just a few of their children into some of the region's best schools of the time. Allison-James in Santa Fé and Menaul in Albuquerque, however, remained as mere dreams for far too many in the Vigil household in Cundiyó.

And post-secondary school, even in short-lived ventures, touched lives of very few in both my Mother's and Father's families. It wasn't for a lack of desire to pursue classroom education. As in the case of my Tía Rosiña and her lost dreams of attending Menaul, needs of the household often held priority.

Both my parents as adults worked as teachers and spoke often of how a college education could improve prospects for a successful life. But I realized early on that if I were to attend college, financial support from home would be very limited.

Mom had stopped fulltime employment to raise her children. There were five of us by the time I entered the fifth grade at Española Elementary School. Dad was earning $9,000 plus change as a shop/industrial arts teacher at Santa Cruz High School. He spent many of his free hours making cabinets and furniture in our garage at home to fill orders that came his way. To further augment his teacher's salary, he also pruned trees for neighbors and accepted almost any chore that cried within earshot for his attention.

Still, family funds were enough to meet monthly expenses and little more. A very serious congenital heart defect accompanied my little sister into this world in 1960, placing new, substantial demands on my parents' resources.

I was in the fifth grade when I secured permission to be dismissed early from class each day just before lunch to begin preparing for chores in the cafeteria. I volunteered as a dishwasher in return for free meals. It didn't amount to much but it saved my parents from having to pay for the meals. Every little bit helped, I figured, all the while recalling my Father's stories about his own times as a restaurant dishwasher while attending Menaul.

As for college days ahead, I knew I would need my own bank account and every bit of luck available while pursuing grants, scholarships and loans when the time came for me to apply for higher education. I arrived at that conclusion well before leaving grade school.

I was ten years old when my inescapable conclusion propelled me into becoming a member of what might have been called The *Tamale* Express. It was an enterprise rooted in the San Pedro kitchen of Sennie García, whose son, Elias "Milly" García, was working his way through Highlands University in Las Vegas, New Mexico, during the 1960s.

Sennie was an accomplished *tamalera*, a *tamale* maker. She had dozens of *tamales* packed and stacked at the start of each weekend. Their numbers soared come summertime.

"Milly" would load his family's 1951 sloped-back Chevrolet with four or five young boys for regular runs into Santa Fé neighborhoods half an hour away. We, the young salesmen, knocked on doors along Santa Fé's Barrio de Guadalupe, Baca Street and side roads of what is now north St. Francis Drive. Thermos jugs packed with *tamales*, we'd often find people waiting for us at their doors as word swept through neighborhoods that we had arrived.

First, though, came the obligatory stop at either the Texaco or Chevron station half a mile from the García's San Pedro home. A buck or two—literally, one or two dollars spent at the rate of 19.9 cents per gallon—was always enough for the round trip and all the meandering that was required in Santa Fé to secure sales.

"Milly" waited to buy gas until we were all loaded in the faded black Chevy and heading out to make our sales. It was as if to remind us that he had overhead costs that kept him from paying more than the three-cent commission on each *tamale* sold.

"Milly" rewarded the two or three *tamale* salesmen toward whom he felt most favorable on any given trip with the Baca Street drop off, which undeniably was the most-profitable of assignments.

Even the worst salesman assigned to Baca Street, just off the old Camino Real, could not keep *tamales* in his jug. People there often figured our visits into their modest weekly grocery budgets.

While other boys worked Santa Fé's surrounding northwest neighborhoods, "Milly" couldn't stray too far from Baca Street where he was needed to provide near-constant refills from the big chests kept in the trunk of his old car.

Countless times during any given day on the beat, each of us kids would bend a knee and remove the lid from our round jugs that resulted in the release of an aroma like few others in this world.

Responding to orders at screen doors, out by mailboxes or alongside cars that pulled over solely to transact business, we'd reach into the jugs and fill our hands to produce whatever numbers were ordered: twenty-five cents a piece.

Sometimes it was just one or two. But usually it was half a dozen, a dozen, even several dozen at a time. The bigger orders required that we scamper back to "Milly's" tired Chevy to refill our jugs.

I was out to make money, not to eat my earnings, so I went most days without buying more than one or two *tamales* for myself.

"Milly" García lost his life to cancer long before he had time to put his teaching certificate from Highlands University to much use. Time spent with The *Tamale* Express wasn't lost, though. Far from it. Along with allowing me to lay down the first dollars on which my own humble college bank account was to be built, Milly and his Mother fortified my already-budding conviction that anything worth wanting is worth chasing.

Ink-stained Hands and Pockets Full of Coins

Like "Milly" García and his Mother, a fifth-grade classmate in Española also provided more than a little inspiration during the period. Tony Vigil, by simply walking into our classroom within one of Española Elementary's converted Army barracks, made it amply apparent that his youthful enterprises were turning out to be more rewarding than mine.

It didn't take a genius to determine why. I was working weekends and summers selling *tamales*. Tony worked daily year-round, excused from class a few minutes early every day to walk the mile or so from Hill Street to local offices of *The Santa Fe New Mexican* newspaper on Oñate Street.

There, Tony filled his arms with the latest edition of the daily newspaper just delivered from the capital city 25 miles away.

Tony was good at his work. Among other hawkers, he staked out the city's best areas for himself and enthusiastically held out the top half of the paper's front page unobstructed by hands or arms so that leading headlines could be read by approaching motorists. (The basic stance seemed to have been lost on later-day news hawkers.)

Skills that Tony displayed daily with *The Santa Fe New Mexican* were put to use on Wednesdays while he peddled the weekly *Rio Grande SUN*.

Tony's family was no better off than mine financially but Tony arguably was one of the school's best-dressed students: nice shirts, ironed and rolled up stylishly once or twice at the sleeves; good slacks; polished dress shoes.

And there was something else about Tony. His pant pockets were always bulging with coins, the kind of money that few of the rest of us saw on a daily basis. And, Tony must have thought, what good were pockets full of coins if you didn't poke your fingers into the money at least once in a while, rattling it around just enough to catch people's attention while also reminding yourself of your fortunes?

I decided I had to try my hand at what Tony was doing so successfully.

In time, I too became a presence on the streets, hawking papers and giving change as quickly as I could so I could move on to the next customer. I got to be pretty good but I never matched Tony's success. He was the master. Like Tony, my hands were ink stained and smelling of coins at the end of each day. More importantly, my little savings account grew along with my prospects for getting through college.

Saddlebags on a Bridgestone then a Yamaha

In a few years, my attention strayed to what seemed to offer bigger payoffs. My focus was still on newspapers but I suddenly was enticed to work at a different level. The enticement: small motorcycles that boys barely a year or two older than me rode along Española streets, slicing through the air while racing purposefully to their destinations.

Those destinations as often as not were connected one way or another to newspaper deliveries on routes carved out of the Española Valley.

The sound of the bikes' motors was music to my ears. The bikes seemed to offer a kind of freedom and status that I had yet to experience for myself. I wanted some of both.

I was nearing the age when I could ask for such a bike to carry on with my newspaper sales. But asking and getting, of course, are two different things. My Mother, in particular, had spoken over and again about the dangers of motorcycles. If I were to stand a chance, I would have to soften my parents' perception of motorcycles as risks best left to others, preferably nobody in the extended family.

It would be a long-term effort, one that I approached with scissors never far from reach. Any account of a motorcycle accident—no matter how far from home—that made it into print and found its way into our family home was cut out and destroyed.

I'd also pounce on any opportunity to tell my parents of boys around the Española Valley, like industrious Johnny Whetsell, who used their motorcycles to tend to needs of their families and those of the broader reading community. Work: I knew that if I could get my parents, particularly my Father, to associate motorcycles with work, I stood a chance.

Eventually, my parents gave in. With little fanfare, my Father drove me a couple of miles to Española's Río Grande Sales, a well-established mom-and-pop business known for marketing Sherwin Williams paint, McCulloch chainsaws and Maytag washing machines. Santiago Martínez, soft-spoken and heavy-set, grew up with Dad in Truchas. He and his wife, Bertha, had owned Río Grande Sales for years. Santiago had shown up at our house in San Pedro at least a couple of times as the Maytag Repairman, tending to adjustments and replacements as needed on Mom's washing machine.

The growing popularity of small motorcycles in Española hadn't escaped his notice. One store that sold only Suzukis motorcycles and accessories had recently opened in town. Yamahas, Hondas and Kawasakis were being purchased and brought in from Santa Fé stores.

Not long before my Father and I walked into Río Grande Sales on an unexplained venture, Santiago had added two Bridgestone motorcycles to his stock of goods. Both looked entirely out of place amid the paint, chainsaws and washing machines. My Father asked me to give each of the two motorcycles a look and then make a choice.

We were going to take one home, Dad said. It would be mine to use for helping to deliver newspapers wherever I was assigned. I was to be a responsible worker, said Dad; no fooling around. I was to make monthly payments on the bike, buy its gas and make sure it stayed in good running condition.

My new bike was painted deep blue and had plenty of chrome touches. It was a 90-cc beauty with a manly kick-start engine. The sale price was around $300. Dad probably leaned on his lifelong friendship with Santiago and his years as a regular customer at Río Grande Sales to knock off a few dollars from the ticket.

My first newspaper route followed soon after I got the Bridgestone home. I became one of a tiny army of boys who in the mid-60s delivered *The Santa Fe New Mexican* newspaper to homes throughout the Española Valley, which spread outward for miles along cottonwood-lined banks of the upper Río Grande between Santa Fé and Taos. Our work kept us busy every day except Saturdays. *The Santa Fe New Mexican* did not publish on Saturdays.

That first route took me through much of Española's eastern edge, including Riverside and Santo Niño neighborhoods.

Other routes and responsibilities followed. I brought home a red 125-cc Yamaha from Santa Fé after paying off and then selling the smaller Bridgestone.

One year on the job turned into two and then three. Work during the warm months was enjoyable. It was brutal come winter. Sundays were the worst. *The Sunday New Mexican* was distributed in the mornings. No amount of clothing at my disposal could stave off the bitter cold that gripped my hands, knees, neck and feet as I maneuvered my motorcycle from home to home before sunrise.

Money that went into my humble account at the First National Bank of Río Arriba depended on how much I collected from my customers in the final days of every month. I got a small percentage from each collection. If each home paid its account as expected, my monthly take would have been between $30 and $40. There was never a month when every subscriber paid as expected so my earnings never were what they were supposed to be.

My savings, thankfully, got a boost from loosely scheduled work I did pumping gas and checking the oil in vehicles of motorists at a Chevron station and a Texaco station (the same ones frequented by "Milly" Garcia) on U.S. 84-285, the main road into Española coming from the south.

Throughout the three years that I delivered *The Santa Fe New Mexican*, I rode my Bridgestone and Yamaha to Española's junior high school campus on Hill Street every day so that after the last school bell rang I could collect my newspapers, roll them up, secure them with rubber bands, stuff them into my white canvass saddlebags and get them to subscribers without delay.

I'd park my motorcycles across the street from the school at the home of Española businessman, Richard Cook, a former U.S. Navy Frogman and one-time Boy Scout leader. Cook was the adult son of W.P. and Sara Cook, who owned and operated Española Mercantile Co., which included a lumberyard that my Father relied upon while engaged in the carpentry that occupied him between his duties as a high school teacher.

My brother, Tim, worked a summer at the Cooks' store, assembling swing sets, sweeping floors and tending to any other duties sent his way. Sara Cook, an Española school board member from 1935–1938, was particularly attentive to making sure Tim had enough to stay busy.

Richard Cook grew to be an integral part of his family's business and was on his way to becoming one of New Mexico's most enterprising and financially successful businessmen by the early 1960s when my Father secured permission for me to park my bikes at his home. I recall thanking Cook in a note that I left at his front door one morning after parking my bike. We were cordial with one another until Cook's death in 2017 at the age of 91.

Cook, the man who once corrected people about his substantial wealth at a town meeting in Velarde, seemed to have a soft spot for anyone who wasn't afraid of work.

At that Velarde meeting north of Española, Cook had just been derided as a millionaire bent on getting his way while surface mining on a nearby hill. He stepped out of the crowd, surprising many with his presence, and offered a correction. According to one of the men there, Cook said: "Excuse me, but I'm not a millionaire. I'm a billionaire."

WHO DELIVERS PAPERS OUT THERE?

Daily responsibilities of my newspaper routes kept me plenty busy but it didn't take long for the bigger world—no, mysteries of the universe beyond—to thrust themselves permanently into my consciousness.

On a cool, dark night near banks of the Río Grande that has snaked its way through centuries of history generated in three U.S. states and two disparate nations, our globe suddenly, unexpectedly got small for me. In just a few seconds, I was drawn into the company of those older and wiser than me who are convinced that life reaches far, far beyond newspaper routes in Española or anywhere else on Earth.

At the tender age of 14, I was pressed to conclude that we on this planet are not alone; that we are being watched, maybe even monitored and judged by beings who move incredibly through time and the heavens. Their movement that night was in aircraft "unavailable to us," as one respected New Mexican would proclaim years later while contemplating his own experiences with unexplained flying objects.

If my beloved brother, Tim, struggled to deal with incredulities of organized religions and competing doctrines of Catholics and Presbyterians who sought to shape our lives, I was left to consider whether such dealings were mere distractions from forces not mentioned in anybody's Good Book.

Further, if even one of the many Gods professed to be responsible for life on this planet truly exists, is He/She also the source of life that I had seen moving unimaginably and seemingly free of constraints in space which most humans have mentally reserved for angels and other heavenly spirits?

Does that Creator also have His/Her ministers of faith working on globes far beyond our own to teach love, peace, hope and compassion? Are those teachings being embraced in the other worlds? Or, are those who come to observe us from those worlds vulnerable to intolerance and aggressions like those that escalate to frightful levels here on Earth?

For generations we have lived in fear of a holocaust ignited by earthly tensions. Might the end of times actually come from quarters that we have yet to discover?

They were profound issues, to be sure, for a boy whose own travels had taken him no further than the plains of Dallas, Texas. And I knew that unless the issues were resolved in my lifetime, the mysteries would follow me to the grave. It was humbling more than frightful.

I didn't face the experience alone. Two other "paper boys" employed by *The Santa Fe New Mexican* were there. So was Nick Naranjo, a sergeant with the Española City Police Department. As a side job, Nick worked as *The Santa Fe New Mexican's* district manager for circulation, tending to "paper boys" and our deliveries.

Nick had a commanding presence even when out of his gray and black police uniform. He also was part of a family that during the previous decade had begun developing a political dynasty that was to assert influence even beyond northern New Mexico for decades yet to come.

One night Nick was with me and the two other "paper boys" in La Mesilla, a neighborhood of middle-income homes still developing along the eastern bank of the Río Grande just a few miles south of Española. We were discussing problems associated with our delivery routes as well as opportunities for developing those routes to include more homes.

But as I recall, most of that was simply an excuse for getting together that night to socialize in a valley that offered few opportunities for socializing. Nick clearly liked the air of authority that followed him through his work as a policeman, which rarely mounted to more than issuing traffic tickets and snagging drunks off Española streets. But he also had a quick sense of humor and enjoyed the joking and teasing that inevitably arose when he got together with young teen boys away from the police force. His wife at home likely found less to like about Nick's absences.

That night in La Mesilla we stood outside Nick's family car, a white Oldmobile Cutlass that Nick seemed to take as much pride in as we boys did in our small motorcycles parked just a few feet away. Our chatter was steady but mostly inconsequential amid occasional bursts of barking dogs that served as sentries in the night below porch lights of their keepers' homes.

We certainly weren't looking for a life-changing experience. But we got one none the less. I forget who was startled first but in an instant we all were looking and pointing incredulously at the dark sky over the Jemez Mountains to the west. Small, bright balls of light, more than half a dozen of them, moved mysteriously above and just to the south of Los Álamos, which is world renowned as The Atomic City.

In truth, to say that the orbs moved does not do justice to the brief display. The bright balls—each one of them—sped freely in all directions. They glided. They darted. They danced. Their motion was smooth like that of a prima ballerina whose routine required that she touch gracefully the entire surface of her stage before exiting for the night.

Some of the bright balls would disappear as suddenly as they appeared only to reappear again.

We were witnesses to an incredible mystery. That it all unfolded above the city where 20 years earlier scientists worked feverishly—and secretly—to develop the horrific atomic bomb and where much of our nation's top-secret scientific research continued only added to the intrigue.

Doyle Akres was *The Santa Fe New Mexican's* Española bureau chief at the time. It was a fancy title for a one-man reporting office. Naranjo suggested that we contact Akres so that he might witness the display for himself and report about it in the following afternoon's paper. But Akres was not to be found.

No matter. The mind-jarring display, having disappeared after we raced off in search of the newsman, would have no reprise. Not that night. Not in that heavenly space.

Still, from that night forward, every news report, movie, television show and campfire story about unidentified flying objects would trigger in me—and others who were with me that eventful night—memories of an experience that likely would have no rival.

Wet Ink on Newsprint and Morning Rounds

No mystery that I came upon on my own was to get in the way of the mysteries advanced over the ages through organized religion. Mom and Dad saw to it nearly every Sunday morning that I was exposed to the belief that the Holy Spirit lives in individuals but works through the community, along with other teachings of the Presbyterian Church.

I had been baptized in the brick-veneered church that is just off the campus of McCurdy Mission School, which was a sister institution of Mom's and Dad's revered Menaul School in Albuquerque.

Weekly church services made Sundays particularly challenging for me.

Sundays for me started long before roosters began crowing on either side of the Río Grande. Nick Naranjo often relied on me to help him with his Sunday responsibilities before I turned to my own. Newspapers, usually tied tightly into bundles of 100, were delivered to Española fresh off the printing press on Marcy Street in Santa Fé just before three a.m.

Nick in his Cutlass and I on my motorcycle would arrive at *The Santa Fe New Mexican's* Spartan office on Oñate Street to meet the deliveries. We then promptly broke the bundles into new numbers to correspond with counts needed for each of the Valley's home delivery routes along with the smaller bundles to be delivered to gas stations and stores throughout the Valley.

Outdoors the smell of early morning air consumed everything in the darkness. Inside the newspaper's office the smell was of wet ink on newsprint. It was a smell that would stay with me—often, on me—well into my adult life.

With the reconfigured bundles marked and tied, newspapers destined for home delivery were picked up later by teens on their motorcycles. Nick and I loaded bundles marked for businesses into his Cutlass then make the rounds, dropping off the papers at doors that weren't due to open yet for hours.

Once those deliveries were made, Nick drove me back to my motorcycle parked outside the newspaper office. There, I cut the twine around the large bundle put aside for my home delivery route and begin stuffing papers into canvass saddlebags that were to straddle the back half of my bike for the next hour or two.

The Sundays of those three cold winters that I delivered newspapers left such an impression on me that the Sabbaths of spring, summer and fall all but faded from memory.

Up since before three a.m., I'd walk stiffly, painfully into our family home around 8:30 a.m. after having braved freezing temperatures to help get the latest edition of *The Santa Fe New Mexican* to hundreds of homes and other designated repositories. It's not that I was a glutton for punishment. But there was that pledge to be a responsible worker that I made to my Father before leaving Río Grande Sales on my new Bridgestone.

Arriving at home, I'd peel off layers of clothing, splash warm water onto my face and too quickly found myself seated in church alongside my parents and siblings for a slow-moving hour that I often spent bent over, elbows on knees and half asleep. Fear of making sleeping noises at my parents' side kept me from dozing off completely. So, too, did the tingling and then the dreaded pain that spread through my fingers and feet as they thawed from the deep freeze inflicted during my early morning rounds outdoors.

We were in the company of people like the tall, gray-haired usher, Mr. Perkins; the ever-confident educator and coach, Dolph Pringle and his family; physician Leonard Akes and his family; as well as the elderly Herrick sisters of Sunday school repute.

The Rev. Richard Campbell led in the singing and gave the sermons. He was a particularly gifted and relevant storyteller whose carefully crafted messages left lasting impressions even in my slumber.

I don't recall, though, that any of the good reverend's stories ever addressed questions about extraterrestrial beings. The prospect of such company in our universe had cast new light for me on all things touched by religion.

The supernatural, to be sure, was no stranger to the lands of my childhood along the upper Río Grande. Mysteries were the fuel of legends, poems and songs, and they followed the grand river to its end.

An impressionable young paperboy, I grew increasingly convinced that there might not be worldy limits to the headlines of newspapers I would dutifully deliver to unsuspecting neighbors the following day or, perhaps, the one after that.

From the Roybal Files...
The Santa Fe New Mexican, Commentary, October 31, 1995
Memory Falls into Ghostly Seasonal Trap

It was the ghost of wicked Felina for sure, I thought, as I drove home under a slender crescent moon that dimly lit the Pojoaque Valley, where old cottonwoods are all but skeletons now in the crisp autumn air.

Halloween approached amid a roar of transformations in this rural hub that sends crossroads reaching toward the newest revelations of the atomic age at one end and toward ancestors of the Southwest's oldest civilizations at the other.

In a season defined partly by fantasies of death, my imagination assumed a life of its own.

I was heading north on U.S. 84-285 just after sundown when a fireball danced across the road toward the hills of Pojoaque Pueblo. Los Álamos, the Atomic City, looked down from a *mesa* to the west.

The luminous ball that appeared before me whirled into a door of an all-but forgotten figure of times past, a long block of a building that seemed to have reappeared from oblivion to give repose that night to a tiny ball of fire. In my inexplicable state of mind, I concluded that the mysterious ball was indeed the spirit of Felina. It had to be Felina, the Mexican maiden whose story I first heard in that creaky, deteriorating structure as a kid probably 35 years earlier.

The building, long ago demolished, was E.D. Trujillo's Trading Post. It stood just off the road of what in the 1950s was called "The Y," a little intersection as sleepy as the Nambé River a quarter of a mile to the north. The entire strip of road between Santa Fé and Española had always been sleepy with evidence of only half-hearted attempts at development.

The façade at Trujillo's Trading Post was two stories high, three stories at the middle of the building where it sloped up over a pueblo-style *portal* that was crowned by a mission bell.

It was a dinosaur of a building, straight out of the Old West. Inside, it had squeaky floors, decent burgers and an old jukebox that countless times a day gave Marty Robbins a chance to tell of a whirling Felina, Rose's Cantina and young cowboys as wild as the west Texas wind.

Trujillo's trading post was where I first heard Robbins' classic ballad, *El Paso*. My dad had pulled his 1952 Pontiac into Trujillo's for an unpretentious lunch one afternoon en route back from one of our family's infrequent excursions into Santa Fé.

For years after first walking into it, I thought that Trujillo's Trading Post *was* Rosa's Cantina. Inside and out, it looked like the perfect hangout for a dashing and daring young woman who inspired love that was stronger than a man's fear of death.

Decades later, long after it was razed, the image of the old trading post was back, even if only in my mind. It rose out of the dusk to capture my attention on the very spot where orange monsters of the state Highway Department earlier that day had worked to lay a new web of roads designed to move motorists to sprouting development just beyond what had been the site of the old trading post.

To the dismay of many, that development included transformation of a low-flung building that had served as an elementary school for my two children and thousands of others. The building that once encased classrooms for kids high on energy and rich with hope was converted into one of the region's first cash-hungry casinos.

The fireball that only seconds earlier had pranced in front of my pickup was now bounding aimlessly inside the darkened, dilapidated old trading post, as if whirling to the tunes of jukebox music and yelps of drunken trail hands.

I spun my truck toward the ghost of the old building just in time to see the fireball's glare fade out. Immediately, dim yellow lights from the ceiling set the dusty trading post aglow from one end to another.

I peeked through cloudy glass beneath the huge wooden staircase outdoors. There in the room where my brother, sister and I once gripped burgers and Nehi sodas, a young lady with the beauty of fantasies danced tirelessly with cowboys whose boots never touched the floor.

It was Felina, and her eyes were true to the song. They were blacker than night, wicked and evil while casting a spell.

Marty Robbins gave way to Faron Young, who gave way to José Alfredo Jiménez. The balladeers changed. So, too, did the ballads. But the crackling 45 spinning in the Wurlitzer stayed the same, song after song.

I pulled my nose away from the pane and looked at a surprisingly stark landscape around me. The casino that was aglow and abuzz with gamblers behind the trading post when I arrived moments earlier was gone. No Dairy Queen, either. No drug store. I drove up in my 1979 Ford but it was my other pickup, my 1954 International that idled, waiting for me a few steps away. The Ford was gone as if never having been on the scene.

Halloween approached, I reminded myself while my imagination continued to defy restraint.

I turned back for another glimpse of Felina but the trading post had vanished as suddenly and mysteriously as it had appeared. The Mexican maiden, too, was gone. Orange highway department machinery was back, parked and waiting for the morning's light.

My Ford had reappeared; the International, gone.

Halloween approached.

I grasped for reality and stepped into my pickup to climb the hills to the east that cradle the old village that I call home. I punched my favorite AM station on the radio and looked into my rearview mirror where I saw Felina's face smiling from behind the letters of the huge, bright casino sign that advertised a Cajun shrimp buffet for a five spot and pennies more.

Patsy Cline was singing "Crazy" on the radio, singing to everyone and there, in my pickup, to no one but me.

Change was gripping the Pojoaque Valley and anxiety was in the air.

E.D. Trujillo Trading Post in Pojoaque greeted locals and visitors for years on the busy route between Santa Fé, Española and Taos. (Photograph courtesy Patrick Trujillo and The Original Chimayó Trading Post in Española)

5
A Career Launched on 25 Cents per Inch
and a Quest for Equal Opportunity

My red 125-cc Yamaha motorcycle and I were all but inseparable by the fall of 1967 when I enrolled as a high school sophomore in Charles Pompeo's journalism class at Española High School.

Somewhere along my newspaper routes I apparently decided that writing for newspapers must be at least as much fun as delivering them. My brother, Tim, had gone through Pompeo's class and spoke very well of the animated storyteller in plaid shirts and soft leather shoes.

I promptly began contributing to the student newspaper, the *Hornet's Nest*, working alongside older students like senior Jimmy Rookard. My enthusiasm apparently wasn't lost on Jimmy, who approached me one day with a surprising offer.

Jimmy was working as a stringer for *The Santa Fe New Mexican* after school and on weekends, reporting on organized sports of some of the area's high schools. He liked the work but his family was moving. *The Santa Fe New Mexican's* Española bureau chief asked if he could recommend someone to replace him before he left.

He turned to me at school and I jumped at the opportunity. It would begin with an introduction to the bureau chief to see if she approved.

It was a Thursday after classes when Jimmy and I walked into the paper's office on Oñate Street about a quarter mile from our high school. Sandra Kincaid was seated at an old desk, pounding away at a manual Royal typewriter that looked like it might have been salvaged from World War II. Common use of office computers was still a decade and a-half away.

In my first year of high school, I couldn't help but guess that high school was more than a few years behind Sandra Kincaid. She was an attractive lady but seemingly not preoccupied with her appearance.

The top of Sandra's desk was a clutter of loose papers and notebooks. A jar of rubber cement used multiple times a day to connect one page of typing with another rose out of the mess alongside a black telephone.

Sandra was a tall lady by Española standards, perhaps approaching five-foot-ten. I could tell that even as she remained working behind her desk. Nor did it take me long to realize that she was direct in her approach and probably at least a bit gruff.

The day had been wet and Sandra apparently had been out in the weather earlier because she was still wearing black old-style rubber boots, unsnapped and open up the front as if she had started to take them off but ran out of time as her day's work piled up.

I stood at the opposite side of her desk where she paused her typing three or four times but only for a few seconds after firing questions at me. She listened to my responses before returning to her typing and the paperwork scattered on both sides of the typewriter. Clearly, I wasn't the priority of her afternoon.

Still, I concluded that her final question was the only one that might be trouble.

"You at least know how to type, right?" she asked, glancing up at me.

"Yes, ma'am," I replied promptly with a straight face.

The response kept me in the hunt.

"Come back Monday after school and I'll give you a closer look," she said.

That meant I had the rest of Thursday, Friday, Saturday and Sunday to teach myself how to type.

My Dad's black Underwood and I became extremely close during that very short period.

Ignacio Monge, a good friend of my Father's who taught typing and other subjects at Santa Cruz High School, came to our family home Saturday morning to go over the basics.

I didn't know much more than the basics come Monday afternoon, but it was enough to land me the assignment as Jimmy Rookard's successor.

Sandra Kincaid must have surmised how I spent my time after our first meeting because I detected a softening in her attitude toward me by the time our second meeting was over.

I was to go to work the following day, dropping in on team practices and preparing to write advance stories on games of the approaching weekend.

My desk was at the opposite end of the horizontal room that served as *The Santa Fe New Mexican's* Española bureau. The desk appeared just as old as Sandra's but smaller. I would sit on a tiny, well-worn office chair that was lightly padded and covered with hard, textured green vinyl. A Royal typewriter as old as Sandra's waited for me to apply my budding skills.

I had seen it all many times before while tending to responsibilities inside the office as one of *The Santa Fe New Mexican's* paper route boys. But now I wouldn't be delivering other people's work. I would be among those producing the newspaper from inside that unpretentious office space, which seemed to me like a station of promising possibilities.

Jim Maldonado was *The Santa Fe New Mexican's* sports editor in Santa Fé. He was a big, gregarious man in his mid-twenties. Not surprisingly, I ended up having more contact with him than with Sandra. Jim took a liking to me and within a few weeks, he had typed a long note for me in which he expressed his expectations.

Jim wanted me to go beyond reporting on teams of the three high schools in the Española Valley: Española Hornets, Santa Cruz Crusaders and McCurdy Bobcats. He wanted me to write regularly about the Elks of Pojoaque to the south and occasionally about teams as far north as the Escalante Lobos in Tierra Amarilla, the Mesa Vista Trojans of Ojo Caliente and the Leopards of Coronado High School in Gallina. He also said he wanted me to write an opinion column once a week that would add depth to the work of teams and players that I covered.

As time permitted, Jim said, he'd like me to write about Little League baseball teams, adult softball and 4-H activities.

All of what Jim suggested, of course, was rich with names. Names sell newspapers, he reminded me. It was one of the cornerstones of this craft that I had begun embracing. Jim ended his note by telling me that he recognized he was asking a lot of me. In the same sentence, he said he was confident I could meet his expectations.

The two of us grew very close.

I was assigned a twin-lens 120 roll film Rolleiflex camera for shooting pictures at team practices and games. I snagged a clipboard from home for recording my notes wherever I went. I'd borrow my Dad's blue Ford pickup for trips out of town.

My camera and clipboard became familiar sights in high school gyms and ball fields over the next three years. Both camera and I took repeated hits while I held my ground on the sidelines so that action could get close enough for my Rolleiflex to record a useable photo. Telephoto lenses for me were but a dream.

I'd dictate my stories by telephone to someone in Santa Fé when deadlines required. Otherwise, a carrier nightly delivered my stories and film to the capital city along with other material from the bureau in a small suitcase.

I was paid 25 cents per column inch for my writings that appeared in the paper; $2.50 for each picture that ran with my stories. Payment didn't change during the three years that I worked as a stringer.

Sandra Kincaid, I learned one day, was leaving the paper by week's end. She said little to me about her departure as the week progressed and was away from her desk late in the afternoon that was to be her last at the bureau. I purchased a drug store card and wrote a very brief note inside to express appreciation. I left the card on the seat of her chair on my way out of the office.

When I returned the following day after school, I found an envelope with my name on it waiting on my desk. Sandra, on her way out of town, had left a card and a few words of her own—along with a five dollar bill.

The money spawned a story that I carried with me for years. My handwritten note on the card that I left for Sandra, if compensated at the rate of 25 cents per column inch, wouldn't have gotten me more than 12 cents. In Sandra's hands, it yielded five bucks. I might never be paid as handsomely for words that I put on paper ever again, I concluded.

At school, the *Hornet's Nest* continued to occupy much of my time, as did student government. I was elected junior class president in 1968–1969 and served as student body president the following school year.

I was the student paper's sports editor during my junior year and editor while a senior. It was during that final year in high school that we converted from a mimeographed publication to one produced by offset printing. Charles Pompeo took responsibility for making sure we had the necessary funds. He effectively shielded the paper's staff from concerns about money.

Highlands University in Las Vegas 100 miles to the east annually organized what it called Highlands Days, which had become a successful recruiting tool for the university. High school students from much of New Mexico assembled on the Highlands campus for several days of workshops in multiple disciplines, journalism among them.

I was elected to serve as a vice president of the New Mexico High School Press Association during the group's annual convention on the Highlands campus. My principal duty was to work later in the 1969–1970 school year as editor of a special edition of the *Highlands Candle*, which reported on events and awards of the 25th annual Highlands Days.

I was up the entire night that the Highlands newspaper was assembled and printed there on campus on an old flatbed press. My work with Jim Maldonado and Sandra Kincaid already had made me aware that newspapering had no hours. For a kid still wet behind the ears, working all night was like a badge of honor.

Even before leaving for Las Vegas, I was convinced that the experience would be useful so I took Eddie López, a junior member of the *Hornet's Nest* staff, with me. I hoped that it might give him a leg up on the student association's activities the following year. Eddie worked with me through the night and into the following morning to ensure that copies of the special edition *Candle* got to where they had to be.

Eddie was a son of an Española schools administrator, who phoned my Father when Eddie and I were a few hours late returning from Las Vegas.

If there was any cause to worry, my Dad offered during the phone call, it was that I might have worked Eddie to death.

Neither Eddie's Father nor mine ever learned that I came dangerously close to going off the road more than once while nodding off behind the wheel of our family's 1962 Pontiac station wagon on the return trip home. Eddie was asleep so he, too, was spared concern.

The wise thing would have been to pull off the road to rest or, at least, walk around and get some air. But 18-year-olds are not known for being wise. In fact, it has been said that before we can be old and wise, we have to be young and stupid. I was being young and stupid. The lucky ones survive that stage. Too many do not.

Late in the 1960s, the upstart weekly *Espanola Express* was founded by a handful of local businessmen to compete with the popular *Rio Grande SUN*. Jim Maldonado was successfully recruited away from *The Santa Fe New Mexican* to edit the *Express*. He promptly put me to work for him part time. When Maldonado left midway through 1970, the paper's owners approached me to take over as editor.

Neither my parents nor my school principal were high on the idea. Principal Robert MacNeely, with whom I had worked closely throughout high school, turned to his well-honed skill of asking just the right questions for as long as it took to lead his pupil to a desired decision.

The decision: I would continue with plans to enroll at New Mexico State University. I had been saving for college, after all, since the age of ten.

My savings grew a little more than expected during the summer leading up to enrollment at NMSU. Jack Sitton, the highly regarded editor at *The Santa Fe New Mexican*, offered me a rare internship at the paper's main office in Santa Fé. Sitton said he would pay me an hourly rate for working multiple days each week, excluding Sundays.

I promptly offered to work Sundays for free. The paper had a small staff on Sundays and likely could use the help, I reasoned. Besides, I told Sitton, I would benefit from the experience.

No, we would stick to his plan, Sitton said firmly.

He must have shared the story with others because when Sitton died years later after having worked as editor of the *Farmington Daily Times*, one of his reporters, whom I had never spoken to, phoned for me in Santa Fé for comments about Sitton's career.

Conservatively Choosing a University

When it came to choosing a university to shape my future, my choice of New Mexico State University (NMSU) in Las Cruces 300 miles to the south of our family home was based on three considerations.

First, my brother Tim enrolled at NMSU and attended classes in Las Cruces for a couple of years before being drafted by the U.S. Army to help plug needs in Southeast Asia.

Second, the University of New Mexico (UNM) 100 miles away in Albuquerque had been the site of much-publicized campus riots against the Vietnam War, Richard Nixon's administration in Washington and even the UNM administration. Drug and alcohol abuse was associated with much of the unrest. None of it tracked with what my tradition-bound Republican parents had worked so hard to instill at home.

Finally, my parents without question remained a central influence in my life but, naturally, the additional separation between home and school offered by NMSU had more than a little appeal for a teen looking to spread his wings.

Campus unrest was spreading across the country at the time. Students along with outside agitators were protesting the Vietnam War on college and university campuses from coast to coast. Drug abuse was mounting. Even NMSU was not spared negative headlines.

In May 1968, *The Santa Fe New Mexican* reported of drug raids and nine arrests made on the New Mexico State campus: Eight were arrested for possession and sale of marijuana; one for possession and sale of LSD.

Two students, the newspaper reported, had been arrested on drug charges earlier in the week at Highlands University in Las Vegas.

Fifty years later, the campus arrests reported by *The Santa Fe New Mexican* hardly seemed like a red-letter day for crime fighting.

But bigger news was ahead. The *Albuquerque Journal* reported in May 1970 that approximately 224 colleges across the country had been closed because of anti-war activities; classes were cut or cancelled at many others.

Amid it all, conditions at UNM were coming to a boil by May 1970. On May 7th, a banner headline in the *Journal*'s front page told of an emotional explosion: "Officials Close UNM as Students Strike."

A smaller headline on the same page read: "3 Stabbed in Clash Over Flag."

The main story in that day's *Journal* told that Governor David Cargo and UNM President Ferrel Heady had ordered the campus closed for the rest of the week. The order followed violence that erupted during a student strike to protest the escalating war overseas and the shooting deaths of four students at Kent State University after national guardsmen opened fire earlier in the week during a disturbance on the Ohio campus of 19,000 students.

That same day several hundred strikers at UNM forced their way into the Student Union Building with the intent of occupying it for the night. Students smashed glass of the front door after employees had barricaded it with furniture, the *Journal* reported. Campus administrators consulted with the New Mexico State Police and others before deciding that students occupying the building would not be evicted during the night.

Governor Cargo ordered 150 national guardsmen and 50 state policemen to remain on alert off campus.

Orders changed for national guardsmen as well as for state and Albuquerque city police the following day.

"The occupation of the UNM Student Union Building came to an abrupt end under National Guard bayonets and state and city police batons Friday afternoon," reported *Journal* State Editor Bill Hume. He said guardsmen had bayonets affixed to their M1 and M14 rifles. State and city police were armed with riot sticks and were helmeted as were the guardsmen, Hume reported.

Richard CdeBaca, then a sergeant with the State Police, recalled how the agency was prepared for a potentially serious confrontation. "I know that I never saw so much ammunition being disbursed out of the property and supply (unit) at State Police headquarters as I saw for that particular civil disobedience. We saw all this stuff leaving headquarters. I thought we were being prepared for a real rebellion," he told me for his 2013 biography, *Chief of Police*.

Unrest of the period could not escape notice of anyone who spent at least some of their time awake. Mom and Dad breathed easier knowing that I would be an Aggie in Las Cruces and not a Lobo in Albuquerque come the fall of 1970.

I enrolled as a journalism and mass communications major at NMSU and promptly began working as a reporter for the student newspaper, the *Round Up*.

I found a conservative administration and equally conservative campus as I moved around. If UNM in Albuquerque was being rattled by hippies and others representing the counter-culture, cowboys and military-related student organizations still held down much of the fort at New Mexico State.

Such groups included the Sabre Squadron, Angel Flight, Corps Staff, Pershing Rifles, Scabbard and Blade, and Counterguerrillas.

Men and women couldn't sit together in the same dorm rooms, not to study much less to visit.

Clothes were ironed, hair was combed and neckties were donned for senior pictures.

Minorities constituted a small fraction of student enrollment that approached 10,000. Hispanics were 14 percent of the total. Blacks and Native Americans were much less than that.

Raucous entertainers passing through campus were few and far between. More often, it was people like Buck Owens, Vikki Carr, the Carpenters and Rod McKuen.

Rock concerts, in fact, were temporarily eliminated by university administrators in 1971 after they objected to student conduct at an Allman Brothers performance at NMSU's Pan American Center. Administrators said they could not tolerate the level of drinking and pot smoking evident at the concert. "What do the students want, to have a concert or do they want to have a big drinking party? ... The odor of marijuana was present throughout the building," said Chancy Van Pelt, director of auxiliary services."

New Mexico State University was very much at home within the larger Las Cruces community, whose economy was fueled largely by agribusiness. Big money in the community tended to be conservative money.

Nearby Holloman Air Force Base, White Sands Missile Range and Fort Bliss contributed to the shaping of attitudes and opinions.

I would in time come to think fondly of both the university and the city. It took a couple of years. I had a rude awakening to overcome. New Mexico State and Las Cruces are where I first experienced bigotry directed at me and others like me.

It wasn't the overt bigotry that I had seen as a pre-teen in Dallas, Texas, where I had accompanied my parents on a mission to save my little sister's life. Dallas in 1964 was one of the few places in the region with a hospital where the open-heart surgery needed by my two-year-old sister could be done. It also was still a city of the old South that refused to accept one of our country's most fundamental principles: that all are created equal.

Our waiting area at the hospital consisted of a row of chairs that were immediately across two small water fountains in a long hallway. One fountain was clearly marked for use by whites only; the other for blacks.

Similar signs designated who was to use nearby restrooms.

Discrimination that minority students faced at New Mexico State as the 1970s began was more insidious than what I had witnessed in Dallas. I easily made regular conversation with Hispanic cooks in the cafeteria and grounds men tending to the large expanses of lawn. But in many other situations, students and university employees alike made me feel like an interloper. There were wonderful exceptions, to be sure, but minority students for the most part were considered to be the "others" on campus despite marketing efforts by the university that professed otherwise.

NMSU was selling itself as an "ethnic university" even though conditions on campus showed that it was not so, said Ray Paz as he stepped into his recently appointed position of Chicano studies coordinator.

My awakening might not have been so unsettling had I been as familiar with the region's not-so-distant past as I was with its history of earlier periods.

School books record that the Mesilla Valley, which is now dominated by Las Cruces, briefly served as the capital of the Confederate Territory of Arizona during the Civil War despite the vow of Hispanic New Mexicans to fight segregationist advances from Texas.

Less known, was a high-profile eruption at New Mexico State in 1952 that could be traced to segregationist views that survived the Civil War. A land grant school, NMSU was still known as New Mexico A&M when a young married couple from Santa Fé had applied for enrollment at the university and for married couple housing on campus. They were approved for both following written exchanges made through the U.S. mail.

"They contact me after they had gotten the blow of their young lives," said Fabián Chávez Jr., who represented Santa Fé in the New Mexico House of Representatives during the period. Chávez spoke with me of the occurrence for his 2008 biography, *Taking on Giants*.

The call for help from Chávez was made by Reginald and Bonnie Barrow. College officials, upon learning more about them, told the couple they would have to live off campus because of their "Negroid extraction," according to a report in *The Santa Fe New Mexican*, Chávez's hometown paper.

"The Barrows, both born of parents having white and Negro ancestry, have been told by a college official that the institution 'shall be happy to try to help you locate satisfactory quarters in Las Cruces' off campus," *The Santa Fe New Mexican* reported on August 3, 1952.

Reginald and his wife Bonnie, both teens, said they would not accept housing off campus. They wanted the apartment-trailer on which they already had paid a deposit.

A&M President John Branson said the university's board of regents would have to deliberate the matter at its next meeting, according to news reports of the period. "The institution can hardly be said to have a policy," Branson said. "We've had two or three similar cases before, and Negroes were welcomed on the campus but were told they'd probably be happier living in Las Cruces ... It's because people are what they are. The community up to now has hardly been ready for a move as drastic as that is," he said of blacks being granted housing on campus.

Republican Governor Edwin Mechem, who lived in Las Cruces before his election, deferred to the university regents.

Fabián Chávez, though, refused to keep his hands off the case. "Jesse Richardson was chairman of the board of regents and was a state representative from Doña Ana County. He also was a friend of mine," Chávez said. "I called Richardson right away and asked him what the hell was going on down there. He says, 'Well, Fabián, you have to understand that we're only forty miles from the Texas border.' That was his answer to me."

"My reply was, 'Damn Texas.' And, frankly, my language was a bit more colorful than that. 'This is a New Mexico state institution supported by New Mexico taxpayers, and they shouldn't be treating this couple that way.'"

The A&M board of regents met in Santa Fé twelve days after the Barrow story broke in the press and unanimously approved a policy that said distinctions among students would not be made based on race, creed, or color. The Barrows obtained campus housing.

Conservative thought and policies still dominated NMSU when I began writing for the campus newspaper in 1970. University administrators for the most part had little to worry about when it came to the *Round Up*. The paper was mostly content to write about clubs, events and sports.

But I began to tweak reporting even as a freshman. And I had support from my editors. Editors named me the paper's "senior writer" my sophomore year and I retained the title as a junior, increasingly taking liberties while selecting topics for my reporting.

Whenever possible, I left stories like those about fraternities, ROTC promotions, benefit dances and approaching concerts to others.

The *Round Up's* editors at the time reflected emerging student leadership that was transitioning from the status quo to more-probing, inquisitive ways. Staff of the student yearbook, *Swastika*, included in their 1972 edition a preface that alluded to the university's recent upgrade of its branding: "Since 1970 the three triangles have been the official symbol of New Mexico State University. The basis for this symbol is the tri-cultural aspect of our geographical area: Indian, Spanish-Mexican-American, and Anglo. To date, there is very little at New Mexico State which reveals any but the Anglo culture. In an effort to serve all three cultures, the *Swastika* is now a tri-lingual book. We feel that the extra effort required to understand that which is not written in one's native tongue will help to achieve the cultural integration that our symbol has ordained."

Sometimes, however, entrenched attitudes instilled at homes and reinforced on campus remained visible even when actions were driven by good intentions. The trilingual reference in the yearbook preface showed up as occasional anonymous quote blocks positioned among pictures in the book. Some that were written in Spanish were more insulting than inspiring.

Upon translation, one of the Spanish quotes read: "I spent my first year in school smoking and drinking. I spent my second year wondering why I was even in school. I spent my third year looking for my true self. This is my fourth year and I'm going to finish school. But what a shame. I still smoke, drink, think, and look but now I have four years of experience."

Another read: "Some who think of themselves as leaders of La Raza yell: The gringos have the best jobs, the best homes and possess the power. To them I want to say: It is not true. I believe that education is the new life, and because of you, the (La Raza) leaders, we have to work harder."

Yet another: "The leaders don't tell us that there are also poor gringos, blacks and Indians just as there are Chicanos, blacks and Indians with money. That's life and if everybody yells nothing is gained."

That last entry was positioned amid photos of students in military uniform standing alongside a sword, a canon and rifles.

Annually, questions arose about the offensive name chosen for the yearbook. *Swastika*, said defenders, is not to be associated with the atrocities of Nazi Germany. Instead, the name was taken from an ancient Navajo idiom meaning that all people should live in harmony, they said.

At the *Round Up*, I wrote about the latest objections to the yearbook's name. And I wrote often about minorities demanding equal treatment. I often wrote about the lack of women and minorities in the administration. I wrote how only three percent of the NMSU faculty was Hispanic. I wrote of a 1971 compliance review by the U.S. Department of Health Education and Welfare that reported of "a dismal picture from the standpoint of aggressive hiring or promoting of minorities."

"Affirmative recruiting, hiring and promoting must be utilized to correct these deficiencies without delay," read the HEW report.

I wrote about the need for student representation on the board of regents. I wrote about angry Arab students who watched from NMSU as their families were being displaced in the Middle East. I wrote of the university's student government asserting increased autonomy over the central administration.

I wrote often about the university's policy prohibiting men and women from spending time together in dormitory rooms. NMSU was one of only two four-year universities in the Rocky Mountain region without some type of inter-visitation for campus residents.

The board of regents in 1972 "shelved" a proposal that would have modified the strict dorm policy. Dissatisfaction among students followed the action and lingered into the next year. My reporting on the subject also continued.

The administration in February 1973 presented a modified Open House By Invitation proposal that would have allowed students (and their parents) to opt out of male-female interaction in dorm rooms. Visitation would be allowed only by invitation and only during set hours. The policy would have been the most-limited among universities in the Rocky Mountains.

Regents rejected the proposal 3-1. "There is an alternative," said board member William Humphries, a Lyndrith rancher. "Students don't have to live on campus."

Regent Avelino Gutierrez, an Albuquerque attorney, cast the only vote in support of the proposal. "We are not treating the students as adults. This university is for the students and I think we are forgetting that very important fact," he said.

Two nights of student demonstrations followed the vote. A State Police force was called in. Clouds of tear gas wafted over protesting students.

NMSU was not accustomed to such things.

Along with my reporting on the subject, I had first-hand experience with the university's policy against inter-visitation in campus dorm rooms. The experience grew directly from my involvement in a sociology class project in the summer of 1972.

I was among several other students who volunteered to work alongside migrant workers on Mesilla Valley farms during the massive onion harvest. Workers arrived at sunrise and labored on their knees throughout the day, plucking freshly unearthed onions from the dirt, clipping their roots and stems with sheers before dropping them into five-gallon buckets that they then repeatedly emptied into large burlap sacks. Migrants left a trail of bulging sacks in their wake as they moved further into the fields.

A foreman would count each worker's sacks at the end of the day and record a tally that would lead to a paycheck later in the week. Laborers were paid 25 cents per sack. Thirty sacks in a day got the worker $7.50.

The hot summer sun beat down relentlessly on the workers. It baked onion juice that dripped from each clipping deep into the skin of workers' hands. Women who brought young children with them onto the fields used those hands stained of onions and dirt to wipe perspiration from their babies' faces, to feed them from barely-chilled bottles of milk and to change soiled diapers.

Older children labored alongside their parents. Food and water was in short supply. Shade was what could be found near aging vehicles. Some—but not all—farms provided portable toilets.

I wrote about conditions and took photographs for a two-part series published in the *Las Cruces Sun-News*. It reflected the darker side of the food production process that unfolded in the Mesilla Valley year after year.

Agribusiness likes stories about big, new farm equipment; record harvests; and advances in fertilizer or herbicides. As many see it, migrant farm workers and the brutal conditions they face for paltry wages are best left forgotten.

A migrant farm worker and her baby wait on an onion sack for the value of the woman's labor of the day to be calculated on a farm in the Mesilla Valley during the mid-1970s.

Near the end of the sociology class project, I agreed to meet with a fellow student in her campus dorm room to compare notes and prepare for a presentation that we were to make to NMSU President Gerald W. Thomas. It was June. Hot. Very few students were on campus. We were aware of the policy that prohibited men and women from being in the same dorm room. But, perhaps, we thought all might be relaxed just a little during the relative stillness of the summer, particularly given the mission that we were on.

We left the dorm room door open so that anyone passing by could see that we were occupied with work and nothing else.

No matter. Someone reported our violation, and I soon found myself standing before the dean of student services. I was told that I should know better. Then I got a slap on the wrist along with an assurance that I didn't want to make the same mistake twice.

My reporting on the migrant farm workers riled some in the community. Displeasure also followed my reports on mounting uneasiness among Hispanic students and their parents who relied on Las Cruces City Schools. A former NMSU student organized a walkout of 500 students in 1972 to protest the lack of Hispanic teachers throughout the district.

More than 16,000 students were enrolled in the district. Fifty-two percent were Hispanic. Among teachers, 632 were Anglos; 73 were Hispanic.

School board Chairman W.B. Darden and other school leaders said little but dismissed the protest as unnecessarily disruptive.

Organizer Jerry Lújan accused school leaders of perpetuating discrimination, even through their silence.

I didn't spend all my time as a student or campus reporter looking for controversy. Nor, though, did I dodge it. At times, controversy was nowhere to be found in some stories, like one I did in 1971 about an old Mesilla Valley farmer named Juan Márquez. But even these stories, I wanted to think, helped move some people away from looking at minorities as lesser human beings.

Márquez was born in Zacatecas, México, in 1898. He came to the United States 21 years later and promptly went to work on Mesilla Valley farms. In time, he developed his own small farm, taking to Las Cruces streets in a horse-drawn wagon made of wooden planks and modified to roll on worn rubber tires. Márquez used the wagon to peddle onions, squashes, and *chile.*

He concluded he had no use for motor vehicles after experimenting with a Model-T for three years.

I visited with Márquez and his wife about their work. He talked of men picking cotton for 25 cents a day during the Herbert Hoover years.

Mrs. Márquez said she often picked more than 100 pounds of cotton and was paid 15 cents for her efforts.

Márquez began making regular trips through Las Cruces to sell his farm products in 1936. He said he used to make an average of ten dollars each trip.

He was thinking of tying up his latest horse for good when we spoke in 1971. There was no more money in his work. People have access to *tiendas grandes* where they can buy anything they want in one place, he said.

This was a noble, hard-working man; a fellow resident of the Americas who deserved respect like any other human being. Equal opportunity grows largely from respect so to secure advances on campus, I concluded that stories about people like Juan Márquez could only help, even if Márquez had never stepped into a college classroom.

I benefited from encouragement of people like journalism department head Harvey C. Jacobs and professor John Dupree. But others, I came to learn, hoped to contain my efforts.

Applications for editor of the *Round Up* in 1973–1974 were being solicited as my junior year neared its end. I had all but decided not to apply. I wasn't aware of a Hispanic ever serving as *Round Up* editor. I had allowed myself to think that the editor's office really wasn't my place, despite my history at the paper.

I would think about it, I told those who inquired about my plans.

Others interested in the position waited.

One evening I walked early into playwright Mark Medoff's creative writing class to inform him that I needed to leave my desk soon after that night's class began. I had been asked to meet with a ranking member of the university's publications board, which would select the next *Round Up* editor.

The man was a long-time, respected member of the NMSU faculty, an insider, a player. And, I came to learn, he didn't want me to become *Round Up* editor. Or, at least, people prodding him from behind the scenes didn't want me to be editor.

I had done so well as a reporter, the professor told me, that it would be sad to see me leave the reporters' ranks. I might not find the same success as editor, he said, delicately.

I couldn't believe what I was hearing from the professor so I thought I'd test him with a less-than-delicate assertion from times past. "It's been said that not all Indians are meant to be chiefs," I offered.

"Exactly!" he replied.

That's when I decided that the *Round Up* was going to have a Hispanic editor in 1973–1974 whether a few of the entrenched big shots wanted it or not.

I returned to Medoff's class and informed him afterwards of how my meeting unfolded. Medoff was a Guggenheim Fellowship recipient and was being referred to by drama critics as one of the hottest commodities in New York theaters.

He encouraged me to disregard what I heard earlier in the night and apply for the editor's post.

My application went in the next day. Other students who applied, or contemplated applying, withdrew.

Our newspaper spent the following year not only prodding the administration and faculty to move beyond old, comfortable positions. The paper also cultivated opportunities to remind students that our responsibility was to achieve our potential because our families and communities relied on it.

That also was the year that Hispanic student leadership commanded an extraordinary presence on campus. While I worked in the editor's office at the *Round Up*, Fernando Macías served as president of Associated Students of NMSU and Christina Chávez was president of Associated Women Students. Each of us sat on the university's board of regents as non-voting members.

Near the end of the year, the *Round Up* won second place in judging of student newspapers throughout the Rocky Mountain region. First place went to the much-larger and better-funded paper produced at Utah's Brigham Young University.

So much credit for the good work was earned by managing editor Gilbert Álvarez of Las Cruces and the staff that worked with us. I hoped that placing Álvarez as M.E. would give him a jump on securing the editor's position the following year, knowing that his abilities were beyond challenge.

Along with my work at the *Round Up*, I was a paid correspondent for the *Albuquerque Journal* through much of the time that I was at NMSU.

I was actively recruited my junior and senior years by Howard Graves, Associated Press chief in New Mexico.

My immediate interests upon graduation, though, were in northern New Mexico and *The Santa Fe New Mexican*, which had given me my first smell of ink on newsprint. I went to *The Santa Fe New Mexican* after a very enjoyable ten-month stint as a reporter for Robert Trapp at the *Rio Grande SUN*. For several of those months, I was the only reporter at the *SUN*. The weekly, which was founded two decades earlier, printed its largest number of pages and greatest number of copies for weeks during that period.

The Santa Fe New Mexican was owned alternately by Robert M. McKinney and media giant, Gannett, during my times with the capital city daily. Gannett recruited me for some of its papers out of state while I worked as *The Santa Fe New Mexican's* editorial page editor from 1980 through 1982.

While serving as editorial page editor, unexpected new responsibilities came my way. *The Santa Fe New Mexican* in May 1982 partnered with Santa Fé's cable television station, KSFE, to begin offering local news reports eight times each weekday. I was asked to be the project's first news anchor. I passed on the offer to have a new wardrobe purchased for me but I couldn't escape the need to rise at three a.m. each day to begin preparing material for the broadcasts.

I was 28 when I began working as *The Santa Fe New Mexican's* editorial page editor. Executives at *The Santa Fe New Mexican* a year earlier offered me the job of city editor. It was the one job that I aspired to since I was a teen but I turned it down when offered. I wanted to excel at the post from which daily news reports are molded and reporters are guided through their rounds. Honored by the offer, I didn't think I was quite ready.

Gannett's overtures to move me to bigger cities at first carried little appeal. Years later, however, I briefly entertained the idea of pinning my future to the media giant.

"Word of your interest ... is the best news I've had all this Christmas season," *USA Today* Editor John C. Quinn wrote to me in a December 1985 letter.

Again, though, I opted to stay in New Mexico where I worked at multiple news media posts.

Beginning in the mid-1970s, I worked as a reporter, Española bureau chief, editorial page editor, capitol bureau chief and columnist for *The Santa Fe New Mexican*. I was a reporter and then capitol bureau chief for KOB-TV; a columnist for the *Albuquerque Journal* and a regular contributor to *Hispanic Business* magazine.

I turned to writing biographies in 2007 and have had four published leading to publication of this book. The book, along with tapping into some of the colorful history that preceded me, is about some of the people and times that figured prominently in my work as a journalist and author beginning fifty years ago.

Experiences collected while working in well-placed state and federal government posts fill out some of the accounts.

6
THE 'KING TIGER' SPRINGS INTO FUTILE BATTLE FOR LAND GRANTS

Real estate broker Virginia Smith and her husband were returning to their Tierra Amarilla home from their honeymoon in June 1967 when men aboard a National Guard tank stopped them near the Río Arriba County Courthouse and told them they could go no further.

Military tanks in pastoral Tierra Amarilla! Leprechauns would have been more believable.

Firebrand Reies López Tijerina, *el Tigre del Norte*, and around 18 armed followers had just shot up the old two-story courthouse. A couple of cops had been wounded, one of them left for dead outside the building. Hostages were taken in a commandeered Pontiac GTO toward the pine-studded hills around the small village of Canjilón to the south.

Tijerina's igniting of the emotional battle over Spanish and Mexican land grants in northern New Mexico during the late 1960s sealed my fate as a newspaperman. It determined what my career would be.

I was a 16-year-old sophomore writing for my high school paper and doubling as a sports stringer for *The Santa Fe New Mexican* as the land grant battle grew amid international attention. I was pulled into photographing and reporting on the unfolding controversy.

The battle, the one led by Tijerina, actually had its roots in New Mexico in 1958. Tijerina purportedly was hit over the head while addressing land grant heirs in Chama in May of that year.

In December 1959 Tijerina and members of a reported 80 families sent a letter to Republican President Dwight Eisenhower, asking for a federal investigation into claims of land grant heirs. Nothing came of it.

Tijerina, born on a Texas migrant farm camp in 1923, was approaching his 40s in August 1962 when he drafted his first plan in Albuquerque for what he called the *Alianza Federal de Mercedes* (Federal Alliance of Land Grants). He was now into a concerted campaign to rouse mostly-impoverished Hispanic villagers from tiny northern New Mexico communities, insisting that the U.S. government and wealthy, scheming Anglos stole land that was rightfully theirs.

Tijerina was volatile, driven, smart, egocentric and an unbridled dreamer. Some in the news media took to calling him "King Tiger." And that was fine by him. Some called him a racist and even worse.

Tijerina, to be sure, had little use for anyone who did not think like him. He repeatedly referred to Anglos as "renegades," the "real undocumented illegal aliens" who crossed the Atlantic without authority and took land that wasn't theirs.

There are two groups in the world, Tijerina told me soon after we first met in the 1960s. One was chosen by God. The other by the devil. According to his account, the Anglo comes from the second group. The Anglo's symbol, Tijerina insisted, is that of "a serpent that always strikes the horse from the rear."

Throughout his battle to reclaim lands awarded by Spanish and Mexican governments on what eventually became part of the United States, Tijerina asserted that he was up against corrupt "Anglo courts" and "Anglo justice."

He was driven by anger and hate, perhaps, as much as he was by a desire for justice.

The *Alianza* in 1963 sent letters to the U.S. and Mexican federal governments, reminding them of their obligations under the Treaty of Guadalupe Hidalgo.

The Treaty of Guadalupe Hidalgo, signed in 1848 at the end of the U.S.-Mexican War, spelled out rights of the people who were on the land when the United States claimed the territory of abundant natural riches for itself. The United States paid Mexico $15 million for a huge expanse of land, including what is now New Mexico as well as territory that became several other western states. It was essentially the northern half of Mexico and it was taken for a paltry sum.

The U.S. government pledged in the treaty to honor property rights of the people who were on the land at the time of U.S. occupation.

Tijerina's immediate focus in the battle as the 1960s unfolded was the San Joaquín Land Grant issued by the Spanish government in 1806. The community grant stretches from just west of Abiquiú north toward the Rio Arriba County seat of Tierra Amarilla. It originally included 472,000 acres.

But the bigger battle, said Tijerina, the battle that he promised to wage till his death, purportedly involved more than 100 million acres from Texas to the Pacific Ocean. By his count, 153 land grants were involved in New Mexico alone. Government officials in the late 1800s listed 204 New Mexico land grants with a total of more than 14 million acres.

"The San Joaquín grant ... was made by Joaquín Alencaster, the governor of New Mexico when it was under Spain," Tijerina said. "There were 39 families as original settlers. They were from Abiquiú, Santa Cruz de la Cañada...those areas. Spain recognized and confirmed the grant.

Mexico confirmed the grant. The United States did not. The United States government was saying that the title was no good, that it was a copy of a copy."

By the early 1900s, much of New Mexico's land grant property had been claimed by people who arrived in the territory after 1848 and manipulated U.S. laws and courts to their benefit. They easily overran natives of the land who were largely unfamiliar with the language and legal system of the newcomers. The U.S. government, itself, ended up with large expanses of land grant property that was then distributed for administration by the U.S. Forest Service or the Bureau of Land Management.

Roberto Mondragón, a Democratic New Mexico lieutenant governor for eight years during the 1970s, was among many who still cried foul decades after the repeated violations of the Treaty of Guadalupe Hidalgo. "Chicanery" was employed to wrest land away from rightful heirs, Mondragon said.

"We continue to survive as a people who have refused and resisted assimilating into this strange and alien society only because we hold a common vision," he told me. "We believe that some day justice will prevail and that we can return to our land."

Tijerina, a gifted orator and former Pentecostal preacher, was convinced that God himself sent him into the mission of reversing transgressions. He asserted as much to anyone who would listen.

Tijerina said he didn't fear taking on wealth and entrenched powers of Washington, DC, He lost his fear as a child, he said, when he was forced to hunt rattlesnakes to help feed his family.

"It all began ... when Tijerina formed the *Alianza Federal de Las Mercedes*," wrote Richard CdeBaca, a New Mexico State Police patrolman at the time. CdeBaca eventually became chief of the agency. He would have direct contact with Tijerina while working as a State Police sergeant and lieutenant and kept personal records of the period. He shared those records with me for his 2013 biography,*Chief Of Police.*

"Tijerina made believers out of people whose ancestors acquired (land grant rights), and soon had a following loyal to him and his preachings," CdeBaca wrote in his records.

The *Alianza* first tried to advance its cause through litigation and formal government channels. By 1966, however, its tactics had turned to demonstration and confrontation.

In 1966, an estimated 100 members of the group marched about 60 miles from Albuquerque to the Capitol in Santa Fé to present a petition to then-Governor Jack M. Campbell.

In October 1966, Tijerina led a group estimated at 350 people who occupied Echo Amphitheater, a roadside park managed by the U.S. Forest

Service. It is a portion of the property claimed by heirs of the San Joaquín Land Grant. The group left after the weekend was over but returned the following weekend and seized two forest rangers who were patrolling the area.

The rangers were "tried" and found guilty at a mock trial of *Alianza* members but were later released.

Finally, on October 26th, law enforcement officers with a federal restraining order escorted the remaining *Alianza* members from the area.

The *Alianza's* activity quieted during winter months that followed but demonstrations resumed in April 1967 in Santa Fé and Albuquerque.

"In May of 1967, Mr. Tijerina and his followers met and voted to re-establish the *Pueblo Republica de San Joaquín del Rio de Chama*, complete with its own mayor, government officials and its own flag ... They declared that the revolution had started and "all the *vendidos* and *gringos* were running scared like cornered dogs," CdeBaca wrote.

Tijerina asserted that his *Alianza* was 20,000 strong during the period, up from 6,000 members claimed in 1964.

There was a series of incidents that May which included property destruction at Echo Amphitheater and the burning of barns and grain belonging to Anglo ranchers in northern Río Arriba County.

"The offenses were never officially connected to the *Alianza*," wrote CdeBaca.

Unrest triggered a federal court order for Tijerina to turn over a list of *Alianza* members. Tijerina tried to maneuver around the order, saying he was disbanding the organization.

With emotions mounting, Tijerina called for a mass meeting of his followers at Coyote in the first days of June 1967.

State Police, who had placed at least one informant within the *Alianza*, learned of potential trouble brewing in the community of Coyote as June began.

"Word got out that the *Alianza* was going to have a meeting in Coyote to plan their strategy," wrote CdBaca. "On June 2nd, District Attorney Alfonso Sánchez gave orders to set up a roadblock on State Road 96 and arrest and confiscate the *Alianza's* records. We arrested 11 members of the *Alianza* on warrants signed by the district attorney, charging unlawful assembly and extortion in connection with past activities of the Federal Alliance of Land Grants."

"The records were confiscated along with some small firearms. Those arrested were taken to the Santa Fe City Jail, then they were transferred to the Tierra Amarilla courthouse, where they were to be arraigned on the charges."

Tijerina and his band were incensed.

First Judicial District Attorney Sánchez was to have represented the state during arraignment of the *Alianza* prisoners on June 5th. Tijerina said he wanted to make a citizen's arrest of Sánchez, who Tijerina asserted was guilty of terrorism and civil rights violations.

But State Police suspected something more was afoot. "We heard that Tijerina and his people were going to grab District Attorney Alfonso Sánchez and take him to Canjilón. There, they supposedly would give him a 'fair' trial and then hang him," wrote CdeBaca.

Tijerina insisted that his goals were far greater than exacting vengeance against one man. He wanted a massive reordering of land ownership through much of the U.S. West.

Whatever the motive, the June 5th, 1967, raid on the Río Arriba County Courthouse was carried out by a loosely knit alliance of small-time farmers, ranchers and forgotten natives of a region as poor as Appalachia. They followed their anger—and Tijerina—into the courthouse well armed and fully determined to grab the bombastic district attorney.

But Tijerina's storming of the courthouse went afoul from the start. Moises Morales, a lanky, soft-spoken 19-year-old mechanic, was the *Alianza's* scout in Tierra Amarilla on the day of the raid. He relayed information to Canjilón, where Tijerina and others had assembled, that the anticipated court hearing was underway.

Tijerina and his band assumed it meant that Sánchez was in the courthouse and vulnerable to abduction. They assumed wrong.

"I wouldn't have recognized Sánchez if I saw him," Morales told me years later.

The raid went sour moments after raiders stormed into the courthouse. State policeman CdeBaca recorded extensive notes:

"Mr. Tijerina and his followers stormed the courthouse about three p.m., armed with weapons and the reign of terror began. State Police officer Nick Sais was standing in the hallway when they entered. He was immediately surrounded and they pointed a gun at him and ordered him to give them his gun. When he started to un-holster his gun, he was shot. Officer Sais fell to the floor wounded and the shooting began in all directions. It was complete pandemonium inside.

"County employees jumped out through the windows for their safety and others scrambled for cover. One of the gunmen took officer Sais' gun and handcuffs. Hearing the shots, Deputy Eulogio Salazar stepped out of the sheriff's office and into the hallway, at which time Tijerina saw him. Deputy Salazar turned around and ran back into the sheriff's office and opened a window to jump out when he was shot in the face and shoulder while straddling the window.

"He managed to jump outside while bleeding profusely from his wounds. Sheriff (Benny) Naranjo lay on the floor and Tijerina and his brother, Anselmo, stepped all over him but didn't hurt him. The gunmen were all over the courthouse shooting and looking for the district attorney. A group of armed men ran upstairs and by this time, District Judge James Scarborough and the prosecutor had hidden themselves in the judge's chambers. The jury, together with Deputy Daniel Rivera, had locked themselves in the jury room. The gunmen tried to knock down the door then fired several rounds with a carbine busting the door lock. Deputy Rivera, who was armed, was kicked and clubbed over the head with a rifle butt. None of the jurors was hurt, only left traumatized.

"Tijerina then led his followers to the courtroom upstairs and into the front office of Judge Scarborough's chamber but for some unknown reason did not enter into the judge's private office. Judge Scarborough said later that someone shot open the door to the hall that led to his chambers. He said it sounded like a machine gun.

"Deputy Salazar stumbled around the corner of the courthouse after he jumped from the window and hid between parked cars. Mr. Solomon Luna, an employee in the county treasurer's office, said he was in the office when he heard several gunshots. He and other employees bailed out the window. Mr. Luna saw Deputy Salazar staggering outside and then bent over moaning. Mr. Luna also saw a gunman ready to give it to Deputy Salazar again. The gunman fired at Deputy Salazar and shot his hat right off his head. Deputy Salazar played dead and they left him there bleeding."

Salazar would say under oath later that it was Reies Tijerina who shot him inside the courthouse. CdeBaca said Luna identified one of Tijerina's brothers as the man who shot at Salazar outside the courthouse and left him for dead.

"The first shot fired inside the courthouse was by Juan Valdez when he shot State Police officer Nick Sais," CdeBaca wrote. "Baltazar Martínez, the so-called Green Beret, said after officer Sais was shot, 'Let me finish the son-of-a-bitch off,' pointing a carbine at officer Sais' head but Juan Valdez, seeing officer Sais bleeding, prevented Baltazar Martínez from shooting officer Sais even though it was Juan Valdez who had shot Officer Sais."

United Press International reporter Larry Calloway was in a phone booth reporting on the arraignment when the shooting broke out. "Larry squatted down on the floor of the phone booth after he saw officer Sais shot," CdeBaca wrote. "He remained on the floor as the gunmen ran back and forth, yelling and shooting...Larry said he could hear officer Sais moaning in the hallway."

"When Larry looked again, he saw Tijerina with pistol drawn and shouting orders. He described Tijerina as 'every bit a revolutionary leader.' Larry then heard footsteps coming toward the phone booth. A man with a pistol opened the door and pulled him out. One man reached in the phone booth and ripped the telephone from the wall. He was taken down the hallway and saw officer Sais lying on his back observing everything that was going on."

Calloway and Deputy Jaramillo were later taken from the county clerk's office and, amid continuing gunfire, were ordered into Jaramillo's 1966 black and green Pontiac GTO. At gunpoint, Jaramillo drove to Canjilón where State Police were waiting, apparently unbeknownst to Jaramillo, Calloway and their two abductors in the GTO.

Tijerina and other raiders had fled back to Canjilón, then into surrounding pine-covered hills, toting tortillas and other hastily prepared provisions before State Police arrived.

Freedom for Calloway and Jaramillo was secured after a tense standoff in Canjilón.

State Police, sheriff's officers and the National Guard, complete with an armored tank, responded to what were almost unbelievable calls for help at the courthouse in Tierra Amarilla. Lieutenant Governor E. Lee Francis summoned the National Guard, acting while Governor David Cargo was out of state.

Even though hundreds of bullets were fired during the raid, CdeBaca said not one was shot by a police officer. He said State Police were poorly prepared. Police presence on the highway and in the courthouse should have been greater knowing that Tijerina and his followers planned some sort of disruption. More than a handful of officers should have been assigned, he said.

Joe Black was State Police chief at the time of the raid. Captain Martin Vigil was commander of the Española district that included Tierra Amarilla.

In fact, only three State Police officers were assigned to the courthouse that day, according to Sais. "We got a call that there was a wreck and the two other (officers) took the call," he told me. "I was left in the courthouse alone. It was a bogus call. Things might have been different if the three of us had been in the courthouse."

Sais said it was both instinct and training that prompted him to move for his gun at the first sign of trouble. "I had been looking at the bulletin board and then I saw these people coming in with weapons," he said. "I went for my pistol and got shot. I wasn't taught in the State Police how to surrender. The guy who shot me was so close that all I saw was a ball of fire come from that weapon."

There was no shortage of criticism following the raid and it wasn't all aimed at men in uniform.

"No sooner did the dust settle down from the raid and Governor David Cargo and the district attorney began blaming each other," CdeBaca wrote in his personal records. The district attorney, Alfonso Sánchez, states publicly, 'Maybe if the governor quits holding hands with them, maybe then they will know they can't take the law into their own hands.'"

"A State Police officer who wanted to remain anonymous because he feared retaliation, told a reporter for the *Albuquerque Journal* that Cristobal Tijerina, while in jail in Santa Fe on Friday night, had made the statement, 'I'll be out of here in three hours. Your boss, the governor, will get me out. We got him 2,300 votes.' That would not be the case."

An angry Cargo, who had listened sympathetically at times to claims of the *Alianza*, said that every person involved in the raid would be held equally liable.

"Governor Cargo emphasized that there would be no more attempts at negotiation between his office and the federal Alliance of Land Grants," CdeBaca wrote. "He said, 'You can't sit down and negotiate with Jesse James, and that's what it amounts to.'

"Governor Cargo expressed his displeasure over the mobilization of the National Guard, and I believe this caused a strained relationship between him and Lieutenant Governor E. Lee Francis, though I thought they were never fond of each other to begin with."

State Police Chief Black directed CdeBaca to remain in Tierra Amarilla and oversee about ten officers who were placed there on special assignment after the June 5th courthouse raid. CdeBaca was to stay in Tierra Amarilla until all suspects in the raid were arrested and calm was restored. To be stationed at the courthouse daily, CdeBaca was away from his home in Santa Fé for weeks.

An entry in CdeBaca's records about an occurrence two nights after the raid tells of the tension that lingered:

"At midnight, the telephone rang and when I answered it, an unidentified man said they were going to raid the courthouse and this time there was not going to be a 'screw up' and he hung up the phone. Then a second phone call came in and the caller said I was going to get visitors. I immediately radioed the State Police officers in the vicinity and instructed them to secure the courthouse and to stop any car that moved in the area. I radioed the dispatcher in Santa Fe and told him to try to trace the anonymous phone calls."

"Suddenly, I heard glass drop somewhere in the hallway. I walked out to the sheriff's office and through the secretary's office armed with my shotgun. The entire courthouse was dark and I couldn't see anything. I waited a couple of minutes before stepping into the hallway. While walking to check the front doors to the courthouse, I heard glass breaking behind me. I turned around ready to shoot but there was no one there."

"I returned to the sheriff's office and got my flashlight and discovered that glass had fallen from a vending machine which had been shot during the raid. I heard footsteps on the wooden floor and turned around to see a man walking in the hallway. I have no idea why I didn't shoot. Fortunately, I didn't because it was the jailer housed in the basement who had heard noises and had come up to find out what was going on."

CdeBaca said he had never stepped inside the Río Arriba County Courthouse prior to being sent there by Chief Joe Black. "I had never seen the courthouse in my life," he said.

He said he did not know that there was a jail in the building or that anyone was in the basement at the time. "Thank God I didn't shoot that jailer. I was really walking on eggshells when I heard that glass fall."

Once captured, several of the raiders were jailed and faced charges. State District Judge Joe Angel of Las Vegas dismissed all charges against nine of the defendants.

A state district court jury in Albuquerque found Juan Valdez guilty of assaulting Sais. He also was found guilty of false imprisonment of sheriff's deputy Pete Jaramillo. Baltazar Martínez, the so-called Green Beret, and his uncle, Baltazar Archuleta, both were declared to have been mentally incompetent at the time of the raid and were absolved of charges that they falsely imprisoned Jaramillo and Calloway.

Valdez was pardoned by Bruce King while King served in his first of three terms as New Mexico governor. Valdez went on to father eight children.

Tijerina was arrested five days after the raid at a roadblock near Bernalillo, He originally was charged with 54 criminal counts tied to the raid. He would be tried on only three: assault on a jail, false imprisonment, and kidnapping. He was acquitted on all three.

State District Judge Paul Larrazolo was on the bench for the November 1968 trial. His instructions to the Albuquerque jury arguably paved the way for Tijerina's acquittal. Larrazolo told jurors: "The court instructs the jury that anyone, including a State Police officer, who intentionally interferes with a lawful attempt to make a citizen's arrest does so at his own peril, since the arresting citizens are entitled under the law to use whatever force is reasonably necessary to effect said citizen's arrest and to use whatever force is reasonably necessary to defend themselves in the process of making said citizen's arrest."

Accusations and tensions mounted through 1968, leading up to Tijerina's trial before Judge Larrazolo. Río Arriba County was on edge as Tijerina's supporters hailed him as their fearless champion and detractors called him a hothead engaged in foolishness, an embarrassment.

Tijerina insisted before, during and after the trial that he was targeted in a "campaign of terror" waged against him by the news media, the FBI, the courts, police and entrenched politicians. He undeniably agitated many.

During the trial, "the *Alianza* headquarters in Albuquerque was riddled with bullets in a drive-by shooting," wrote CdeBaca. Tijerina sympathizers accused police of the attack.

Previously, plate glass windows at Tijerina's Albuquerque headquarters had been smashed twice on separate nights; an off-duty Bernalillo County sheriff's deputy had attempted to throw a bomb into the building only to have the device go off prematurely.

Tijerina's home and office in Coyote also had been attacked.

Eulogio Salazar, Río Arriba County jailer at the time of the raid, was to have testified at the trial that it was Tijerina who shot him in the face while inside the courthouse. But Salazar never made it to the trial. His beaten body was found in the first days of January, 1968, off a county road about two miles from Tierra Amarilla. Evidence suggested that Salazar was abducted in the dark from his driveway not far from the courthouse.

CdeBaca wrote in his records: "In the next few minutes when his car was driven through Tierra Amarilla and west of El Vado road, Deputy Salazar was brutally beaten. Blood stained the inside of his car, soaking the seats, headliner and windows. The overhead lamp in the car was broken. He must have put up a good fight. West of Tierra Amarilla, his assailants stopped and threw his body into the front seat and stuffed it down onto the floorboard. The car was then pushed over a 40-foot embankment as if to make it appear that he had lost control of the car."

State Police Chief Black and District Attorney Sánchez made it clear that Tijerina was the prime suspect. Tijerina repeatedly denied involvement, asserting that he had no motive; Salazar already had testified under oath that Tijerina shot him during the raid. Tijerina accused police and other government officials of the murder, alleging they would use the brutal crime to discredit him and quash his land grant movement.

CdeBaca does not think Tijerina was responsible for Salazar's murder but suspects that someone associated with him committed the crime, with or without Tijerina's knowledge.

The murder remains unsolved.

Tijerina was tried a second time on charges related directly to the courthouse raid. His lawyers alleged that protections against double jeopardy were being violated but Judge Garnett Burkes in Las Cruces said the charges in his court were different from those that Tijerina faced before Judge Larrazolo in Albuquerque. Tijerina was convicted of false imprisonment of a deputy and assault with intent to kill or maim Eulogio Salazar.

Even before the Las Cruces convictions, jail sentences had been secured for Tijerina in another courtroom. He was confined in federal prisons in Texas and Missouri from 1969 to 1972 on convictions growing out of his occupation of Echo Amphitheater prior to the courthouse raid. Tijerina said he wanted to be arrested at the roadside park in the possession of the U.S. Forest Service, anticipating that he would be charged with trespassing. That, he figured, would force the U.S. government to prove in court that it was the rightful owner of the land. Trespassing was not included among charges.

"They sent him first to La Tuna prison in Texas, then to the prison in Springfield Missouri, where all the crazy people are," Tijerina's former wife, Patsy, told me years later. "A psychiatrist told the parole board in Missouri that Reies was a man no-one could change. He wasn't crazy, but he's always been very strong about what he believes in."

Sports Editor Jim Maldonado at *The Santa Fe New Mexican* in Santa Fé couldn't help but be drawn to Tijerina and the land grant stories that continued unfolding seemingly without end well past the June 1967 courthouse raid.

Doyle Akers, *The Santa Fe New Mexican's* Española bureau chief at the time of the raid, reported on developments before leaving the bureau. He was succeeded in Española by Sandra Kincaid who had limited interest in chasing after what must have seemed like crazed anarchists speaking of revolution in a tongue that she did not understand while roaming the hills an hour or two north of her already-busy station.

Maldonado and I by then had grown very close while he mentored me in sports reporting and the unique role of newspapermen in their communities. Maldonado was the only member of *The Santa Fe New Mexican's* editorial staff in Santa Fé who spoke Spanish fluently. He had come to learn that I, too, could communicate well in Spanish. He must have sensed that I was more than eager to assume additional responsibilities, broader responsibilities as a budding reporter.

Land grant drama after the raid drew Jim and me into hills and arroyos between Coyote and Tierra Amarilla as our time permitted. We were, after all, still assigned to sports. And Jim's responsibilities, of course, were far greater than mine. Still, he seemingly looked for every opportunity that allowed him to drive north from Santa Fé in his cherry red 1966 Chevrolet coup and chase intriguing stories that had nothing to do with hard courts, gridirons or baseball diamonds.

Invariably, Jim would pick me up in Española so that upon arriving at our destination, I could follow and shoot photos while he interviewed men in sweat-stained hats, faded blue jeans and scuffed work boots. When my small talk with the men began producing useful information or colorful quotes, I'd reach for my own notebook and record what would later add to Jim's stories. We grew closer with each day.

Reies Tijerina addressed followers in 1977 to commemorate the tenth anniversary of the Tierra Amarilla courthouse raid.

Tijerina through the years continued with his attempts to get the U.S. government into court so that he might force it to prove ownership of contested property. I regularly had direct contact with Tijerina during the period.

Tijerina's confidence in his position grew in March 1979 when state Historian Dr. Myra Ellen Jenkins found the original title to the San Joaquín land grant while looking for other papers in the state records center.

Prior to that, Dr. Jenkins had publicly asserted that Tijerina's claims

Reies Tijerina confronted U.S. Forest Service officials near Coyote while still fighting for land grant property years after the 1967 courthouse raid.

to the grant were weak because there were no papers to any "genuine" San Joaquín grant. She said that copies of records were "very suspect" and that the San Joaquín grant case was one of the most dubious among all the grants in New Mexico.

Tijerina and Dr. Jenkins had sparred over the issue more than once. After Dr. Jenkins found the original title, Tijerina said he gleefully told the elderly Dr. Jenkins, "If you were here, I would give you the biggest hug and the biggest kiss I have ever given to anyone in my life."

With Tijerina serving as "principal adviser," a San Joaquín town government had remained in place and was quick to respond to the discovery of the original San Joaquín grant title.

"Since we got the title of San Joaquín, and the title is genuine, we're figuring that the land is ours," said San Joaquín "judge," Uvaldo Velásquez.

To that, Tijerina added, "This merits a White House conference."

And why not? he argued. Then-President Jimmy Carter had granted meetings to runners and basketball players. How could he turn down land grant heirs hoping to tend to serious business that dated back to official decisions of the Spanish crown?

New Mexico land grant scholar Malcolm Ebright asserted at the time that two U.S. courts had adjudicated the San Joaquín title but that

Reies Tijerina met with representatives of the San Joaquín Land Grant in one of numerous gatherings during the 1970s designed partly to summon attention to the protracted battle over land grants in northern New Mexico.

decisions recognizing the grant as having less than 1,500 acres were reached improperly to the benefit of corrupt and politically connected land speculators.

With the original title in hand, Tijerina said, rigged adjudications of the grant could be disregarded. He said that the original title meant that heirs have "perfect" title to more than 472,000 acres. The "perfect" title along with continuous occupation of the land by heirs mandates that land held by the U.S. government be turned over immediately to heirs, Tijerina said.

And if the U.S. government wanted to dispute that assertion, Tijerina argued, then a fair court battle surely would end with ownership being awarded to those who hold the rightful title.

Tijerina asserted that his position was rooted largely in the 1848 treaty signed between the United States and Mexico. There is no expiration date to the treaty, he said. If the United States wants to act as if the treaty is no longer valid, he argued, then it should return all the land that it took from Mexico through the treaty.

The 1979 New Mexico Legislature petitioned the U.S. Congress to review the property rights of San Joaquín grant heirs.

In the end, Tijerina's attempts to gain immediate possession of the

San Joaquín grant went nowhere. Plans to contest the issue of ownership in court also withered. There was no meeting with President Carter, and the U.S. Congress as a whole has been mostly silent.

Nearly each of New Mexico's congressional members during three decades beginning in the 1970s publicly called for action intended, at least in part, to appease land grant activists. Republican U.S. Representative Manuel Luján Jr. in 1979 drafted a bill proposing that Congress confer jurisdiction for examining legal questions of the San Joaquín land grant to the federal courts in New Mexico.

Republican U.S. Senator Harrison "Jack" Schmitt that same year said he was not convinced that the simmering San Joaquín Land Grant dispute could be satisfactorily settled in the courts. Monetary compensation to people adversely affected over the years may be the best way to make up for alleged losses, he told me.

A few years later, Democrat U.S. Representative Bill Richardson said at a congressional hearing that the federal government was the principal foe of those trying to resolve land grant disputes. He sponsored a bill that would have empowered the U.S. Justice Department to examine chains of titles to land grants, but he couldn't even find a co-sponsor for the bill.

"This is a long, complicated problem that has been opposed by the federal government," he said.

Republican U.S. Representative Bill Redmond in 1997 submitted legislation that called for creation of a presidential commission to study land grant claims and recommend to Congress steps for restoring property to land grant groups.

A bill introduced in 1998 by Democrat U.S. Senator Jeff Bingaman called for establishing county-level committees to examine the validity of land grant claims stemming from the 1848 Treaty of Guadalupe Hidalgo. The seven-member county "settlement committees" would include representation from federal and state agencies, local residents, area Indian tribes and land grant heirs. They would recommend settlement packages to Congress when claims were determined to be valid.

Democrat U.S. Representative Tom Udall in 1979 called for creating a federal commission to investigate land grant claims before reporting to Congress on the best ways to redress them.

Influential Republican U.S. Senator Pete Domenici had been largely quiet on the land grant issue. But in 2003 he spoke of what would have been a momentous step following years of study by the U.S. General Accounting Office. Senator Domenici suggested that rights to possibly two million acres in New Mexico could be transferred away from the federal government and into the hands of land grant heirs. Reparations might be made elsewhere in the state, he said.

In the 2003 New Mexico Legislature, Senate President Pro Tem Richard Romero of Albuquerque said the nation had 155 years of "unfinished business." He referred to the Treaty of Guadalupe Hidalgo through which the U.S. government pledged to respect the rights of indigenous landowners. Soon after the treaty was signed, said Romero, U.S. colonizers began rampant stealing of lands that they came upon.

People of the New Mexico Territory "became strangers in their own homeland" and suffered at the hands of "an alien government with alien laws and alien courthouses," Senator Romero said,

Long-time House Speaker Ben Luján of Nambé pledged to help lead a push for change.

Arguably, little of the activity in government halls would have surfaced if not for Tijerina's activism beginning with the 1967 Río Arriba Courthouse raid, even if many thought Tijerina went too far.

The violence likely set back the land grant movement, said Bruce King, a three-term Democratic governor in New Mexico.

King was seen as a friend by land grant activists, or, at least, as someone who was not hostile toward their efforts. But as hopes waned, Tijerina felt pressed to express disappointment. He wrote in a letter to King that injustice surrounding the history of the San Joaquín Land Grant "can no longer be tolerated" by heirs to the land. "We gave you our votes, hoping and trusting that you would represent everybody according to their Constitutional rights," the letter read.

A letter to Senator Domenici from Tijerina read, "The U.S. government has never shown anything to the people of San Joaquín showing the federal government's right to legal possession. The people have a firm, sincere and honest belief that they, and not the government, own the land given to them by Spain in 1806."

In truth, none of New Mexico's elected government officials could have felt optimistic about securing for Tijerina and his followers what they demanded. In the U.S. Congress as in the New Mexico Legislature, elected members have long been known to introduce legislation that they recognize from the start will have no chance of adoption. Such bills, nonetheless, let lawmakers appear responsive, even empathetic, to blocs of their constituents.

The land grant issue, in crude terms, is one of those cans of worms that few like to open. A big part of the problem is that multiple states have land grant heirs who claim that so much of their land was stolen. Tens of millions of acres are involved in the U.S. West. Congress, indeed the federal government, has wanted no part of a movement that could officially cloud titles on what are now private lands in such a large span of the country.

Nor is the government inclined to battle with environmentalists and others who are opposed to large-scale losses of forests and other public lands.

U.S. Representative Sam Gejdenson, a Connecticut Democrat, years ago sided with New Mexico's Representative Richardson in saying that the federal government holds acreage taken from land grant claimants without sufficient documentation.

But, Gejdenson wondered, even if solutions for correcting the problem could be found, how would they be managed when so many people are involved?

"Once we figure out who has a right to what, we better have a program for how we're going to deal with it," he said.

New Mexico Senator Bingaman had his own terminology. "We've had 150 years of history since the Treaty of Guadalupe Hidalgo and undoubtedly some of the land now is in private ownership. You can't unscramble the egg. You can't move owners off of property they have purchased legitimately," he said of people who in good faith bought lands from those who were involved in original fraud. "You have to be realistic about the kinds of remedies that you propose."

Moises Morales, the young scout for Tijerina on the day of the courthouse raid, in time concluded that time was misspent while working with Senator Bingaman and others elected to represent New Mexico in Congress. "Our mistake after the raid was to rely on our government officials in Washington to carry on the job," he told me.

Intermittently in the 1970s and 1980s, Tijerina iced out the press for months. He saw the Anglo-dominated news media as part of the supposed conspiracy that was being waged against him. There were spells when I was the only reporter with whom he would talk. He recognized that he needed publicity to keep his movement alive and must have figured that I was the least of evils.

Among my work, I reported on assemblies organized by land grant activists to commemorate key dates associated with the 1967 courthouse raid. I was at a loosely organized gathering in Canjilón in 1992 to commemorate the raid's 25th anniversary.

By then, the "King Tiger" was 65 and seemed all but spent.

He had been a hero to some, an outlaw to those whom he cursed and threatened with both fist and gun.

He appeared disinterested in all of that in 1992. He was no longer a firebrand in scuffed black combat boots. He was a grandfather in tan soft-leather shoes, carrying 15-month old Diana, among the youngest of his offspring, in his arms.

When excited during that day, he still punctured holes in the air with a strong forefinger as he spoke. But if one were to have counted, the score likely would have shown that for every poke into the cool mountain air, little Diana with the big Tijerina eyes got two kisses planted firmly on her cheek.

A photographer approached Tijerina and two of his more-recognized raiders, Juan Valdez and Morales. "Do you mind if I take your picture since the three of you are all together?" asked the photographer.

"If they don't mind, I don't mind. I'm too old to mind," Tijerina replied with a smile.

Moments later, another photographer coaxed Tijerina to walk away from the crowd for another photograph but the walk was interrupted when a man of Tijerina's age urged him to stop under a tree to listen to a Spanish ballad recently composed to commemorate the courthouse raid.

The balladeer already had begun the song, reading lyrics from a piece of paper held before him. As he moved through the lyrics, he misstated the year of the raid.

"I'll listen, but the year was nineteen sixty-seven, not nineteen seventy-seven!" Tijerina scolded.

The balladeer now timidly studied the rest of the lyrics quietly to himself, reluctant to begin the song anew. Tijerina grew impatient.

"Go ahead, begin," he ordered with a wave of his hand. "Anyway, you'll get it right once you start."

The versus unfolded, telling of bravery and injustice. Tijerina seemed unmoved. Midway through the song, he yawned loudly, demonstrably, then walked away to talk to others. He did not join in the cheers and applause when the song was completed.

It was a sign, perhaps, that a tiger's temperament, no matter how old, doesn't die easily.

"I don't know if he's a changed man. Songs don't turn him on, though," Tijerina's wife, Patsy, told me. She was 19 at the time of the raid and told me she would have "given a leg and a foot" to be in the Río Arriba County courthouse during the raid. "I would have been so proud. But Reies didn't want me to get involved."

She said Tijerina had grown to enjoy talking about world issues. "Oh, he talks about Tierra Amarilla but you've got to move on and you've got to talk about something else."

God still figured into much of what the former Pentecostal preacher talked about. Remember, he long had insisted that he was doing God's work while leading land grant activists. "I slowed down because I felt that I was getting ahead of God," he told me that day.

He proclaimed victory in the land grant fight. "The fight already has been done. The price already has been paid," he said. "All hundred and fifty-three land grants are coming back. It will happen before the year two thousand."

Tijerina had never shied from unrealistic predictions, seemingly unconcerned that time likely would prove him wrong.

At the raid's 25th anniversary he predicted that a radical change in the nation's government soon would be responsible for restoring property rights to land grant heirs.

"This will all be settled now without us sending letters and telegrams and all that shit," he said.

"I'm going to be like a grandfather for it all. I will advise them not to precipitate, not to use violence. My main role has already been done. But I don't think any of this can be done in the future without consulting Reies."

Following a divorce from Patsy, Tijerina remarried and lived alternately in Mexico and El Paso, Texas.

He had been largely unnoticed in New Mexico until showing up in Albuquerque in October 1999 to donate his archival materials to the University of New Mexico.

Tijerina died in El Paso in January 2015.

Hardly an unbridled admirer of the government, Morales eventually was elected to two terms as Río Arriba County commissioner. He also was elected county clerk.

It was in the wake of the courthouse raid that I was given an opportunity to sit in on my first governor's press conference at the state Capitol. True to politics, it was a favor that placed me in the company of Republican David Cargo. It was a returned favor, actually, from a lady named Leslie whom I met while she was Los Álamos bureau chief for *The Santa Fe New Mexican.*

One cool autumn night, the woman seemingly couldn't muster the enthusiasm to cover a Los Álamos High School football game, as had been expected. I was reporting on sports in nearby Río Arriba County so I must have seemed like a logical stand-in. She called for help just hours before the game.

Sure I could help, I told her, but added that as a high school student reliant on his Father's pickup for transportation, I couldn't drive to Los Álamos on such short notice.

I reported on the game by listening to it on the radio from my San Pedro bedroom. Nobody detected any major gaffes, and one day after Leslie left her job at the paper to work on Governor Cargo's staff, she saw to it that I got an invitation to one of the governor's news conferences.

I don't recall walking out of the news conference with information of any real value. Still, it was my first lesson on the importance of a newspaperman having friendly contacts in high places.

It was the beginning of a bond between Cargo and me that lasted decades. Cargo, deep into his life, phoned me periodically from his Albuquerque home simply to talk about current events or old times, beginning each phone call with the greeting, "Hey, how's my *tocayo?*"

Jim Maldonado, *The Santa Fe New Mexican's* sports editor who enthusiastically mentored me as if he were my older brother moved on to report briefly for the *Denver Post* and the Associated Press before his young, promising life took a catastrophic turn on the punishing back of substance abuse.

At the age of 31, Maldonado walked into the Las Vegas, New Mexico, police station on a particularly hot day in June 1977 and confessed that he had beaten and probably killed his father, Manuel, in the home they shared on Columbia Street. Less than two months later, Jim Maldonado was among several men involved in a break from the San Miguel County jail but his attempt to escape charges related to the murder was short-lived.

Maldonado's influence followed me not only while I continued reporting on the land grant issue and many others. It has followed me through life. Nobody—in or out of school—taught me more about newspapering.

The real estate business around Tierra Amarilla, Canjilón and Coyote, would never be more than tepid for people like Virginia Smith, the newlywed real estate broker whom authorities turned away from Tierra Amarilla immediately after the Río Arriba courthouse raid. The protracted land dispute wasn't good for business.

Smith had lived in Tierra Amarilla since she was two. It was safe to say she had never seen anyone quite like Tijerina in those parts.

No one had.

From the Roybal Files...
A novel in progress, untitled, 2018

It was said that in Río Arriba County, dead men not only voted routinely, but many of them voted at least twice each election. For inexplicable reasons, dead women were not nearly as faithful to their civic obligations, yet surfaced at least occasionally in especially close elections.

Sheriff Jimmy Silva often suspected that's part of what was meant when it was said that someone had gone on to a better life after death. If you hailed from Río Arriba, where people long had been told how to vote, the better life in the Mysterious Beyond not only meant that you got to vote for whomever you liked come Election Day. It meant you were free to vote for your favorite candidate until your finger got tired of pressing the button alongside his name in the voting booth.

Sheriff Silva didn't know how many—if any—dead votes he got, but five years after his first election, here he was on a beautiful autumn morning driving the best cruiser assigned to the Río Arriba Sheriff's Department, accompanied by its most reliable deputy and weighed down by the realization that as of 9:30 a.m. the previous day, he had another homicide to solve.

It's what had him on the road that morning traveling between the opulence of Santa Fé's northern hills and the more-burdensome realities of his own county just ahead. And he sensed in his bones that this murder was different. Even this early and from a county away, the musty odor of the region's old land grant struggle hung over this homicide. And it was going to stir people up, probably for no good in the end.

7
NEW MEXICANS PERSEVERE AMID POVERTY'S RELENTLESS GRIP

Reies López Tijerina wasn't a natural fit for northern New Mexico, where most Hispanics for generations had lived quiet lives in homes that embraced respect, humility, frugality and the virtues of hard work.

"*Honor y provecho no caben en un mismo lecho.*" (Honor and gain do not fit in the same bed). So says an old Spanish proverb about values.

Still, anyone looking in could argue that something had to change along regions of the upper Río Grande. And it's precisely what Tijerina, the firebrand, did as he swept into Río Arriba County during the 1960s

The median school year completed by residents 25 years old and over in the county during the period was 9.7. In neighboring Mora County, it was 8.2 years; in San Miguel, 9.1 years; and Guadalupe, 9.5 years.

These were among the poorest counties but poverty was a serious statewide problem. New Mexico had the nation's seventh-highest poverty rate in 1969, according to the U.S. Census Bureau. Nearly 23 percent of New Mexico's population reported incomes in 1969 that were below the poverty level. The state's poverty rates were more than 20 percent during most of the previous quarter century.

Time went on and no intervention—not Tijerina's convulsive campaign nor the more-measured approaches of New Mexico's political leaders—made much difference.

New Mexico in 1994, reported the Census Bureau, was the only state where poverty increased over the previous two years. More than 25 percent of New Mexico residents lived in poverty in 1994.

And there was a growing trend of disparate income. Where growth occurred, the poor saw less of it, said Lawrence Waldman, a University of New Mexico economist at the time. The trend continued into the new millennium.

By 2016, *Albuquerque Journal* columnist Winthrop Quigley wrote insightfully: "The most intractable problem New Mexico faces is poverty. From low-birth-weight babies to violent crime, poverty is either a cause, an effect, or a complicating factor in the state's many dysfunctions."

And evidence suggests the problem is getting worse, Quigley wrote.

Much of my time as a journalist was spent in some of New Mexico's most-isolated communities while addressing pressing needs of education, health care, government accountability and crime prevention. I came upon some very admirable people in the process; some rather incredible stories, too.

One from the 1970s grew from the stew that is concocted when poverty, isolation and anemic law enforcement are stirred together.

It started when bullets rang out, making it frighteningly clear to the Río Arriba County sheriff's dispatcher that trouble had erupted in distant hills of northern New Mexico. It would be a while before she could get help to the site.

That's what's wrong with the many isolated expanses of the region. When trouble erupts, help often is far away. By the time it arrives, the gun smoke already has cleared and all authorities can do is assess the damage.

Former Republican governor and U.S. senator, Edwin Mechem, in 1978 sat stoically and listened to the latest story about how people in northern New Mexico can feel chillingly abandoned at times. Mechem was serving then as a U.S. District judge in Albuquerque. High-ranking Río Arriba County officials were buried in allegations of assorted misconduct, including unlawful retaliation against political opponents.

The testimony in Judge Mechem's courtroom that day came from a former Río Arriba sheriff's deputy. He had been one of two deputies assigned to monitor a political rally of what was then a spirited chapter of La Raza Unida Party, which had become a pain in the neck to the county's Democratic Party machine of Emilio Naranjo.

The rally of perhaps two dozen people was in a remote area more heavily inhabited by furry critters than people of any political persuasion.

The pair of deputies assigned to the stake out watched from a hill as the crowd chanted slogans, thrust fists into the air while boasting of potency and otherwise carried on wildly, as any self-respecting political organization would do in the heat of a campaign.

Relations between La Raza Unida and the Río Arriba Sheriff's Department already were bad. Terrible! Many of the accusations of misconduct leveled against county officials were leveled by Raza Unida members. Several members of the party in turn had been arrested by sheriff's deputies. One of them, land grant activist Moises Morales, was stopped on the road near his Canjilón home by Naranjo and the sheriff's department's two ranking officers who first pulled Morales away from his pickup then planted marijuana in the vehicle.

"If they had stopped me for poaching a deer, maybe people would have believed them. But marijuana? Everybody knew I don't smoke marijuana," Morales told me then.

At the La Raza rally, when people spotted the deputies atop the hill, nobody could have been surprised by the taunts that followed.

Outnumbered, the deputies wisely sat still. But as taunts from the distant crowd grew louder and more threatening, one of the deputies reached for the police radio and called for help.

No one was available to help way out there, came the response. Stay put. What could happen? the deputies were counseled.

But the crowd grew louder. Again the deputies pleaded for backup but none was promised. Finally, some in the taunting crowd started inching their way up the hill and toward the deputies.

That did it. One of the deputies reached for the radio and excitedly told of a life-threatening situation. Leaving the radio mike live, he promptly stepped out of the cruiser, pulled his revolver from its holster and fired more than once into the car door.

The deputy again grabbed the radio and announced that he, his partner and their cruiser were taking fire.

The sound of shots having just rung through the radio surely would prompt the dispatcher to summon help, thought the deputy. The bullet holes in the cruiser would serve later as evidence—albeit fabricated evidence—of just how bad the situation became.

If it was far from standard operating procedure for the sheriff's department, it wasn't far by much, representatives of La Raza told Judge Mechem.

By the time the deputy on the stand finished his story, people throughout the large courtroom were struggling to keep from laughing out loud. Many failed. Even the stone-faced Mechem cracked more than a smile from the bench in apparent disbelief.

"Some of the department's activities during recent years had precious little to do with law enforcement," Tony Tupler, an assistant district attorney at the time, told the judge.

Indeed, law enforcement for the most part has been stretched thin in northern New Mexico, often leading some in the isolated communities to take the law into their own hands.

I was in the thick of northern New Mexico's rural communities in November 1987 while working on a series for *The Santa Fe New Mexican*. I visited with people along narrow dirt roads that wind below steeply pitched tin roofs. The corrugated tin shields homes of thick adobe walls and irregular floor plans by modern standards. They're frequently forgotten villages where life largely has escaped the atomic age and the digital age that followed, rooted still in more-basic routines of human survival.

During my visit to these villages 20 years after the Río Arriba courthouse raid, signs posted off the road didn't advertise estate sales or deals on used Volvos.

"Native Worms" was scribbled on a small board outside a Tierra Amarilla home near the Río Arriba courthouse where the vendor sought to lure passing fishermen.

Not far away the entire wall of an abandoned home long served efforts to attract slightly bigger money. A makeshift ad, spray-painted over the crumbling adobe read: "Need workers?" The question mark was followed by a long, crooked arrow pointing interested readers toward equally old adobe houses to the rear where men once waited to dig trenches, mix cement, load bailed hay.

"Goats 4 Sale," read one sign that was staked near Llano at the tip of the Río Arriba-Taos County border.

Many of the New Mexicans who live in poverty do so in communities like Tierra Amarilla, Llano, La Madera, Truchas and other communities in New Mexico's beautiful but often-exacting northern mountains.

"I use wood to cook here ... I have butane for the water heater but I don't have no stove yet," said Martha Gallegos, who was recently married and expecting a child in Vallecitos when I visited. Her husband worked hard, she said. It's the isolation that made things more trying in the mountain village between Española and Tierra Amarilla.

It was a life far more deprived in material goods than what it is in most of the world's recognized Land of Plenty. Chants of "U.S.A., U.S.A...." heard increasingly at national political rallies or international sports events ring hollow here.

Poverty rates in some of these isolated communities are more than double the national average. Poor people don't stand out in these communities. Too many are in the same condition. Many have accepted their lives as the way life is meant to be. They won't accept pity, having developed a rare sense of pride and dignity that comes, perhaps, only from maintaining a family in the face of stiff daily odds.

"They have learned to make a living out of their land and out of their surroundings, and they're not about to bow to anybody," said longtime Democratic state Representative Nick Salazar of Ohkay Owingeh Pueblo.

Salazar referred to the small, self-sustaining farms and ranches that fuel life for residents of isolated villages. Many in these villages like to note how their families couldn't tell when the nation's Great Depression of the 1930s came and went because subsistence living already was the norm for them. Their vegetable gardens continued producing. Livestock was butchered as needed. Game was taken from the forests, fish from the streams.

In these villages, every eye-catching photograph of a child hauling water in a bucket for use indoors has a story of a home without plumbing. Where large piles of chopped wood rise over back yards, nearby bedrooms frequently go cold at night after the fuel of old stoves runs out.

Poverty in northern New Mexico luckily isn't represented by long lines of children with bloated bellies reaching out for rice and milk. It isn't represented by entire families rummaging daily through recently dumped garbage to retrieve the most salvageable waste.

Poverty along the northern Río Grande isn't even like that found 350 miles down river in what have come to be known as *colonias*, communities often identified by hastily built shelters and filled mostly by relatively recent immigrants from Mexico who arrived to work on huge farms of the Mesilla Valley.

Still, poverty amid northern New Mexico's adobe homes and its small farms and ranches is as well rooted as the area's reverent attitudes toward the land. It is reflected every time a family finds education unattainable at more than a basic level, every time a family must treat medical attention as a last-ditch alternative to disability or death, every time unemployment rates hover around 30 percent. It is represented in every child who recognizes hunger and inadequately treated infections as unshakable companions.

Perhaps more importantly, poverty is reflected every time childhoods that inescapably result from such surroundings rob youths of optimism and confidence of what they themselves can attain.

Government assistance programs had multiplied beginning with President Lyndon Johnson's War on Poverty in the 1960s. They lightened the load for many yet failed to do much for those hidden away in nooks and crannies of rural America.

In Río Arriba County during the mid-1980s, more than 45 percent of the rural poor were not served by food stamps, according to Public Voice, a non-profit research group based in Washington, DC,

Numerous reasons were cited, including isolation of the people in need and a bureaucracy so cumbersome that it discouraged participation particularly among those who face language barriers and barriers posed by limited education.

More than a few who qualified considered government assistance to be something intended for those with greater needs than their own.

The study showed that no matter the reasons, noble or not, many poor people in New Mexico did not sit idly waiting for others to take care of them. These are people, after all, who descend from families like those in Truchas who 250 years ago dug by hand the *Acequia de la Sierra* along a mountain ridge high in the *Sangre de Cristos*. Huge rock faces often had to be blasted to make way for the *acequia* that flows from high in the mountains to feed multiple ditches in Truchas. Those community ditches are then relied upon to keep alive small vegetable gardens and grassy meadows that sustain livestock from year to year.

Men and boys worked over generations to keep the mountain wonder running. "That's where a lot of kids learned how to use a shovel," Truchas *mayordomo* Henry Romero told me amid recommendations to line the *acequia* with plastic pipe.

"Having learned to use a shovel." It was high praise to have that said of you in northern New Mexico's mountain villages. It meant that you knew how to work. More importantly, it suggested that you weren't afraid of work.

Squeezing sustenance from mountain villages had become a way of life for many in northern New Mexico. "We are lucky," 77-year-old Vidal Maestas told me in his small kitchen in Rodarte north of Truchas in 1978. He had just walked into his home after having shoveled foot-deep snow on property that had sustained his family for generations. "We have our animals to provide meat and get use out of them. When they established welfare, I never applied because I knew there were people who needed the help more than me."

Nearby during the same period, 92-year-old Perfecto Gonzales didn't allow himself to see much poverty at all in his tiny mountain village just east of Peñasco, where people's daily lives were a lesson in making do with what they had.

"In the old days people around here were very poor. Not now," said Gonzales, disregarding conditions that so many outsiders surely would consider unbearable. "Now, we're all rich. There's not a poor person here. We all have money. Some get welfare. Some get pensions.

"Sometimes you feel sorry for those who misspend their money so you give them three dollars or five dollars," said the man with a soft face and gentle eyes. Rancor seemed foreign to this man who tended to a small store at the front of his quiet home.

The store had only half a dozen cans of soda in the refrigerator. There were three loaves of bread and two or three half-filled boxes of 3 Musketeers and Milky Way bars on display behind the counter. A homemade fly swatter hung on a nail to fend off the occasional pest and ensure customer comfort.

"I sell mostly candies and cigarettes now—and Coca-Cola when I can get it," Gonzales said.

Half an hour after we had begun talking while stooped head to head across his store's counter, Gonzales reached behind him for a small wooden box and shuffled for military papers he thought were important for me to see. He unfolded them and stood proudly at my side as he waited for me to read. The papers didn't tell of individual honors or extraordinary conditions of combat. They told simply of his service as a U.S. foot soldier from 1918 to1920 and of his honorable discharge from the military that took him in.

Service to the country and honorable release at the end of an assignment clearly said plenty for a man who had grown accustomed to life being simple.

Personal responsibility, like that reflected by Gonzales, is very much a trademark of residents throughout northern New Mexico. When practiced by people of very modest means, personal responsibility can inflict considerable expenses.

I think of a story that unfolded some time ago near Abiquiú. While Georgia O'Keeffe painted New Mexico's scenic beauty, little more than a stone's throw away a family in Cañones went through the kind of social strain that typifies deprivation and loss in northern New Mexico.

A son of that family recalled how, with most of his years of schooling still ahead, his parents decided to sell their modest ranch in Cañones and move closer to Española in pursuit of a better base for educational opportunities.

The education was secured and the son, after years of community activism, went on to work as Río Arriba County manager.

But Lorenzo Valdez, while appreciating his parents' sacrifice, regretted that his education carried such a steep price: loss of family land. Land, after all, remained a critical element in defining security and preserving the threatened culture of the region that Valdez fought to protect both as a community activist and county administrator.

As the new millennium unfolded, increasing attention was paid to deprivation faced by U.S. families who worked entire lifetimes without benefit of health insurance. For too long it had been an overlooked form of want. It was prevalent in northern New Mexico.

"A lot of people can't afford to have health insurance. I get the feeling that they have more-pressing problems, like feeding themselves, clothing themselves and getting heat for the winter," Dr. Gershon Bergeisen, medical director of Health Centers of Northern New Mexico, told me during the 1980s.

Getting health care, let alone paying for it, has always been hard for the state's northern villagers. "Eighty percent of all physicians and medical facilities in New Mexico are within a three-mile radius of the (interstate) interchange here in Albuquerque," Dr. Jaime Salazar, a visiting professor at the University of New Mexico, told me in 1979.

Dr. Scott Obenshain, UNM's assistant dean of undergraduate medical education during the period, said obstacles between rural residents and adequate health care were systemic. "When you're talking of physicians, most of us are trained in highly sophisticated systems ... in large cities and big university hospital complexes," he said.

Many health care professionals prefer not to be associated with rural health care, which is regarded as inferior to what is practiced in urban areas, Dr. Obenshain told me.

"Many medical students see it as less important, either less important or less honorable," agreed Dr. Arthur Kaufman, associate professor of family, community and emergency medicine at UNM at the time.

Physicians were recruited to rural clinics during the 1970s in exchange for help with their education loans. The clinics helped with basic needs but when more was needed, trips to communities beyond the mountains had to be arranged.

"Most of the old people in the mountains don't drive so they have to find a neighbor to drive them down and they have to reimburse them for gas. Even that can become too expensive," said Dr. Bergeisen.

Federally subsidized rural clinics were hurt in the 1980s by substantial cuts to federal funding for rural health care during the presidency of Republican Ronald Reagan and his policies that came to be known as Reaganomics.

Independent clinics, like those that served much of northern New Mexico, were constantly engaged in grant writing and in pursuit of donations to supplement patient fees that usually were based on people's ability to pay.

Alternatives to rural clinical care were prohibitively expensive. Emergency room care at the time was four times more expensive than clinical care; hospital care, 20 times more costly, according to independent national studies.

It's sad and frustrating, Representative Nick Salazar said at the time. "I, myself, still wonder how these people make out. I really do," he said.

Always underlying much life in rural northern New Mexico is the land. But even the land continued running out on many, as it had in Cañones for the family of Lorenzo Valdez.

Santa Fean Jesús Rios was 87 years old when I visited with him at his home in 1987. Santa Fé families and their land were once inseparable. Big money changed that.

Rios himself lived comfortably on his own land at the corner of what is now Santa Fé's chic Canyon Road and Camino Monte Sol. He had been offered as much as $1.5 million for his property, situated amid trendy galleries and restaurants. There he dealt firewood and reclaimed goods ranging from bathroom sinks to full-length mirrors.

Once, residents throughout the neighborhood were engaged in similar pursuits. But when I visited with him in 1987, Rios and his property stood out like a sore thumb. Still, he proudly and defiantly resisted pressure from those who would have supplanted piles of wood and kindling with racks of canvas and pastels. He had seen others in Santa Fé take a different course.

"Some couldn't resist the unusual amounts of money they suddenly were offered," he told me in Spanish on an early morning outside his home. "But others didn't have a choice. And many still don't. They have little money. They don't have insurance. They have nothing to help them when they get old or sick so they sell what they have."

He made his point in a story he shared about an elderly woman who drove more than 30 miles to Rios' home only a few weeks earlier. "This wood, here," said Rios, pointing to dry blocked pine, "was brought in by the lady who drove up in her truck around dinner time. She asked if I wanted to buy it.

"Her husband is going blind and she needs whatever money she can get to keep things going. I asked her to back in her pickup and told her that if she comes again, she should come before five because that's when the men go home. They could help her unload the wood if she came earlier," Rios said.

"You know what she told me? She said it was no problem. 'I loaded the wood onto the truck myself. I can unload it the same way,'" she said.

A little more than an hour's drive north from Santa Fé that same autumn, I came upon an elderly couple in Llano at the foot of the Rockies as the season's chill had begun to work its way in. Sixty-five-year-old Ricardo Medina sat under the opened hood of his 1968 Chevrolet pickup, crouched on top of its tired engine.

As cold weather blows in so, too, does the realization that getting around roller coaster dirt roads is going to become a whole lot harder for a few months.

Medina was fixing his only form of transportation for yet another time. His wife, Lucía, stood by his side while he strained through the repairs. She alternately handed him all the necessary tools and parts: pliers, bailing wire, an empty can of Hawaiian Punch.

Medina had sheared off the top and bottom of the small can, then cut through the side so that the can formed a curved sheet of thin metal. His wife held another similarly transformed can just in case repairs grew complicated.

The faded green pickup showed signs of having rubbed up against a tree or two over the years. Medina, from his perch under the hood, leaned deep into the guts of the truck, twisting tightly a short length of bailing wire around the disfigured can of punch. He had wrapped the can around the exhaust pipe that looped down from near the bottom of the engine.

"It's been making a lot of noise," said Medina, talking to me in Spanish as he worked. "This isn't going to fix it, but maybe it will hold for a while.

"Actually, I think the engine is cracked," Medina said as he came up for air from the depths of the old engine. "This isn't the right engine for the truck. The other engine gave out, and this is the engine that a mechanic in Peñasco put in. I don't know if it's going to work."

The 1968 Chevy pickup was parked in the Medina's front yard. There, weathered wood of assorted lengths and widths formed several animal pens that stood empty. Secured to one of the pens was a narrow basketball rim that was tilted forward slightly only about six feet off the ground where a few chickens walked freely and pecked at the dirt.

Three piles of chopped, neatly stacked firewood rose over the entrance to the yard ready for heating and cooking indoors as the year's chill grew stiffer. A fire of a different sort was planned for dry kindling that had recently been loaded into a wheelbarrow that stood near the rear of the pickup. The kindling would become part of a project to be taken on once repairs to the truck were completed.

Work was not uncommon to the Medina family. Ricardo, Lucía and their six children at home were sustained by one project after another. Some projects made money. Some saved it. The morning's work on the pickup saved money. So, too, did an outing by a couple of the Medina children who traveled deeper into the mountains to pick piñon for the winter. The wheelbarrow full of wood was to be pushed to the back of the house where a grunting pig waited his inevitable fate.

"I'll use the wood when we kill the pig," Medina said. "We'll need a fire for hot water to peel off the hair and to cook *chicharones*."

Republican Garrey Carruthers was nearing the end of his first year as governor as I visited with Medina while he sat atop his old pickup's engine. Carruthers had long been a fan of old vehicles. He likely never would have looked twice at Medina's battered pickup, though. Carruthers' favorite was a well-maintained 1967 Mustang convertible that he took out for spins from time to time.

It's all but certain that Carruthers never made it up to Medina's neck of the woods. The washboard roads would have been murder on the Mustang's alignment. Medina could have told Carruthers that from personal experience.

Carruthers liked to say that being governor was some of the best fun he ever had. All governors ought to have fun, but perhaps there should be a rule that before the fun begins, the state's chief executive each day had to talk to just one person like Medina.

New Mexico's Capitol could benefit from such visits because for many in our land of sharp contrasts, fun still doesn't come easily.

Infrastructure—libraries, schools, health clinics, roads, water systems, senior centers—have always been essential to the well-being of rural communities. Successive New Mexico governors have touted their efforts to address such needs even if those efforts haven't resulted in long-term reversals of fortune.

"A hot meal is there if they need it in almost every community around the state," said Jacob Block, a planning director for the State Agency on Aging in 1993 during the third gubernatorial term of Democrat Bruce King.

Lucía and Ricardo Medina of Llano de San Juan southeast of Taos moved on to other chores in the autumn of 1987 after having finished repairs to the engine of their battered 1968 Chevrolet pickup.

Adonay Gonzales in the 1980s walked among the woodpiles he kept outside his home in Llano de San Juan southeast of Taos. Gonzales was known to carefully stack wood depending on its size and age.

Eduardo Lucero in the 1980s walked the back roads of La Madera north of Española, knowing it would not always be an easy path that rose to greet him.

A lonely flag flutters in La Madera.

Jobs, however, remained perhaps the most-critical element required to sustain families and the villages that they call home. Carruthers was out of state in the late 1980s when he opined that there was little hope for substantial economic improvement in many small, rural communities of New Mexico. If residents of those communities want to better their financial standings, they'll likely have to move, Carruthers was quoted as saying.

He wasn't being mean-spirited. He simply saw slim chances of major employers moving into tiny villages whose very appeal is rooted in their isolation from most everything that businesses need to survive.

Carruthers entered office in 1987 promising to put in place a five-year plan to boost economic development in the state. Governor King began his third term in 1991 and said there was no meaningful evidence of such a plan to be found.

King during his third term directed his lieutenant governor, Casey Luna of Belen, to look for ways around obstacles to rural economic development. Fabián Chávez Jr., a former state legislator from Santa Fé and director of the state's Economic Development Department from 1975–1977, had been given the same task as a consultant to Democratic Governor Toney Anaya during the 1980s.

Chávez failed to find solutions and he didn't see much hope for Lieutenant Governor Luna's efforts.

"I tried very, very hard but it's a real difficult task," said Chávez, whose resume included six years on the state's Economic Development Board. "Almost invariably, the prospective industrial investor has chosen to locate in Albuquerque or Las Cruces because of their access to major transportation arteries for shipping materials and products."

Mike Cerletti, Governor King's tourism director in 1991, hoped to find ways for rural villages to reap greater benefits from the state's ever-growing flow of tourists even while aware of villagers' sensitivities. Like Indians who usually seek privacy in their pueblos, rural villagers for the most part didn't want tourists trampling outside their kitchen doors and interrupting a lifestyle and routine that set their communities apart in the first place.

Bah, said others.

There were those, for example, who talked of a ski resort or dude ranches in the beautiful mountain slopes and meadows around Tierra Amarilla.

Too much, countered opponents, who instead preferred help like that which might develop traditional industries, such as wool growing and marketing.

Cerletti proposed having seminars in small communities to discuss "reasonable tourism."

"We would like people to know that having visitors and maintaining the environment are not necessarily mutually exclusive. You can have both," he said.

Perfecto Gonzales in 1987 worked the wooden counter of his small store in the front room of his house along foothills of the southern Rockies, while former Governor Garrey Carruthers saw little hope for economic growth in some isolated communities.

Tourism, he asserted, is an industry and, as such, is much like mining, ranching and manufacturing. "There's no industry that isn't without some degree of problem," he said.

The affable Cerletti got points for good intentions if not for success on a significant scale.

Well aware of government's limitations, longtime Española Mayor Richard Lucero suggested that tenacity and local enterprise mustn't be abandoned. "Every community in northern New Mexico has to pick itself up by its own bootstraps. Communities can't just wait and cry the blues," he said. "State development commissions can't be magicians. If communities help themselves, they will get help from the Legislature and the governor's office."

Perhaps. But such talk was akin to whistling in the wind for many. By 1993, the dead ends left people like 28-year-old Marcos Maestas of La Madera torn as he saw no hope for change in northern New Mexico's economy, which had been traveling uphill and against the wind all his life.

Maestas spent most of his young adult life fighting forest fires, hauling firewood and peeling *vigas*. He was no stranger to his own bootstraps. Nor was he stuck in the perception that opportunities had to come to him. He lived for a while in Oakland, California, but felt compelled to return to northern New Mexico even though he knew his employment options would be very limited.

"The people over there would rather shoot at you than wave at you," Maestas told me. "It's hard being broke all the time. I'm not the richest person in the world but I'd rather be here than in the big city. If I didn't, all I'd have to do is pack my stuff and go."

His heart was at home even if the jobs were not.

Hard times have taught many that home is where you make it. As a young boy, Leveo V. Sánchez learned that lesson well while new job assignments kept him and his mother, Victoria, moving from one tiny northern New Mexico community to another.

Born in Lamy, Leveo followed his mother to her early assignments as a New Mexico public school teacher in Lamy, Galisteo, Glorieta, Nambé and Las Vegas. Pay was poor and money was tight at every stop.

Leveo's father, a state highway department employee, died in an auto accident just months before Leveo was born. Hardships faced by Leveo and his mother were very apparent while the two lived in small rented quarters in Nambé about 15 miles north of Santa Fé.

Leveo was only 11 when his mother received an unexpected offer to leave Nambé and work for the Las Vegas City Schools.

"The job offered me a substantial raise in salary, the chance to work

Residents of isolated communities like Vallecitos north of Española struggle to find economic opportunities while trying to preserve their lands and culture.

for the first time in a large, urban school setting, and the honor of being one of the first Hispanics invited to teach in the Las Vegas school system in New Town," Victoria D. de Sánchez wrote in her memoirs. "It was an offer I couldn't afford to turn down, but it was contingent on my renewing my teaching certificate by attending the first session of summer school at New Mexico Highlands University."

Victoria had recently remarried. She, her husband and Leveo had planted a huge vegetable garden and seeded several acres of wheat as well as a third of an acre of chile near the small house they rented. They also were responsible for an orchard with around 100 fruit trees.

"The orchard soon would be bearing cherries, apricots, pears, plums, peaches and apples," wrote Victoria. "The plantings, orchard...laying chickens and numerous hogs made up the major part of my assets ... At this point, my husband had left us to find work in California."

Victoria wrote that the work her husband left behind was overwhelming. And suddenly she had to contemplate what to do about that work as a promising teaching opportunity knocked on her door. She and young Leveo faced big decisions.

"Should Leveo and I leave the crops unharvested and go to Las Vegas

Child's play in Vallecitos

together? Should I leave my eleven-year-old son alone to tend to the crops and animals? Or should I turn down the teaching post in Las Vegas?" Victoria wrote.

She accepted the job in Las Vegas and committed to summer school at Highlands University. Leveo was left alone on the Nambé farm to assume a man's responsibilities. Mother and son cried together, Leveo admitted.

Victoria left for Las Vegas at three a.m. each Monday and returned

Marcos Maestas found the economy of northern New Mexico to be traveling uphill and against the wind throughout his young life in La Madera. He earned money as a young adult fighting forest fires, hauling firewood and peeling *vigas*.

to Nambé by eight p.m. on Fridays. She remembered: "I would make a pot of beans and a large stew for my son, leaving him to do the balance of the cooking each week. The experience was extremely difficult and we missed each other terribly. I worried about Leveo constantly but there was no way to check on him since the phone service in Nambé was very limited.

"Leveo carried out his responsibilities as effectively as a mature man. He arranged for the use of irrigation waters every other week on the night I returned from Las Vegas. It was a two-person job to spread the water evenly over the fields, and we would water all night long. He hoed daily,

Tunes of hope for Marcos Maestas.

fed the hogs and chickens, picked the ripened vegetables and collected the eggs. My son was very lonely during this period and later informed me that he often cried himself to sleep. It was only the thought of the new opportunities awaiting us that made this ordeal bearable."

In a way, Leveo had prepared himself for the responsibilities. He was nine when he and his mother moved into a two-room house in Nambé.

"Every morning, Leveo ... would haul enough water in lard buckets to fill the cistern in the kitchen and to water the hogs and the chickens," Victoria wrote. "He spent another hour each afternoon after school making trips to the well two blocks away. Each day he also carried home the slop over from the school lunch program so that we could feed it to our pigs."

As an adult Leveo went on to work, mostly as a ranking administrator, in government programs under U.S. presidents Dwight Eisenhower, John Kennedy and Lyndon Johnson. Much of his time was spent overseas fighting global poverty in programs like the U.S. Alliance For Progress and the Peace Corps. At home, it was LBJ's War on Poverty, which administered programs like Head Start, Job Corps, VISTA and Upward Bound.

Leveo left government in 1968 and soon started his own management consulting firm that focused on social, educational and economic programs worldwide. It would become one of the country's largest such firms owned by a Hispanic. The firm, Development Associates, plus Leveo's investments made Leveo a very rich man.

Rural tranquility and faith in higher powers often get northern New Mexico families through their days.

The poverty that Leveo left behind in New Mexico's rural areas where he grew up faded little during the years he spent away. "People have more cars and TVs these days but progress hasn't gone much beyond that for a lot of people," he told me for his 2015 biography, *Nerve of a Patriot*.

Indeed, automobiles likely have become more prevalent in northern New Mexico's rural communities as elders have passed on and younger generations have stayed behind. Automobiles and cell phones undoubtedly have helped those younger people feel more connected and have increased their access to health care and other assistance. Piercing poverty statistics, though, haven't gone away.

The nation's War on Poverty that occupied so much of Sánchez's time, arguably, was more successful at tending to symptoms of poverty than at getting solutions to take hold long term for the well-being of families in New Mexico and across the country.

Sadly, for so many who live in poverty, learning to deal with it might be all that can be expected.

I think of a five-year-old girl who early in the new millennium was among scores of kids tempted by the wonderful smell of cupcakes, cookies and other sweets of a bake sale at an elementary school in south side Santa Fé.

Most of the classroom's kindergartners stirred as they waited for a chance to spend a quarter or two on at least one of the objects of their temptation. This particular little girl, though, wouldn't be getting a treat that day. In the Spanish language used by her family at home, she offered a very simple explanation to a classmate who had asked what the girl was going to buy at the bake sale.

"Nothing," replied the girl. She then opened her lips enough for her tiny teeth to show. "See, I have a loose tooth but it hasn't fallen out yet so I don't have any money. Maybe it'll fall out in time for the next bake sale," she said.

From the Roybal Files...
The Santa Fe New Mexican, December 1978
Excerpts—Northern New Mexico Lifestyle Story Shared

Eighty-four-year-old Max Cruz of Trampas speaks proudly of his age and of how he is still able to weather a cold morning. Wearing patched jeans and a work shirt, he visited with me in the snow outside his home near a pile of juniper logs he had chopped that morning.

He talked of the work he has known since before New Mexico became a state:

"I worked first as a sheepherder, back around 1910 in Trinidad, Colorado. We would go from here on foot and with burros. The burros would carry our food and beds and everything. We went on foot wearing moccasins, not shoes like this. It was mostly young boys who would go. I was about twelve when I went for the first time with an older brother.

"From here we would go on foot and sleep in Taos. Then we would leave the next day and sleep in Cimarron, then the next day we would sleep in Raton and we would keep going like that—on foot. Now you only have to take your suitcase and go wait in the station for the bus or the train.

"We were taught to make our moccasins because in those times the people were real poor. There was hardly any money. We would go work in Trinidad for fifty cents a day ... We would bring the money back to our father ... The father and mother would stay behind on the ranch, taking care of the crops. When we would come home, we would find a lot to eat, much more than where we were herding sheep. Here, when we came, there would be meat, there would be everything. We would butcher pigs. We would butcher cows.

"In those days, people wouldn't buy flour in the stores. The homes had plenty of flour, corn, wheat and everything. There were fat pigs, fat cows. It was just a matter of rounding them up, butcher them and eat. We didn't have a lot of money, but we had a lot to eat."

Cruz said he got tired of working as a shepherd and worked later laying ties for the Santa Fe Railroad in southern Colorado. He again compared the work to the wages that were paid, laughing occasionally as if finding his own story hard to believe.

"I worked for the railroad when I was already grown for one dollar and ten cents for ten hours of work. I was well worked. There was no monkeying around. And that was the company that paid the most."

Cruz was proud of the work he had done and spoke with admiration for the work of his father and others whom he called *"los viejitos."*

"They were even better than us. They did even more," he said. "My grandfather would go to Kansas in a wagon drawn by animals. When he came back he would have the wagon filled to the top with meat that he had already dried. People were smart in those days.

"Today, experience is lacking, and it hurts us sometimes. I tore up the very wagon used by my grandfather. It was a thing of value. It was one of those things people today would like to see to learn how things used to be. But I myself tore up the wagon for firewood."

8
FUGITIVES IN THE NIGHT AND SECRETS OF A FEDERAL GOVERNMENT

"Aircraft unavailable to us" were likely being used in a growing string of mysterious cattle mutilations discovered largely on northern New Mexico ranches beginning in the mid-1970s, said State Police officer Gabe Valdez.

By themselves, the mutilations of precise incisions and bloodless surroundings had been enough to make news reporters reach for their notebooks. Valdez's tantalizing pronouncement about extraordinary aircraft took interest to another level.

Valdez, an awarded, soft-spoken cop posted in the small community of Dulce near the New Mexico-Colorado border wasn't referring to aircraft unavailable to New Mexico State Police. More and more, he said, it appeared that aircraft not available to anyone on Earth were being used. They were being used to lift and transport cattle prior to being mutilated and then used again to deposit the carcasses in corrals or open fields with very little, if any, evidence left behind with which to track the perpetrators.

The aircraft from all indications worked speedily and quietly, usually escaping anyone's notice. They also must have possessed considerable power. Victimized cattle often weighed 900 pounds or more. Faint tripod markings on the ground near some of the carcasses were among scant evidence.

High levels of radiation found on some of the mutilated animals added even more to the intrigue.

It was all plenty to capture and retain my attention while working as *The Santa Fe New Mexican's* Española bureau chief. It had been little more than a decade since several of my companions and I had seen unidentified flying objects moving mysteriously over the hills rising above Los Álamos and within eyesight of a 1978 mutilation near Santa Clara Pueblo.

It was at that site in Santa Clara that Valdez told me cattle seemingly were being moved by alien aircraft prior to and following mutilations.

Valdez during the previous three years had worked on 32 livestock mutilation cases in New Mexico—all but six in Río Arriba County—and was recognized as New Mexico's chief information source on mutilations.

Santa Clara Pueblo policeman Roger Naranjo, New Mexico State Police officer Gabe Valdez and Los Álamos National Laboratory scientist Howard Burgess found northern New Mexico's cattle mutilations draped in mystery.

Mutilations in New Mexico, at least, were all very similar. The eyes, ears, tongues, sex organs and chunks of flesh around the rump were taken. Clean incisions, as opposed to tears or jagged cuts, were typical.

"The cow's a perfect test animal," *Boulder Monthly* magazine reported in January 1979. Information and comments were collected from three Colorado UFO researchers. One of them offered this: "(Mutilators) ... take the genitals, which pick up any generic aberrations. The genitals would give the best sampling of a genetic screw-up due to technological contaminants or radiation. They take the sperm, or the genitals of a bull. Or, if it's a cow, they take the milk.

"The other thing they take is tissue, the basic types of tissue in the body that give you its record. Tongue, rib, eye—they take the eye. We're learning from iridology right now that the eye contains a record. Everything that goes into the body shows up in the eye fourteen days later—in a cow at least."

By February 1979, Santa Fé District Attorney Eloy Martínez was seeking federal funds to investigate livestock mutilations in Río Arriba County, which was within his jurisdiction. Martínez said in his application to the Law Enforcement Assistance Administration that 8,000 to 10,000 mutilations had been reported across the country since 1970. More than

60 had been in Río Arriba County, he reported. (In fact, a total of 76 stock mutilations had been investigated in New Mexico between February 1975 and June 1979.)

Martínez's office that April was granted $44,000 for the investigation. The district attorney's application for funds described the mutilations as bizarre crimes against expensive property of defenseless ranchers. Animals killed and mutilated "for some reason tend to be the best livestock in a rancher's herd," the application said.

The FBI stepped in because of the apparent criminal element involved.

Crimes or no crimes, New Mexico Republican U.S. Senator Harrison "Jack" Schmitt, an Apollo 17 astronaut who walked on the moon, said the mutilations had become a serious economic threat to New Mexico ranchers.

Valdez was kept busy in 1979. Mutilations were reported in Truchas on July 21st, September 13th and September 28th. Other communities with reported mutilations during that three-month period were Lindrith, Tierra Amarilla, Socorro, Questa, Tomé, El Cerrito and Medanales. Communities were scattered within the top half of the state.

But mutilations had occurred elsewhere in the country, apparently since 1967 when a prized horse was found mutilated in southern Colorado. Reports of mutilated livestock came out of Kansas, Minnesota, Nebraska and Oklahoma in 1970 and 1971. Ranchers in Illinois, Iowa and Missouri in the spring of 1973 reported strange helicopters buzzing their herds. Cows then turned up mutilated, Colorado researcher David Perkins wrote in 1980 in *Taos The Magazine*.

Dulce rancher, Manuel Gómez, in the summer of 1975 reported some of the earliest mutilations recorded in New Mexico.

About 60 miles down the Chama River basin, Abiquiu-area rancher Alva Simpson reported his loss of a prized bull from the same ranch where he was known to host some of New Mexico's most-prominent Republican politicians.

Ranchers in Portales, Springer, Clayton and Raton also reported mutilations in 1975.

Mutilators seemingly were not concerned about a rancher's politics, ethnicity or status. But they did appear to want the best young stock that could be found.

Perkins, the Colorado writer who began researching mutilations in 1977, said reports of mutilations had come in from across the country near sites with nuclear power plants. In some states, mutilations ring the area of nuclear power plants. Other mutilations have been found "right at the gate" of power plants, said Perkins, who was president of what was then a two-year-old organization called Animal Mutilations Probe.

Perkins added support to Valdez's supposition about alien aircraft, claiming it is possible there is "concern about our use of atomic material among extraterrestrial beings."

"It could be a manifestation of their survival instincts to protect themselves from us," he told me in May 1979.

An Arkansas couple during the same period was asked by the Benton County Sheriff's Department to investigate cattle mutilations reported in northwestern Arkansas. The couple, anthropologists and faculty members at the University of Arkansas, said concern had increased as losses mounted for cattle farmers in Benton County along the Ozark Plateau.

Speculation was running wild in Arkansas, said Nancy Owen, who had come to northern New Mexico as part of her research. Some were linking mutilations to witchcraft, she said. Others blamed them on foreign students at the University of Arkansas. Others, still, expressed fear that a child would be the next target for mutilation.

By May 1979, Valdez was retreating from his comment about alien aircraft. His change of opinion came after a widely distributed tranquilizer was among two drugs discovered in the carcass of a young bull mutilated two months earlier in New Mexico's Torrance County.

The tranquilizer's generic name is Chlorpromazine. A second drug, apparently used to clog the blood, was also found during an analysis of carcass remains by a Los Alamos chemist.

The Torrance County bull's carcass was found by the owner within two or three hours after it was killed. That's why the drugs were able to be detected, Valdez said.

He said of the growing number of mutilated cattle, "We know they've been tranquilized, which we suspected. They're immobilized by a tranquilizer ... and the other drug is used to clog the blood and remove it through the jugular vein.

"We know this stuff is made here, and it isn't from outer space. Whoever is doing it is highly sophisticated and they have a lot of resources. They're well organized."

It all left open the mystery about the aircraft being used. The mystery grew as more information was reported.

Torrance County Sheriff Bobby Chávez said the young bull's carcass that was found in February 1979 seemed to have been dropped from the air because there were no tracks in the area.

A second mutilation case was reported in Torrance County about a month later. Chávez said tracks of a tripod were found about 25 feet away from where the carcass of a five-year-old cow was lying. The cow weighed about 900 pounds and also appeared to have been dropped where it was found.

"They did not kill it within the area," Chavez said. "It had clamp marks on the hind legs, and if they dropped it, they dropped it very carefully inside the corner of the corral."

It was inside the corral where the tripod markings were found.

Valdez, too, had reported finding tripod markings near a mutilation site in Dulce.

Operators of an unidentified aircraft in April 1979 were apparently surprised by tribal police while spotlighting a herd of cattle near Dulce, prompting State Police to investigate. The aircraft was seen around two a.m. on the Manuel Gómez ranch, where eight cattle had been mutilated that year.

Valdez said the two Jicarilla Apache tribal offers were on routine patrol with their vehicle lights off when they saw the aircraft approach. The craft reportedly was hovering about 50 feet off the ground with a powerful spotlight aimed at the cattle. The spotlight was turned off and the craft rose swiftly then sped away when the tribal officers turned on headlights of their cruiser, Valdez said.

He said he was about four miles away from the sighting when the Jicarilla officers alerted him by radio. The aircraft flew silently over him, he said, and turned on small green and red lights as it headed south.

Valdez said radar at the Air Traffic Control Center in Longmont, Colorado, apparently detected the mystery craft as it was flying at an altitude of 5,800 feet at about 300 miles per hour. The craft disappeared from radar about 20 miles north of Albuquerque, Valdez said.

Anxiety mounted. Threats were made for no good reason at all. Jicarilla Apache tribal leader Raleigh Tafoya said threats had been made against several ranchers whose cattle had been mutilated. "I'm wondering whether the lives of human beings will be next," he said. "We don't know what we're dealing with."

A decidedly no-nonsense approach, however, would be charted for the federally funded investigation of stock mutilations for which funding was secured by the Santa Fé district attorney's office.

Kenneth Rommel, a 28-year veteran of the FBI, was selected to head the investigation. His previous assignments had taken him to Puerto Rico, New York City, Chicago, San Francisco, Cincinnati and Santa Fé.

Rommel left work as senior resident FBI agent in Santa Fé in May 1979 and began the year-long mutilations investigation in June. His salary for the year would be $27,500.

Rommel said that because the investigation was to be funded by a law enforcement grant, his attention should be directed at determining whether crimes were being committed. "If we don't have a crime committed, then as a law enforcement matter, we don't have a problem," he said.

He referred to a state law that prohibits the unauthorized killing of livestock. "If we don't have anyone killing stock, then we don't have a violation under the statute," he said. "If we do have a violation, how many violations do we actually have and who's doing them?"

Should he come upon little green men, he'd bring them in by the ears, he said flippantly.

Four months into the investigation, Rommel said that 76 stock mutilations reported in New Mexico from February 1975 through June 1979 had been reviewed and indexed and that additional investigation would follow in cases "where feasible."

He pledged to work closely with the New Mexico State Police and other law enforcement agencies.

Little useful historical information would be available to investigators. Dr. Myra Ellen Jenkins, working then as New Mexico's highly regarded state historian, said she was not aware of any information on mutilations that was dated before 1970.

"I know of no documentation of similar mutilations of carcasses in New Mexico until ... what has been going on for about five years," she told me as Rommel began his investigation. "I have never seen anything concerning same in the folklore of New Mexico."

With a ranching background developed in central Colorado, Dr. Jenkins said a "practical down-to-earth point of view" tends to discount consideration of something extraterrestrial. From a historical view, extraterrestrial involvement is "a little far out," she said.

In the end, Rommel's findings dropped with a thud. Animals—scavengers and predators—were responsible for the livestock deaths and dismemberments, he reported. There were no crimes, no mysterious aircraft involved, no little green men.

So much was left unexplained, critics asserted.

Dr. Jenkins, the state historian with a ranching background, discredited assertions that predatory animals were responsible for the mutilations even before Rommel's conclusions were released.

"This particular rather bizarre type, if it were predator attack, I've never seen any documented records of such attack in Western history," she said. "I have not seen documentation in Spanish records or Mexican records or even Territorial records of this type of mutilations that would have been done by predators before."

Valdez dismissed Rommel's conclusions, suggesting that the retired

FBI agent's closest encounter with cattle prior to his latest investigation might have been a steak in a New York restaurant.

An Earthly Accent—From Chimayó

Valdez retired from the New Mexico State Police in 1995. He was State Police officer of the year in the late 1970s, not for anything associated with UFOs or livestock mutilations. It was for astute police work late one evening that led to the identification and capture of a Chimayó man who was wanted for murder in Española and had escaped capture for years while hiding out in San Francisco, California, and Salt Lake City, Utah.

Amadeo Martínez, a handsome 43-year-old man with a full head of black hair, had entered New Mexico in the dark of night and had maneuvered his car to the side of U.S. 84 after it ran out of gasoline six miles west of Chama. Valdez was on patrol in his cruiser just eight miles south of the Colorado border when he came upon the motorist and his stranded vehicle at around 2:30 a.m. on September 24, 1977. The two men visited for a few moments alongside the cars before Valdez offered to siphon enough gasoline out of his cruiser's tank to get the man's car into nearby Dulce. There, Valdez told the man, he knew the owner of a filling station who would open his door and unlock a pump long enough for them to purchase fuel.

Valdez was engaged in more than conversation during those first few minutes with the stranded motorist. He took note of tattoos and of the man's accent and manner of speech. To Valdez, the man spoke with inflections distinct to Chimayó, the small farming community about 100 miles to the southeast.

Valdez radioed in a description of the man as they drove west in separate cars alongside large meadows, rolling hills and towering Ponderosa pines en route to Dulce.

It wasn't long before Valdez was informed that he likely was in the company of Amadeo Martínez from Chimayó, a suspected murderer who had escaped capture and detection by authorities for nearly four years.

Martínez stood accused of shooting to death Elizabeth Sanderson, 50, from the Española Valley, on Thanksgiving night of 1973. The woman and her husband, 58-year-old Wesley Sanderson, worked as private security guards. Having just returned from Santa Fé, they began making their nighttime rounds on Española's westside when they came upon what was later reported to be two men stealing tires from the small car lot of Hunter Motor Company. It was alongside well-lit Oñate Street perhaps a quarter mile from the Española City Police station.

Elizabeth Sanderson was shot twice in the chest with a .38-caliber pistol and once near her right hip. She died quickly. Wesley Sanderson, shot in the head and a wrist with the same pistol, survived. Martínez apparently escaped in his yellow Ford pickup.

Just short of four years later Valdez made his spectacular arrest in Dulce.

"I didn't know who he was, but he looked real nervous and suspicious," Valdez testified later, referring to Martínez. I conned him into going to Dulce to get some gas for him."

"When he was following me to Dulce, I called to Española (State Police field office) and got information about Amadeo Martínez. Española gave me a full description on him, tattoos that he had and everything. We got to Dulce. I lured him into the service station and arrested him. He started to give me resistance, but I didn't give him a chance."

Martínez had escaped capture for years because he had been careful. He deliberately drove into New Mexico late into the evening of September 24, 1977, as part of his caution. It purportedly was the first time he had returned to New Mexico since fleeing after Elizabeth Sanderson's murder. He came to visit his mother.

Martínez had expected to find an open gasoline station in Chama to refuel his car so that he might pull into the driveway of his mother's home in Chimayó before daylight. Though cautious in his planning, his execution of plans failed him. More precisely, caution might have been doused by blurred judgment that night. A Salt Lake City woman traveling with Martínez said he drank more than a pint of whiskey and smoked as many as ten joints of marijuana on the drive from Utah to Chama. Martínez had not been careful to ensure that he had fuel for the last leg of his trip.

Chama stations closed, Martínez must have anticipated trouble. If he were to find an open station that night, it wouldn't be until Española, some 85 miles away, well beyond the reach of fuel remaining in his car.

The sight of Valdez's cruiser surely fanned Martínez's anxieties. But they must have waned as he began talking with Valdez. Valdez in his entire career likely struck few people as a threatening cop. A native of the tiny community of Cebolla about 25 miles south of Chama, his demeanor made him seem more like everybody's favorite uncle. His eyes were soft, not piercing; his voice, friendly; his manner, relaxed.

Valdez was accompanied by state policeman Ramon Suazo as Martínez was driven from Dulce directly to the Santa Fé city jail. Both Valdez and Suazo would testify months later that Martínez was talkative, even boastful, during the two-hour drive. Both officers testified that Martínez admitted to killing Sanderson and supposedly claimed to have killed others over the years.

"He started bragging, boasting ... that I was lucky; that he had had many opportunities to kill me or do away with me," Valdez testified.

In fact, Valdez said, Martínez told him that he did not kill Valdez out on the dark roadway because he liked the cop's Spanish accent.

So important can be one's manner of speech. Out on the roadway near Chama that night of September 1977, Martínez sounded like someone from Chimayó and it contributed to his arrest. Valdez sounded like an Hispanic who never shed his own manner of talking and, apparently, it saved his life.

Martínez pleaded innocent in the Sanderson shootings. He accused Valdez and Suazo of lying about his supposed confession on the drive from Dulce to Santa Fé. Prosecutors based their case on so many lies, he said, that he feared jurors at his trial would wrongfully deprive him of his freedom.

A lesson on lying was at the root of a brief discussion that Martínez had with an acquaintance during a recess in his trial at the Río Arriba County Courthouse in Tierra Amarilla. The two talked at the wooden railing that separated spectators from principals in the trial. Martínez, neatly groomed, wore a three-piece suit and a broad smile as he talked away from the presence of the judge, jurors and prosecutors. Reporting on the trial, I slowly positioned myself close enough to hear the discussion.

One of the jailers downstairs was in the habit of arriving late for work, Martínez said. Worse, said the accused murderer, the jailer kept giving supervisors the same excuse for his tardiness.

Martínez said he counseled the jailer. The advice: Don't blame it on a flat tire every time if you want people to believe you. Change your story. Nobody gets a flat tire every day.

Courtrooms, of course, tend to be filled with lies, even as so many inside swear to tell the truth.

Wesley Sanderson had grown ill, and it became evident that he would not be able to attend the trial in Tierra Amarilla. He gave a taped deposition in December 1977 from Irving, Texas, in which he identified Martínez as the man caught stealing tires at Hunter Motor Company on Thanksgiving night 1973. But Sanderson could not say that he saw Martínez fire the gun.

Wesley Sanderson died a month after giving his deposition of causes apparently unrelated to the 1973 shooting.

A Río Arriba jury of nine men and three women sat through the week-long trial in Tierra Amarilla then deliberated for 16 hours before reporting that they could not reach verdicts on any of the charges.

State District Judge Santiago Campos of Santa Fé declared a mistrial, and prosecutors pledged to do it all over again.

The second trial was scheduled for August of that same year. As both sides prepared, Judge Campos won appointment to the federal bench in Santa Fé. State District Judge Louis DePauli of Gallup was assigned to preside over Martínez's second trial. This time, there were less than four days of testimony. Jurors deliberated for two and one-half hours before finding Martínez guilty of first-degree murder, aggravated battery and theft.

Judge DePauli sentenced Martínez to life in prison.

"Madness" and Death Among the Sleuths

After retiring from the State Police, Valdez in 1998 went to work as a field investigator for the National Institute for Discovery Science, which was based in Las Vegas, Nevada. The institute was founded in 1995 by real estate magnate and tea entrepreneur, Robert Bigelow. It was devoted to sponsoring research into UFOs and other paranormal phenomena, such as cattle mutilations.

Valdez developed information related to cattle mutilations around the clock, much of the work done independently. He was consumed and had been for years. He and I had maintained contact over the years so he wasn't caught entirely by surprise when I phoned him at his north-side Albuquerque home early in 2010 and asked that we visit so that I might catch up on his investigations.

Valdez in 1988 had moved from tiny, remote Dulce to a large home in Albuquerque's rural North Valley.

He agreed to meet with me but made it clear that he was constrained in what he could discuss. And then he asked two perplexing questions: 1) Was I certain that I wanted to dig deeper into the subject of cattle mutilations? 2) Was I willing to take risks that could come from our visit?

We agreed to meet on January 8, 2010, a Friday. We'd visit over lunch at Tomasita's Restaurant on the Railyard in downtown Santa Fé.

I arrived about ten minutes early and asked for a small table in a corner of the building away from the main dining room. I took a chair that allowed me to see patrons as they arrived and was more than a bit surprised when I saw a small man walking purposefully toward me.

It was Gabe Valdez all right. But he bore little resemblance to the man with whom I had developed a trusted working relationship that had spanned more than 30 years. Our last face-to-face meeting had been a couple of years earlier, a chance encounter along an isle of an Española grocery store soon after he began working with the National Institute for Discovery Science.

It was a 66-year-old ex-cop who I rose to greet that Friday at Tomasita's but I couldn't help but wonder, at least briefly, if I was about to sit down with an old friend in the midst of a battle with a serious disease.

Valdez's thick dark black hair was gone. What little hair remained was gray and short, forming a rim around his bald crown. He appeared shorter and had lost a considerable amount of weight. The once-soft eyes had become jumpy, restless. So had his demeanor. At least they had that day.

Valdez's livelihood and mine both had been rooted largely in our impulse to read our company, our surroundings. Still, neither one of us spoke that day about the changes we undoubtedly saw in one another. Neither one of us had escaped telltale signs of advancing age.

Valdez offered almost immediately that his investigations had kept him quite busy and that what he had turned up was more than a little unsettling. Forget extraterrestrial involvement in the cattle mutilations, he said, reasserting the conclusion that he first reached in 1979. Clandestine operations of the U.S. government are behind the mystery, and secret agents have been all too happy to divert attention away from the government's research by fanning suspicions about UFOs, he said.

The air around the subject of cattle mutilations was filled with disinformation carefully propagated by federal agents, he said. That campaign of disinformation had ruined the reputation of a friend and fellow researcher and likely drove him to the point of near madness, Valdez said.

Very, very few in the government, itself, even know about the clandestine operations, he said.

He appeared nervous as he spoke, glancing periodically to both his flanks.

Maybe five minutes after he began talking, Valdez asked if I was sure that I wanted to continue the discussion. He long had suspected that he was under surveillance, he said, and his suspicions were confirmed in 1984 when he discovered that the phone in his Dulce home was bugged.

He had been both bugged and tailed over the past 25 years, he said, adding that the Jicarilla Tribal Police and the Dulce home of much-targeted rancher Manuel Gómez also had been bugged.

We probably were being watched even as we ate lunch that day, Valdez asserted. He had photographs and documents that he wanted me to see but he intentionally left them inside his car out of concern for who might be inside the restaurant, he said. We would go to his car in the parking lot later if I chose to, he offered.

"You and your family could be subjected to surveillance," he warned. "You could have a tail wherever you go."

We finished our lunch and walked out to his car where several fat envelopes waited. I read documents that seemed to tell of purported covert operations. I also saw photographs of lights considered to be suspicious captured for moments in dark skies as well as photos of deformed livestock, the result of government experiments gone bad, Valdez surmised.

He said I was looking at information that he had compiled while working independently or as a State Police officer and that going to others to confirm information would prove fruitless; no one would talk.

He was right. I never expected that any of my inquiries would get someone to acknowledge existence of supposed top-secret operations of which even select members of Congress purportedly were unaware. But even attempts to get someone to confirm or deny lesser information were futile.

Valdez had photos supposedly from 1963 that showed unusual lights in various positions over the community of Ojo Caliente about 20 miles north of Española. Photos were taken by a man in a red Chevy pickup, which appeared in at least one of the photos.

"I looked at the photographs to try to analyze what was going on," Valdez said. "I determined that it was a small spacecraft that had come out of a bigger spacecraft. Some scientists would tell me this: The small craft apparently went back up to a hovering ship."

Valdez said he didn't link the sightings to the string of livestock mutilations that surfaced in northern New Mexico a decade later. Nonetheless, it was 1967, four years after the Ojo Caliente photos were taken, when one of the region's first cases of inexplicable livestock mutilations was discovered. Rancher Harry King in Alamosa, Colorado, just north of the New Mexico border and less than 100 miles on a straight line from Ojo Caliente, had ridden out looking for a missing horse. He found it, dead and mutilated, its brain and stomach removed.

There were circular "exhaust marks" around the carcass as well as a substance that burned the skin when touched, Gregory Bishop wrote in his book, *Project Beta*. The book was published in 2005 by Paraview Pocket Books, a division of Simon & Schuster, Inc.

Rancher King promptly associated the mutilation with mysterious "floating" lights that had been seen in the area, Bishop wrote.

A growing number of mysterious aerial sightings and seemingly related mutilations inevitably drew international attention to the region. As time went on, Valdez became engrossed in such phenomena.

He and Jicarilla Apache authorities in Dulce pursued orbs in the night skies. "(Tribal leader) Raleigh Tafoya, David Osuna (of the State Police) and I spotted an orb near Dulce. Orbs were being used to monitor Dulce. They're very effective, I guess, because they're being used all over (war zones) in Afghanistan."

Valdez said a mysterious round ball had been found by Jicarilla tribal authorities one year around the time that laptops and cell phones were rendered temporarily useless.

Another similar ball supposedly turned up in 2009. Valdez said he was called to a site in El Vado just southeast of Dulce where a woman purportedly found the small ball. "The lady didn't want to be identified but she told me that aircraft hovered over her trailer the night before. The next morning she found the ball and she called me."

"The war chief in Dulce wouldn't let us analyze anything. He said it was against their culture. We don't know what they are. They're buried in the ground somewhere near El Vado."

Valdez showed me a photo that he said he shot during that period in El Vado that appeared to show four saucer-like crafts in the sky.

Valdez was certain that saucer-like crafts were being secretly stored on Air Force bases in Albuquerque and Alamogordo and at White Sands Missile Range.

"Flying saucers were sent to Dulce to confuse people and make them think that UFOs were involved while the government went on with its top-secret research with the cattle mutilations," Valdez said.

Valdez and retired scientist Dr. Howard Burgess learned through nighttime experiments on cattle of Dulce-area rancher Manuel Gómez that select cattle had been marked by a bluish substance detectable only with ultraviolet lighting.

"Manuel Gómez's ranch had been targeted and the cows that we found marked with that glowing substance were approximately the same age and from the same breed. They were similar to the ones that already had been mutilated on Manuel's ranch," Valdez told me.

"Those cattle first were selected as targets then they were marked with that substance that could only be seen later with a UV light. The animals were disabled and a fast, very quiet aircraft that could hover and lift heavy weight would then take the cows away. They were taken to a place where their organs could be removed. Their carcasses were then anchored to the craft by their ankles and flown back to the pastures where they had been taken. Often there were no tracks anywhere close to the dead animal, not even tracks of the animal that had been killed."

Valdez teamed up with Albuquerque physicist and successful entrepreneur, Paul Bennewitz, to explore Dulce-area sites around which suspicious activity had been reported. Principal among sites was Archuleta Mesa on the New Mexico-Colorado border. In Bennewitz, Valdez met his match and more on UFO-related issues.

Valdez said Bennewitz found evidence of what could have served as a small airstrip as well as something that might have been used as an airshaft on the conifer-covered mesa.

Valdez and others already had surmised that there were substantial tunnels within Archuleta Mesa and beneath surfaces nearby.

"There are three tunnels. Helicopters were landing on a strip near what appeared to be the entrance to a tunnel," Valdez said.

Even as he reached perplexing conclusions, Valdez was wary of the disinformation campaign that supposedly surrounded the mutilations.

Bishop wrote that the Air Force improved small dirt roads in remote areas above Dulce and airlifted "mothballed equipment up to the Archuleta Mesa by night" as part of the campaign of disinformation. "They placed old storage tanks, equipment shacks, and engineless Jeeps in clearings next to the primitive roads. A small area was cleared for helicopter landings."

One former secret agent acknowledged that fake air vents were positioned around the large mesa to fan suspicions of an underground base, according to Bishop. That same former agent supposedly also acknowledged existence of underground rooms that were used for elaborate subterfuge that included projecting "flying saucer"- like shapes in clouds over the area.

Subterfuge was everywhere in the cattle mutilation story, as far as Valdez was concerned.

It all was very "bizarre and weird," said Assistant Santa Fé District Attorney Tom Fiorina in 1979. He used the words while visiting with me only a few months before former FBI agent Rommel began his superficial investigation for the district attorney's office.

If events were bizarre, they also appeared to be well coordinated even if very few people knew of the coordinators.

Valdez told of shredded aluminum found on the ground near a mutilated cow in Colorado. "We found the same thing at one of the mutilations in Dulce. The tailings serve as radar chaff. It served to knock out radar towers in Albuquerque and Longmont, Colorado. That way, people couldn't tell when the mystery crafts were flying in."

"In the late 1960s, people around Dulce said they were having little earthquakes. We believe that's when the tunnels were being built. I learned that an engineer who had worked on the tunnels died later in Oregon. I was told he was strangled."

Valdez was among a small number of people who speculated that a research base of some sort existed within Archuleta Mesa and that it was used by Los Álamos National Laboratory for work that was even more-sensitive than most of what was being done in the atomic city.

A laboratory as far away as the East Coast was also involved in the secret work, Valdez said.

His own work over decades had drawn him to two jaw-dropping conclusions.

"We think cattle were being used for human cloning," he told me. "Separately, some of the work is used for research into antidotes for bio-germ warfare."

"Human cloning was being done as early as 10 years ago," he told me in 2010. "Twenty or thirty people have told me they've seen clones in Dulce. They were short. They looked different. They walked different."

Dulce was selected for the supposed extraordinary research because Indians keep to themselves and rarely complain; when necessary, reports could be written off as Indian superstition. So speculated some who got close to the mysteries.

"The cloning, as far as we knew, had nothing to do with research into bio-germ warfare but it likely was being done in the same place," Valdez said. "The U.S. military went into Iraq (in 1992) looking for weapons of mass destruction. We were looking for bio-germs that we gave to Iraq before they became our enemy. Our government developed the deadly virus for germ warfare but it hadn't come up with an antidote."

"Paul Bennewitz and I stayed in contact but we knew we were being bugged by the government. We relayed our information through the State Police," Valdez said.

Bennewitz alone was the subject of an incredible mystery until his death in Albuquerque in 2003. He was seventy-five. The mystery from all appearances was orchestrated by the U.S. government.

Not only were government agents determined to conceal very sensitive information from this well-positioned sleuth, they had gone so far as to destroy Bennewitz's reputation and, seemingly, even drive him out of his mind, Valdez said

Bennewitz in 1969 started a small company, Thunder Scientific, to manufacture specialized temperature and humidity instruments for clients like NASA, the U.S. Navy and the Air Force, Gregory Bishop wrote in his book, *Project Beta*. The company was located just outside the border of Kirtland Air Force Base in Albuquerque.

Bennewitz's life took a troublesome turn ten years later when the electronics expert and his wife began recording strange occurrences from their home in the city's Four Hills neighborhood.

Bennewitz compiled hundreds of photographs and thousands of feet of 8-millimeter film showing "multi-colored lights floating and swooping about the small mountain range inside the base about a mile from his home," wrote Bishop.

"At times, the lights streaked away as quickly as a magician's slight of hand, only to reappear seconds later, apparently miles from where they had just been. To Bennewitz this was irrefutable proof that something unearthly was playing cat and mouse with the human race."

The mysterious lights were moving freely around the Manzano Weapons Storage Complex, which was then the largest underground repository of nuclear weapons components in the Western World, Bishop wrote.

(The *Albuquerque Journal* in June 2010 reported that an estimated 2,000-plus nuclear warheads were being maintained at Kirtland Air Force Base in an underground weapons storage complex.)

Bennewitz presented his mass of data to authorities, whom he thought would move quickly to confront the threat, Bishop wrote.

Instead, he wrote, Bennewitz was subjected to a campaign of disinformation that spanned decades. The campaign apparently was directed by the Air Force Office of Special Investigations, relying heavily on special agent Richard Doty, a former base security guard.

"The events and organizations that were called like moths to the flame that Paul Bennewitz had lit were there to make sure that whatever they were trying to protect would never see the light of public truth," wrote Bishop. "National security was on the line, and all is fair in love and spooking ... The men and women whose job it was to keep things buried did not want the graves disturbed, or the underground tunnels leading to them breached."

"Bennewitz had put his total trust in the (Air Force Office of Special Investigations) at Kirtland and had been led astray about almost everything nearly from day one ... Kirtland Intelligence had told quite a pack of lies to Paul Bennewitz."

Multiple government agencies, including the CIA and FBI, were actively spying on Bennewitz to ensure that he was not digging into their undercover work or violating national security, Bishop wrote.

He wrote that the U.S. government had grown adept at fanning suspicions about UFOs to deflect Bennewitz and others from probing into actual top-secret activities.

"The (Air Force Office of Special Investigations) had done its job so well that Bennewitz was seeing UFOs everywhere ... The counterintelligence plan was working almost too well," Bishop wrote.

Bennewitz, he wrote, had reached the point where he was certain that aliens came out of the walls of his home at night.

"What was all this fuss about? How did a man who was so worried about alien invasion become such a concern to the Air Force and their secret tenants at Kirtland? Paul Bennewitz must have been on to something mighty important to warrant all this attention. The simple fact is that he was, but aliens and UFOs had very little, if anything, to do with it."

Bennewitz, Bishop wrote, reportedly had faced so much stress and fear by late summer 1988 that he barricaded himself in his home and had piled sandbags around all the windows. His family checked him into nearby Anna Kaseman Mental Health Facility for nervous exhaustion. He was confined there for just more than a month.

Valdez acknowledged that much of what Bennewitz professed was considered suspect. He argued that the federal government went to great lengths to ensure that it was, and that it was done to protect the nation's secrets.

Valdez arrived at some extraordinary conclusions of his own. He stood by them during my last meeting with him at his home in Albuquerque's North Valley. I took my wife, Marlene, with me to that meeting. I told her, a lifelong public school teacher and principal, that I wanted fresh eyes and a fresh mind on the subject. I had read of Bennewitz's story and I wanted to know if my wife thought that maybe Valdez, too, had been driven to "nervous exhaustion" or worse.

Marlene left with questions about some of what she heard in Valdez's living room but still impressed by the sincerity of the honored former state cop.

Just a few months later in that same clean, orderly home, Valdez went to sleep and never woke up.

"As it got late, dad rushed people off to bed," said Valdez's adult son, Gregg, also a former state policeman.

"We have to go to church tomorrow," the elder Valdez reportedly said.

"He said he was going to stay up and watch TV. He died on the couch in his street clothes, his shoes off," said Gregg Valdez. "The coroner's report ruled it heart attack."

Gabe Valdez was 67.

Only a week earlier, he reportedly told a friend in Cebolla that Los Álamos National Laboratory had developed a weapon that could shoot through a wall to kill someone and make the death appear due to a heart attack.

Gregg Valdez declined to speculate about the assertion. "Dad had siblings who died of heart disease before the age of 68. They eat a lot of sheep up there (in Cebolla)," he said, alluding to the animals' greasy meat.

"My father had lost a lot of weight in the past year. He had high blood pressure. He might have had diabetes. He craved sugar."

Retired national laboratory scientist Howard Burgess, who consulted with Gabe Valdez on the cattle mutilation issue, wrote me a letter following my report about a mutilated cow near Santa Clara Pueblo in the winter of 1978. Burgess was there to measure radiation along with Valdez and Santa Clara tribal officer Roger Naranjo.

"My wife and I were very much impressed with your story on the cattle mutilations in the November 15 issue of *The Santa Fe New Mexican*," Burgess wrote. "It was done in a very objective and thoroughly unbiased way. That is something that does not always happen with mutilation-type stories."

Restraint in reporting wasn't always easy while following livestock mutilations and the assertions that grew from them. It became harder as assertions—both wild and credible—swirled like so many suspicious saucers and orbs in the sky.

9
SPIRITS IN THE HILLS

Earthly disruptions rooted in the supernatural for generations have injected themselves into lives of mortals along the Río Grande, paying little more than scant attention until recently to possible intergalactic interlopers.

Organized religions have sought to frame thoughts and behaviors in matters of the supernatural. Impressions rooted in religion have moved through northern New Mexico like the precious water that flows in *acequias* along farms to nourish life and fuel labors that are built on the faith of better tomorrows.

But not all has been tidy in those teachings. Disruptions rooted in religions have been known to emerge—sometimes frightfully—along the

La Morada de Alto in Abiquiú overlooks the Río Chama Valley.

way. Considerations aren't always confined to the credible and incredible. At least occasionally, they're locked within arenas of the inexplicable, certainly not to find their explanations as part of the daily rounds of mere newspapermen, no matter how enterprising.

Vandals in September 1992 burned and vandalized an 18th Century *adobe morada*, built and used for generations by the secretive Catholic *Penitente* brotherhood, *Los Hermanos*, on a hilltop in Abiquiú, which was once New Spain's northernmost settlement within the New Mexico Territory.

Vandalism of *La Morada de Alto* included demonic-themed scrawls painted inside and outside the building. The fire required massive restoration that unfolded over six months.

New Mexico *santero*, Charles Carrillo, is a member of *Los Hermanos* in Abiquiú and was among those principally involved in the *morada's* restoration. He told me soon after work was completed that an unknown evil appeared to have inflicted ailments on several people who contributed to the restoration, including himself.

Both of Carrillo's legs became swollen, blemished and suffered unusual pain. He said an Apache friend from the Jicarilla Reservation in

Award-winning artist Charles Carrillo, whose work hangs in the state Capitol, was among people struck by ailments after working to repair damage to *La Morada de Alto*.

Dulce called him out of the blue one day and asked if he was suffering from an ailment of the legs. He said he learned of Carrillo's mysterious troubles in a dream.

Doctors, meanwhile, didn't know what was making Carrillo sick.

"I don't know how he could have known, but I've had an infection in both my legs for some time," Carrillo said. "They're red and swollen and have spots that seem to be coming from the inside. I've been to all kinds of specialists but I still don't know what it is."

"A lot of us who worked on the *morada* have come down with ailments," he said. "It's an evil. We always dismiss such things because we live in such a modern world ... But this other stuff is out there."

Alberto Parra, a successful architect and *adobe* builder in Albuquerque, suddenly became deathly ill after helping with *adobe* work and hauling *vigas* to restore the *morada's* roof.

"I had some kind of infection that caused paralysis down the entire left side of my body," Parra said. "It was a stroke-like illness. I couldn't move my eye, my arm, my leg. I even had to use my right arm to move my lips so I could talk. The doctors gave me brain scans and every type of test. But there I was: paralyzed for a week in the hospital and then told that it was probably just stress."

Parra said he remained in that condition for weeks at home, rigging up a rope and pulley in his garage so he could use his good side to exercise the limp one.

An herbalist in Albuquerque's South Valley sent Parra numerous *remedios*, teas and ointments." That's what started to work: the herbs and the prayers of the brothers at the *morada*," he said.

Jerome Luján, a *santero* and son of Ben Luján, a longtime elected leader in the New Mexico House of Representatives, worked with Carrillo and Parra on restoration of *La Morada de Alto*. He was principally involved in installing electrical wiring for the building.

Within months he developed thyroid cancer.

"Jerome is the spitting image of health, and out of nowhere he got this ailment," said Carrillo, fearing that he and others had been bewitched. "Have we been *embrujados*? That's what I think, and it all has to do with the burning of the *morada*."

Carrillo was careful to stress that he did not think the *morada* was possessed. "The evil is not coming from the *morada*. The *morada* is a sacred building," he said.

"We don't know how evil manifests itself. In this case, I'm saying it's an evil coming from someone who doesn't like what we do with the *morada*."

An herbalist and nurse from the tiny mountain community of Mora gave Carrillo a root of *cachana* (Blazing Star) to help him through his mysterious ailment. *Hermanos* reportedly have used it to keep *brujas* (witches) away.

Hermanos supposedly split open the root and carve a little cross on the opposing faces of the opened root and then close it up again so they could wear it on their clothing.

Keeping with custom, the senior brother of the Abiquiú *morada* was to carve the crosses on the root to be used by Carrillo.

The Catholic priest in Abiquiú conducted an exorcism at the *morada* to ward off evil.

Internationally acclaimed artist, Georgia O'Keeffe, for years made her home just below *La Morada de Alto* after being enthralled by the region's landscape. Rich in scenic beauty—sometimes majestic, sometimes raw—New Mexico is equally endowed with diverse human richness.

Witches in the hills? Evil spirits? Some people believe so. Stories and songs for generations have been built around them in this region of *mesas*, owls, serpents and village cemeteries where tumbleweeds lean restlessly against forgotten sun-bleached wooden crosses.

Mysteries, like that of the wailful *la llorona*, are almost drawn to the entire region that is touched by the storied Río Chama and Río Grande.

Some mysteries, to be sure, press up against reality more than others.

Life is often explained by people in their own cultural terms, said Carrillo.

It is fuel for the work of storytellers who can be left to discern between the mythical, the mystical and realities that at times can seem to be out of this world.

And when they can be meshed together, apart from the objective reporting on routine daily events, ¡*ah caray!*

10
THE POLITICAL REIGN OF EMILIO NARANJO

For decades it probably wouldn't have taken much to convince at least a few citizens of northern New Mexico's Río Arriba County that the sun came up each morning only after winning approval from Emilio Naranjo to cast its light on the world below.

It's the opinion I drew while reporting on the political boss and his expansive organization over 30 years beginning in the 1960s.

For more than 40 years until 1995, Naranjo was chairman of the Río Arriba County Democratic Central Committee. Democrats outnumbered Republicans in the county by as many as seven to one during that period.

What county Democrats won in June primary elections was theirs to keep. Republicans were more of a nuisance than they were serious competition.

Along with his post as Río Arriba Democratic chairman, Naranjo held multiple local government positions, including county manager and sheriff.

It was Emilio's county. And in that county, he was without question the boss, the *patrón*. Just about everyone in and around Río Arriba knew it. Most—if not all—state legislators knew it. Successive governors and all the state's members of Congress knew it. So, too, did State Police chiefs, district attorneys and state judges. Heck, it was known by at least two U.S. presidents who made it their business to recognize Emilio Naranjo's clout and reward his support.

Discussions of political dominance in New Mexico invariably turn to Manuel Armijo, who as constitutional governor, commandant of all troops and colonel of militia, held sway over the New Mexico Territory through much of the period of Mexican rule (1821–1848). They turn to the Santa Fé Ring of the late 1800s. They also turn to Emilio Naranjo.

Beyond the state's boundaries, Naranjo's name was mentioned alongside those of New York City's Democratic Tammany organization of the late 1800s; Leander Perez, "boss of the Louisiana Delta" for more than three decades through 1969; and Richard Daley, Chicago mayor from 1955–1976.

The East Coast Kennedy family, aware of Naranjo's influence in northern New Mexico, brought John Kennedy's 1960 presidential election campaign to the region. JFK became a champion to its people, and Naranjo successfully pinned his political credentials to the Kennedys from that campaign forward. Kennedy family members campaigned for Democrats in Río Arriba County years after JFK was felled in Texas by an assassin's bullet.

Emilio and his closest political associates campaigned enthusiastically in 1964 on behalf of Democratic presidential candidate Lyndon B. Johnson, at times standing alongside a small black and white spotted donkey bedecked with printed campaign material. "LBJ for the USA" read large posters strapped like saddlebags across the animal's back. Bumper stickers promoting Joseph M. Montoya's election to the U.S. Senate and Jack M. Campbell's re-election as governor flanked the LBJ posters. An orange bumper sticker promoting Naranjo as county sheriff was affixed across the donkey's forehead.

Naranjo and the others won their races but Emilio promptly moved out of the sheriff's office in 1965 to accept Johnson's appointment as U.S. marshal in Albuquerque. He returned to serve four years in the county sheriff's post after he was replaced as U.S. marshal in 1969.

From his long-held post as Río Arriba Democratic chairman, Naranjo determined who would be nominated and then elected for the county's plum political posts. County commissioners, county managers, county clerks, treasurers, assessors and probate judges all recognized that they owed their fortunes to Naranjo. They knew that they were to dance to his music or they wouldn't dance at all.

Naranjo thrived while orchestrating it all. He controlled jobs, roadside arrests, jail releases, tax assessments, roadwork and many other acts of consequence on everyday lives.

Long-time Democratic state Repesentative Nick Salazar of Ohkay Owingeh Pueblo once told the *Albuquerque Journal*, "When (Naranjo) called for a job for somebody, he was listened to. If he recommended somebody, that person better be hired ... He would call the school superintendent or the school board or county commission or a state agency and things would happen."

Salazar knew of such things. Early in his political life he served on the Río Arriba County commission and responded to Naranjo's directives.

Democrat Toney Anaya, a reform-minded attorney general from 1975 through 1978, said in an official report during that period that Naranjo had a stranglehold that "enables one (political) faction to control all county offices."

Benny Chávez, a popular Santa Fé County commissioner from Chimayó, observed in 1982 that the Democratic Party machine in

Emilio Naranjo, serving as Río Arriba County manager, worked with county attorney Lanny Messersmith of Albuquerque during a meeting in the Tierra Amarilla courthouse. Naranjo was a master at working behind the scenes while keeping a tight grip on Río Arriba County government for decades.

neighboring Río Arriba County "elects whoever they want to no matter what."

Each Río Arriba County office, of course, had its own well of employment opportunities, and they invariably were awarded to Naranjo loyalists.

County commissioners and county managers often worked off of scripted instructions at public meetings in the isolated Tierra Amarilla courthouse. Commissioners customarily were nominated to seek election not for their knowledge, education or experience but for their loyalty to Naranjo's agenda and their willingness to follow his scripts.

A grand jury foreman in 1981 confirmed that his panel had been asked to consider corruption charges against two Río Arriba County commissioners only to find that insufficient time was allowed for a thorough investigation. The foreman, José G. Salazar, said one of the two commissioners under investigation didn't seem to know anything about his responsibilities and that the second commissioner knew little more.

The Río Arriba Sheriff's Department payroll often swelled with deputies, many of the young men having been plucked out of unemployment or underemployment before being issued a uniform, a gun, a badge and a cruiser. All were required to get through firearms courses, driving courses and other special preparations at the state law enforcement training academy within a year after their hires. For more than a few, it meant that employment at the Río Arriba Sheriff's Department didn't get beyond the twelfth month.

Still, a year's worth of paychecks couldn't be taken lightly in a county where employment historically has been nearly as hard to find as an elephant weighed down with Republican campaign material.

Naranjo's clout as well as the region's sparse economic landscape both were visible in 1977 when the Río Arriba County commission named Emilio county law enforcement coordinator. It was a newly created post; Naranjo's idea, many suspected. No one else was given the opportunity to apply for the new job. The coordinator supposedly was to work with lawmen of all agencies in the county and beyond to beef up crime fighting. Naranjo's annual salary was set at $14,000.

It promptly became clear, however, that the other agencies had not been consulted about creation of the new position. Nor did any of their leaders think that Naranjo could offer much from his new post.

Derisive names soon were attached to the position and even to the man who was picked to fill it.

"For fourteen thousand a year they can call me anything they want," I overheard Naranjo tell a county employee as the two huddled in a small office in Española.

Enjoying total control over Río Arriba County government for decades, Naranjo's organization also competed for dominance in operations of the substantial Española public school district. Control bounced between Naranjo's group and the so-called Salazar faction among county Democrats. With control, went the spoils of patronage. Winners rewarded their friends and punished their enemies.

Naranjo, of course, didn't invent political favors, payoffs and punishments. The system was honed within Tammany a hundred years earlier in New York City, in Chicago and in so many other communities where, as journalist and historian Alistair Cooke assessed, politicians were familiar with the "primitive needs of people."

Loyalty to those in power often determine how so-called primitive needs are addressed.

Tim Salazar, a longtime member of the Española school board and a leader of Río Arriba's Salazar faction of Democrats, visited with me during the late 1970s moments after the newly realigned school board voted on employee assignments for the following year. Salazar had regained control of the board's majority, which translated into bad news for Naranjo loyalists in the expansive school district that is spread across two counties.

Salazar told me how his faction had approached a school employee from Chimayó for support during the recently completed election campaign. Overtures were rebuffed, though, by the tenured employee who at the time was assigned to Chimayó elementary, minutes from his home. The employee reportedly told the Salazars that he was sticking with Naranjo, convinced that it was in the best interests of students.

The Chimayó man following the election was assigned to work at Abiquiú elementary, about 30 miles from his home.

"Let's see how much he thinks about the students while he makes that long drive every day," Salazar told me through a broad smile.

Audaciously into the State Senate

Unexpected spoils came Naranjo's way in 1977 when the Río Arriba County commission selected Emilio to fill the vacancy in the state Senate created upon the sudden death of popular veteran legislator, Matias Chacón. Chacón over the years had found ways to work with both the Naranjo and Salazar factions.

County commission Chairman Juan Martínez of Abiquiú said the commission prevailed upon Naranjo to make himself available for appointment to the District 5 Senate seat. Naranjo "reluctantly agreed," Martínez said, ignoring the widely recognized courtesy of first offering such a vacated position to a family member of the deceased.

"It was a very boss-manner way of doing things," said Matthew Chacón, eldest son of the deceased senator. "The fact that (Naranjo) callously appointed himself senator, in essence, so soon after the death even without a call to our family to express condolences signaled that he suddenly thought he was in complete control."

Naranjo easily was elected to the Senate post later in 1978. His strategy was to build alliances within the Senate, speaking only when spoken to while allowing veteran Democratic lawmakers to articulate and otherwise advance his interests. He had little desire to engage in tedious committee work.

Serving in the New Mexico Senate would be one of the great honors of his life, Naranjo told me. His father would be proud, he said.

But Naranjo's first years in the Senate were stormy. Naranjo was convicted of perjury just days before the 1979 Legislature convened on January 16th. He was fined and sentenced to jail. Presiding Judge Ray Hughes of Deming, in what was considered an unprecedented order, also directed Naranjo to relinquish his hold on Río Arriba County politics.

Naranjo skirted his punishment pending appeal. But the state Senate, because of the felony conviction, was compelled to deny seating Naranjo in 1979. Naranjo successfully got Senate leaders, though, to keep the position unfilled until his appeal was resolved.

It all stemmed from a lawsuit in which Moises Morales, a county La Raza Unida leader and Naranjo nemesis, claimed that Emilio and his top two sheriff's deputies planted a grocery bag full of marijuana in Morales' pickup in 1975, then promptly framed him on a drug charge.

"In my career I've never seen such an obvious case of evidence being planted on an innocent suspect for purposes of political retaliation," said Robert Rothstein, a Santa Fé lawyer who represented Morales.

The county government paid $10,000 to settle the lawsuit out of court. But the perjury conviction, which grew out of testimony associated with the lawsuit, followed.

Naranjo vowed quietly to return to the Senate and carefully orchestrated steps in Río Arriba designed to fulfill that promise. The Senate's decision to temporarily keep the District 5 Senate seat vacant drew controversy. So Naranjo veered from his original plans. Rather than keep the Senate seat vacant, he resigned from the post and got the county commission to appoint his son-in-law, Abedón López Jr., to succeed him.

López had served on the Española school board and was among Naranjo lieutenants who battled perennially to spread the influence of Emilio's machine throughout the district.

Naranjo was so certain that he would return to his coveted seat in the Capitol that he took pains to ensure that his successor would willingly give up the post when the time came.

So much had been orchestrated ahead of time. Naranjo enlisted help from Senate Majority Leader C.B. Trujillo, a Taos Democrat, to ensure that Naranjo's resignation would take effect moments before López was installed. It would leave no room for interlopers eyeing the Senate seat for themselves.

"I worked it out with the secretary of state so that the resignation would be simultaneous when the county commission was appointing Abedón," Trujillo told me.

Naranjo's resignation came in a letter in which Emilio reasserted his innocence and his intent to appeal the perjury conviction. The District 5 Senate seat was formally declared vacant on February 5, 1979, opening the way for López's brief tenure.

Emilio's adult son, Benny Naranjo, spoke of his father's state of mind during the period. "He's not the happiest man in the world. He's hurt. He's hurt at the news media. He's hurt at a lot of things. But he's strong."

Lopez's entry to the Senate had its own controversy. La Raza Unida filed a lawsuit in state district court the day after the Río Arriba County commission selected López to replace Naranjo in the Senate. The suit sought to nullify the appointment, alleging correctly that commissioners selected López in a closed meeting.

Commissioners met on February 22nd and appointed López again, this time ensuring that there was proper public notice of the meeting.

On his first day, López was escorted into the Senate chambers by Trujillo, the Senate majority leader, to be sworn into office by Lieutenant Governor Roberto Mondragón.

Trujillo was closely aligned with Senate President Pro Tem Ike Smalley of Deming. Smalley noted from the Senate floor that Naranjo was in the chamber's gallery while López was administered the oath of office. Naranjo stood from his seat in the gallery and waved to senators as his presence was noted by Smalley.

Smalley moved without objection from other senators that Naranjo be extended "the courtesy and the right to come into the Senate at any time and at his pleasure."

Emilio's perjury conviction was overturned by the state Court of Appeals in November 1979. The court said that state Attorney General Toney Anaya lacked jurisdiction to prosecute the case and that there was insufficient evidence to support a conviction. The state Supreme Court in May 1980 affirmed the Court of Appeals decision. Heads shook after each decision.

López unwisely flirted with the idea of trying to keep the District 5 Senate seat for himself before coming to his senses.

When Naranjo returned to his state legislative post in 1980, Trujillo again was there to help.

"I was the one who worked out the resignation ... so Emilio called me and said, 'If I was to come back, what would be the deal?'

"I said, 'I don't think there would be any deal. I don't think there would be any problem if you decided to come back," Trujillo said.

López said he resigned from the Senate reluctantly, citing unspecified personal reasons. The Río Arriba County commission promptly appointed Naranjo to fill the vacancy. Commission Chair Cecilia Valdez nominated Naranjo. Naranjo's older brother, Ramón, voted to approve. Emilio was seated at the commission table during the meeting but left to an office upstairs when it came time to fill the Senate vacancy. He said later that he did not know that he would be nominated and that he was informed of his appointment in an interoffice phone call moments later.

The whole process took fifteen minutes.

Trujillo told me he was more than happy to pave the way for Naranjo's re-entry to the Senate. "A guy helps me and I never forget," Trujillo said. "Early in my political career in 1970, I was in the state Senate and ran for lieutenant governor. I didn't know Emilio. I knew of him. Everybody said you got to go see him. Everybody said take money and all that.

"I went to see him hat in hand. I told him, 'I'm going to run for lieutenant governor and I would appreciate your help.'

"I remember he said, 'Forget about campaigning in Río Arriba County. We've already decided that you're our candidate.' I carried Río Arriba County with his blessing big time and I never forgot that. I reciprocated several times, including trying to help him through that troubled era."

Nick Salazar, the Democratic state representative from Ohkay Owingeh, said Naranjo moved beyond that difficult period to become "by far one of the most effective senators that we've had."

"Emilio and I were in politics together for a long time, even before we were elected to the Legislature," Salazar said. "I was a county commissioner in Río Arriba and my order (from Naranjo) was not to have reappraisal of property values at the time. So we didn't. Emilio didn't want taxes to go up.

"The state finally ordered us to do reappraisal but in time the state has made changes in how property is taxed so that people, especially those in rural areas, are not overburdened."

On this issue, Naranjo was ahead of his time, Salazar suggested.

Salazar said Naranjo's friends in the state Senate, like Trujillo, ensured that Emilio's interests were addressed.

Naranjo was still in the Senate when Salazar talked with me in 1996. "Emilio does most of his legislating through the leadership. He's not active in committees. You'll see him introduce bills and then have the leadership pretty much fund what he asks for. He sets his priorities and he's pretty much guaranteed what he requests."

Alex Naranjo, Emilio's nephew from Española, agreed. "What my uncle has mastered in his own way is to have other senators work on his behalf for the benefit of Río Arriba. I think he has gained the respect of other senators where they do things on his behalf. They respect him as a man and, in all due respect, as a legend in New Mexico politics."

Republican Walter Bradley was a state senator from Clovis before serving two terms as lieutenant governor. He observed Naranjo's conduct and effectiveness firsthand. "He's always very respectful. He follows the rules. He never introduced a lot of legislation but he was successful primarily through his ability to work with his leadership," Bradley said.

"One that just blew me away, one that none of us on the Republican side of the aisle thought he would get, was eight hundred thousand to start the monument for don Juan de Oñate north of Española. It was a tight budget year (nineteen ninety-one) and here came this eight hundred thousand dollar request from Emilio Naranjo. How did he pull that off we don't know because we thought it was dead for sure."

What did Naranjo provide in return for special attention from Senate Democratic Party leaders?

"He was a reliable vote when they needed him," Salazar said.

Naranjo's respectful nature within Senate chambers noted by Bradley reflected the gentlemanly side of the Río Arriba political boss. But he had another side that so many in his county knew all too well. A conservative Republican senator from Albuquerque got a glimpse of it one day amid floor debate that eventually alluded negatively to Naranjo's pet project, the Oñate Center.

Senator Bill Davis got one of those looks from Naranjo that some people in Río Arriba County had come to dread and go far out of their way to avoid.

Davis rose in the Senate during the closing hours of the 1991 legislative session to oppose a bill that called for making the Senate clerk and the House clerk positions full-time jobs. He told how lawmakers already had the Legislative Council Service to tend to staffing needs year-round and said he didn't know what was left for chief clerks to do once lawmakers go home.

The New Mexico Legislature meets for 60 days on uneven-numbered years and for 30 days on even-numbered years.

With nothing else to do, maybe fulltime clerks could monitor construction of the Oñate statue that Naranjo asked to be built in his district, Davis suggested sarcastically.

Naranjo, usually still and silent, turned around and looked directly, coldly at Davis until he finished his remarks. Davis was one of those lawmakers who clearly liked the sound of his own voice so his remarks went on for a while as Naranjo glared in his direction. More than happy to talk under any circumstance, Davis also likely wanted to let Naranjo know that he was not intimidated by the glare.

Intimidated or not, Davis' sarcasm probably meant that the Albuquerque senator likely would never win a unanimous vote in the Senate as long as Naranjo was in the chamber.

"The Hell With Newspapers"

Crossing Naranjo's organization had been costly over the years for those bold enough to challenge the political *patrón*. And the organization could have a long arm when it came to retaliation.

Río Arriba activist and La Raza Unida Party member, Antonio "Ike" DeVargas, had been a thorn in the side Naranjo's organization dating back more than a decade before Emilio's Senate brush-up against Davis. DeVargas, through his protests, had been as responsible as any single person for curbing civil rights violations in Río Arriba since the mid 1970s.

County sheriff's deputies had arrested him multiple times on charges ranging from disorderly conduct, possession of small amounts of marijuana and possession of supposed subversive literature.

A federal court jury in October 1978 deliberated less than two hours before finding that Naranjo and four of his former deputy sheriffs violated DeVargas' constitutional rights and awarded DeVargas $55,000. The lawsuit stemmed from a 1976 raid of DeVargas' La Madera home by sheriff's deputies working for Naranjo in his capacity as sheriff.

DeVargas was arrested on drug charges, which were later dropped for insufficient evidence. DeVargas also was accused of possessing subversive literature. Among "subversive" material taken from his home was Dee Brown's *Bury My Heart at Wounded Knee*.

State Judge Gene Franchini of Albuquerque signed the search warrant but testified later in the federal court that he directed sheriff's officers not to search for so-called subversive literature. He said there is no such thing.

Naranjo and his men showed a "reckless disregard for our system of law," DeVargas attorney Steven Farber told the federal court. "Dasterdly deeds" were directed against DeVargas because of his political opposition to Naranjo, Farber said.

Naranjo refused to answer questions 49 times in court while invoking his Fifth Amendment Right against self-incrimination. The under sheriff who directed the search invoked the Fifth Amendment 31 times.

"They jealously guarded their rights ... but they were so cavalier about the rights of the defendant," Farber told jurors.

DeVargas, bolstered by the federal court decision, doubled down on his opposition. He and other Raza Unida Party members battled Naranjo's organization almost continuously.

The wheels of Naranjo's powerful political machine seemingly had begun to wobble. Financially costly and embarrassing defeats in court during the late 1970s fueled speculation that Naranjo was headed for his last hurrah as the state's 1978 Democratic primary approached.

Perjury charges growing out of the bogus marijuana arrest of Moises Morales were yet to be resolved. Allegations of absentee ballot misuse and other election fraud had begun swirling into the state attorney general's office in Santa Fé.

Naranjo's political brand had been battered for 20 months. Alleged—and proven—claims of civil rights violations were at the heart of Emilio's problems. Surely, newspapers in the region editorialized, Río Arriba voters would not support more of the same.

But Naranjo had the last laugh after the 1978 primary. Voters endorsed his earlier appointment to the state Senate and Naranjo claimed victories for his organization in each of the county's contested positions. He retained control of the county commission, which meant he retained control of county government. That was the central issue of the 1978 primary.

"This is the greatest victory I have ever had in my life," Naranjo told cheering supporters who packed into the Española Laborers' Union Hall. "The hell with newspapers!" Naranjo shouted. "They played against me ... They played against people that are close to me. Whether they like it or not, we have power and we're going to stay in power."

Cheers were nearly deafening.

As a reporter in *The Santa Fe New Mexican's* Española bureau, my assignment for the night was to report on the local Democrats' victory celebration. I had reported on the long, controversial campaigns leading up to the primary election and also had taken a lead in reporting on the court battles that had enveloped Naranjo's organization. I recognized that the target on my back couldn't be bigger as I walked into the union hall.

I took my girlfriend, Kay Cordtz, to the hall to witness it all. She had been a news reporter in Santa Fé and previously held similar positions in New York and California. Her father had been in the news business all his life. Still, I suspected that she never had witnessed raw political fever like what I knew would fill the union hall that evening.

Our arrival seemingly fanned the defiant, alcohol-laced jubilation. Fists were shaken, fingers were pointed. One municipal official who had long enjoyed Naranjo's support stood at my side and likened reporters to noisy coyotes. Noisy coyotes end up smashed alongside the road, he told me.

It took only a few minutes for me to realize that my companion's stay in the union hall had lasted long enough. I drove her to *The Santa Fe*

New Mexican's Española office about a mile away on Oñate Street before returning to finish my work.

That night was a springboard for Naranjo's political organization. The swagger was back, at least for a while. So, too, was the recklessness that only recently had brushed the organization up against trouble.

One day in 1981 Naranjo's lieutenants on the Española school board went after Antonio DeVargas' mother in an apparent attempt to silence one of Emilio's most-relentless critics.

Louise DeVargas had helped raise her family of 11 children while working as a cook with the Española schools for 17 years. But she lost her contract in 1981 after her son, Antonio, organized or supported numerous complaints against the school board.

Louise DeVargas sued the board and in 1982 settled with the district for $65,000 and a contract for her old job.

Yet again, a case could be made that the Española school board and the Río Arriba County commission had fallen into a pattern of spending too much money defending themselves against lawsuits arising from their own misconduct and then settling those suits for large sums.

Naranjo and his followers blamed it all on homegrown troublemakers and outside agitators. The latter term came to be recognized as code for Jewish lawyers from the East Coast.

AN OLD FRIEND SUFFERS A SWIPE

Longtime Truchas Postmaster Ruben Tafoya fell out of favor with his old friend, Emilio Naranjo, and wound up losing his hold on the community's post office.

As time went on, Naranjo himself unwittingly began punching holes in his organization's defense that outside agitators were determined to thwart wishes of local voters. Truchas merchant and long-time Naranjo ally, Ruben Tafoya, found himself pushed into the ranks of detractors. He fell victim to swift, one-sided judgment, the kind not too uncommon in Río Arriba County of those times.

(Tafoya's father, Celso, was a brother to my paternal grandmother, Juanita Tafoya Roybal.) Ruben Tafoya for 30 years operated a branch office of the U.S. Postal Service out of his general store in Truchas. He was told in August 1990 that he'd have to shut down postal operations in the store. He didn't know why at the time but he suspected it was because his son, Ray, ran in that year's June primary for a county commission seat in opposition to the candidate backed by Naranjo.

Naranjo's son, David, was postmaster in Española, from where postal operations in Truchas were overseen. David Naranjo said he had gotten complaints about Tafoya and that Tafoya, himself, at one point indicated the work was getting too tiring. The decision to relieve Tafoya of postal duties was clear cut, nothing political, insisted the postmaster.

Crazy, said Ruben Tafoya. "We who live in Río Arriba County know how things are here. In Río Arriba, we're like Iraq. If you don't do what you're told, you're quickly punished," he said in the midst of mounting conflicts along Mesopotamia.

I wrote an opinion piece about the unexpected political break up in Truchas, and told about a story that had recently come out of Iraq. President Saddam Hussein reportedly summoned close advisers to discuss one of his ideas for a military operation. One aide dared to opine that the operation would lead to heavy casualties. Saddam supposedly invited the aide into an adjoining room to discuss the matter further. The door was closed and a gunshot rang out. Saddam was said to have emerged packing his pistol into his holster.

Punishment takes many forms, to be sure, and Ruben Tafoya knew that what he faced fell far short of what he and others in the United States were hearing about Saddam Hussein's Iraq.

Still, Tafoya remained stung by what he insisted was political retaliation, Río Arriba style.

He recalled for me the day that David Naranjo came into the Truchas store with a couple of postal inspectors from Albuquerque. "They wanted to look at the books. They said they knew they'd find something wrong," Tafoya said. "I looked at David and asked him how he could be doing something like this.

"I told him I remembered years ago when I went to his dad's house in Española on my way to a party. David came up to me and sat on my knee.

He peed on my leg and stained my pants. I ended up borrowing a pair of his dad's pants, which were way too short. But that's the way I went to the party."

Close enough to share a pair of trousers: That's how close Ruben Tafoya and Emilio Naranjo once were. But when Tafoya's mother was buried in 1993, Naranjo was nowhere to be seen.

"Emilio's a man who likes to have things his way," Tafoya said simply.

THE BEGINNING OF THE END

Naranjo was up to his neck in challenges as Río Arriba politics moved rather sloppily into the 1990s. Arthur Rodarte, a soft-spoken Ojo Caliente businessman, upset a Naranjo-backed candidate and claimed a position on Río Arriba's three-member county commission in 1990. A year later, Rodarte challenged Naranjo for his long-held post as county Democratic Party chairman. Naranjo trounced Rodarte, 68-4, in secret voting by precinct representatives selected in Democratic meetings held in communities around the county. But even in defeat, Rodarte brought new embarrassment to Emilio and his group.

Well-publicized challenges to secret proceedings of precinct meetings were raised in four communities.

In Córdova, Naranjo opponents said the meeting was not held at the site advertised and that a long-time Naranjo ally was elected precinct representative at an improperly organized meeting.

Two separate meetings were held in Alcalde at the same place but at different times, with each group challenging the other's actions.

Olivia Olguin, a long-time county official who recently had bolted from Naranjo's fold, said the precinct meeting she called in Canjilón was shunned by Naranjo loyalists who met elsewhere and had their own election.

El Guique residents met as one group but had a tie vote in their selection of a precinct representative.

In each case, Naranjo's credentials committee settled disputes and dissidents argued that they lost out in every decision.

"This is the first time in 36 years that another name was placed on the floor to challenge Mr. Naranjo," Rodarte said of his ill-fated nomination. "This gives the message that change is just around the corner. This is the beginning of the end."

Not everyone was buying the argument, though. Democrats who controlled the New Mexico Legislature considered Naranjo to be such a safe bet that in 1991 they expanded his state Senate district to include two precincts of neighboring Los Álamos County. The two precincts at the time were 90 percent Anglo. As previously charted, Naranjo's Senate district was more than 70 percent Hispanic.

Democratic legislators gambled that adding two Los Álamos precincts to Naranjo's district would not threaten Emilio's re-election chances. Too, they reasoned, reducing the number of Anglo votes in future Los Álamos Senate elections might improve prospects for Democratic candidates there.

Except for political considerations, pairing Río Arriba with Los Álamos made no sense. Home to one of the nation's most-prominent national laboratories, Los Álamos has benefited from years of special treatment by the federal government. The 1990 unemployment rate in Río Arriba was 13.4 percent. It was less than three percent in Los Álamos. High school science laboratories in Española floundered for lack of equipment. By comparison, school labs in Los Álamos stood out as if coming from another age.

Simply, Río Arriba was among the poorest counties in one of the poorest states in the nation. Los Álamos was among the nation's wealthiest counties.

Pairing Naranjo with two Los Álamos precincts in time proved costly.

In the meantime, though, Naranjo had little trouble reaching out for help from another wealthy corner of the nation while campaigning for Democratic victories in 1992. U.S. Senator Edward Kennedy arrived from Massachusetts in October of that year to wave the party flag during several stops in northern New Mexico, including Española.

"Ted Kennedy is the most-influential politician among Hispanics," Naranjo proclaimed to anyone who listened.

Kennedy first campaigned in northern New Mexico in 1960 at the age of 28 while promoting the U.S. presidential bid of his older brother, John. Naranjo was instrumental in securing a large margin in Río Arriba for John Kennedy, who beat Republican Richard Nixon in New Mexico by less than 3,000 votes en route to one of the slimmest national margins in U.S. history. The Kennedys seemingly never forgot.

In 1992, Bill Clinton was the Democratic presidential candidate. Naranjo was en route to re-election to the state Senate, having won in the June primary. His orgnization, however, suffered serious blows in some of the other primary races.

Kennedy keynoted a fundraiser in Santa Fé as part of his 1992 campaign swing through northern New Mexico. He arrived an hour late to the $100-per-plate dinner at the Inn at Loretto, immediately working the large assembly upon his arrival. "Good to see you. Good to see you," Kennedy said repeatedly as he shook hands with admirers while working his way to the lectern at the front of the dining room.

It was near the front of the room where Naranjo stood silently at his table, almost lost amid the commotion. Would Kennedy see him? The dinner, after all, was out of Naranjo's political territory. This was the state capital, and other dignitaries accustomed to special treatment were in the room. Naranjo seemed at least a bit anxious.

Kennedy continued his slow walk toward the lectern. Suddenly, he veered to his right and opened his arms to offer his first embrace of the evening. Naranjo was on the receiving end. Others could only look on, at least a little envious, no doubt.

"It's amazing," Kennedy said moments later from the lectern as he recalled his first visit to New Mexico more than three decades earlier. "Emilio Naranjo was chairman then. He's chairman now."

People in Massachusetts, one of the original 13 colonies, think they know about politics, but they could learn much from Río Arriba, Kennedy said.

Naranjo glowed.

Clinton won the U.S. presidential election a couple of weeks later, and Naranjo was elected to his fourth term in the state Senate. But it was in that summer's primary election that two of Naranjo's three candidates for the county commission were upset. The commission losses were stunning defeats for Naranjo. It meant the commission that Naranjo had used to dictate employment decisions and direct spending since the mid-1950s no longer would dance to his tune. The man called *patrón* for the better part of four decades had been stripped of his power.

TAFOYAS LIVE FOR ANOTHER DAY

Ray Tafoya of Truchas, who narrowly lost his bid for the county commission as an anti-Naranjo candidate in 1990, was among the two Naranjo opponents selected in the primary of June 1992. Alfredo Montoya of Alcalde was the other.

It might have been easier to imagine nobody showing up for opening night at the Santa Fé Opera or Zozobra going up in flames at an empty Fort Marcy Park than to picture Emilio Naranjo getting drubbed on election night in Río Arriba County. Río Arriba County and the Tierra Amarilla courthouse had belonged to Naranjo since 1956, a year before the opera in Santa Fé was founded. The figure that Emilio cut in Río Arriba political circles had been even more imposing than that of Zozobra towering over the opening of Santa Fé's annual fall fiesta.

Ray Tafoya and Alfred Montoya beat Naranjo's county commission candidates as part of a slate organized largely by Estanislado "Tiny" Vigil of Chimayó. Since 1957, Vigil had worked at Naranjo's side, amid multiple controversies, as they set affairs of Río Arriba County government.

Vigil's work in the Tierra Amarilla courthouse had included 12 years as county assessor and four years as treasurer.

With Naranjo's support, Vigil also served six years on the Española school board during the 1970s. But when Vigil ran again for a school board post in 1991, Naranjo gave his support to another Chimayó man, incumbent Leo Martínez. Martínez beat Vigil and, incredibly, the old bond between Naranjo and Vigil was broken.

"I was hurt in a way," Vigil said. "Emilio and I had always been aligned together. I had always supported him. I operated on his behalf. I was sincere. I went out to support him because I believed in the man.

"I was really surprised when he told me during the (1991) board of education election that he was not going to support me. I figured it must be the end of the line for me with him. I figured he doesn't need me anymore."

Although Vigil lost his 1991 school board race, three people beat candidates supported by Naranjo in that year's school election.

"Maybe we were lucky, or maybe people just wanted change in the schools, too," Vigil said.

Splits even within Naranjo's family surfaced as candidates began lining up for the fateful 1992 Río Arriba Democratic primary. Nick Naranjo, a nephew to Emilio, filed to run for county sheriff against Naranjo's handpicked candidate. (Nick was a former Española City policeman and while working parttime for *The Santa Fe New Mexican*, was my supervisor as I delivered newspapers as a teen 25 years earlier.)

Nick and his brother, Alex, both had been loyal lieutenants within Emilio's organization. Alex, while serving on the Española school board, for years had taken the lead in carrying out Emilio's wishes within the schools.

Alex tried but failed to talk his brother out of bucking their uncle's organization in the sheriff's race. Alex then said he felt compelled to support his brother, who wound up losing in the primary.

Hard feelings lingered. When I talked with Alex Naranjo in January 1996 for a story about his uncle's work in the state Senate, he confessed that he had not spoken with Emilio in more than a year.

If frayed ties among family members waited to be fully mended, Emilio nearly a decade earlier incredibly had begun moving toward peace with some of his fiercest adversaries. Moises Morales welcomed the turn. Morales had fought Naranjo since before 1975 when Emilio and his two top deputies framed Morales for marijuana possession as he drove his pickup home after work.

Morales and Pedro Arechuleta of Los Ojos were among leaders of La Clínica del Pueblo in Tierra Amarilla, a floundering medical and dental clinic that for years was denied funding by Naranjo's county government. The clinic was organized through a cooperative that consisted largely of Naranjo adversaries so Emilio saw no need to help keep the clinic afloat, much less boost its standing among voters of the region.

To Naranjo, La Clínica came to represent foul-mouthed radicals; drug-taking, Marxist-reading troublemakers bent on stirring disruptions at any cost.

But in 1989 Naranjo introduced legislation in the state Senate to appropriate $274,000 from the state's general fund to renovate and enlarge La Clínica del Pueblo. He asked that money for La Clínica be appropriated on an emergency basis so work to improve the facility could begin immediately.

A few years earlier, Naranjo reversed long-held opposition and freed county funds to pave a quarter-mile dirt road leading to the clinic that turned impassable in bad weather and often kept the clinic's ambulance from tending to emergencies.

"I've seen what they do for the people of northern Río Arriba," Naranjo told me in his Senate office on the Capitol's third floor. "They're doing a tremendous job. They inspired me to help them."

Adversaries were especially pleased when Naranjo got the county commission, during a period when he still controlled the panel, to adopt some of New Mexico's most-stringent subdivision regulations. Morales, Arechuleta and others had argued vocally against proposals to use the region's verdant meadows and other unspoiled lands for summer homes or condominiums. Land use regulations crafted by Naranjo addressed those concerns.

Morales said his loosely-knit group of adversaries and Naranjo probably suffered from the same problem until they mended fences.

"Maybe it was too much *machismo* on both of us," said the soft-spoken mechanic. "I think we were both trying to reach the same goals. And a while back, we just kind of made the peace."

"I'll tell you one thing: He treats us well," Arechuleta said. "There have been problems in the past. But now you see your county government trying to do something to help your county so you support those ideas.

"I'm not saying Emilio Naranjo is on our side. I'm not saying I support Emilio. But you support those ideas that are good for the county."

Morales said simply, "The past is water under the bridge."

Naranjo in our meeting away from the others agreed. "The past is the past. I'm looking to the future. I review my days and I admit my mistakes. This is the only way that I can improve myself."

After losing control of the Río Arriba County commission in 1992, Naranjo vowed to "come back like a lion." He tried but failed.

Naranjo voluntarily relinquished his position as county Democratic Party chairman in 1995. It was like Rockefeller Center losing Rockefeller; like green beans losing The Jolly Green Giant, I wrote of the transition.

Naranjo handpicked his successor as party chairman. But in time, the upstart Democrats for Better Government would lay claim to the post, and Naranjo adversaries continued to move into various elected positions of county government.

In 1996, Emilio lost his bid for a fifth term in the state Senate. He was upset by Ojo Caliente businessman Arthur Rodarte. It was Rodarte who Naranjo trounced, 68-4, in 1991 while retaining his post as county Democratic Party chairman. The county commission seat that Rodarte surprisingly won in 1990 was taken from him in 1992 by a Naranjo-backed candidate.

But according to the county clerk's first tally of the 1996 primary election, Rodarte beat Naranjo by 19 votes in the race for the state Senate's District 5 seat. A crushed Naranjo blamed results on conditions long associated with his own organization: error and fraud.

But Rodarte's victory stood. He won the nomination on the strength of votes from precincts in Los Álamos and Sandoval counties.

The profoundly loyal following that Naranjo developed over four decades might best have been described by Leonard Ludi, an Española man who dared to run for the Río Arriba County commission against Naranjo's organization in 1978. Ludi acknowledged his uphill battle by telling how he might not even get the vote of his own father.

"He is one of those fellows who is under the spell of Emilio Naranjo," Ludi said of his father. "He is under the impression that Emilio Naranjo is God."

I reported on Naranjo since the late 1960s in four newspapers, one television station and a book. Naranjo was known to ice out certain reporters for substantial periods when he felt their news coverage was particularly unfair. He and I had a hot-cold relationship but anger that he occasionally expressed toward me on his radio program, at public gatherings—and in private settings, no doubt—rarely lasted long.

Many of his ardent followers were friends of mine or parents of friends of mine. One was my former supervisor. Some were members of my extended family. One of his step-daughters was the administrative assistant in *The Santa Fe New Mexican's* Española bureau where she worked dutifully and where I served as chief.

Still, at least a handful of Emilio's most-enthusiastic admirers likely wouldn't have lost sleep had they learned that I had been crushed like a coyote on the side of some back road, as one of them taunted drunkenly during a raucus election night celebration.

"*¡Deja Emilio solo!*" a man shouted at me one day as I walked on my daily rounds along Oñate Street and he passed along in his white utility van from which he delivered Lays potato chips to local stores.

One of Naranjo's county managers and most-controversail lieutenants took a wild swing at me in the late 1970s as he walked out of the Española City jail, where he and two county commissioners had just been booked on charges of fraud. I used my large box camera and its substantial stick strobe to fend off the punch immediately after snapping a photo that captured the man's anger and ran in the next day's paper.

Moments after I shot the photo, as I returned to my office on Oñate Street, the accused felon pulled over in his pickup and stopped along the sidewalk long enough to shake his fist and shout menacingly through an open passenger's side window, "*¡Te chingo, joto cabrón!*"

My editor in Santa Fé, learning of the encounters outside the jail and alongside the public street, promptly assigned one of his Santa Fé reporters, John Robertson, to write a story telling of the incidents. Only 25 miles away, Santa Fé newsmen long had been dismayed by what their compatriots often encountered in Río Arriba County.

In the midst of Naranjo's mounting troubles, one of Emilio's lieutenants warned me against getting caught up in the county's political battles that often revolved around signs of mismanagement or outright fraud. Mauricio Chávez, an El Rito rancher, was elected to the Río Arriba County commission in the late 1970s as part of Naranjo's ticket. He declined to seek re-election after witnessing disturbing operations in and around the Tierra Amarilla courthouse.

Chávez told me how the same political opponents that I quoted hurling accusations at each other one day can easily make at least a temporary peace a few days later, leaving me and other reporters susceptable to the wrath of all sides.

"Be careful," he advised.

I had an unexpected encounter with a close Naranjo ally one night in 1976 in Española's popular bar, Saints & Sinners. U.S. Senator Joseph M.

Montoya and I both had been at one of Naranjo's county Democratic central committee meetings half a mile down the street. Montoya, already victorious in three Senate races and running for a fourth, addressed a packed room of the faithful. But he had no interest in staying for the mundane business of central committee assemblies so he excused himself. Sadly, he needed to rush to an important meeting in Albuquerque, he explained.

I left the meeting about half an hour later only to find Montoya seated and relaxed in the tiny, smoke-filled quarters of Saints & Sinners. Embarrassed as I approached his table, he was in no position to deny me an interview. My notebook was resting on the seat of my pickup outside so I reached multiple times for napkins on which to record notes. Montoya that night equated Harrison "Jack" Schmitt, his moon-walking Republican opponent in 1976, with the monkey thrust into space by NASA years earlier. Montoya did it again in ensuing days, likely contributing to Schmitt's election.

A decade after Naranjo's departure from the state Senate, I sought out the former political boss at his San Pedro home. I wanted his insights and comments for my first book, *Taking on Giants, Fabián Chávez Jr. and New Mexico Politics*. The book would offer a close look at our state's political world so, naturally, Emilio's presence within the pages was all but required.

Alone in his living room, Naranjo greeted me with a broad smile. We hadn't seen or spoken with each other for years. "Why, look who's here," he said in Spanish. "Come in, come in, Johnny," he added quickly in English. "I read your columns all the time. In fact, I was going to call you the other day because I really liked something you wrote."

Old age wasn't to blame for Naranjo calling me Johnny. He had occasionally called me Johnny going back to the 1970s. (I'm sure he had called me names much worse than that over the years.)

I asked Naranjo about former Republican Governor David Cargo's assertion that he enjoyed Emilio's support in the 1968 gubernatorial race in which Democrat Fábian Chávez Jr. contested Cargo's re-election bid and narrowly lost.

"I have never helped any Republican in my life," Naranjo told me.

Maybe not. But he had kind words for Cargo, who built a reputation for helping small communities and disadvantaged residents of northern New Mexico. Cargo, said Naranjo, came looking for him at his Española businesses to say farewell when Cargo's second term as governor ended in 1970.

Said Naranjo: "I was cleaning the stove in my restaurant one day when Cargo walked in and said, 'I don't know what I'm going to do now, Emilio.'"

Futures of politicians young and old once passed through Naranjo's door. But like most things, Emilio's tenure of unrivaled political influence in New Mexico came to an end. He had made peace with it all by the time of our last meeting shortly before his passing.

Emilio Naranjo died in November 2008 at the age of 92. He was at a son's home in Albuquerque. There were no thunderous closures to his long political life. His loudest thunder had sounded years earlier.

From the Roybal Files...
The Santa Fe New Mexican, Column, June 12, 1994

The fun's all but over now for sure.

That's got to be the inescapable conclusion of Emilio Naranjo, northern New Mexico's political boss who during four decades decided almost single-handedly when the fun would begin in his territory and when it would stop.

It was as fine a display of old-time politics you could expect to see anywhere.

Naranjo's consecutive victories in Río Arriba County became too many to count. Now, in contests to control the county commission in Tierra Amarilla, Naranjo has suffered consecutive defeats.

His candidates lost two of the three commission races in 1992 to a Democratic Party faction of younger blood, all three of the races in Tuesday's primary. Naranjo vowed after his first defeat to come back like a lion.

But the lion's roar is gone.

Naranjo's people likely will get another two years to run several Río Arriba County offices, having just defeated Democratic opponents for posts like assessor, sheriff and clerk. (Republicans in general elections up north are more of a nuisance than a threat, so Democrts winning in June have only the oath of office to worry about.)

County victories that don't include the commission, however, are hollow.

Naranjo's assessor gets to send voters their property tax bills while his sheriff doles out traffic tickets.

County clerks, who count votes on election day, long have been accused of being behind controversial Naranjo victories. But after two major defeats, people in the clerk's office clearly aren't doing more than hanging around musty old property deeds all day. That can't be much fun.

Today, it's the new party faction—the one that controls the

commission—that decides how all the money is spent and who gets favors along the way.

That's where the fun is; that's where the power is.

For well more than a decade, a northern New Mexico historian has worked on a Naranjo biography. Naranjo has talked of the project fondly over the years, as if to emphasize his unrivaled role in shaping the course of the region's politics.

But the long-awaited book apparently is still in the making. Perhaps, it's the ending that's awaited.

Unless it is death itself that is required, material for that final chapter appears to be at hand.

At 77, Naranjo seemingly is hardy and could live well into the next century. Many would vote for that.

But it's doubtful that Naranjo has many more political campaigns to engineer. And it's not just age to be considered.

Narano for the most part failed to bring new faces into his team this year. One wonders if he can anymore.

Voters twice now have indicated they want to give opportunity to a new political era. The politicians seeking to shape that era, of course, could fail at any turn. Too many failures and Naranjo might still get another chance.

But even that is unlikely to provide any thunderous closures to a long political life.

One has to figure that Naranjo's loudest thunder already has clapped.

Perhaps the final words of the unfinished biography could be about a graceful relinquishing of the batan, if not to the opposing Democratic faction, then to a new leader of the group that for so long has belonged to the man whose very name, Emilio, has meant politics.

11
Changing Santa Fé

Molly Ivans, the *Fort Worth Star Telegram* columnist during the 1990s who was known nationally for her biting wit, visited Santa Fé in the summer of 1993. She returned to Texas to profess that her oft-whacky state hadn't been declared a large lunatic asylum because the Lone Star State appears nearly normal compared to what she encountered in Santa Fé.

"For one thing, in Santa Fé, there are now twelve-step groups for those recovering from pet-loss grief," Ivans wrote.

Historic Santa Fé along the Río Grande, at the time of Ivans' visit, was well into its transformation as a favorite city of the U.S. Southwest, change defined largely by an influx of money carried in by new arrivals; change that the city still wrestles with today.

Santa Fé, home sweet home to many, annually is recognized among the nation's most-popular tourist destinations.

"For reasons not entirely clear, but probably involving the fact that rich people can afford to be dippy, northern New Mexico is now the woo-woo center of the universe," Ivans wrote. "Envision, if you will, every fruitcake New Age notion that's ever come along magnified and taken seriously ... (listening) to someone going on for hours about the dreaded low self-esteem and how to cure it ... Shirley MacLaine now lives here—need I say more?"

Oh, change was, indeed, taking hold in Santa Fé—again. Change was strongly encouraged more than 100 years earlier when a self-assured representative of the U.S. government warned that if the city's inhabitants remained the way he found them, they might soon find themselves in the company of dinosaurs.

U.S. General William Tecumseh Sherman was as direct as he could be in 1880 when he addressed an assembly in Santa Fé.

"You must improve your land and develop the vast resources of your country, or the new race will come and displace you," he scolded. "I hope and pray that the next time I come here I shall surely find the old race of Mexicans that we found here long, long ago in the past, improved (and) brought to a higher degree of improvement and cultivation. Without that they will be displaced, not by force, injustice and violence, but by a better, stronger, higher race."

The Santa Fé Trail, after 60 years of use as a major wagon route between the U.S. East and West, was in the process of being closed even as General Sherman spoke. The railroad with all its promise had reached New Mexico, which had been a U.S. territory since 1848. Previously, it had been governed by Spain, then by Mexico.

Missourian William Becknell in 1821 began what became heavy trading traffic along the Santa Fé Trail. Different classes of people had begun arriving in the New Mexico Territory's rather isolated capital. Becknell, a 34-year-old salt maker, was among them. Change was afoot, to be sure. And it wasn't all good. Becknell, himself, headed west to escape mounting debt. Drunkards and roughians rode the trail that wound through prairies and mountains.

But there also were people like John M. Kingsbury and partner James Josiah Webb who came to own one of the largest merchantile companies in Santa Fé during the mid-1800s. They considered Santa Fé to be plagued by too many swindlers and too much drunkenness, brawling and killing among natives and newcomers, alike.

Kingsbury in September 1859 wrote to Webb in the East. "We got safely through Election Day without any serious fights, only one man killed in Santa Fé over the election."

A deadly Independence Day celebration at the Exchange Hotel, the forerunner to today's La Fonda, was described by Kingsbury this way: "On the night of the 4th the Americans gave a *baile* at the Exchange which the Mexicans chose to break up. They succeeded and closed by killing Finnigan the blacksmith ... we have positive proof that it was done by Tapia, the one who was convicted in San Miguel county for cutting a woman, sentenced for three years and broke jail first night."

An early trader wrote to a partner back east, "It is really unsafe here for a quiet man. If I escape with my life, I shall consider myself lucky."

Historians have noted that crime in the region just before the opening of the Santa Fé Trail in 1821 often went unpunished. According to one account, people arrested and put in jail often came and went from a plain adobe room as they chose. If errands begged attention, prisoners usually were allowed out. And if music of a *fandango* was heard, it was not uncommon for those confined to be freed so they might join the dance.

Most early traders on the Santa Fé Trail were said to have had little interest in staying in the territorial capital. Much of what was gained in profits from commerce on the trail also left the area, taken back to Missouri and Kansas, where trading businesses were often based.

And yet Santa Fé couldn't escape becoming a repository for the ventureous, the curious, the fugitives and the people who simply had grown bored with what they once had called home east and west of the Mississippi. The much-publicized end of the Santa Fé Trail was what had been founded by Spanish and Mexican colonists who beginning in 1610 dug in between the Río Grande to the west and the feet of the southern Rockies to the east. And beginning more than two centuries before William Becknell, Santa Fé had come to be recognized as the last major stop for traders and travelers coming north from as far away as Mexico City along *El Camino Real*.

Before *El Camino Real*, Pueblo people inhabited the lands upon which Spaniards and Mexicans later imposed themselves.

"Santa Fe is Tewa Land," read a placard held by a protester in 2017 amid complaints about how Hispanics continue to assert themselves while defining the city's complicated history.

Indeed, Hispanics of the 1600s found the Río Grande region just north of Santa Fé inhabited by Tewas as represented by pueblos of San Juan (now Ohkay Owingeh), Pojoaque, Santa Clara, San Ildefonso, Nambé and Tesuque. Life as known by the Indians was promptly placed at risk by the colonists who insisted on change.

The Pueblo Revolt of 1680 became inevitable, learned Antonio de Otermin, governor of New Mexico during the consequential uprising. Governor Otermin, wrote historian Rubén Sálas Márquez, learned from Indians captured after the Revolt that Indians for more than 70 years had resented the Christians because they had destroyed native religious objects, prohibited ceremonials, and humiliated or punished tribal elders. Forced labor became so burdensome that the Amerinds didn't have time to work for themselves.

Change that was visited upon the Indians during the Seventeenth Century would resurface continually in various forms as the nation's oldest capital city moved well into the Twenty-first.

"There are all kinds of people in the world and twice that many in Old Santa Fe," proclaimed *The Santa Fe New Mexican* in October 1927.

A Newspaper Plows Unsettled Emotions

Pita Gonzales wore a broad, infectious smile when at the age of 18 she was crowned queen of the 1943 Fiesta de Santa Fé. The annual fall fiesta has commemorated what is promoted as the peaceful reconquest of Santa Fé by Spain's don Diego de Vargas following the Pueblo Revolt of 1680. Beginning in the early 1900s, the fiesta was staged intermittently and became an annual event soon after statehood in 1912.

Pita Gonzales was the proud queen of the Fiesta de Santa Fé in 1943. (Photograph courtesy Bernadette García)

The fiesta for the most part has been a celebration of *Hispanismo*, as reflected in this old account in *The Santa Fe New Mexican* about an event that spilled over into the small community of Lamy well beyond the capital's borders:

> "The mariachi de Jalisco, fourteen native musicians from Guadalajara, thrilled a crowd on the platform at Lamy and passengers on the southbound train last night with the crescendo finale of their stirring song of home entitled *Guadalajara* ending a short farewell concert at the (Ortiz) saloon ... As happened four years ago, this group of Jaliscienses from the most beautiful ancient city of Mexico found their visit to Santa Fe a high spot in their lives; and in Guadalajara it is the dream of every musico to go and play for the muy buena jente of Santa Fe, who are incredibily simpatico, en la Fiesta mas alegre del mundo."

The annual fiesta's gaiety has few critics but it is the repeated assertion of a peaceful reconquest that has swept relatively small numbers of protesters onto downtown streets during recent celebrations.

Still, even as some object to how Hispanics choose to remember local history, the Hispanic families who have made Santa Fé home for generations have grown to lament that they barely recognize their own city anymore.

For generations everyday life in Santa Fé came to be what was defined by families with names like Gonzales, Delgado, Chávez, Otero, Ortiz, Trujillo and Vigil.

Institutional guidance came largely from the Catholic Church, its private St. Francis Parochial School, Loretto Academy for girls, St. Michael's School for boys and St. Michael's College.

"*Mi casa es su casa,*" proclaims a welcome sign long popular within homes of northern New Mexico Hispanics. Many of those same Hispanics in Santa Fé beginning in earnest during the 1970s came to conclude that the sign's friendly words were being taken literally by people moving in, often with pockets full of money and seemingly bent on transforming the historic city to fit their own desires.

Like the Indians three centuries earlier, Hispanics came to feel displaced by people moving in.

Resentment mounted because of the attitudes and conduct of some of those who arrived.

"They're taking things that should be shared," said internationally acclaimed artist Frederico Vigil. "I used to go pick piñon around Wilderness Gate near St. John's College. All of a sudden I find these big pillars that say, 'Keep Out', 'No Trespassing'."

There was no escaping the resentment, to be sure.

"I felt like this town belonged to me," Gonzales told me in 1993 for a series of articles in *The Santa Fe New Mexican* that the newspaper titled "Saving Santa Fe".

The newspaper's bold, front-page headline over the story about Gonzales read, "Strangers in Their Own Town". The subhead read, "Money and growth have made Santa Fe a place natives barely recognize".

"I used to tell everyone this was *mi lindo Santa Fé*. Now it no longer belongs to me. It no longer belongs to the people who grew up with me, and it makes me very sad. I only regret that my seven children didn't get to see this lovely town the way I knew it," Gonzales told me.

Biddle Duke was among other reporters who helped collect information for the series. Duke, himself had recently moved to Santa Fé from the East Coast and is part of the founding family behind Duke University in North Carolina.

Pita Gonzales, twice elected Santa Fé County clerk, became unsettled by transformations of her hometown. (Photograph courtesy Bernadette García)

Duke visited with people who had moved to Santa Fé in the 1980s and 1990s, lured by its charm but also aware of its needs. Change would be required if the city was to remain a place where people want to live and raise their children, said one woman who asked not to be identified.

"The schools have to get better," she said. "The rich people who are moving here can send their kids to private schools. What about the rest of us?"

Santa Fé's school children could benefit from those moving into the city, said teacher Jeanette Larragoite. "Our children don't know there are people out there who they could emulate, people who they could pattern themselves after," she said.

Many newcomers promptly developed a sense of responsibility for the city and became active in community, school and cultural affairs, Duke reported. He told of the four women who established the popular Children's Museum in 1985, combining fun and education for children of all backgrounds.

Duke also reported that some recent arrivals had their own sense of resentment. Jerry Nachman, former editor with the *New York Post*, moved to Santa Fé around 1990 and said he found community hostility toward newcomers. "What did we do wrong?" he asked. In public speeches, Nachman said he thought he was moving into a tolerant community but criticized Santa Fé residents for intolerance.

New Mexico's internationally acclaimed fresco artist, Frederico Vigil, says people never should feel locked out of their own home. (Photograph courtesy Frederico Vigil)

So many long-time residents were more than ready to tell Nachman and others what they thought too many newcomers were doing wrong.

WARY OF BECOMING A "TOURIST TRAP"

Pita Gonzales in the late 1970s sold her family home in Casa Solana only about a mile northwest of the capital's historic Plaza. She spent much of the remainder of her life in a trailer park off Airport Road more than five miles from the Plaza, which she remembered fondly as having been a vibrant center of community activity.

It had been that way for a long, long time, said Fabián Chávez Jr., an influential state legislator during the 1950s and 1960s. "The downtown Plaza was the place," Chávez told me for his 2008 biography, *Taking on Giants, Fabián Chávez Jr. and New Mexico Politics.*

"Ninety-five percent of Santa Fé's activity was scattered around the Plaza, say about an eight-block area," he said. "As a boy I remember the occasional horse-drawn wagon coming onto the Plaza with *sacos de arina* and *papas.* People from the area would come in and buy their flower, their potatoes and drive them back where they came from, usually into the hills around Río en Medio.

The Plaza, indeed, had been the heart of Santa Fé since soon after the community was established as a villa in 1610. Caravans of merchandise arriving from Mexico or from U.S. states on the Plains and beyond were unloaded on the Plaza to the content of receptive locals. The periodically controversial soldiers' monument in the Plaza's center was used as a starting point for partitioning the Santa Fé land grant. The Ft. Marcy band gave concerts on a wooden bandstand during territorial days when the Plaza was encircled by a white picket fence.

But by 1980, much of the commotion around the Plaza came from owners of the commercial buildings who scurried to get the most out of their newly acquired properties.

Old Santa Fé families long owned much of the commercial space around the Plaza, offering storefront space for two to five dollars a square foot. Rental prices soared after new owners arrived.

Among victims: Raul's Café, which for years served inexpensive native foods, including $1.75 *burritos,* just off the Plaza. Raul's closed its doors in March 1981 amid rising rents.

Escalating rents forced out other businesses that long attracted Santa Fe's traditional shoppers, the community's long-time residents. Stores and shops whose emphasis was on the tourist trade took over.

The well-established store, Kahn's Shoes, in 1981 got a new neighbor that sold $175 western boots and $350 chamois tops to go with them.

Jewler Paul Shaya, a 36-year tenant of West San Francisco Street, said owners of neighboring stores were being squeezed to death by the new landlords.

"It's going to end up as one big tourist trap. And when it gets that reputation, it will kill it," he said of the Plaza.

The wave of change that Shaya and others feared could not be stopped. Its consequences weren't as dire as some predicted. Nor, though, could they be overlooked or dismissed as insignificant.

A middle-aged man with a Texas twang in the autumn of 1990 burst out of one of the Plaza's trendy shops wide eyed and with more than a bit of feigned imbalance before declaring to a companion waiting on the sidewalk: "I've never seen so many things I could do without in a single place!"

A day or two earlier an elderly couple visiting from the Plains stopped me on a street just off the Plaza and asked politely where they might find some "regular food" close by. "You know, mashed potatoes and, maybe, a chicken fried steak," the man said. He not only was looking for "regular food." He was hoping for "regular" prices.

Regular prices are what Julia and Carlos Castro sought to provide near the Plaza when they opened Café Castro in July 1993 on Lincoln Avenue. Their stay there lasted only nine months. They couldn't afford the monthly rent of $3,500 in La Esquina Building, which was being managed by Santa Fe's Territorial Properties for an out-of-state owner.

La Esquina Building went up only a few years earlier adjacent to the old home of Sears department store. Sears departed and the building was remodeled to accommodate several smaller and trendier businesses as part of the New Santa Fé.

Shingles for stores on the ground-level row leading up to Café Castro carried names like Talbots clothing, Mati jewelers, Eddie Bauer, Kent Galleries, J. Crew and Ann Taylor clothing.

Out of place in that atmosphere, the Castros offered *enchiladas* for $5.50 a plate. They hoped they could sell enough *enchiladas*, beans and *chile* at reasonable prices not only to pay the rent but also for something else that they considered at least as important. "I wanted to be a part of getting longtime, local people back into the downtown," Julia Castro told me. "I guess I could stay here and cater to tourists. I could sell four ounces of trout for about sixteen dollars, but I really don't want to do that. If I did, the money would just be going to the landlord, anyway."

The Castros, instead, focused their attention on their other restaurant, *El Comal*, on Rodeo Road, miles south of the Plaza. There they paid $1,500 a month to rent more space than what they had downtown at nearly three times the price.

The area around the Plaza very simply used to feel like home, said Pita Gonzales, the former county clerk and fiesta queen. But no more. "I moved after I got a divorce and saw I simply could not afford to maintain the home and take care of seven children, too. The mobile home park is fine, but it's way on the other end of town from where I grew up and where a lot of people have been pushed because they can't afford the high prices of homes and land downtown anymore."

If $175 Western boots dropped jaws only ten years earlier, downtown, as Gonzales visited with me, had become home to $12 *enchiladas*, $800 boots and oil paintings that cost more than the cars of some longtime residents.

Even Sam Pick, one of the city's most-reliable cheerleaders and Santa Fé mayor from 1976–1978 then again from 1986–1994, wondered out loud why even simple *enchiladas* cost so much in the City Different. Pick had just returned from Española 25 miles to the north, where he said he got an exceptional *enchilada* without having to take out a loan for it.

With distinctively local features that looked as if they sprouted from the very earth of the city's old downtown, Pita Gonzales said she had grown to feel "like I'm on the outside looking in."

HOME PRICES SOAR, CITY'S SOUL PUNCHED

Money brought in by newcomers, without question, fueled displacement. Prices readily paid for land and homes in some parts of Santa Fé were "outrageous," said Gil Tercero, county manager during the early 1990s.

Reporter Bob Quick told how the average price of a Santa Fé home jumped by 12 percent to $171,243 during the six-month period ending June 30, 1990. The average price was one thing, but more than a few homes were selling for far more.

As early as the 1980s, it wasn't hard to find home listings in newspapers encroaching on the one-million-dollar mark, mostly properties bought for far less by recent arrivals and then placed back on the market to make a tidy profit. Still, property owners and Realtors seemed reluctant for a while to ask for a full million. Once the reluctance was overcome, though, multi-million dollar listings weren't far behind.

Prices of vacant land by the early 1990s, especially on the city's east and north sides, were rising at a "feverish pace," real estate agents told Quick.

"My observation, having been here in the real estate business for 30 years, is that this is the biggest six months ever experienced by the City of Santa Fé," Santa Fe Properties owner Wally Sargent said at the time. "Every six months beats the previous six months."

Mike Hall, owner of The Prudential Hall and Fenn Real Estate, added, "I thought last year was good, but this year is even better. Business is excellent."

As real estate sales mounted, longtime Santa Fé residents found themselves pushed further away from the coveted center of their town; some by choice, some be necessity.

And if Pita Gonzales felt like a stranger in her own town, she had plenty of company. Numerous longtime residents expressed their pain and frustration for *The Santa Fe New Mexican's* series of stories on a changing city and in other reporting of the period.

Manuel Romero, a retired pipefitter with the Gas Company of New Mexico, recalled when native Santa Feans, mostly Hispanics, set the town's course.

"Our people used to rule, from Cerro Gordo all the way out in this direction," Romero said, talking in his mobile home off Cerrillos Road.

Romero once owned two houses on large lots on Hickox Street, about two miles west of the Plaza. But costs and pressures associated with growth proved to be more than he could deal with. Romero sold one of his houses. His daughter sold the other.

"As I got older, I didn't have the money to keep them up," he said.

It was a problem faced by far too many, said former Lieutenant Governor Roberto Mondragón. "Let's face it. A bunch of old-time Santa Fe is already gone: Canyon Road, Agua Fria, Alto Street, the Plaza; land and water that has been taken over for the purpose of making money," he said.

More than ten years earlier, in 1981, then-Santa Fé Mayor Art Trujillo expressed concern that New Mexico's historic capital city was on the verge of becoming "another elitest community."

Trujillo, an architect who served as mayor from 1978–1982, exploded when he got an advance peak of photographs that *National Geographic* was preparing to run along with an article about Santa Fé. Neither the article nor the photographs portrayed the city accurately, he and multiple city council members asserted.

I agreed with their incredulity while serving as editorial page editor of *The Santa Fe New Mexican* from 1980 through 1982. We were being misrepresented yet again as the home of leisurely bathhouses, leather pants, crystals and inescapable incense, I asserted in a December 1981 editorial. We had every right to feel as distressed as the proverbial public official who was home sick in bed during a meeting of his panel only to find that he had been quoted at length in a news story about what transpired at that meeting, I wrote.

"Santa Fé is not a community that only recently has been cut out of the Mexican landscape, lifted over the border and dropped onto Yankee soil," I wrote. "Nor are we a city that has been taken over by the 'beautiful people' and whose native residents hide sleepily behind *sombreros* until some passerby drops word of a *fiesta* or a low-rider car show.

"Santa Feans do more than pass the day away eating Reuben sandwiches while sitting in hot tubs; we do more than customize '57 Chevys; we do more than wait for camera-toting visitors to walk by so we can take a bite of our *tamale* in hopes that our image will be captured for a wall hanging or the next trendy article on the history-laden community we call home."

Some longtime locals would have preferred for *The Santa Fe New Mexican* to have gone even further in its editorials. But the paper's mission wasn't to stop growth or forbid change. It sought, instead, to remind people of Santa Fé's well-established profile, the long-standing cultures and values that had molded the city, and to show how so much was being threatened by ill-considered and, at times, heartless transformations.

I wrote in a May 1981 editorial: "Growth is changing the city's identity. Change can't be avoided, nor must it be destructive. It can be planned to preserve what is both attractive and equitable. It can't be done, though, by sacrificing the old for the new."

The artist, Frederico Vigil, said as much while he cautioned longtime Santa Feans against painting all newcomers with the same brush. "We were newcomers when we came. It depends how a newcomer comes and what a newcomer has to offer," he said. "I think we have both kinds coming here: those who come and give and come in respect of what is here, and those who come without respect and only take. They are the ones we have to fear."

His words told of serious issues facing the community. But even as those issues were building, a 1982 poll by a local mayoral candidate reported that Santa Feans considered potholes on city streets to be the most-pressing concern of the period.

Potholes? Really? I asked in an editorial.

Maybe that's why so many people were coming in and wanting to "Aspenicize" Santa Fé, I wrote.

"It's enough to make outsiders believe we're a virgin community standing still, without a substantial history, without real problems, without real vision, aching to be transformed into somebody else's dreamtown—which for some reason frequently seems to be Aspen, Colorado ... We're not Aspen. Not Vail. Not Boulder. Not Back East. We're Santa Fé, a community with very distinctive roots that was founded as the seat of government for the vast Southwest ten years before the Pilgrims landed at Plymouth Rock."

Yes, potholes played heck with our tires and vehicles. But Santa Fé's very identity had come into serious play. Perhaps more than ever before, the city was being divided. How would those divisions determine the community's growth and its allocation of resources, not just for potholes, but for housing, land, water, schools, health care and access to so much of what had defined the city for so long?

Some feared that merely asking such questions and giving voice to those who felt displaced encouraged divisiveness. Others complained that those questions weren't being asked often enough.

Popular Santa Fé County Sheriff Eddie Armijo (third from left) turned to tracking and other old-time police methods while fighting crime in the 1980s.
(Photograph by Barbaraellen Koch)

Art Trujillo, the former Santa Fé mayor, told me years after leaving city hall that longtime residents shouldn't look only at what the community used to be. "The community has to determine what is best for the future," he said. "I think the natives have to articulate their issues and concerns. They're verbalizing it but they haven't done a whole lot about it.

"When I was mayor, you never saw the natives come out and protest or say they were for something. It was always the outsiders who came out and dictated the issues. The natives have to have some leadership within their own culture. They have to become a part of the process."

The artist, Frederico Vigil, told me that native residents took too many things for granted as change occurred around them during the 1970s and 1980s. "What once were *barrios* on the east side, are now very elitist. It's frightening to see how it all could change so fast," he said.

"BROTHERS, HOW AM I GOING TO PAY YOUR TAX?"

The *Barrio Guadalupe*, on the southern banks of the Santa Fé River and just blocks from the city's Plaza, was among regions transformed with head-spinning speed. Fred Sánchez, born in 1896, had owned and operated Sánchez Market in the heart of the *barrio* since 1945. He talked to me in 1975 in his small store situated in one of the old buildings across from the Santuario Guadalupe. He told me at the time how he and other oldtimers of the region couldn't help but see change at their doorsteps.

Money was driving change and they predicted they wouldn't be able to stop it.

John Bott, editor of *The Santa Fe New Mexican* in the mid-1970s, also sensed the changes coming to the *Barrio Guadalupe*. Bott was a former editor of the *New York Post* who showed a willingness to straddle the increasingly evident divide between old Santa Fé and new Santa Fé to which his very presence contributed.

I was one of Bott's youngest reporters, two years out of college. But I also was one of only two in his entire editorial crew who knew his way around the Spanish language. Bott asked me to go into the *Barrio Guadalupe* and tell its story.

At the time, predominantly Spanish-speaking populations were distinguishing characteristics of Santa Fé's six designated *barrios*.

"The people from here are good. There's a lot of (Hispanic) people. That's why I like it," 81-year-old Thomas Sandoval told me at the time from a wooden bench on his front porch at 739 Dunlap Street. Sandoval had settled into old age after years of ranching, shepherding and railroad work.

Aurora C de Baca was born and reared in *Barrio Guadalupe*. Two of her 11 children still lived with her in 1975 and a third one lived with his family just a block away. "My family comes to visit me a lot," she told me. "There's always one or two of my children around. My (12) grandchildren are also here often."

A lot of the old folks from those days were gone by the time Santa Fé's changing profile was getting concerted attention during the early 1990s. Some had died. Some had moved away as part of the change that they couldn't stop.

Sánchez Market was closed. The building served as a credit union for a while and later was remodeled to serve multiple other uses. The area during the 1980s was transformed into one of Santa Fé's most trendy.

What was once an old auto upholstery shop became Zia Diner. The Palace Swiss Bakery opened up nearby as did Pranzo Restaurant and the e.k. mas fine food restaurant, where patrons could get lamb shanks or soft shell crabs for $14.95 on special. Those offerings surely appealed to some. But few, if any, residents of the old *barrio* likely ever walked in and asked for a table or a menu.

I wrote of the gentrified *Barrio Guadalupe* in a 1991 column for *The Santa Fe New Mexican*. A grandiose proposal was getting attention at the time. The San Francisco-based Catellus Development Corp. was proposing a $180-million development of the old railyard along the heart of Guadalupe Street. Plans included six-story buildings and what one person called New York corridor-type views.

Fred Sánchez and Thomas Sandoval recognized 15 years earlier that change was coming. But they never could have imagined anything like this.

Sandoval and his neighbors didn't call meetings in the 1970s to try to moderate change. They didn't hang handbills or lobby City Hall. They were among those referred to generally by the former mayor, Art Trujillo, when he said that the city's native residents tended to hold back and allow others to dictate the issues.

Outcomes were predictable. Displacement was an issue that inevitably fueled others. Clarence "Porky" Lithgow, a Santa Fé city councilor during the 1980s, said soaring prices set the value of his own family home so high that if he had been forced to move out for a week and then return to purchase the house at its new market value, he couldn't afford to buy it.

"The people who made Santa Fé what it is ought to have the right to stay here," he told me.

Indeed, ever-rising property values and soaring property taxes associated with them fanned the flames of resentment of many longtime residents as the 1990s unfolded.

Raul Martínez paid $13,500 in 1958 for his Santa Fé home near the popular Capitol District. Some of his neighbors recently had sold their homes for $90,000 to $100,000, he said. His own home recently had been valued at $117,000.

Those prices would seem like peanuts in the Capital District as the new millineum unfolded.

Martínez said he had no plans to sell his home so he didn't benefit from its rapidly rising value. He simply was stuck with much-higher property taxes.

Valentín Valdez, who built his house himself in 1957, said his tax bill had grown six-fold in the previous decade to more than $700, wiping out a significant chunk of his fixed income.

"I didn't make this happen. Why should I pay for it?" he said.

Longtime resident Francisco Romero said he paid $1,500 in 1969 for his small house in the central part of town and 25 years later was paying taxes on a valuation of $98,000 on the same house.

"If I were selling my property, I would be very grateful. But I'm not selling," he said.

Gaspar Naranjo for years had owned a small upholstery shop in north Santa Fé. He said he could not keep up with property taxes on the home that he and his family bought for $11,000 and had grown to be taxed on a market value of $150,000.

"Brothers, I'm still making fourteen thousand a year. How am I going to pay your tax," he told state legislators meeting to hear mounting concerns.

State Representative Ben Luján, a Nambé Democrat who would go on to become speaker of the House, was among lawmakers who heard Naranjo. So, too, was influential Santa Fé Democratic Senator Edward López. The two in time successfully sponsored legislation that limited growth in tax valuations for properties that stayed off the real estate market.

A Sign Signals Changing Times

Without question, the image of Santa Fé as a hometown was being redefined.

The perception was comicly expressed in 1991 by Felipe Cabeza de Vaca, a Santa Fé plumber, painter, garlic farmer, space enthusiast, political gadfly and reportedly a descendent of the first European to stumble onto the U.S. Southwest.

Felipe hung a hand-scrawled sign outside his Space Science Center on South St. Francis Drive that led to passers-by innocently camping out in his back yard. Felipe's sign read: "SF: Newcomers Promoting Newcomers".

"It's a sign about what Santa Fé has become, not a sign offering help to newcomers," Felipe told me at the time. "Through the years, people of all cultural backgrounds have come to Santa Fé and they do not work with the locals. They do not hire local people. Their management positions do not go to local people. A lot of their profits are exported out of the community."

Felipe's sentiments were not known to everyone, though. Some concluded that his sign advertised a haven for recent arrivals in search of advice, counseling or directions to the nearest Realtor.

"Three or four people rolled out their sleeping bags in my backyard the other day," Felipe said. "A lot of people come by and say they want to join the club. I have to tell them there is no club."

A periodic entry in municipal political races, Felipe in 1991 was serving on the city's cable television advisory committee. "It's another one of those committees that's designed to do nothing," said the outspoken maverick who was convinced that the historic old capital city was becoming a grand façade.

Felipe had allies in spirit, even if he didn't get their votes on election days.

"It's been about a year since I've gone into the downtown. They push you around over there," longtime resident Manuel Romero told me during that period. "They think you're a stranger from outside, or I don't know what.

"On New Year's Day, some friends and I would get together with guitars and go to all the houses that had men named Manuel. New Years is known as the Day of the Manuels. We would sing them *Las Mañanitas* and play the guitars. You can't do that now in Santa Fé. People would think you're crazy and they'd throw you out of town or throw you in jail."

"It's not that I don't want people to come in. But when they come in and push you around as if you don't belong, then forget it."

Paul Ortega, a retired truck driver from Lafayette Street, said simply that he felt robbed. "I feel like they stole my town," he said.

Jobs, Money and the *Acequia Madre*

Pita Gonzales acknowledged that Santa Fé's economy benefited from the city's changing population. "Sure there are more jobs now and more money," she said. "There was a time when we didn't have much money, but we had feelings for one another.

"It went through every family. When people needed help, we came with food, with clothing, with what was needed to put up a building. And we did it with love and respect. This used to be a lovely town. But it is very, very changed." Gonzales eventually moved out of her trailer after buying a small home in the city's southside Bellamah area, welcoming friends and family there until her death in 2015.

David Cargo, Republican governor from 1967–1970, was embraced by many established New Mexico families while he worked from the Capitol in Santa Fé. He spoke plainly about what he saw in the capital city during the early 1990s. "I must tell you, I like Santa Fé the old way," he said. "I don't think you had the kind of conflict in Santa Fé that you see today. People have come in and they tell the guy who has been there for a long time that his life ought to be made a little tougher for him."

Cargo, himself a Michigan native, said it was easy to feel tension of the period in Santa Fé. "It's getting nasty," he said.

The change was undeniable, said Fabián Chávez Jr., the former state tourism director and a contemporary of Gonzales'. Chávez grew up on ten acres along Acequia Madre, which morfed into one of the most-exclusive neighborhoods on the city's eastside. Near the south bank of the Santa Fé River, it was an unpretentious rural area settled by some of Santa Fé's most-established families during Chávez's childhood.

"We had apple trees, peach trees, apricot trees and wild crab apple trees," Chávez told me for his biography. "My brother, Eugenio, and I used to come here to the *acequia* and we carried a tub between us and a pail on our free side and we would go water the trees as a regular routine ... There was so much around us: water from the *acequia*, fruit trees, vegetables, *milpas*. The soil itself was rich and the *adobes* that were made for the family home came from that very patch of land."

The ditch referred to by Chávez is the same one—*Acequia Madre*—from which the neighborhood street draws its name. More than 400 years old, the *Acequia Madre* winds through the city's core historic district and long carried irrigation water under rights claimed by property owners.

Changing times all but put an end to that. The Sangre de Cristo Water Co. served Santa Fé's water needs from reservoirs in the eastern foothills and released water into the *Acequia Madre* only intermittently, when company administrators thought they had water to spare. Such times grew increasingly infrequent as the city's population grew.

But in 1990, state district Judge Art Encinias ruled from his Santa Fé bench that the water company must annually release water from its reservoirs to the *Acequia Madre*. Water in the ditch is critical to the vitality of the local culture, Encinias ruled.

The local culture along the *Acequia Madre* is a far cry from what it used to be. In his boyhood days, the Acequia Madre neighborhood "was just a place to call home," Fabián Chávez Jr. told me.

"A large majority of the property in (the) neighborhood now is owned by people who moved into the city much more recently. What can I say? It's changing times. To own a place on Acequia Madre, on Sosaya Lane, really has come to be equated with moving to the Hamptons back East," he said.

Gentrification by no means was limited to Acequia Madre and Sosaya Lane, as noted earlier by former Lieutenant Governor Mondragón and others. Jesús Rios, the seller of firewood and recycled materials at the corner of Canyon Road and Camino Monte Sol, continued running his large wood yard and salvage business late into his life, resisting the onslought of change fueled by outside money.

As Rios spoke to me in 1993, his home and business stood out almost like a Third World island among galleries and restaurants of the gentrified neighborhood.

Rios, to be sure, benefited from the money-fueled transformation of Santa Fé. Just as newcomers drove up the cost of homes, they raised the price of firewood that Rios sold to those homes. Every house that was sold and remodeled became a potential reclamation site for Rios' salvage business.

Similar dissonance thrust itself into the life of 35-year-old artist Orlando "Gabby" Leyba during the early 1990s. Raised in Chimayó, Leyba at the time painted and taught art in Boston, Massachusetts. He returned to northern New Mexico for a visit in 1993 to soak in the culture that runs through his blood—and his paintings.

He walked inside his great grandfather's adobe house in one of the area's mountain villages and marveled at how the region's cultural essence still flowed through the community, only half an hour drive from Santa Fé.

"Boy, I hope this never changes," he told me from within two-feet-thick adobe walls.

A few days later, Leyba opened a monthlong show of his works in a Truchas gallery frequented by tourists reaching out from Santa Fé for new excitement.

Tourists were dropping chunks of money into the Santa Fé area economy during the early 1990s, more than $800 million a year, according to some official accounts. Without tourists and the changes afoot, there would have been little hope for Leyba's show. He knew that as much as anyone. Still, he like so many others couldn't help but wonder how to keep a productive stream of change from becoming an uprooting flood.

An Old Bordello and a Treasured Adobe Home

Gentrification, no doubt, was abloom on the southeast side of the capital's historic Plaza, but the summer of 1993 revealed displacement had few limitations. Inescapable tensions that accompanied growth usually had been expressed in terms of "locals" and "newcomers." But in time, the issue pitted rich against poor, with some newcomers falling among the displaced.

In July 1993, more than two dozen people who in recent years moved to Santa Fé were directed to leave a funky, if somewhat run-down, adobe apartment complex on Park Avenue on the city's north side. Frequented as a popular bordello soon after statehood in 1912, the 16-unit complex for years had offered affordable quarters to artists, waiters and such at a site sandwiched between trendy West San Francisco and Guadalupe streets.

Change was signaled after an opera singer bought the property. Tenants were asked to leave their quarters of worn hardwood floors, crooked doorways and leaky roofs so the complex could be made over for use as luxury rentals.

Cheryl Goodman lived in the complex after moving to Santa Fé from Florida. "It was love at first sight," she said.

She said her forced move out of the complex gave her a firsthand look at how longtime Santa Feans feel when their lives are turned upside down by those who are driven by the time-honored American practice of pursuing a maximum return on investments.

"Now I know how people who have grown up here their entire lives feel," Goodman told me. "But people like us also work here. We support community projects. I feel like we can also be a part of a place. It's hurtful when you see your own neighborhood treated this way."

Paula Romero, a 26-year-old lighting designer and electrician, joked about being the "token local" at the Park Avenue apartment complex, where her neighbors had roots in places like Germany, Israel, Los Angeles and San Francisco. "Most of the friends I grew up with, if they haven't moved out of state, they live with their parents," she said. "The people around me now I consider locals. These people are a part of Santa Fé. They're trying to keep Santa Fé as it is."

Back at Acequia Madre, Fabián Chávez Jr.'s own family had become among the displaced. But their departure from the increasingly coveted and pricy neighborhood was voluntary. The Chávez family home, which was designed and built in 1926 by Fabián's carpenter father, was sold as part of the neighborhood's transformation.

The Chávez family decades earlier had lost the four-bedroom home during the Great Depression when Fabián's father was unable to make good on a $5,000 debt incurred for the home's building materials. He was able to buy back the home after the Depression through a new federal program intended to promote recovery.

Losing the home hurt his father dearly, said Fabián; getting it back several years later was pure joy.

That treasured adobe home with French windows was sold again out of the Chávez family in 1993. A Chávez sister, Nora, had inherited the house and Fabián, himself, encouraged her to sell.

Eventually, she did but only after struggling financially to hold on. A retired school teacher, Nora Chávez said taxes on her home rose from $537 to $1,019 in 1991 and then rose again to $1,209 in 1992. Her retirement income, meanwhile, rose two and one-half percent annually, she said.

She said speculators with little or no interest in staying long in Santa Fé were hurting the city's permanent residents.

"Santa Fé is now the Wall Street of real estate and that is not fair," she said.

Brother, Fabián, took a different view and encouraged Nora to stop fighting the inevitable change.

"I told her, 'Oh, go ahead. Sell it. Enjoy your life,'" Fabián said.

"When she sold it, she got three hundred thousand dollars for it. You couldn't touch it for that now," Fabián told me in 2007. "With the money that (she) got from the sale, she was able to buy another house for her and her daughter and still had two hundred thousand left that she could use to travel and enjoy life."

A 2018 map of the city showed that only 14 percent of the people living at the time in what used to be the Chávez neighborhood were Hispanics, 25 percent in the downtown area, and 16 percent in the area immediately north of downtown. The southern half of the city was predominantly Hispanic with most concentrations ranging from 54 percent to 89 percent.

Fabián told me without hesitation that he would not have stopped Santa Fé's transformation even if he could have. The city's people are better off for it, economically, for sure, he said. "I don't feel bitter about the changes because there's nothing I could do about it. And you can't just look at what's bad. My dad and mom never drove a car. They had ten children and thirty-five grandchildren and every one of us owns a car. It's prosperity. Times change."

I watched those changing times begin to unfold during the 1970s from my post as a newspaperman in Española 25 miles north of Santa Fé. I became a victim of the times in 1980 when I was hired to work as *The Santa Fe New Mexican's* editorial page editor. It would mean long hours spread over six-day work weeks so a move to Santa Fé seemed inescapable.

I began looking for a home near the newspaper's offices on East Marcy Street, just blocks north of the plaza. Walking to work would have been convenient, and there were plenty of small, old homes in the area. Surely, I thought, I could find one that was affordable. I didn't need anything new. Old would be fine. Näiveté didn't last long.

My house search went on for weeks as I made larger and larger circles extending beyond the Plaza. The first affordable home I found was on Rodeo Road near the city's southern edge. Dusty. Few trees at the time. Little landscaping.

Rather than walk to work, I drove 15 to 20 minutes each way and at times couldn't help but feel as if I was the hired help driving in to apply my craft amid the affluence of the transforming historic little city.

Santa Fé was well on its path of redefinition. I liked much of what I saw and encouraged more than a little of it from my new post as an editor at the city's daily newspaper. Amid the change—good and bad—it was abundantly clear that Santa Fé had moved well beyond the community where in the 1960s, not that many years before, I had walked through old northside neighborhoods and between cars lined up at Fort Marcy park during burns of Zozobra to sell *tamales* at 25 cents a piece for a neighbor who was working his way through college.

Alas, Western boots selling for $800 a pair had come to define downtown Santa Fé. It would have taken sales of 3,200 *tamales*, at 1960 prices, to buy those boots.

Snakes, St. Francis and "Environdog"

Molly Ivans, the newspaper columnist, likely would have gotten as much of a kick as I did from the dismay expressed to me in the Nineties by a man whose life was spent in a rural area outside of Santa Fé. From his unassuming post he, too, had watched neighboring Santa Fé go through remarkable changes.

He called my attention one day to a brief letter to the editor in that morning's *New Mexican*. Standing in a meadow alongside gurgling water running through a small *acequia* and leaning on an old shovel that seemed to be a constant companion, he asked if I had read that day's paper.

"Did you see it, the letter from that woman?" he asked in his native Spanish. "Now these people don't even want us to kill snakes! Imagine what the world is coming to!"

Old Molly also might have marveled at the crowd at a Santa Fe rally during that same period, a rally organized to commemorate St. Francis Day. St. Francis has long been Santa Fé's patron saint but few people at the rally looked like they had been in the city for a very long time.

They assembled to speak for peace, nuclear safety and recycling.

Who could stand in opposition?

Children and well-groomed dogs pranced softly—for the most part—on the trimmed grass of Pérez Park. Placards poked above people's heads. One read: "Help prevent a nuclear accident here". Another read: "Be a friend of the Earth—recycle". A small sign posted near the speakers' platform read: "Sound stage powered by Flowlight Solar Power".

Brazilian, Zamba and New Age music filled the air.

A Labrador-cross dog sported a red doggie pack on its back on which was attached a cardboard label that identified the black pooch as "environdog".

From the beginning, divisions being created by the city's transformation didn't escape the attention of city politicians. Nor did they as time went on. As recently as the 2018 municipal elections, three-term city councilor Ron Trujillo, of Santa Fé's southside, waged a campaign for mayor in which he openly promised to act on behalf of locals before anyone else.

Trujillo, a Santa Fé native, had built a reputation as a likeable, reasonable and articulate official. But his appeals to the "locals" during the mayoral campaign got him nowhere. They alienated many. Alan Webber, a progressive East-Coast-educated entrepreneur who moved to Santa Fé 15 years earlier, beat Trujillo two to one.

Webber drew endorsements from some high-profile Hispanics and pledged inclusion. He told supporters at his election night victory party that too many of their neighbors feel left out, promising immediate change.

Webber's energy and reputation gave hope to that promise, although the approximate 100 people who assembled for his victory celebration did not look anything like a representation of the city's diversity.

A ranked process of recording final vote totals made Webber's strength seem greater than what was reflected in the night's initial, traditional tabulation. Still, if Trujillo's resounding defeat suggested anything, it likely was this: The time when candidates in a citywide election could pin their hopes on "locals" vs. all others was over.

A large plywood sign posted just off busy Cerrillos Road probably spoke more of intentions than reality as the 2018 municipal campaign came and went. "In our Santa Fe, ALL are welcome!" read the sign. The message was attributed to two unions: the American Federation of State, County, and Municiple Employees and the American Federation of Teachers.

The self-proclaimed City Different long has touted its diversity. Assertions like, *"Mi casa es su casa,"* and "ALL are welcome," suggest kindness, cooperation, inclusion. But no matter the proclamations, whether posted in small, cozy kitchens or outdoors alongside busy entries to the city, Santa Fé remains a community where people of diverse backgrounds mostly work and play apart, sticking to their kind when conditions do not require them to be together.

Often, it has had piercing ramifications. Under the guise of tranquil diversity, too many walls and fences have been built on prejudices and fortified by access to wealth and influence. Past wrongs are getting in the way of new overtures.

There is work to be done. If there are any who consider themselves to be a part of that "better, stronger, higher race" that Tecumseh Sherman predicted would come to Santa Fé to make the community right, they probably ought to be escourted to the city's boundaries then allowed to ride off on their high horses.

From the Roybal Files...
The Santa Fe New Mexican, Column, October 31, 1993
No Candidate Will Declare as 'Pick's Boy'

Let's make one thing clear as we embark on Santa Fé's 1994 mayoral election campaign: Sam Pick won't have any boys asking for your vote.

There are four candidates so far. Pick isn't seeking re-election, and speculation mounts over who our increasingly embattled mayor and his traditional supporters will endorse.

Youthful-looking City Councilor Peso Chávez went out of his way to stress, while announcing his mayoral candidacy that he isn't "Pick's boy."

"The only boy that I am is my mother's boy," the 42-year-old Chávez declared.

So the...um...self-proclaimed mamma's boy, always well-coiffed and meticulously dressed, has hit the campaign trail. Bets are that whenever the trail veers off onto Santa Fé's trendy unpaved roads, Chávez will pause before ringing doorbells to rub his shoes against his pant legs so dust doesn't dull his spit shine.

Tony López, a true salesman at heart who for years pitched the U.S. Navy as a recruiter, followed his mayoral campaign announcement with a large newspaper ad that listed dozens of his affiliations.

Nowhere did the ad say that López is Sam Pick's boy.

Pugnacious City Councilor Debbie Jaramillo was first to announce that she is running for mayor. For obvious reasons, she is the one candidate who commands immediate believability when she says she isn't Pick's boy. And Jaramillo, if caught on a bad day, is likely to pound into the ground anyone who doesn't heed the command.

Smart reporters covering the campaign will heed caution, at least while approaching Jaramillo and Chávez. Jaramillo's disdain for the Fourth Estate is well known.

Jaramillo, if she had her way, likely would ban reporters from City Hall, break their pencils, burn their note pads and dispatch them to keep company with Realtors and developers, all of whom she thinks grew out of the same seed.

Chávez is a bit more restrained than Jaramillo while expressing his disappointment with the press. Everyone is more restrained than Jaramillo when she's expressing disappointment.

Chávez's criticisms of the press aren't original. Chávez, one might say, doesn't burst with originality. Leave it to a lifelong news person to draw that conclusion, Chávez would say. He thinks the press is quick to criticize and far too reluctant to praise.

Chávez believes there is much to praise in this lovely old town. He proclaimed it boldly in his announcement speech.

"Let's preserve what's good about our city ... but let's fix what is wrong," he urged.

Gosh! How can reporters not see originality in that?

Thomas Montoya, a city Parks and Recreation Department employee, is the latest to announce his mayoral candidacy. He tossed originality aside this past week, saying he would encourage people to feel good about themselves.

Pick for a long time made the mayor's job in Santa Fé look easy. He swept the sidewalks, clipped the grass and told anyone who would listen that this town is the best thing south of Heaven's gate.

Enchantment, Pick professed once on national TV, is a good taco and a better margarita.

Heck, the only time Pick took off his cheerleading uniform was when he asked delicately why enchiladas cost so much in Santa Fé. He had just returned from Española, where he said he enjoyed a tremendous enchilada without having to take out a loan for it.

Why can't the same be true in Santa Fé restaurants? Pick asked.

If Pick's luster has dulled recently, it's because Jaramillo and others assert that Santa Fé under Pick has been sold to the highest bidders.

So with Pick on his way out of City Hall, the definition of enchantment in Santa Fé is about to change. Enchantment one day might come to mean not only affordable enchiladas but affordable homes, too. It might become the word uttered most by native residents who no longer feel squeezed out.

From the Roybal Files...
The Santa Fe New Mexican, Column, August 19, 2004
Fancy Names, Fancy Prices Not For Me

Oh, I might quibble about one or two of the colors. Otherwise, I think the new bandstand on Santa Fé's historic Plaza is a wonderful addition to the fabulous city.

The price tag? Well, the price tag is something else. See, the problem with paying $400,000 or so for a bandstand is that it makes us all look like sitting ducks.

The cost of the structure, which is about the size of an ample den in an average home, exceeds by about $50,000 the latest median price of entire Santa Fé homes, which themselves are out of reach for many. And the homes usually come with the land around them. The little bandstand doesn't even come with walls.

It's important to emphasize that money for the bandstand was collected from civic-minded donors, who like so many others had grown tired of the tacky-looking portable structure it replaced. Still, the whopping price tag marks us all.

It marks us for people like that audacious showerhead salesman from Southern California who made it into the news recently. The guy is selling $125,000 shower "systems", and he might well figure that there's too much wealth here to be left untapped. Yup, $125,000 for a shower. It's what the maker, architect TAG Galyean collects. So far his collections are mostly around the West Coast.

The SilverTAG Shower uses 18 heads to target six different zones of the body, say promoters. They say water fluctuates from warm to hot, then cool, then hot again to deepen muscle relaxation. A new version claims to reduce cellulite by using a series of pressure variations to supposedly increase circulation.

Until recently, we were told, one could only experience such treatment at major resorts like the Broadmoor in Colorado Springs. (I drove by the Broadmoor as a young man but couldn't muster the courage to walk in.)

The funny thing is, people in most parts of New Mexico could have one of these extravagant showers installed while purchasing a new home and still pay less for the entire package—home and shower combined—than what was paid in Santa Fé for the new bandstand.

Oh, I know. We don't really refer to it as a bandstand. It's a gazebo in many circles. But perhaps that's where the problem starts. Maybe it's our fancy talk that gets us into trouble.

I recently bought a car in Albuquerque after first shopping for weeks in Santa Fé. I came to like a nice, new sedan that I thought stood out in a sea of other beauties. The two Santa Fé salespeople I dealt with alternately—while kicking the dirt and otherwise working down the price—said the sedan's color was "desert mist."

As nice as the name sounded, it became clear after a while that representatives of the Santa Fé dealer weren't going down further on their price. That's when I hit I-25 south for Albuquerque.

There the first saleman out of the showroom door heard me say what I was looking for as I pointed to a couple of cars on the lot that fit the description perfectly. "Oh, yeah," he said. That's a nice gold color. It's one of our most-popular colors."

Turns out the amiable salesman was originally from Hobbs near New Mexico's southeastern border with Texas. He learned to play football there, he said. He also learned in that no-frills town, I suspect, that calling gold "desert mist" can get you onto pretentious fronts that merely interfere with business when folks are simply looking to get the most for their dollar.

We struck a deal within an hour—for nearly a thousand dollars less than the bottom price in Santa Fé.

Calling Santa Fé's nice new gazebo a bandstand from the start probably wouldn't have affected the price. But we seemingly need to be alert to all the angles these days, nonetheless. After all, showerheads can get downright expensive if we allow ourselves to call them something other than what they really are.

12
When Talk of Diversity Moves Beyond Tourism Campaigns

It was a very thin line that emerged between adversaries in discussions over Santa Fé's changing profile beginning late in the 1970s. Constructive debate sprouted on one side. Divisiveness tainted at least occasionally by bigotry was on the other. It extended into the 1990s and beyond.

Former Republican Governor David Cargo wasn't whistling Dixie when he observed, "It's getting nasty." It was as if anger commonly associated with our nation's Deep South wanted to get its foot in the door that led to the lovely old town which long had called itself the City Different.

New Mexico's capital, Santa Fé was largely a government town. Along with Taos 70 miles upriver, Santa Fé also was one of New Mexico's most-liberal communities. And as the 1990s approached, new wrinkles in the capital's social fabric surfaced, stoking emotions and adding new dimensions to old debates about diversity.

Santa Fé and much of New Mexico had grown fond of their internationally publicized claims of tri-cultural diversity. References were to Hispanics, Anglos and Native Americans. Little or nothing was said about blacks. Little or nothing was said about others who also knocked on doors in pursuit of equal opportunity.

James Lewis beginning in the early 1980s became a familiar figure in the capital and emerged as a solid pioneer for blacks in New Mexico.

But controversy and disruption followed Donald Grady as that young black man entered the Santa Fé scene from Albuquerque a few years later.

Mary Walters blazed trails in the state's legal profession while recalling that her parents assured her that no one in her family would consider her any less capable or confident simply because she was a girl.

Liz Stefanics in 1992 was the woman in a field of men who offered themselves as candidates for a newly carved district in the New Mexico Senate. But there was more to Stefanics, I was told by a man who approached me in the aisle of a grocery store. "She's a lesbian," the man said as if springing on me news of which I wasn't already aware. "What if more people knew she's a lesbian?"

Blacks constituted only two percent of the state's population in 1985 when then-Governor Toney Anaya appointed 37-year-old James Lewis state treasurer. Lewis' parents divorced when he was one-year-old. His mother was a domestic worker; his father a retired railroad engineer. Lewis was 27 before he met his father.

Governor Anaya entered the state's top executive office in 1983 as only the second Hispanic to serve as governor in New Mexico since 1920. Determined to open doors for minorities and women, it was during his first year in office that Governor Anaya appointed Michigan native Mary Walters to the state Supreme Court. Walters became the first woman ever to serve on the state's high court. She was elected to a full term on the panel in 1984.

Lewis also was elected to the office to which he was originally appointed by Anaya. He previously had been elected Bernalillo County treasurer in 1982. Lewis, by winning election as state treasurer in 1986, became the first black man elected to a statewide office in New Mexico.

In 1991, Lewis became chief of staff to then-Governor Bruce King. The governor appeared slow to allow Lewis into his inner circle but Lewis went on later to excel in other elected and appointed government posts.

Blacks already had risen as leaders in Albuquerque, New Mexico's largest city. Lenton Malry for years served as Bernalillo County commissioner after having first been elected to the state House of Representatives, the first black to be elected to that chamber. Bill Gooden during the 1980s was a ranking aide to then-Mayor Harry Kinney. And there were others.

But if Lewis emerged with the highest profile in New Mexico's black community, the controversy that followed Donald Grady through his brief tenure as chief of the Santa Fé police department during the early 1990s often deteriorated into divisive discussions about race.

Democrat Liz Stefanics said she had been openly lesbian since arriving in New Mexico ten years prior to her surprising election to the state Senate. Governor Anaya in the mid-1980s appointed Stefanics to the New Mexico Gay and Lesbian Political Alliance, where she served for years.

"Because of (my) sexual preference, I certainly know what discrimination is," she told me following her 1992 election to the Senate from a newly structured District 39. "I do not tolerate discrimination against anyone based on religion, class or sexual preference."

The Democratic-controlled state Legislature in 1991 carved out the Senate's District 39 to include all or parts of six counties.

"I don't think I was who the party in Santa Fé County or the party in San Miguel County wanted. I was told very concretely that (the seat) was meant for a Hispanic male Democrat," Stefanics said.

After defeating four men with Hispanic surnames in the Democratic primary, Stefanics faced moderate Republican Lou Gallegos in the general election. Gallegos declined to make Stefanics's sexual preference an issue.

"I thought if we took it up in the political arena, we would not add anything meaningful to the dialogue," he said. "I've always considered these to be private matters, and I think they should stay that way."

I wrote in a post-election column: "Some will criticize the news media for not mentioning that Stefanics is a lesbian as part of her background reported during the pre-election coverage. We probably would have had we concluded it would affect how she served as a senator."

Stefanics in 1993 was among vocal supporters of Senate legislation that called for extending protections of the State Human Rights Act to homosexuals. A statewide survey done for the *Albuquerque Journal* by Research & Polling Inc. showed that 50 percent of adult respondents favored extending human rights protections to homosexuals. Thirty-nine percent were opposed and 11 percent were undecided.

Bruce King, governor at the time, said his office was taking as many as 2,000 phone calls and dozens of letters daily on the controversial Senate legislation. Opinions in the phone calls and letters ran about 75 percent against the bill, the governor said.

Passed in the Senate, the bill worked its way through the House of Representatives while King declined to say whether he would sign the legislation. "I'm a pretty good cowboy. I can do this or do that," he said.

Still, there was little room for guessing about where King stood while he suggested the legislation might appear to grant special treatment to homosexuals. He said his job would be easier if the bill never got out of the House. "Whatever develops, the sun comes up the same. I don't think it would have very far-reaching effects either way it goes."

Some who contacted King's office pledged to campaign against anyone who supported the legislation. Did that bother the governor?

"Oh, well, it always concerns me," he said. "I wouldn't want to turn enough people against me that I get beat."

The 1993 legislation sought to move protections beyond the 1985 executive order signed by then-Governor Anaya that prohibited discrimination in public employment.

Expansion of protections didn't come until 1993 when legislation passed by both state legislative chambers was signed by then-Governor Bill Richardson.

None of the new friction emerging around diversity was to suggest that old tensions had gone away. The All-Indian Pueblo Council late in 1991 announced that it would not meet with a descendant of Christopher Columbus who was touring the United States to mark the beginning of a yearlong celebration of the 500th anniversary of Columbus' landing in the New World.

Cristobal Colon de Veragua, also known as Christopher Columbus XX and the Duque de Veragua, was to arrive in Santa Fé in mid-October. The All-Indian Pueblo Council hoped that Colon would bring with him an apology for the subjugation of Native Americans following Columbus' arrival. But the pueblos learned that their time with Colon would be very limited and that an apology was unlikely.

Colon said later he was in no position to apologize for what occurred following Columbus' landing in 1492. "Neither you nor I were present to witness (the) first encounter between the Spaniards and the Indians," Colon said in a statement released in Taos.

"The first Admiral Columbus never reached this land nor did he meet its inhabitants. Pure fate has entrusted me to meet them after 20 generations and almost 500 years since the first Columbus landed on the small island off San Salvador in the Caribbean."

Colon's goodwill mission was largely successful. But when he left, incessant tensions remained barely concealed in and around Santa Fé, not only between Hispanics and Native Americans but between Hispanics and Anglos as the age-old issue of displacement spread through much of the community well into the new millennium.

ON FIRES, PIZZA Y EL "BUEN SABOR" DE ESPAÑOL

It was autumn 1993 and Santa Fé City Councilor Debbie Jaramillo was among several candidates running to succeed Sam Pick as mayor the following year. Jaramillo was angry about what the city had become under Pick's charismatic and often-freewheeling leadership.

If people like onetime mayor Art Trujillo had used terms like "natives" and "outsiders" while referring to the city's transformation during Pick's multiple terms as mayor, Jaramillo injected derisiveness as part of her campaign.

People who "just got off the bus" should not chart the city's future, she insisted.

In the final weeks of 1993, Jaramillo said so much discontent had built up and so many people had come to feel oppressed that she knew longtime residents who were ready to set fires and shoot their guns to stop the city's transformation. She made her remarks to a San Diego, California, columnist.

I figured her campaign for mayor might be doomed. She couldn't keep shooting from the hip at everything that moves, I wrote, and still expect to become the first woman to be elected Santa Fé mayor.

The 41-year-old Jaramillio eventually came to the same realization. She took a hard look at the path she was on and seriously considered withdrawing from the mayoral race. Instead, she toned down her rhetoric, picked her battles and talked about "celebrating diversity" while committing herself to thoughtful discourse of controversial issues that had kept her at the fore of public attention for years.

She took the oath as mayor in March 1994 and couldn't steer away from controversy any more than she could bring herself to smile upon her critics.

John Dendahl, New Mexico Republican Party chairman at the time, was among many who considered the new mayor to be more than abrasive. Jaramillo's rhetoric and thinking were racist, plain and simple, claimed Dendahl, himself a sharp-tongued Santa Fé resident whose family was well established in the city.

Dendahl spoke for many on the issue, not just Republicans.

Yet, Jaramillo had her own substantial following, some supporters standing enthusiastically at her side; others cheering her on from a distance to avoid fallout for themselves and their families.

The undercurrents of tension had flowed for years, claiming as victims a former Santa Fé mayor and his family in the late summer of 1991.

George Gonzales, mayor from 1968–1972, filed a complaint with the state Human Rights Division, accusing a local Pizza Hut restaurant of asking him for identification to prove his U.S. citizenship before being allowed to order.

A manager at the restaurant denied the charge, saying it was the business' policy for servers to ask all customers for identification—but only to ensure that they were legally old enough to consume alcoholic beverages.

The legal drinking age was 21. Gonzales was 54 at the time. And, he told me, the waitress demanded to see his identification before anyone in his family ordered anything to drink or eat.

"It seems barbarous to me. Nothing like that has ever happened to me in my life," he said.

Long active in Santa Fé-area Democratic politics, Gonzales was master of ceremonies at the inauguration of Governor Bruce King in January 1991. Working from behind the scenes, he helped Republican Governor David Cargo win re-election in 1968.

Gonzales had been part owner of KDCE-AM radio in nearby Española, and just months before the Pizza Hut incident, he and his family launched their own radio station, KSWV-AM, in Santa Fé.

Gonzales said he and his wife, Celine; sons, Anthony and Stephen; and a four-year-old grandson walked into the Santa Fe restaurant around seven p.m. on a warm August evening.

"The first thing the waitress said is, 'I need to card you.' I said, 'What do you mean?' She said, 'It's policy. I need to card you.' My wife said, 'Here's my driver's license.' The waitress said, 'No, I don't want yours. I need his.'"

The waitress supposedly motioned toward the former mayor.

Gonzales objected and the restaurant's shift manager came to the table. "He said (the waitress) was only doing her job," Gonzales said. "I asked them what they were trying to do and finally my wife showed them her driver's license and they threw the menus on the table."

"I'm very dark complected and my impression was they wanted a so-called green card. But even if they thought I was Mexican, why would they need to ask for a card?"

Gonzales said he and his family wrestled with the issue for four months before deciding to file a complaint with the state government agency assigned to combat race discrimination.

"We thought about how I was born and raised here and about how this kind of thing shouldn't happen here," he said.

He said he filed the complaint because he wanted an apology and because he wanted Pizza Hut stores to prevent such incidents from happening again.

Gonzales got his apology. A company spokesman reasserted that it all was a misunderstanding and pledged that steps would be taken to prevent recurrences.

One of the Gonzales' sons, Javier, would serve as Santa Fé mayor from 2014 to 2018.

That a former mayor and his prominent family could feel the pangs of what they considered to be overt discrimination told of how pervasive tensions had become. Fuel remarkably was still being added to those tensions 15 years later.

It was March 2006 and I almost felt compelled to apologize to Jorge Serrano, a waiter at one of the city's Starbucks coffee shops. It seemed I likely contributed to his suspension supposedly for speaking Spanish while on the job.

Fabián Chávez Jr. and I had taken to meeting at the Starbucks shop for interviews while I worked on the biography of the civil rights champion and former government official. The interviews had turned to how Chávez in the 1950s boldly stood up to fellow state legislators and others while battling institutional discrimination against a young black couple at New Mexico State University in Las Cruces.

I had long before been convinced that a culture's survival depended largely on keeping its language alive. So I have commonly greeted Hispanics with familiar Spanish expressions as we come upon one another. If brief discussions in Spanish ensue, all the better.

"Buenos días, caballero," I recall telling Serrano as our paths crossed in the coffee shop.

"Que le vaya bien," I offered multiple times to the waiter as Chávez and I walked out after our meetings.

Serrano's responses usually were in Spanish, even if only to say, *"Gracias,"* or *"Vuelven."*

Serrano, a naturalized U.S. citizen from South America, later said he was suspended by a Starbucks manager who purportedly directed him not to speak his native language on the job.

This was in a shop within a city that carries a beautiful Spanish name meaning holy faith. The DeVargas Mall in which the coffee shop prospered is named after one of Santa Fé's Spanish colonial governors. So, too, is one of the city's main thoroughfares, Paseo de Peralta, which fronts the coffee shop. New Mexico's governor at the time, Bill Richardson, played as a youth in the streets around Mexico City, where his proud Mexican mother and his father, who had business and political ties in much of Latin America, were prominent members of the community.

I didn't know Jorge Serrano from Pedro de Peralta when I first started dropping into Santa Fé's northside Starbucks for occasional interviews. But I made Serrano out for a Hispanic who had no interest in concealing his roots.

Serrano wouldn't have been much of an employee—or much of a Hispanic—if he had not responded to my own comments in the same Spanish language that not only expresses pride in our backgrounds but in the culturally diverse community in which we found ourselves.

Then I came to learn that our brief exchanges might have contributed to his suspension.

¡Que lástima! ¡Que desgracia!

A Starbucks spokesman in Seattle called it all a misunderstanding. Nonetheless, Serrano missed two days of work.

Around the same period, the stirring movie, *The Three Burials of Melquiades Estrada*, was playing at the same Santa Fé mall where Serrano worked. Viewers of the movie might recall the old, blind rancher living out his final days in near-isolation along the U.S.-Mexico border. He's seated alone listening to ads and music of a Spanish-language station playing on a radio positioned directly in front of him when he is surprised by men making their way on horseback to Mexico.

Apparently sensing that he owed his visitors an explanation as they settled in front of him, the old rancher offered something like: "I don't understand a word they're sayin' but it sure sounds nice, doesn't it?"

I suggested in a column that if managers of trendy coffee shops in Santa Fé happen to hear Spanish spoken during the course of business, they shouldn't cringe. They ought to smile and acknowledge that it sure sounds nice, even if they don't understand a word of it. In our parts for sure, I wrote, if they don't understand a word of Spanish, that's their misfortune.

The beauty of the Spanish language is becoming lost in too many quarters. Fabián Chávez Jr. shared how his own father told family members more than once that the Spanish language far exceeded English in its ability to convey meaning and feelings. "He loved to read. He loved books," Chávez told me. "He especially liked reading out loud in Spanish. I'd ask him why he seemed to read mostly the Spanish out loud. He'd say because the words in Spanish *'tienen buen sabor.'* He read and savored every word. That's the best way to describe it."

Santa Fean Leveo V. Sánchez, a U.S. foreign service veteran, told me of a deathbed conversation he had with a close friend and mentor as I prepared his biography, *Nerve of a Patriot, Global Trails of Leveo V. Sánchez*.

"I knew that Jack Vaughn was ill. I called him at his home in Tucson a day or two before he died," said Sánchez.

Vaughn, like Sánchez, helped lead U.S. diplomatic efforts of presidents John Kennedy and Lyndon Johnson throughout Latin America and the Caribbean. A Montana rancher, Vaughn spoke fluently in Spanish, French and English. Sánchez chose to speak only Spanish for the half hour that he visited with his longtime friend while reliving perilous and productive times they spent together.

"I did all this in Spanish. The Spanish language so often can carry more meaning, more fealing," Sánchez said. "You think differently when you talk in Spanish."

The Spanish language and the culture that enveloped it was under fire well beyond Santa Fé, of course, as the new millennium approached. The proprietor of a bar in the south-central Washington town of Union Gap drew some heat in 1996 when it was reported that she had a wooden sign hanging above her cash register and bottles of liquor that read: "In the U.S.A. it's English or adios, amigo".

Joyce Ostrander ejected three Hispanics shooting pool and drinking beer when they refused to quit talking to one another in Spanish. "This is

America, where English is supposed to be the main language. We don't want Spanish gibberish here, and we mean it," she told the Yakima *Herald-Republic.*

Murky Waters of College Campuses and Swimming Pools

If teaching Americans to do better by one another was expected amid diversity's unease, little such teaching was occurring where it might have been expected most.

Hispanics have been cut off from the "life" of U.S. institutions, scholar Arturo Madrid told me in 1989. Madrid, who grew up in northern New Mexico's Tierra Amarilla, was serving at the time as president of the Tomás Rivera Center, an institute in California for policy studies on Hispanic issues.

Rather than find role models, encouragement and support at the nation's colleges and universities, Hispanics often encounter environments that are either hostile or indifferent, said Madrid. Madrid already had served as a university professor and went on to become a distinguished professor at Trinity University in San Antonio, Texas. He was honored at the White House in 1996 for his contributions to the humanities.

The dearth of minorities in meaningful positions on campuses of higher education was hardly a secret. It simply was something that most in authority did not like to talk about, doing so only when pressed into making comments.

It was April 1981 when the state advisory committee to the U.S. Commission on Civil Rights stated in an official report that women and minorities were lacking in faculty and top-level positions of New Mexico's six public colleges and universities.

University of New Mexico President William Davis said at the time that too few qualified minorities were available to be hired.

But eight years later another UNM president offered what to many was a stunning acknowledgment. Racism and bigotry taint hiring practices at UNM, Gerald May told state legislators. "We acknowledge that there is subtle racism and other forms of bigotry in our society, and UNM is no exception," he said.

May said that 78 percent of UNM's service and maintenance crews were Hispanic in 1987. In contrast, seven percent of the university's faculty were Hispanic in a state where nearly 40 percent of the population at the time was Hispanic

As bad as critics found hiring practices at UNM, May said, conditions historically have been worse at the state's other major universities and elsewhere. Among schools with worse records were New Mexico State University, the University of Texas at El Paso, the University of Texas, the University of Arizona and Colorado State University, May said.

Statistics seemed to support May. A 1985 state government report showed that 90 percent of all UNM employees earning at least $30,000 were Anglos, 6.8 percent were Hispanics. At NMSU it was 91.2 percent Anglos, 4.7 percent Hispanics; at New Mexico Tech it was 98.7 percent Anglos, 0 percent Hispanics; at Eastern New Mexico University and Western New Mexico University it was 95.6 pecent Anglos, 0 percent Hispanics.

Albuquerque Senator Manny Aragon, who was Senate president pro tem at the time, said universities were quick to complain about small pools of minority job applicants but far to slow to cultivate prospective job candidates. Among UNM graduate students in the spring of 1989, he said, there were 852 school-related jobs intended to support the students through school but only 65 were held by ethnic minorities.

Toney Anaya, the New Mexico governor from 1983–1986, used his position like few if any others ever had to press for greater opportunities for women and minorities at the state's higher education campuses.

And, Anaya said, not every university graduate wants employment on education campuses. For those who choose to pursue their growth and success elsewhere, New Mexico's banks needed to make more money available for loans to women and minorities, he said. It was time for institutional discrimination—subtle or otherwise—to end, he insisted.

Anaya was persistent in his calls, to the consternation of many, including ranking members of the education, banking and business communities.

The governor in a pair of good shoes stood no more than five-foot-eight and soon became derided as "the little Mexican." Bumper stickers called Anaya a "runt." Another called him a "pigmy."

Senate Majority Leader Michael Alarid of Albuquerque complained during a private meeting with Anaya and ranking Democratic senators that some in the Legislature were dismissing them as "sheepherders."

Bigotry, indeed, was evident in much of society, just as Gerald May, the former UNM president, asserted.

Just across the Río Grande from UNM, the university drew many of its students and more than a few of its employees from the city of Río Rancho. Río Rancho was a fast-growing city of 35,000 in 1990. It had its share of problems. One was that many people in the relatively young community didn't like Mexicans.

The city's mayor himself, Pat D'Arco, told me so in 1990 while we visited at a conference in Taos.

And when he said "Mexican," he referred to Hispanics in general, not Mexican citizens who in increasing numbers were crossing the international border.

Not many politicians speak so frankly. Very few spoke so frankly in those times about such a sensitive issue.

D'Arco only a few months earlier was elected mayor of the sprawling city west of the Río Grande. Many of Río Rancho's residents moved to that community directly from out of state.

"There's a lot of bigotry in Río Rancho," he said. He said he would not condone bigotry in a state where more than one-third of its citizens were Hispanic and about half were minorities.

D'Arco might have stepped into a hornet's nest in his young city but such nests had existed in New Mexico at least since the wagon trains began arriving in the territory from the Plains and further east.

"Much of the (bigotry) has gone underground. It's usually not so open anymore," one of New Mexico's former state auditors told me in the mid-1990s. Al Romero was auditor from 1983–1986 and worked as chief clerk of the state House of Representatives from 1959–1982.

Romero told me how as a teen growing up in Roswell during the 1940s, blacks and Hispanics were allowed to swim in the public pool just one day a week.

"The blacks and the Mexicans could swim on Friday because the water was going to be changed anyway on Saturday," Romero said.

By winning a seat on the Roswell City Council in 1955, Romero became the first Hispanic elected to a public post in Chaves County.

"They isolated *Hispanos* on the east side of town," he said. "First Street was a dividing line. You couldn't go to the barbershops on the other side. In the restaurants, they wouldn't feed you. The bars, they wouldn't let you in. Even the Catholic church was that way."

From the Roybal Files...
The Santa Fe New Mexican, Column, November 19, 1993
Angry Outbursts Might Cost Jaramillo Election, and More

There's a difference between spirit and anger. That's why I figure City Councilor Debbie Jaramillo will not be elected mayor of this lovely old town come March.

Too bad. She could have been a fine mayor had she not allowed herself to become her own worst enemy.

Jaramillo has spirit in her eyes and charm in her smile. But her talk—the words she expresses publicly and behind closed doors—too often reflects a woman bursting with anger.

Many in Santa Fé have cause to feel angry about the gentrification that has extended its tentacles across the prime parcels of our town with increasing fervor during the past dozen years.

Jaramillo is not alone in feeling that anger. She probably should be proud that so many have rallied behind her to tell Mayor Sam Pick, Mayor Pro Tem Phil Griego and Santa Fé Realtors that their enthusiasm for development ought to be bridled.

Many rallied behind Jaramillo largely because she was among the first to publicly and repeatedly challenge power brokers over the issue. She should be proud of that, too.

But fanning anger is inexcusable in a public official.

Spirit ought to be the driving force behind elected leaders of any town, particularly a town that could find its fortunes dipping as sharply as they rose after passing fancies move on to other quarters.

Pick has been a spirited mayor while championing Santa Fé as an "in" spot. He has stirred interest, pride and building activity. We're a bustling town with a relatively strong economy.

And it's not people with BMWs and Range Rovers who are out there hammering nails into two-by-sixes. The well-to-do were not the only ones to find opportunities under Pick.

But growth should mean more than new houses and new shopping centers. A small town that sheds its sense of community as it grows needs to re-examine how it is growing.

We're doing that, in a sense. Increasingly, we're meeting to acknowledge we have a problem, that important first step required to address most trouble. But outside of City Council meetings, antagonists generally are meeting separately. You don't find many of the city's middle class and poor meeting with the wealthy. And Anglos rarely assemble with minorities.

If we are able to resolve our problems without working on them together, we're destined to become a textbook study for community planning worldwide.

Clearly, we've got to change if we're not willing to become—and forever remain—Santa Fake. Pick is bowing out, at least partly because he's tired of being the target of criticism. Jaramillo wants to take over while preaching change like a fiery minister convinced damnation is just around the corner.

Sometimes, as if having scared even herself, Jaramillo retraces her steps and reaches a bit for moderation. It might work if she didn't invariably fall back into her reckless ways but, oh, she does.

Towns shouldn't be scared into change. Anger must not be our primary motivator. Anger breeds hate, and the City Different is too proud, too wise to become a hateful town.

If Jaramillo, as she said in our paper earlier this week, knows people who feel so oppressed that they are on the verge of bringing their shotguns down from the hills to change our community's course, then she has discovered some very dark corners, indeed.

But before you lock your doors and close your shutters, talk to others who consider themselves activists. I'd bet my only hat no one needs to hole up.

Spare us leaders whose most profound thought of the day is represented by their pledge to study an issue carefully and then try to do what is best. On that count, Jaramillo is right. We don't need more people who are content merely to play it safe for fear of making a mistake.

Jaramillo never could be a member of that crowd. But too bad she had let the spirit in her eyes and charm in her smile go to waste. Many people—minorities and Anglos—who have seen those qualities in Jaramillo have been willing to be convinced that this unorthodox politician is poised to inspire change, to skillfully orchestrate harmony where dissonance now exists.

Jaramillo lost a lot of those folks this week, though. If her destiny, before her remarks about mad men with shotguns, was to win the mayoral election by, say, 500 votes, her loose tongue probably cost her that victory margin, plus a good bit more.

Retracing her steps won't help this time. I'll bet my hat—and my boots—on it.

From the Roybal Files...
Albuquerque Journal column, September 2, 2007
Alberto Gonzales' Failures Are His Own

Disgraced Alberto Gonzales was the first Hispanic to serve as U.S. attorney general. He won't be the last. Nor should it be long before we see another Hispanic leading our nation's justice department. Overreaching and blind loyalty are human traits not limited to any particular race, gender or ethnic group.

From the start, President Bush earned my respect for his appointment of Gonzales. Why not, at long last, turn to a Hispanic? Competence and the ability to succeed are not withheld from any particular race, gender or ethnic group.

No, Gonzales' failures were his own. That he had a quick smile and easy gait made him no less a concern to the rest of us than attorneys general John Mitchell and Richard Kleindeinst of another era gone bad.

Mitchell was "as charming a conversationalist as one could meet," wrote historian Theodore H. White in "The Making of the President—1972." But, he added, Mitchell was "hardest of all the hard men around the President, by far."

Frequently at odds with Congress and the laws of our nation, Mitchell resigned as attorney general in 1972 to become chairman of the committee to re-elect President Richard Nixon. There, he added via the Watergate scandal and other misdeeds to a tarnished record seemingly driven by his loyalty to Nixon and because, White wrote, he was "bound into the President's affections."

As Mitchell's successor at the justice department, Kleindeinst promptly became embroiled in his own controversies, which included alleged collusion in anti-trust cases and lying to Congress.

Lying has a way of sinking careers in government, Thomas Jefferson observed more than 200 years ago. "He who permits himself to tell a lie once finds it much easier to do it a second and third time, till at length it becomes habitual; he tells lies without attending to it; and truths without the world's believing him," Jefferson said.

Along with his other shortfalls, Gonzales had reached the point where far too many in Washington and beyond did not believe him. No one less than the director of the FBI, who serves under Gonzales, testified before Congress in recent weeks and directly contradicted sworn testimony by Gonzales.

Gonzales has not been charged with perjury but one too many members of Congress have very publicly told the outgoing AG that they simply don't believe him anymore.

And just short of perjury, doubts were fanned by Gonzales when he appeared before members of Congress and repeatedly insisted that he did not know or could not remember information that someone in his position should have known or, at least, should have recorded so that it might be retrieved later.

Gonzales, we have learned, was among architects of President Bush's policies that have eroded our civil liberties, have promoted the inhumane abuse of others abroad that we would not tolerate for ourselves and which, in fact, expose our own defenders overseas to new, grave risks when captured.

Without question, our much-needed vigilance against terror (calling it a war helps justify abuse and creates more enemies eager to harm us) since 9-11 has made us all re-examine the rights we have promised one another; Gonzales seemingly was among those who dawdled little before plowing through some of our nation's most treasured principles.

Because Gonzales is Hispanic, New Mexico Governor and presidential candidate Bill Richardson has acknowledged that he was slow to call for the attorney general's resignation even while others began demanding it in the spring. It's because Gonzales is Hispanic that he wanted to give the AG ample opportunity to pull himself out of his tailspin, said Richardson, whose mother is Mexican.

It was generous of Richardson.

Count me among those who are more inclined to set the bar higher for trailblazers so that their conduct might disarm the lingering few who are still reluctant to admit that particular trails needed pioneering. (Please take note, governor, the next time you wonder what generates occasional heat from this corner.)

A native of San Antonio, Texas, Gonzales says he "lived the American dream" by being able to serve as U.S. attorney general. His worst days on the job were "better than his father's best days," he said, alluding to his family's struggles.

We all can be thankful that as head of the justice department, Alberto Gonzales was no John Mitchell. Gonzales is not a bad man. But he was not a good attorney general. The prominence that Hispanics are gaining at all levels of our society will ensure that Gonzales' performance does not preclude others with his background from ascending to The Dream, just as Mitchell's performance did not block the paths of others more accustomed to being tapped for top roles in government.

13
A Fuller Meaning of National Security

Institutionalized discrimination against minorities and women during the 1990s might not have been so overt as it was during Al Romero's times in southeastern New Mexico. But as events in the state capital, university campuses and beyond reflected, debilitating discrimination was still defiantly embedded.

In one major arena, it was both denied and defended under the guise of national security.

Several longtime employees of Los Álamos National Laboratory invited me to meet with them in a warm Chimayó home one cold night in February 1995. They were very unhappy and were poised to shake things up.

The nation's premier nuclear weapons lab since its secretive beginnings in 1943 had been run as if it were a little universe of its own, tethered to reality only by expectations that it was to maintain our nation's superlative position in the frightful global nuclear arms race.

If LANL had other missions, they seemingly were pushed to the rear where they wouldn't get in the way or where they might be forgotten altogether.

Arrogance had long been one of LANL's inescapable characteristics. It had grown thicker than the pine forests that surround the secluded laboratory positioned within the Jemez Mountains about 25 miles northwest of Santa Fé.

The lid was about to blow but some of the lab employees with whom I met that February evening in Chimayó at first insisted that they not be identified in my reporting. They feared for their jobs.

Their concerns were understandable but the evening's meeting, I told them, would have been a waste of time if I couldn't attach names to the comments and information they had just provided. I would need names and plenty of information directly out of laboratory records, I told them, if their story was to have legs, not only for a one-day report but for a long-term effort that would be required if even incremental changes at the lab were to be expected.

Once they committed to such an effort, I had to do as much myself.

"The laboratory is run by white, male, arrogant people," Loyda Martínez told me in that Chimayó meeting. "In this setting, where our jobs and livelihoods are at stake, our people have been easily intimidated."

Martínez, a lifelong Chimayó resident, worked as a systems manager with the Facilities, Security and Safeguard Division at LANL. She was among the fortunate ones. Records showed that Hispanic women made up less than .05 percent of the lab's large technical staff.

When Martínez and others meeting with me in Chimayó spoke of "our people," they for the most part referred to women and minorities who lived in the valleys below Los Álamos and commuted daily to help keep the weapons facility operating.

"I like my job but I've become an advocate for change because we've had enough," Martínez said. She was just one of a number of lab employees who had been meeting regularly to plan how to get LANL to do better by women and minorities.

I had spent much of the previous 25 years pressing for equal opportunity while working as a newsman along the length of New Mexico. So the group must have seen me as an obvious phone call when they decided to publicize concerns and the inequities that sparked them.

LANL at the time had a budget of around $1 billion and employed 7,000 people. An additional 3,000 worked for contractors retained by the lab. The lab's total annual economic impact to New Mexico was routinely estimated to be around four billion dollars, or about one and one-half times more than the entire state government budget at the time.

Lab Director Sig Hecker said more than half of all lab employees were either women or minorities. But the lab's own records showed that women and minorities fared much better at lower-level, lesser-paying jobs. Worse, it seemed as if they were meant to stay there.

The lab, for example, had 1,186 officials and managers at the upper end of the employment scale; 186 were Hispanic.

There were 3,001 employees classified as professionals; 396 were Hispanic.

Tom Baca, a former Santa Fé city manager and former state environment director, was the only Hispanic among ten program directors listed by the lab.

There was only one Hispanic among 63 directors or deputy directors in 1994.

Of 2,750 employees with salaries of $60,000 or more, four percent were Hispanic.

A 1993 audit by the U.S. Department of Labor found LANL out of compliance with portions of an executive order on affirmative action, including failure to monitor whether women and minorities were given "full and equal opportunity."

The lab late in 1994 was still out of compliance with federal guidelines on the employment of women and minorities in mid- and upper-level positions, according to a report filed by a ranking U.S. Energy Department official who visited the lab in August of that year.

If change were to be expected, it would require more than gentle prodding, said Chuck Montaño, a Los Álamos resident at the time and a longtime lab auditor.

"For sixteen years I played by their rules but I can't stay quiet anymore," he told me.

He wrote later, "I can tell you from personal experience, racial discrimination exists at the laboratory and is particularly pervasive in the way certain people are groomed for advancement and given recognition while others, minorities in particular, are forced to endure the indignity of chronic disappointment and denial."

Montaño in time told of one occasion when his treatment was particularly upsetting. "The person chosen over me ... had been with the laboratory for less than a year; prior to that he was a manager of a hamburger franchise."

Hecker argued repeatedly that the pool of qualified women and minorities was too small to accomplish everything that Montaño and others wanted.

Montaño countered, as he often did, with specifics from LANL's own records. He said Hecker and others liked to imply that PhDs were required for designated "managers" at the lab yet only 54 percent of the lab's managers had PhDs. At least 33 Hispanics had PhDs but none was in top management, Montaño said.

There also were 141 Hispanics with master's degrees and another 344 with bachelor's degrees. Why then, he asked, was there only one Hispanic among 63 senior-level managers; only three Hispanics among 83 program managers and other managers; only 17 Hispanics among 311 designated group leaders and project leaders?

Hecker said LANL, while still needing improvement, actually was doing better by minorities than other national laboratories across the country.

Okay, but how many of those laboratories had such substantial pools of well-educated minorities ready and eager for promotions? Montaño asked.

Amid the debate, the truth could not be escaped: Scientists and mathematicians were not needed—nor were they the ones hired—for many of the lab's top jobs or for those in the next tier down. Minorities and women for the most part were kept out of the mix.

In the opinion columns that I wrote to track with the numerous news stories that I submitted regarding LANL's controversial personnel practices, I was careful to stress over and again my allegiance to the lab's core mission and to its very substantial contribution in sustaining northern New Mexico's economy. But the lab's mission, like it or not, was very closely aligned with the lofty goal being embraced by many minority and women employees, I asserted.

"The lab's job," I wrote, "is nothing short of helping to ensure the nation's security—protecting the very ideals upon which our country was founded. Equal opportunity is primary among them. Allow me to say that again for emphasis: Equal opportunity is primary among them."

If lab employees who boldy set out to demand equal rights—not special rights—felt hopeful while turning to me to write about their mission, they confessed later that they approached me because they didn't think they had much choice.

"No one in New Mexico's mainstream news media has done more than David Roybal to promote equal rights and equal opportunity," wrote Chuck Montaño while his group's battle was picking up steam.

Gene Hill, owner of Añoranza Press in Albuquerque, described me to others during the period as "a paladin in the fight for our (Hispanic) rights and culture."

DARING TO LOOK INTO OUR OWN HOUSE

If the unsettled LANL employees had confidence in me, it was rooted at least partly in my aggressive approach to reporting on the discriminatory personnel practices at UNM and other New Mexico universities. Their attention also was caught by a lengthy opinion column I wrote for *The Santa Fe New Mexican* in the summer of 1993 telling of similar discriminatory practices within the news media.

The July 9, 1993, report was 43 inches long, 18 of them running across the bottom of Page B-1 in an eye-catching irregular column width ("bastard measure") 15 picas across.

The headline read: "Minorities find 'no room at the top' of news room management".

The lead paragraph read: "*The Santa Fe New Mexican* just named a new supervisor of reporters and in the process left undisturbed the long record of newspapers nationwide of keeping their news room management staff's largely free of minorities."

That record had very recently been documented by the National Association of Hispanic Journalists. A study by the group found that Hispanics made up just four percent of full-time news room employees at 57 of the country's largest newspapers. Hispanics accounted for 2.4 percent of news room managers at those papers.

Santa Fé County at the time, I reported, had what deomographers call a minority-majority population, nearly 50 percent of it being Hispanic.

Then I wrote, "Amid Santa Fé's substantial minority population, these are the names of news room managers hired or promoted at *The Santa Fe New Mexican* since mid-1987. Cousland, Mitchell, Blair, Taylor, Cole, Gaussoin, Friedenberg, Northup, Dean, Datko, Thornton, Walker, Scott, Dolan, Albano, Swibold and now, again, Datko.

The last Hispanic at the time to hold a news room management job at *The Santa Fe New Mexican* was Donicio Flores, who was editor for a year until mid-1987 while the paper was owned by the Gannett media group. Few—if any—other Hispanics had held newsroom management jobs since 1937 when the paper was sold by Jesús Baca.

Karen Datko came to Santa Fé in 1992 when she was hired by Rob Dean. Dean had arrived from Tacoma, Washington, to work as *The Santa Fe New Mexican's* assistant managing editor. Dean and Datko previously worked together in Montana and Washington State.

Dean before long was promoted to work as *The Santa Fe New Mexican's* managing editor and Datko was elevated to city editor.

Billie Blair, an Alabama native who arrived in Santa Fé via Taos, worked as the paper's associate publisher. Santa Fé CPA Stephen Watkins was its president.

All of us worked for the paper's owner, Robert M. McKinney.

I got along well with all of them. In fact, I used to joke that McKinney, a former U.S. ambassador to Switzerland under President John Kennedy, hired me three times to work at his newspaper: first, during the 1960s to deliver the paper to homes and businesses throughout the Española Valley as a young teen; then to report and work on the copy desk a couple of years after I graduated in 1974 from New Mexico State University; then to return to the news room staff as one of McKinney's first moves after he regained full control of the paper in the late 1980s following a brief, contentious partnership with the Gannett media group. (I worked for Gannett, including two years as *The Santa Fe New Mexican's* editorial page editor before leaving in 1983 to work as a Capitol reporter for Albuquerque's KOB-TV and later as an executive assistant to then-Governor Toney Anaya.)

To Rob Dean's credit, he remained fair and professional with me even after I had spoken frankly with him about the need for more minorities in his news room. We had those talks first in private and then, eventually, when I raised the subject in an open meeting of the news room staff after I grew increasingly disappointed with the lack of movement.

Months later I approached Dean and then Blair to inform them of my intent to surface from relative oblivion the National Association of Hispanic Journalists report about media hiring practices and add to it facts and comments to show how New Mexico's newspapers were doing by minorities.

I wasn't asking for their permission; I was giving them advance notice, knowing all the while that they might simply spike the column after I turned it in. That bridge, I concluded, would be crossed if we came to it.

I would, in effect, be using my bosses' own newspaper to prod them as well as managers at other publications around the state to face and improve on their shortcomings. Responses among my superiors were icy even though everyone knew there was nothing they could do, short of my termination, to keep me from engaging in the report.

Each of the managers was aware of at least half of my motivation: Dean in our private meetings had seemed receptive to my arguments about the need for greater inclusion. He was neither dismissive nor retaliatory when I felt compelled to aggressively express those arguments in an open staff meeting—but still inhouse and not aired within the greater community. Although I sensed that Dean would become an important ally, it was apparent even after the staff meeting that more was needed to move management beyond what it had long considered to be satisfactory practices. It was time for a balanced, well-researched story to be distributed within the community.

But I had another motivator, nearly as important as the first. And it was this one that I focused on while telling my superiors why I thought it would be smart for us to print and distribute the column that I proposed. They couldn't help but acknowledge that my earlier stories on discriminatory personnel practices at the state's universities and other institutions helped them sell papers. Further, they knew I wasn't going to back away from stories about discrimination in the future and, in fact, would dig to find more of them. We needed to pre-empt those who would try to turn the tables on us by publicly inquiring about conditions within our own house, I argued. To deflect negative attention from themselves, I said, these people would ask how minorities fare with personnel decisions at *The Santa Fe New Mexican*. Let's rob them of that ploy by reporting on ourselves first and publicly making commitments to do better, I implored; let's signal that we're going to look at them hard because we've already looked hard at ourselves.

No one jumped up and down with excitement.

In time, word came back from Watkins, who along with serving as the paper's president, was a close friend and confidant of Robert McKinney.

The paper's owner wouldn't object to the column that I proposed but he probably wouldn't be very happy if I did something like it more than once, I was informed.

I promptly went to work. Dean was among the first to be interviewed. His comments further fed my budding optimism that change would come to *The Santa Fe New Mexican*. The paper's pursuit of minority applicants for top posts, including his own recent hunts for city desk leaders, had been inadequate, he acknowledged.

Dean, since arriving at *The Santa Fe New Mexican*, had filled seven news room management posts. None went to a minority.

He said that responding to questions for my report made him more aware of the need to recruit and cultivate prospects, not simply advertise when job vacancies occur.

"It's a problem that we don't have minorities in our news room management and something should be done about it," he said.

The paper that reports on a community should "reflect the community," he acknowledged. "If your newspaper is to be ... a heartbeat of the community, the paper has to be of that community."

By those standards, *The Santa Fe New Mexican* was not the only newspaper in town that fell short. The *Albuquerque Journal North*, which began publishing in 1980, had yet to hire a Hispanic news room manager. Nor had the *Santa Fe Reporter* since it was founded in 1974.

"Our managing editor is our only news room manager and we don't get many applications from Hispanics for that position," said Hope Aldrich, who had been publisher of the *Santa Fe Reporter* since 1988.

Albuquerque Tribune Editor Tim Gallagher sounded much like Dean in his comments about minorities and newspapers even though the *Tribune*, too, was short in its numbers. The Tribune had two Hispanics on its news room management team.

"A newspaper, if it is to be a mirror to the community it covers, ought to look like that community, ought to have the same experiences as that community," Gallagher said. "We shouldn't do it to be politically correct, but for reasons that you accurately cover what's going on in your community."

At the state's largest newspaper, the *Albuquerque Journal*, Editor Gerald Crawford suggested that news room conditions were dictated by what was available. "I think there hasn't been a pool of Hispanic journalists from which to draw for management," he told me. "The pool obviously is getting larger now but all of this stuff takes time."

The *Journal* had one Hispanic on its news room management staff—the arts editor.

Crawford expressed a view different from those voiced by Dean and Gallagher when asked if accuracy and depth might suffer in news reporting and editorial advocacy without something close to a fair representation of minorities.

"Obviously you can cover the community without having a quota of minorities," Crawford said. "But it doesn't mean we don't have minorities on our staff and it doesn't mean that we can't improve our coverage because we can and have improved our coverage by having minority members who do represent different cultures."

Zita Arocha, a former reporter with *The Washington Post* who became a consultant to the National Association of Hispanic Journalists, disputed Crawford's contention that a lack of Hispanic journalists had made it hard for newspapers to include Hispanics in news room management.

"That's spurious. The pool is there," Arocha said. "Job fairs are one of the prime draws for Hispanic journalists. Hundreds attend these fairs every year. The problem is these people are not getting an opportunity to move up."

My own experience during decades of work in and around news rooms was that editors sought out others with whom they had worked in the past. It was evident in how Dean and Datko arrived and then advanced within *The Santa Fe New Mexican*. David Mitchell was brought in to work as managing editor prior to Dean, resulting in at least three of his prior acquaintances following him to Santa Fé.

My own experiences also told me that concerted efforts to find well-qualified minority applicants often came with rewards. As *The Santa Fe New Mexican's* bureau chief in Española during the late 1970s, I had three opportunities to fill reporting vacancies at the bureau. Working closely with then-Managing Editor Mike Stepanovich, we hired two young Hispanics and one Native American. A woman who made it to the final round of interviews ultimately had second thoughts about moving to New Mexico.

From the hires, Ed Moreno eventually advanced to become Capitol bureau chief for the Associated Press. Dan Herrera later became editorial page editor and then managing editor at the *Albuquerque Journal*.

Felix Gutierrez, who was vice president of The Freedom Forum in Arlington, Virginia, affirmed that newspaper managers usually didn't like to stray from what was familiar to them. "People tend to hire as managers people in their own image, people they are comfortable with, people who look like them, people who have their tickets punched in the same places. Few of us Hispanics fit into any of that."

Gutierrez's words reinforced an argument I had made to Dean in previous months about how a lack of minorities in the news room couldn't help but be reflected in what the paper put forward every day. I pointed Dean to the "citizen on the street" surveys that *The Santa Fe New Mexican* published regularly. Despite Santa Fé's substantial minority population, minorities were noticeably underrepresented in the photos and opinions printed as part of those surveys.

It wasn't bigotry, I told Dean. Reporters and photographers sent out to do those surveys simply approached people who looked like them, people who they were comfortable with.

Though there was nothing villainous in that particular work, I said, it easily could convey the impression that minority opinions don't count or, at least, that they don't count within offices of *The Santa Fe New Mexican*.

Dean bought into the argument and so did photo department chief Clyde Mueller, who followed Dean to Santa Fé. They began making changes in their hiring and recruitment as well as in how citizens were approached in the community.

Newspapers each day spend their time and efforts publicly exposing what others do, I wrote at the end of my July 1993 column. "So it's probably only fair that we tell folks once in a while what's going on in newspaper offices behind those fancy slogans that describe papers as the biggest, the best or the oldest."

MOVEMENT AROUND LANL AT LAST

In the end, pre-empting those who would have challenged us to look within our own house before confronting others about their shortcomings was successful. Hecker and others at LANL repeatedly defended themselves by insisting: 1) There are insufficient numbers of qualified women and minorities, 2) LANL does better than so many other federal institutions, 3) Unsettling statistics about personnel practices alone don't tell the full story.

Hecker said he could produce favorable statistics about the lab's work for every statistic that is unfavorable; pleasant stories from lab workers for each story that is unpleasant.

Democratic state legislative leaders weren't satisfied. Senate President Pro Tem Manny Aragon and House Speaker Raymond Sanchez, both Albuquerque Democrats, wrote in a letter that the record of minority hirings at the lab was "absolutely dismal." The letter was written to the chairman of the University of California Board of Regents. The university, under a non-competitive contract with the U.S. government, had managed LANL since its creation five decades earlier.

"Unusual if not disconcerting," a university spokesman said of the letter, seemingly suggesting the New Mexico legislators lacked standing. LANL received 99 percent of its annual $1 billion budget from the federal government. Hecker reminded legislators of that when the state Legislative Finance Committee scheduled a meeting in Los Álamos in June 1995 to discuss the lab's personnel practices.

"I can't remember when I felt less welcome, even in my own place," Hecker admonished state lawmakers who did little to hold their verbal punches despite Hecker's thinly veiled attempts to minimize their standing in what he clearly asserted was his place, not theirs.

Even a soft-spoken Representative Max Coll of Santa Fé couldn't restrain himself after acknowledging to Hecker that it was unlikely any of the state's universities could "pass the same litmus test we're asking you to pass." Coll described the lab's employment record as "pretty dismal" and even "abominable" in some cases.

Both Coll and Representative Luciano "Lucky" Varela, also a Santa Fé Democrat, openly expressed doubt about information provided by the lab.

Varela said Hispanics tend to be "tolerant and passive" but added he was not surprised by the sort of pressure increasingly being brought to bear on the issue.

Senator Ben Altamirano, a Silver City Democrat and perhaps even more mild-mannered than Coll, told Hecker that continued pressure from state legislators could be expected. "I think for a long time we've rolled over and played dead," he said.

Stories about conditions at LANL began multiplying to the consternation of many.

"This is a place filled with minds that can solve any problem, except the oldest one—how to get along with your neighbor," Jim Carrier wrote in the *Sunday Denver Post* in June 1995, four months after my lengthy series of reports began appearing in *The Santa Fe New Mexican*.

Carrier, too, was caught by startling disparities at the lab.

"Women from pueblos in the valley cleaned houses and did laundry (in Los Álamos)," he wrote of the lab's early days. Hispanic women were secretaries, and Hispanic men began working as guards and technicians, jobs they still dominate."

Anglo men at the top; almost everyone else below.

And in more ways than one, the system as it was structured fueled disparities. Los Álamos public schools for years had received support from the federal government—seven million in 1995—to go along with state funding.

Art Blea, superintendent of the Pojoaque Valley Schools in 1995, said the additional money going to Los Álamos schools allowed the district to spend 38 percent more on each pupil than neighboring districts. He said the statewide average operational fund expenditure per pupil in 1993–1994 was $3,508. It was $5,715 in Los Álamos.

The average returning teacher salary statewide that year was $27,922. It was $38,624 in Los Álamos, Blea said.

"Scientists' kids (get) the best education in New Mexico, thanks to federal subsidies," Carrier wrote for the Denver paper.

Although slow to jump into the fray, most of New Mexico's U.S. congressional delegation eventually added to the pressure being placed on the lab.

U.S. Representative Bill Richardson of Santa Fé, the self-proclaimed "Fighter for New Mexico," had been remarkably silent while hundreds of his constituents did battle with the lab on multiple fronts. He was about to be criticized publicly by some of those constituents for his uncharacteristic silence when in November 1995 he sent a letter to the U.S. Energy secretary saying he was unconvinced that the University of California's contract to manage LANL should be renewed in 1996.

Richardson said there was "a real disconnect" between the university and residents of northern New Mexico.

Richardson was finally moved to publicly address concerns after 600 LANL employees were fired or were urged to take early retirement early in the autumn of 1995. The lab said it had to streamline its workforce amid new budget constraints. Because most of the lost jobs were in support staff positions, many who were pushed out were minorities, including some who called for better opportunities.

U.S. Senator Jeff Bingaman, an ever-cautious Santa Fé Democrat, initially said he wasn't in a position to thoroughly look into complaints about LANL coming from constituents but he publicly urged Energy Department officials to "continue the process they started (in August 1994) to promote diversity."

U.S. Senator Pete Domenci, an Albuquerque Republican and New Mexico's senior member in Congress, largely refrained from addressing mounting concerns but fumed about negative publicity aimed at the laboratory. Support for the lab, not negative publicity, was needed to ensure that the lab's budget was not jeopardized, he insisted. He was irate that we all did not fall into line.

"Pleas for aid fall on Domenici's deaf ears", read the headline over a column I wrote in February 1996.

The column began: "Outwardly, U.S. Sen. Pete Domenici has lent little, if any, help in response to the cries of discrimination ringing today from corners of Los Álamos National Laboratory.

"He didn't change his course this past week while addressing about 150 people in Española about management practices at LANL, including the messy termination of hundreds of employees last year."

There was little mystery to the senator's approach. With the end of the Cold War, Domenici and others in New Mexico's congressional delegation worried about losing the lab, or big parts of it. Military tensions had eased and there were increased calls for fiscal restraint.

The University of California had done everything required by its contracts while overseeing LANL's management, Domenici insisted. If more was needed out of the lab and the university, then a new contract with UC could reflect that, he said.

I used that February 1996 column to remind Domenici that we were not in total disagreement. Mutual respect had run through our association dating back to the 1970s.

"Three cheers for Domenci's unflagging support for LANL," I wrote. "The lab, indeed, has been instrumental in defending America. But the defense has not just been of America, the land: the mountains, plains,

New Mexicans pressing for change at Los Álamos National Laboratory expressed displeasure with what they considered lack of support from U.S. Senator Pete Domenici.

deserts and beaches. The defense largely has been of America, the ideals. Principal among those ideals is the concept of equal opportunity for all.

"People in this country in pursuit of equal opportunity are not supposed to have to wait for new provisions to be inserted into old contracts.

"Raw numbers out of LANL suggest such opportunity has been sorely lacking at the lab. Domenici is far too good a politician, far too good a persuader, to think he could not aggressively stand up for some constituents who have been left to feel like second-class citizens without jeopardizing the future of a national laboratory that few here want to lose."

What did Domenici think?

He had read enough from me and he met with my superiors to try to get me fired.

One man with whom I visited regularly expressed his displeasure directly to me. It was during a time when people could walk right off the street into *The Santa Fe New Mexican's* news room and start talking to people as if they had stepped into the local post office or Sears department store. I liked the openness because along with the entry of colorful characters from within the community, it led to more than a few good news tips.

"I read your column the other day," a bearded Colonel George R. Hawthorne told me one morning after walking directly to my desk. "I read you once in a while even though I think you're a racist."

Hawthorne had served in the U.S. Army Corps of Engineers for 38 years. He was assigned to Los Álamos in 1945 to work as part of the Manhattan Project—development of the atomic bomb.

Comments like the left-handed compliment expressed by Hawthorne did nothing to move me from my mission. I was reminded regularly of my purpose by others who walked into *The Santa Fe New Mexican's* news room several times a week. Santa Fe ad man, radio personality and former state senator, Edmundo Delgado, was among them.

"What have you done for the little guy today?" Delgado would begin each of his approaches to me no matter how early in the morning. It's how he greeted many people, as if to remind us that, no matter what our mission, leaving people behind shouldn't figure into the mix.

Support took more-formal channels in other quarters. The Hispano Round Table of New Mexico, which claimed to represent 40 organizations with 36,000 members statewide, presented me an award in 2003 as recognition of my reporting to promote equal opportunity.

As reporting unfolded, LANL's need to be a better neighbor to surrounding communities became a central theme among those who finally acknowledged that a change in course was needed. Rather than merely complain that there weren't enough minorities and women to fill more than a relative few of the lab's most-rewarding positions, LANL needed to devote more resources to prepare residents of Española, Pojoaque and beyond to further contribute to the lab's mission and share in its rewards.

Even Hecker in time was pressed to acknowledge that LANL could not "live as an island" within northern New Mexico.

Helping to further the education of its workforce and the workers' children would be an important first step.

If the Los Álamos School District had long been the prince of the region's public education, surrounding schools had been the paupers.

It wasn't just the seven million in federal aid the Los Álamos schools received annually because of the lab. The lab's proximity to schools on the Hill assured ready access to considerable high-tech equipment and to the scientists who make it all work.

"My brother-in-law teaches at Alcalde Elementary and he doesn't even have access to a computer at that school," said Albert Jirón, an Española resident who worked for the lab as a community relations specialist. "We (at the lab) should at least be able to help him with a computer."

I wrote in a February 1995 column, "That Los Álamos National Laboratory has been allowed to thrive on the Hill for so long while all but neglecting its neighbors in key areas of development is unbelievable."

Three months later I wrote: "The substantial federal aid funneled annually to Los Álamos schools is rooted in the desire to make public education there exceptional, better than what might be expected in the state's other 88 school districts.

"The Department of Energy is obligated under contract to allot millions to the Los Álamos schools to 'provide an education program at a level which will not impede the recruitment of personnel essential to DOE's program' at the national lab.

"Stated simply, if Los Álamos schools were no better than those in surrounding districts, the lab might not be able to attract all the top-level employees it requires.

"Needless to say, the policy for decades has bred resentment among educators, students and parents outside Los Álamos."

Something had to change.

Even the University of California began to acknowledge as much. University administrators suggested that Hecker needed to take much of the initiative to address local concerns, including mounting calls for greater so-called economic outreach into surrounding communities.

Hecker pledged to press for greater educational outreach but at the time took comfort in $12,000 that had just been put aside by the lab to boost scholarship awards for New Mexico students. Creation of the financial pot was trumpeted from as far away as the president's office at the University of California.

"It's a start," university spokesman Rick Malaspina said of the $12,000.

It also was about the size of the salary raise granted that year to just one of LANL's ranking officials, Deputy Director Jim Jackson.

Loyda Martínez, the lab employee and advocate from Chimayó, asked in one of our first meetings of 1995 why Los Álamos schools shouldn't be pressed to share with surrounding school districts the federal wealth bestowed upon them annually. Martínez told me she likely was thinking big by voicing the idea. But she quickly was encouraged to think bigger by a ranking Energy Department official.

"Why share? Why not ask for separate funding? That's what I was told," said Martínez.

Months later, Domenici began recommending the same kind of neighborly cooperation that Martínez proposed.

Domenici, without acknowledging the resentment that had accumulated over years, wrote a letter to then-Energy Department Secretary Hazel O'Leary. He told O'Leary that parents of 414 students in the Pojoaque Valley Schools work in Los Álamos. And there were more in the Española Valley.

At long last, Domenici said Los Álamos no longer could be treated as "a lone city on a hill."

Our reporting on the disparities continued, and in 1997 the Los Álamos National Laboratory Foundation was created. In June 1998, *The Santa Fe New Mexican* applauded the foundation for issuing grants that totaled three quarters of a million dollars to 68 community organizations serving northern New Mexico. The foundation awarded $1 million more to educational enrichment grants to school districts within the lab's workforce area.

The foundation was created as a public-benefit corporation governed by a board of trustees representing the University of California, LANL management, corporate partners and communities of northern New Mexico. Its contributions grew handsomely over the years.

Hecker, who had been LANL director since 1985, was replaced in 1997 by John Browne. Browne was LANL director until 2003 when he was replaced by Peter Nanos. Nanos held the post for just two years. First Browne then Nanos claimed they had ushered in new, positive eras for the lab's workforce but critics dismissed the assertions as bogus.

One-third of the lab's workers were said to have salaries of $100,000 or more. Hispanics still made up less than three percent of those workers, said Ralph Arellanes, a former chairman of the Hispano Round Table.

Some complained that even if Browne was sincere about changing the lab's culture, too many managers below him were slow or unwilling to join the effort.

Within LANL's better-paying jobs, hirings and promotions continued to benefit Anglo men over minorities and women, the U.S. General Accounting Office reported in 2002.

A beleaguered Browne saw his successor, Nanos, similarly unable to change the lab's culture to the satisfaction of those who felt neglected—no, violated—for so long.

The University of California in 2003 for the first time was required to compete for LANL's management contract. The university partnered with three other parties to form a private company that eventually was awarded a seven-year contract.

Some New Mexico leaders, including former Governor Toney Anaya and Santa Fé state Senator Roman Maés, lobbied for the University of New Mexico or one of the state's other universities to be included in a LANL management partnership. Something like that was needed, they argued, to help ensure that concerns of New Mexicans were adequately addressed during a new long-term contract.

Hecker wasn't sure that any of New Mexico's universities were ready for what he considered to be the big leagues. He met privately with then-Governor Gary Johnson to ensure that the proposal didn't get far.

By 2018, LANL's annual budget had grown to two billion dollars and the lab's importance to the nation's security was taking on new meaning. Tensions among global powers that eased following the end of the Cold War festered anew. Those who worried that the lab might be lost entirely should a lasting world peace break out fretted needlessly. Those who hoped that the lab would become a bright example for equal opportunity found themselves hoping for too much.

Cover ups that had abounded on the Hill since the secretive lab's opening continued to the surprise of perhaps only a few. Chuck Montaño, the longtime LANL auditor who was part of the Chimayó meeting in February 1995, wrote a book that told of such cover ups and their consequences. Several of the chapters in Montaño's book, *Los Alamos: Secret Colony, Hidden Truths*, were at the core of an hour-long CBS news report that aired in the summer of 2018.

Back at *The Santa Fe New Mexican*, Editorial Page Editor Inez Russell Gómez in 2018 used a facebook post to trumpet yet another general excellence award for the paper. Her post expressed pride not only in the award but in what she described as the most-diverse newsroom in New Mexico.

General excellence awards became commonplace during Rob Dean's tenure as a ranking editor of *The Santa Fe New Mexican.* In time, he recognized that diversifying the paper's staff, like excellence in reporting, had to drive his decisions. If *The Santa Fe New Mexican* could boast of having the state's most-diverse news room in 2018, it was because concerted efforts were made to get the paper onto a path that it previously had not seen as its own. It took a while. Once found, the path was not to be abandoned. People like Russell Gómez helped ensure that it wasn't.

Strides undeniably were made since the late 1970s when I was pulled out of my post in the Española bureau to drive my pickup nearly 80 miles one way to report on a horrible story that had just scarred the Catholic church and a tiny Hispanic community along the Pecos River in San Miguel County. Editors concluded no one in their own Santa Fé news room could speak enough Spanish to communicate effectively with villagers or even approach them with much confidence.

I dutifully tended to the story even while recognizing that the newspaper to which I was so emotionally attached had to do better. I first came to the conclusion as a teen during the 1960s upon seeing that *The Santa Fe New Mexican* had to rely on its sports editor and its high school stringer in Española to effectively speak the language most relied upon by men and women engaged in the budding land grant movement.

This book's author questioned Bill Clinton after his handlers kept him from meeting with assembled Hispanic leaders in Albuquerque. (Photograph by LeRoy N. Sánchez)

Pressing for change consumed me at times during ensuing decades.

One day in 1996 then-Publisher Billie Blair called me into her office to say that my salary had reached the highest point in *The Santa Fe New Mexican's* pay scale. Newspapers everywhere were hurting, she said. At *The Santa Fe New Mexican*, pay raises that year would be small. My pay would stay the same.

The Santa Fe New Mexican was still making good money, just not as much as it was accustomed to.

I had told Blair and others years earlier that as long as the paper was making money, my signal for leaving would be a flat salary, a salary that failed to acknowledge even in the smallest way that I was contributing to the paper's earnings.

My time was up.

Rob Dean and Karen Fuhrhop, my longtime dear companion and fellow employee at *The Santa Fe New Mexican*, organized a fond farewell party.

I promptly opened a small government and public relations office and was retained parttime by the *Albuquerque Journal* to write weekly columns.

I was working PR under contract with the Santa Fe Indian School during the late 1990s when Senator Domenici and I found ourselves seated at the same private meeting with Superintendent Joseph Abeyta and other school administrators. Early, controversial phases of the school's campus expansion were a central topic. Senator Domenici asked some questions then offered his thoughts in a few sentences before turning to me and saying, "Clean that up for me. You'll know how to make it sound good."

Billie Blair moved on to consulting after leaving *The Santa Fe New Mexican*. She was appointed to the LANL Foundation Board of Trustees in 2016. It was an ironic twist.

I keep on my desk at home a small photo of Robert McKinney and me as a reminder of my long association with the state's newspaper baron. A company party was organized at the Santa Fé Country Club to celebrate McKinney's birthday while I still worked at the paper. Employees mingled with one another on one side of a swimming pool while McKinney and his wife, Marielle, visited at a distance with a handful of well-wishers at the opposite side. After a while, a frail Marielle McKinney walked slowly to where employees had assembled and gently placed a hand on one of my arms. Her husband, she said, asked if I would stand with him for a picture.

McKinney, to be honest, didn't hire me three times. He had little if any interest in the young teens enlisted for home delivery of his paper back in the 1960s. But there was contact between us beginning in the mid-1970s as my years as a reporter began unfolding. His high-profile dispute with Gannett leading to his resumption as owner of *The Santa Fe New Mexican* was rooted in the refusal of Gannett's local managers to endorse Democrat Bruce King in the 1978 race for governor. U.S. District Judge Santiago Campos of Santa Fé noted in his records that McKinney insisted that editorial page editor Robert Storey be replaced. He eventually was. At the age of 28, I was brought in from my post as bureau chief in Española as Storey's successor with both McKinney and Gannett agreeing on the move.

Nearly 40 years later, McKinney's daughter, Robin, walked me through part of the family's 100-acre ranch in Nambé as we discussed information for an informal family memoir. Robin had assumed ownership of the ranch and the paper years earlier. Her father, she said, planted many of the trees on the ranch, Rancho Las Acequias. I think he liked trees more than he liked people, she said, acknowledging her father's reputation in some circles as a difficult man.

I've kept the pool-side photo of Robert McKinney and me, my left arm resting across his shoulders, for good reason. It speaks to so much time in my life, not all of it accompanied by rhyme and reason. McKinney, just as he had nodded to reluctantly authorize my reporting about inequalities in his news room staff a few years earlier, might well have nodded when the time came to tell me that I had reached the limits of the paper's pay scale.

From the Roybal Files...
Albuquerque Journal, Column, April 17, 2007
Painful War Souvenir Trumps Unreturned Salute

My dad, Amos, spends a lot of time these days sitting at the edge of his bed or at his chair alongside the kitchen table massaging his left leg as if he's trying to rub life back into an old friend. For months now, most of the rubbing has been in vain. Cold days are particularly difficult for this man whose body and mind are under assault by age.

The leg is stiff, like a board. It has been since my 83-year-old father was 21. Dad was wounded in World War II, his knee shattered and rendered as useless as a military amphibian tractor had it strayed onto the back yard meadow of the Truchas home that he left for battlegrounds overseas.

Ken Burns isn't a part of dad's world. Nor is the controversy stirred by Burns' new documentary about the war that so affected my father's life.

Mention the name Ken Burns and dad is liable to search his memory of students whose respect he earned during 38 years of high school woodworking classes or perhaps someone who, during his proud days in the Lions Club, might have helped him hang Old Glory throughout the Española Valley on holidays.

For more than six decades, dad has hauled around a leg left bum on a bloody theater of World War II, where he served his country with pride. Most of the time since returning, he all but refused to acknowledge that the leg was bad, rejecting even a special parking permit for his vehicles until a few short years ago when simple walking began to take its toll.

Dad is one of the thousands of forgotten patriots who suddenly, unexpectedly are being discussed alongside Burns' 14-hour war documentary to be aired on KNME-TV later this year.

"Hispanic veterans will see no reflection of their service and valor in World War II," this newspaper said referring to the documentary in a recent editorial. "How can such a gaping omission be explained?"

The omission strikes at half a million Hispanics who fought in WWII and at their families who struggled through their absence. Hispanics have fought on the front lines of U.S. wars in numbers disproportionately larger than what is reflected in our nation's general population.

Burns and those who worked with him on the long film said veterans interviewed were selected from a few "quintessentially American" towns. It's America as defined by old, exclusionary terms.

Hispanic groups around the country threw up their arms in disbelief upon learning of the documenatary's omission. Finally, last week pressure forced concessions from Burns. He won't reassemble the documentary to include Hispanic contributions and sacrifices, but he pledged to append the film so that Hispanics are recognized, perhaps at the beginning or the end.

My father took little, if any, note of it all. Dwelling on slights or on those who might treat him as an afterthought has never been his way.

Dad earned a bachelor's degree at Highlands University after the war and settled to raise a family in the quiet neighborhood of Lower San Pedro just south of Española. Residing a few houses away in one direction was one of the area's top auto body repairmen, Luis López, a survivor of the 1942 Bataan Death March, where 1,800 New Mexicans were among the tortured captives.

Just down the road in the opposite direction lived another Bataan survivor, Paul Trujillo, a highly respected, softspoken agricultural extension agent. Other neighbors included Augustine Martínez, himself a WWII veteran and officer of the American Legion who took great pride in helping to coordinate graveside military ceremonies for the region's many war vets.

Shocking images of WWII will forever be etched in my uncle Mauricio Chávez's mind as he still tends to ranching duties at his El Rito home. My uncle was among U.S. sailors who helped recover bodies from ships that were sunk during the 1941 enemy attack on Pearl Harbor.

Hispanic veterans of WWII get the same treatment in Ken Burns' film that was long accorded by our nation to the Tuskegee Airmen, the all-black fighter squadron that served with distinction during WWII. The airmen were deprived of nearly all recognition until earlier this month when they were awarded the Congressional Gold Medal in the Capitol Rotunda.

Separately, President Bush saluted them, saying he hoped it helped "atone for all the unreturned salutes and unforgivable indignities."

Unreturned salutes and unforgiveable indignities: There should be no room for them in our lives.

Back at home it's controversy that finds little room for mischief in my father's life as he tends faithfully to his leg. His massaging seems aimed at both rubbing out pain and rubbing in strength. I imagine him talking silently to it in his mind, not cursing it for wanting to give up but coaxing it with the confidence of an old soldier: We've come this far together; we can make it the rest of the way.

14
A Stench at the Back Door

A stinky surprise greeted students at Santa Fé's southside Capital High School minutes after they stepped outdoors one day in April 1991 in search of environmental pollution.

"We found it, big time," said Christina Howard, teacher of the school's gifted and enriched projects class.

Ten minutes into their walk amid high desert flora and fauna, the 25 students came upon raw sewage bubbling up in an arroyo on the school grounds.

Howard said there was a pool of sewage—some of which was beginning to rot—about half the size of her classroom.

"Some of it was running down the slope and it apparently had been there for a while because there was green grass growing around it," she said.

The teacher and her students were accompanied by a guest speaker, Kathy Buehler of the Santa Fé Sierra Club. Buehler told the teens the discovery should serve to show not only that environmental problems exist right at home but that each one of the students could do something to correct them.

"We walked out about 50 feet and suddenly the smell hit us," Howard said. "When we got closer, the students said things mostly like, 'Oh, gross!'

"'Oh, this is making me sick!'

"'Oh, we can't believe this!'"

Howard said it had been difficult rousing interest among students for the environmental excursion.

"One of the other teachers had told them, 'Come on, you never know what's going to happen.'"

Discovery of dumped septic waste certainly wasn't supposed to happen.

Disposal of wastes—multiple kinds of waste—increasingly had drawn attention in New Mexico since the early 1970s, spurred along by adoption in Washington of the national Clean Water Act in 1972. Among its many provisions, the federal law funded construction of sewage treatment plants across the country. Revisions in 1981 led to federal-state partnerships intended to improve wastewater treatment and discourage illegal dumping.

In New Mexico, legislation adopted in 1971 authorized creation of a state agency to more-closely monitor environmental protection. State regulations governing pumping and disposal of septic waste drew particular attention in 1978 revisions, which were continuously modified through 2013 when an administrative code for the state's Environment Improvement Department was adopted.

For decades, it wasn't entirely uncommon for people out on a stroll in remote areas to come upon the kind of smelly, unhealthy surprise that Christina Howard's students encountered in their excursion.

Septic wastewater disposal was poorly regulated in this state of vast open spaces. Neighborhoods and entire communities not served by municipal sewage systems rely on private entrepreneurs to empty septic tanks and grease pits into their modified tanker trucks, more than twice a year at some homes.

Waste, once collected by the truckers, didn't always end up in established wastewater treatment plants. Fees are charged at those plants. And driving to those plants could translate into a roundtrip of an hour or more. So truckers often unloaded what they collected in hidden sections of arroyos, atop prickly pear cactus on sandy slopes of isolated foothills or on alfalfa fields where owners felt discharges fertilzed their plants.

Changes became inescapable as New Mexico's population grew and an increasing number of residents became concerned about potential ground water contamination.

It was October 1989 when a Santa Fé County government official said publicly what many had known or, at least, suspected for years. "We're aware that there's a tremendous amount of (illegal sewage) dumping," county Field Operations Director Ron Martínez told the Santa Fé Board of County Commissioners.

He reported that at least seven of the 35 sewage-hauling companies based in Santa Fé County and perhaps others that work out of Bernalillo and Río Arriba counties were dumping wastes illegally in Santa Fé County arroyos and other off-road sites

County commissioners went to work on an ordinance that would make such acts of illegal dumping criminal acts punishable by jail time and substantial fines.

Until then, illegal dumpers could be taken to court only on civil charges, and then only if action were initiated by the state attorney general or the state engineer. Clearly, the threat of civil action was not enough, Martínez asserted.

Jacob Viarrial, then governor of Pojoaque Pueblo, said illegal sewage dumping had become a serious threat to ground water through much of the region extending from Santa Fé to Chamita north of Española. He pledged to build a new treatment plant on pueblo land to cut travel times of truckers.

"It's a very serious problem and it's not going to get any better unless we address it today," Viarreal said.

Eventually, regulations set hefty fines for anyone found to be disposing wastewater anywhere except at designated treatment plants. Because of the fees charged at those plants as well as the time and fuel spent to get to them, costs rose for truckers, who then passed along expenses to homeowners. The fee for emptying residential septic tanks, long set at around $100, soon nearly doubled in some cases.

That's Waste of a Different Color

In 1979, waste of a far different kind was drawing attention. Radioactive waste for decades had accumulated at Los Alamos National Laboratory only half an hour drive from Santa Fé. Conditions were unfolding simultaneously in New Mexico and in the U.S. Capitol that would lead to construction of a controversial road for handling disposal of that dangerous waste. To many New Mexicans, the waste was much-more disgusting than what Capital High School students came to find so repulsive.

The road for transporting the transuranic radioactive waste around populated Santa Fé would pass within a mile or so from Capital High. It would be used by large trucks, each carrying multiple large cylindrical containers specially designed to transport the dangerous waste accumulated at nearyby LANL since the early 1940s.

Transuranic radioactive waste included plutonium-contaminated material like gloves, clothings, rags, tools, machinery, demolition rubble and sludge that came in contact with radioactive substances during research and production of nuclear weapons.

As the nation's premier nuclear weapons lab, LANL had tons of such waste and at least some of it had been stored carelessly, exposed to the elements, for far too long.

The U.S. Congress in 1979 authorized construction of the massive Waste Isolation Pilot Plant in the Chihuahuan Desert about 26 miles east of Carlsbad near the Texas border in New Mexico's southeastern corner.

It was to spread over 16 square miles and come to include multiple large rooms buried within ancient salt beds approximately 2,000 feet below the surface. It would be the world's first deep geological repository for radioactive waste.

WIPP was planned to accept defense-related radioactive waste from Los Álamos and more from other federal installations in the West.

It would stir heated debate for years among more than just environmentally conscious high school students.

Democrat Jeff Bingaman, while serving as state attorney general, filed a federal lawsuit in 1981 to ensure that the federal government didn't merely move in its equipment, dig a deep hole then send a letter to the Capitol in Santa Fé to inform New Mexicans the radioactive waste dump was finished, safe and ready for the glowing garbage.

A court settlement of the suit assured the state that specific tests would be conducted at the WIPP site throughout construction. Dr. George Goldstein, state Health and Environment secretary at the time, won assurances as part of the suit that New Mexico would get more than just reports. Feds promised certified data (information scientifically proven to be reliable and valid) along with raw test samples for its own analysis.

Bingaman, Goldstein and others had to be resolute. Promises from the U.S. Department of Energy charged with overseeing the project were hard to obtain and they didn't come without considerable double-talk from Washington.

WIPP, simply, was not one of those plums the federal government periodically dishes out to states—an Air Force base or, perhaps, a hydroelectric dam. It was officially described as a repository for the federal government's transuranic waste but many in New Mexico knew that it very quickly could be designated to receive more-dangerous, higher-level radioactive waste. It was the type of government project that most people in other states had fought to keep out of their midst.

Bingaman and his staff drew at least some comfort from the way New Mexico's lawsuit against the feds was settled. Assistant Attorney General Joe Canepa said the federal government no longer could act like a big train that rushes by, offering the state only an occasional post card telling New Mexicans where it is.

Bingaman said the lawsuit pulled the feds away from being able to tell the state that it's going to get a fair trail...and then be hung.

Among assurances wrung out of the legal settlement signed by then-Governor Bruce King, was a right retained by New Mexico to go back into court should it ever feel wronged. Not surprisingly, though, the state would not have veto power over the project. With such power, it was doubtful that any state would allow a huge dump for radioactive waste to be constructed within its boundaries.

New Mexicans in much of the state pressed their elected leaders to secure as many safety assurances as they could from the feds. Still, those same leaders as well as the locally elected officials in southeastern New Mexico recognized that many of their constituents in communities near the planned WIPP site looked upon the project as an economic boon that should not be chased away.

An early federal document projected that the total direct impact from both construction and associated non-construction WIPP activities would approach $129 million in Eddy and Lea counties during a three-year construction period. Indirect effects within the private sector would total an additional $115 million, according to the projection. Some 140 to 150 employees would be needed at the site once the plant opened, and the feds projected that $35.6 million would be spent annually during its operation, which was estimated to be 35 years.

Ah, but costs of federal projects have a way of soaring beyond projections. This particular project, because of its nature, was followed by legal challenges, site accidents and other delays. Testing at WIPP was scheduled to begin in 1988 but was delayed until the early 1990s. Costs after 20 years of construction soared beyond $1 billion.

And large sums also had to be spent on New Mexico roads in preparation for waste shipments. The State Highway Department by 1982 had asked for nearly seven million in federal highway funds for major repairs to at least eight roads that would become WIPP transportation routes.

Jimmie Glenn, a maverick Republican serving then on the state Corporation Commission, called upon the feds to provide thousands of dollars to study how transportation of hazardous wastes could best be regulated.

"We need to know how to route. We need to know what to do in case of a spill," Glenn said in January 1982.

Waves of new concern spread in the summer of 1991 when an independent oversight agency reported that nuclear waste planned for storage at WIPP would pose a greater threat of fire and explosion than previously reported by the federal government. Numerous spontaneous ignitions at waste sites operated by the U.S. Energy Department supposedly had been disregarded in the government's latest safety report.

Richard Miller with the group, Concerned Citizens for Nuclear Safety, considered the WIPP project to be a terrible idea. "It's Stone-Age technology to dig a hole somewhere and cover up your waste, hoping that everything's going to be fine," he said.

Democrat U.S. Representative Bill Richardson of Santa Fé over time became increasingly vocal while pursuing safety assurances and funds from the Congress. He took the brunt of the criticism generated in Washington among those who grew impatient with mounting demands while the $1 billion waste dump remained unused.

If WIPP's opening was to face continued delays, maybe the nation's nuclear waste should be dumped in Santa Fé, said an exasperated U.S. Representative John Rhodes, an Arizona Republican.

The battle over WIPP's opening went on and by the end of 1991, it was proposed in Washington that New Mexico be paid a lump sum of $387 million in return for housing WIPP.

Bingaman, who in 1982 was elected to the U.S. Senate, and Democratic Governor Bruce King worked to get all they could from Washington while trying not to further antagonize Washington. Bingaman referred to King as one of New Mexico's most pragmatic politicians. If so, Bingaman wasn't far behind. Both knew that pragmatic politicians couldn't expect the U.S. government to walk away from a billion-dollar project without ever using it.

Nor, though, did they want to be seen as pushovers in a battle where so many of their constituents felt bullied and at risk. King at one point suggested he might use the State Police to block waste shipments from entering New Mexico. His threat came late in 1991 after U.S. Energy Secretary James Watkins said he would send the first waste shipment to WIPP before the feds had secured all necessary state permits to dispose of radioactive waste in New Mexico. State Attorney General Tom Udall filed a federal lawsuit in Washington to block shipments.

Eight more years went by and in the end Governor King sought to assure New Mexicans that everything possible had been done to protect their safety as well as the environment.

The first shipments of waste arrived from LANL in March of 1999.

Protesters followed the WIPP project through all its phases. They became a common sight at key Santa Fé intersections. Some pledged to lie across roads to block shipments to the plant near Carlsbad.

Initially, the first shipments were expected to come from out of state. Republican U.S. Sen. Pete Domenici of Albuquerque speculated that the actual opening of WIPP could be rather anticlimactic. Protesters would not be able to block caravans of waste coming in because only one or two trucks would be ready for transport when the plant opened, he said. He seemed to imply that more than one or two truckloads of waste would be needed if a human blockade of roads were to successfully capture attention of the news media and the general public.

Controversy that swirled for years prior to WIPP's opening at times moved along boundaries of the incredulous. Bitter feelings mounted during the period between U.S. Representative Bill Richardson and state Economic Development Secretary John Dendahl. The two exchanged increasingly hostile letters in 1989 while Richardson was among principals behind the delays to WIPP's development and Dendahl pressed for the plant's progression.

Richardson described Dendahl's letters as "emotional" and "venomous."

"You lower the standards of public service with your participation. Perhaps that is why you have trouble keeping a job very long," Richardson wrote on his congressional stationary to Dendahl.

Dendahl replied: "I can't believe someone in the position of a congressman reducing himself to writing a note of that low caliber."

Governor King in mid-1992 himself meandered beyond the edges of worn debate over WIPP by proposing that the plant's mission be expanded from a mere dump to a major scientific project worthy of the nation's best minds.

Opposition would be reduced sharply if WIPP became identified as a national mission comparable to the Manhattan Project that produced the atomic bomb in Los Álamos, said gubernatorial spokesman John McKean. The idea was to put scientists to work at finding safe, productive uses for radioactive waste that was proposed to be buried at WIPP.

"Let's see if WIPP can be turned into a kind of waste disposal Manhattan Project that can make some of these wastes less toxic and more useful," said McKean.

Sasha Pyle, a board member with Concerned Citizens for Nuclear Safety, accused King of trying to package a lion in sheep's clothing. "It seems like a desperate and irrational attempt to market the facility and create a false sense of political harmony," Pyle said. "I don't think it has any basis in science. If there were any possible use for this waste, why in the world have we spent so much money planning to sandwich it between layers of salt where the only place for it to go is into the water table?"

"What we really need is leadership to protect the resources of our state. Clean air and clear water will be worth more than gold in a hundred years."

STOPPING THE "LAND OF ENTRASHMENT"

Even as the WIPP issue festered unresolved, concerted attention suddenly was drawn in 1988 to the disposal of common trash in New Mexico.

State Senator Roman Maés, a 45-year-old Santa Fé Democrat, received a phone call that year from a private garbage hauler looking for land near Santa Fé for a private dump.

Proudly pro-business, Maés must have seemed like just the person to approach.

The senator followed up on the phone call and learned that New Mexico had few regulations governing landfills or their placement. Only two state rules protected ground water from garbage: 1) Landfills had to be at least 20 feet above the groundwater, and, 2) Landfills had to be located and operated so that they did not cause a public nuisance or create a hazard to public health or welfare.

No public hearings were required before landfills could be opened, and state inspectors did not test the ground water near landfills because they lacked personnel, money and legal authority.

New Mexico was said to be the least-protected state on issues involving solid waste.

"There's really nothing looked at to see if (landfill operators) are protecting public health or the environment or anything like that," said Richard Mitzelfelt, serving then as director of the state Environmental Improvement Division.

The state's failure to regulate its landfills left New Mexico ripe for exploitation of its land and possible pollution of underground water supplies, Maés said.

He introduced a comprehensive bill during the 1989 legislative session to go about addressing concerns.

"We wanted to throw a rock out there and see if we hit anything," he said of his effort to measure interest in the issue. "We apparently hit a lot."

Maés' measure proposed regulating the collection, storage, transportation, separation, recycling and disposal of solid waste statewide. It would apply to individuals creating the trash and to government bodies that handle it. The bill became one of the most-talked about measures of the 1989 session. Supporters and opponents alike sought out copies of the massive bill.

The senator presented his controversial legislation well armed not only with information but with patience and a sense of purpose that even his detractors could not disrupt even as days grew long deep into the session and patience among other lawmakers was short.

Consideration of the bill drew additional weight when it was learned that a Maryland company, Driggs Corporation, already had proposed to build a 36-square mile landfill near Lordsburg in southern New Mexico to handle waste from other states. The dump would be about the size of the city of Santa Fé and would be the largest in the nation. It would straddle Interstate ten and tracks of the Southern Pacific Railroad between Lordsburg and Deming on land owned by Casas Grandes Cattle Company and the Kipp Ranch.

Driggs Corporation would do business in New Mexico under the name of Innovative Environmental Systems of New Mexico. Former New Mexico senator, I.M. "Ike" Smalley, was the company's lawyer in New Mexico. Smalley was a conservative Deming Democrat. Before leaving the Senate, he served for years as president pro tempore earning the nickname "the bear" because of his bulk as well as his substantial influence.

Smalley at first was keeping much information about the proposed landfill close to the vest. When I asked in mid-January 1989 for the names of his clients, he replied bluntly, "I can't give you that."

Maés complained that he was having trouble getting basic information even from state administrators who Smalley had approached.

Maés and Representative Max Coll, an environmentally conscious Santa Fé Democrat, introduced memorials in their respective legislative chambers. The memorials would not have the effect of law but would express an official position from the Legislature about the proposed Driggs dump.

Maés and Coll alleged that dump proponents had sought to keep their activity confidential. The two lawmakers said the proposed landfill would be large enough to take waste generated by New Mexico at 1989 levels for 300 years, or the city of Albuquerque for 1,000 years.

There was mounting concern in multiple quarters about the inescapable need to secure open spaces for the nation's garbage.

The U.S. Environmental Protection Agency projected that the United States would produce more than 190 million tons of municipal solid waste by the year 2000. That compared to 87 million tons produced in 1960.

Much of the waste is produced in large East Coast cities, but more than 50 percent of East Coast landfills would be closed by 1993, Maés said. He said cities and states in the East would look for open spaces, such as those in New Mexico, to dump their trash.

Maés' 1989 solid waste bill said New Mexico received "increasingly large amounts of infectious, dangerous and undesireable solid wastes and hazardous waste from other states by persons and firms who wish to avoid the costs and requirements" imposed elsewhere.

Carting garbage into New Mexico from other states also concerned

Joe Mercer, who was chairman of the Governor's Organized Crime Prevention Commission in 1989. "We are concerned, with dumps closing every year in the East, that we're going to see New Mexico scouted for potential dump sites," he said.

A report from Mercer's commission said "traditional organized crime has long been involved in (waste disposal)."

"It is a simple matter, and a logical expectation that organized crime will extend its solid-waste property rights system to hazardous waste," the report said. "Indeed, numerous mobsters have been charged and convicted of commingling hazardous waste with solid waste and illegally dumping it in solid-waste landfills."

But Smalley and the men he represented sought to get around such concerns. Smalley arranged for his clients to meet privately with then-Governor Garrey Carruthers, a Las Cruces Republican who previously served as an assistant secretary in the Interior Department of former President George H. W. Bush.

Upon learning of the planned meeting, Maés insisted on being present and eventually was invited by Smalley. Maés had objected to Smalley bringing in his clients to meet privately with Governor Carruthers and the state's Envronmental Improvement Division director. The director would be among those acting on the dump's permit application.

Maés called it all a high-level lobbying effort and in the end was accused of disrupting what Smalley had organized. The meeting ended abruptly.

"I think the meeting was torpedoed because (Maés) didn't want to listen to any of the facts," Smalley said. "It was a little unruly, but the governor handled it pretty well."

Maés saw it differently. He said the result of the brief meeting was good. "They have to go through the process like everybody else and not try to go through the governor's office first."

Coll joined the meeting at Maés' request and said he thought Governor Carruthers ended the meeting abruptly because he did not want the dump's planners to skirt the state's application process.

Maés' comprehensive solid waste bill that would have imposed strict regulations on landfills eventually was passed by both the 1989 Senate and House. The bill also would have discouraged—but not prohibited—importation of waste from other states. (Federal legislation was required to completely block interstate shipments of solid waste.)

Maés bill was vetoed by Carruthers who said he found technical problems with the legislation.

The Legislative Council promptly approved creation of a 16-member

Environment, Land Use and Solid Waste Study Committee to begin hearings statewide that would lead to new legislation the following year. Maés was named chairman. He said he hoped legislation in 1990 would not be too late to stop what would be the nation's largest landfill planned for the Lordsburg area.

Senator John Arthur Smith, a Deming Democrat who succeeded Smalley in the Legislature, sought to ease Maés' worries. The stormy political climate stirred by the huge landfill proposal ought to discourage the Driggs outfit from moving forward with plans, Smith said.

Maés again was tenacious during the 1990 legislative session while advancing a solid waste bill of more than 100 pages. Debate again was complicated and sometimes rancorous en route to being passed by both the Senate and House. The second effort escaped a governor's veto.

Along with setting new, substantially stricter regulations for collecting, disposing and storing garbage, the state's new Solid Waste Act assured that anyone considering hauling garbage into New Mexico would have to jump through numerous discouraging hurdles. The law killed plans for the massive Lordsburg-area landfill.

The Solid Waste Act stood as landmark legislation alongside revisions to the New Mexico Children's Code, ethics laws and DWI laws of the period.

From the Roybal Files...
Albuquerque Journal, Column, September 9, 2008
My Climate Change Theory Croaked—Or Not

For the sake of us all, I can only hope there's more than a bit of overreaching in this business about global warming. I, myself, might have been about to indulge in it recently while preparing to comment about Sarah Palin's incredible position on global warming before my mother-in-law in Española unwittingly gave political cover to the Republican vice-presidential nominee.

Unwittingly, I say, because mom has remarked that with very few exceptions, she wouldn't support a Republican even if he/she "were the last dog running in town." (I'm not sure that she's joking.)

Palin, the first-term, 44-year-old Alaska governor, is not convinced global warming can be tied to human activity. "I'm not one ... who would attribute it to being man-made," she told a reporter just last month.

It's a startling position these days, for sure, because even President

George W. Bush, the great ostrich in fields of science, has come around to acknowledge links between global warming and decisions made by the globe's inhabitants. John McCain, who incredibly picked the ill-prepared Palin to join him on the Republican presidential ticket, himself calls for changes in how we all live to curb global warming.

Alarms about global warming—big and small—can be noted just about everywhere. (Think of collapsing glaciers in Palin's own home state.) I've wondered this summer if the alarms around our family's home in the foothills of the Sangre de Cristos aren't represented by a certain silence. Actually, I've grown to wonder if evidence of trouble wasn't already making its presence known in our community's night air last summer.

Frogs. The absence of frogs and toads around our home is what has turned me both curious and somewhat anxious. A nightly chorus of croaking amphibians was very much a part of each evening when I first moved into the community 20 years ago. I'd sit in the small screen porch every night to marvel at the starlit sky above the darkness that enveloped our isolated village and listen to a serenade of countless crickets, frogs and toads. If only more people could experience such glee, I recall thinking.

Much of the croaking came from along the small stream a hundred yards away but some was much closer. Walks around the yard at night had to be approached delicately to avoid stepping on brown toads that had leaped out of flower gardens and onto pathways. Rainfalls brought out armies of toads big and small. And just as puddles were inescapable evidence of passing rains, so too were the squashed carcasses of toads on the two-lane road that winds along our village and on the driveways that branch off the unpretentious thoroughfare.

But it all started diminishing last summer. This summer, the nocturnal croaking has been missing entirely. Crickets have the night stage to themselves. All summer, one single toad has turned up in our yard. Rainfalls have left only puddles behind. No jumpers.

The local disappearing act unfolds as unsettling news reports come in from around the world. Rising temperatures are pushing dozens of frog species over the brink of extinction, the *Washington Post* reported early in 2006. Earth's amphibians have been vanishing from their usual habitats over the past quarter century, the paper said while telling of findings by a team of Latin American and U.S. scientists.

"Disease is the bullet killing frogs, but climate change is pulling the trigger," the study's lead scientist said. Amphibians are disappearing in Costa Rica, South Africa, Seattle and beyond.

Yeah, but here in a tiny, innocent little village in northern New Mexico? Our little valley is just half an hour away from New Mexico's state capital yet wonderfully isolated. This old Hispanic village that still has little more than 30 homes has experienced relatively few lifestyle changes over generations. No factories; few cars. Amid fears of global warming, our days are often cool; the nights even cooler.

None of that, though, exempts us from being part of the greater world. I was going to say so at my in-laws' home last week as my contribution to a meandering political discussion. Nothing had been said yet of global warming. The subject was mine to raise there at the dining room table. I would cite the mounting scientific evidence about disappearing frogs worldwide then turn to my anecdotal accounts from home. I'd stress that I wasn't sure global warming was behind disappearing frogs at home but if it was, I would assert, we could only imagine what might be happening in communities with environments far more threatening to good health than ours.

My mother-in-law had no idea what I was poised to express. No matter. She made it unnecessary before I got my first word out with her own declaration: "Boy, I couldn't sleep last night. I had to get up and close all the windows," she said. "The noise from the frogs and the crickets was as loud as I've ever heard."

Sarah Palin surely would have smiled.

Not so for those with a little more information at their disposal. Frogs truly are disappearing at alarming numbers, said Gerald Chacon, an Española resident who recently retired as associate vice provost for outreach services with the New Mexico State University Cooperative Extension Service. "It was a little disconcerting to me for a while but frogs appear to be returning to at least some northern New Mexico water systems," he said. "I don't think we understand completely what's going on."

15
The Irritant of Ethics Reform

Hear the one about the reporter who offered a state legislator ten bucks if he would answer a few questions about ethics in government?

Twisted humor abounds when talk turns to ethics in government. Ethics in government is a touchy subject.

Albuquerque Democrat Raymond Sánchez, longtime speaker of the New Mexico House of Representatives, blew up at me when I approached him one day in one of the lesser-used corridors of the state Capitol.

"You're a cop-out!" Sánchez sternly informed me that day in December 1991 as he walked into a closed meeting of the Legislative Finance Committee. "I don't know what I'm going to do with you."

Sánchez shared his newfound opinions about me for several minutes as we stood toe to toe. I call them newfound opinions because the House speaker in the past had gone out of his way to compliment me.

The main irritant on the day that Sánchez and I exchanged opinions was a news story I recently wrote in which I quoted a state government worker who said people shouldn't expect legislators to impose new restrictions on themselves governing how political campaign money is collected and spent.

"It never ceases to amaze me how a group of unethical people can sit down and spend so much time talking about ethics," the state employee told me at the end of a day-long ethics seminar called by Sánchez for lawmakers.

Renewed attention had been given during the previous two years to how some legislators conduct business, even amid constant recognition of the considerable work that Sánchez and most other lawmakers take on. Very few lawmakers—certainly not Sánchez—had been accused of anything illegal. But Sánchez and other legislative leaders were used repeatedly as examples of how influential lawmakers could raise large sums for political campaigns year after year, prompting serious questions of propriety even while they operated within the law.

Repeated assertions from multiple quarters: The laws needed to be changed.

Sánchez fumed each time anyone suggested he was dragging his feet. The year before he squared off with me in the Capitol, he grabbed *New Mexican* reporter Peter Eichstaedt by the lapels of his coat in anger. I got off with a tongue-lashing and, frankly, probably gave as good as I got, as it is said.

It might have been said about anybody pressed into my position. Debates about ethics in government tend to agitate adrenaline meters. It's that kind of subject.

Senator Roman Maés, a Santa Fé Democrat, was among a handful of state lawmakers who openly spoke about the need not only for campaign finance reform but also for improved decorum within legislative chambers. He proposed creation of an ethics commission to oversee conduct of government officials.

Tim Jennings, serving then as the Senate Democratic Whip from Roswell, said if such a commission were to be created, it should supervise the news media, too.

"There should be a system of checks and balances for everyone," he said.

Senate Republican Leader Les Houston of Albuquerque said problems

Toney Anaya, an aggressive state attorney general from 1975–1978, antagonized members of both major political parties while pressing for open, clean government.

put forth by the news media "aren't as profound as the perception."

Democrat Shannon Robinson, an Albuquerque Democrat, was more blunt. "Our relationship with the news media is so bad that we're losing control over how the public perceives us," he said. "We're being denied the ability to be loved by our people. I can't compete if the press chooses to report only negative things about me."

Senate President Pro-Tem Manny Aragón, an Albuquerque Democrat, told legislators they should not count on getting a "fair shake" from the news media.

When Washington Sets the Pace

Some of my early exposure to issues linked to government ethics grow from a school-related trip to Washington, DC, in 1969. I was a high school senior and had just been accepted into one of those excursions to the nation's capital, organized at least in part to give teens wondrous feelings about their government.

President Richard M. Nixon and Vice President Spiro T. Agnew were atop the executive branch of that government.

Agnew was a rising prospect within the national Republican Party. We swung by his empty office one day while on a tour. I was asked by a secretary if I wanted to sit on the vice president's high-back leather chair so I dropped my slim frame onto what was one of the historic city's many seats of power.

I had no idea that in four years Agnew would become the only U.S. vice president to resign his office while under criminal investigation. He was being investigated for alleged widespread graft while a Maryland officeholder prior to becoming vice president.

Two decades after resigning, Agnew was up to his stunts again. He said in the mid-1990s that he was asked at least a hundred times per month for his autograph. For an alleged bribe taker, it had to seem like opportunity knocking. Agnew began charging for his autograph. Fifty bucks got people a signed photo of the disgraced former veep.

He said all money collected would go to the University of Maryland library, which was organizing a repository of Agnew's papers. It prompted me to write in a column, only partly in jest: "Sounds like a bribe to me. It would be a mighty ungrateful university that took $60,000 a year and didn't manage to bury a lot of what made Agnew reek."

I wondered in the same column if I couldn't make a tidy sum of my own by getting Agnew to sign prints of the 1969 photo taken of me at his desk. I was told that day that the vice president was out tending to business.

Having come to learn what kind of business Agnew was prone to tend to, I wrote, perhaps his autograph over my likeness in his Washington office would have at least a small market. I could title the photo "Innocence Lost" then sell copies to county clerks and high school principals around the country.

County clerks could hang the photo over every voting booth come election days as timeful reminders of what can come when electors don't take their responsibilities seriously. The photo could get high school principals to recognize that the babes in the woods they send out to learn more about their grand nation might not always end up entirely aglow with pride and unbridled patriotism.

Agnew wasn't the only one of President Nixon's scoundrels who figured into my rounds. John Ehrlichman, who was President Nixon's top domestic affairs adviser, was convicted of conspiring to obstruct justice, obstructing justice and multiple counts of lying under oath.

He served 18 months in a federal prison camp in eastern Arizona in 1977 and 1978 for his role in trying to conceal White House involvement in the Pentagon Papers case and the Watergate scandal that forced President Nixon to resign in disgrace rather than face expulsion.

Ehrlichman moved to Santa Fé soon after resigning from his White House post amid the scandals and returned to the city upon his release from the federal prison camp. He lay low initially, quietly enjoying Santa Fé's blossoming charm and cultural life. Then controversy struck again. Oh, it was nothing like Watergate, but Ehrlichman hit the papers nonetheless when he began arguing over a five-square-foot parcel of land that he contended went with the 100-year-old house he bought on Montoya Circle.

Once calm was restored, he settled into writing books and travel articles and said he did not miss any of the power and prestige that was his while serving as one of President Nixon's top men.

Then, before you could say Deep Throat, Ehrlichman was gone. He moved himself and belongings to Atlanta, Georgia, in 1992. There was no explanation for his departure from the lovely old town that he professed to enjoy so much.

In time I got word from knowledgeable sources that Ehrlichman was angling for a presidential pardon for his crimes before outgoing Republican President George H.W. Bush turned over the White House to Democrat Bill Clinton. Ehrlichman, who was a successful lawyer before joining government, supposedly left for Atlanta so he might engage in high-profile do-good work. Simply sitting back and enjoying Santa Fé charm somehow doesn't seem to be the stuff from which U.S. presidential pardons grow.

With a pardon in hand, Ehrlichman could go back to lawyering. In his late 60s at the time, he wouldn't have many years of work ahead of him. Still, at the rate of $100, $200, $300 an hour, money could pile up for retirement rather quickly.

Ehrlichman had been tough to reach in Santa Fé so it was no surprise I couldn't contact him in Atlanta. The U.S. Justice Department, approached for information, said only that the process for obtaining presidential pardons is pretty confidential.

Indeed, any attempt by Ehrlichman to secure a pardon would likely die on the vine if his efforts became public because of the profound public disgust that followed him out of the White House and then mounted as more became known about the incredible crimes and cover-ups of the Nixon administration.

Work leading up to an Ehrlichman pardon would have had to unfold without catching public notice.

Ehrlichman was not at all happy when I wrote a column November 15, 1992, that told how he apparently was angling to have his name effectively expunged from the nation's list of felons.

He phoned me from his new home in Atlanta after someone in Santa Fé sent him a copy of my column in which I reported that acquaintances Ehrlichman left behind in New Mexico told me Ehrlichman wanted President Bush to pardon him for his crimes.

"Lazy, incompetent journalism," Ehrlichman called it during our brief conversation. "Any cub reporter could have found me if he tried to get his facts straight," Ehrlichman scolded. "You don't even achieve the level of a cub reporter."

He didn't want to hear during that phone call that I tried multiple ways to reach him in Atlanta. He didn't want to hear that my attempts to reach him in Georgia were accompanied by several phone calls I made to well-positioned sources in Washington who I thought might know how I could reach Ehrlichman.

This man had a well-earned reputation for guarding his privacy except when he saw an opportunity to promote himself or his work.

I bit my tongue to keep from playfully making a cub's purring noise over the phone while Ehrlichman scolded. It would be more productive, of course, to press on with the real issue at hand.

When Ehrlichman finally allowed me entry into the phone conversation, I asked the former White House aide to put aside his anger with my column and tell me directly whether he was interested in securing a pardon from President Bush as his term moved into its final month.

"I'm interested in a retraction," said the man who became known for dodging federal investigators' questions before being convicted of downright perjury.

"Are you interested in a pardon?" I asked again.

"I have not applied for one," he finally replied.

"Will you apply for a pardon?" I asked.

"I don't intend to apply for one," he replied, leaving the door open for him to do later what he said he did not intend to do at the moment.

"What are your plans?" I asked.

"That's none of your business," he said.

Sidestepping. Refusing to respond. A proven record of lying to people with far greater standing than me. It almost made me regret having spent so much time trying to reach him earlier.

I wrote a second column that told of my phone conversation with Ehrlichman.

The following day, Ari Fleischer, the long-time press secretary of Republican U.S. Senator Pete Domenici, penned a note to me from Washington on Senate stationary. "As one of those Washington sources who took your usual 'check-it-out-get-the-facts-before-you-write-it' phone calls, I offer you my praise for your Ehrlichman column," Fleischer wrote. "You did what every good reporter does—you heard an interesting story, you checked it out, and you wrote what you knew."

"Here's to wishing that all those journalistic animals out there were as fair, thorough, and thoughtful as a 'cub' like you! If you're a cub, then I'm a Democrat!" said the man who went on to work as a respected national Republican political strategist.

There's no way of knowing if the publicity derailed any plans Ehrlichman might have been cooking. In the end, though, he went to his grave without ever having been pardoned for the crimes he committed in and around the White House.

Potholes Full of Trouble at New Mexico Highway Department

For a while beginning in the late 1980s it appeared as if crimes were surfacing in and around the New Mexico State Highway and Transportation Department as often as potholes on roadways following a cold, wet winter.

Robert Ringer, for years the third-ranking administrator at the state highway department, in June 1990 made wide-ranging allegations of misconduct and wrongdoing with the highway department in a lengthy affidavit to state and federal investigators.

Investigators said Ringer confirmed much of what they collected from other sources during the previous year and that his high-ranking position gave credence to the allegations.

Ringer, an employee at the highway department for 22 years, was demoted eight months after he made his allegations of wrongdoing.

By then, two men had been indicted on fraud charges and a special prosecutor working under state Attorney General Tom Udall was reviewing other cases for possible presentation to a grand jury.

Udall said multiple times that if information compiled by state and federal agents at the highway department were true, the scandal would be the biggest in the history of New Mexico state government.

I, myself, began looking into allegations in 1989 when mismanagement—not criminal acts—appeared to be behind problems. The problems increasingly were driving a substantial wedge between the highway department's administrative chief and the state Highway Commission charged with overseeing the agency's administration.

At the heart of the conflict was an eight million dollar court settlement made by highway department Secretary Dewey Lonsberry in 1989 to settle a fight with a Minnesota contractor over roadwork on the Mescalero Apache reservation. Payments were made without approval of the Highway Commission.

Lonsberry took over as highway department secretary in January 1987 at the beginning of Republican Governor Garrey Carruthers' administration.

Testifying before a state legislative committee about the settlement, Lonsberry said respected legal advisers told him not to throw out a nice round number while negotiating a settlement. The other side would think it's superficial and try to get the figure higher, he said. Lawyers representing the state, who themselves wound up with $2.2 million in fees from the deal, reportedly told Lonsberry to throw in a few threes, fives or sevens after the number that designates millions so opponents would think that it all actually represented something.

All those threes, fives and sevens that eventually got rounded off added up to the largest court settlement ever cooked up by the state road agency after lawyers' fees were included.

Two years earlier, Lonsberry failed to notify the Highway Commission that $65 million was taken out of the ever-important road fund to cover overexpenditures in another fund.

Projects around the state were disrupted because of multiple administrative decisions that increasingly drew negative attention to Governor Carruthers. The Highway Commission repeatedly cast votes of no confidence in Lonsberry. The governor late in 1989 ordered his highway chief to "tighten up" management of the massive agency with an annual budget of more than $450 million.

By then Republican state Attorney General Hal Stratton had begun an investigation into alleged criminal wrongdoing. It involved "a whole number of matters," said Deputy Attorney General Stephen Westheimer. Federal investigators also became involved.

In August 1990, James Scarentino, a former assistant state attorney general, alleged in a court affidavit that the Attorney General's Office was covering up allegations of criminal conduct at the highway department.

Bid rigging and attempts to secure kickbacks from contracts awarded through the highway department were among allegations.

As part of their work, investigators looked into a three-year-old case in which an Albuquerque contractor sued the highway department, alleging he was harassed by state employees when he rebuffed what he said were repeated extortion attempts.

A lawsuit alleged that T. Brown Constructors resisted "shakedowns" at a $1.5 million job in sourthern New Mexico in 1985. It further alleged that because of the resistance, state employees were instructed by their superiors to harass Brown's operations and personnel.

Scarentino alleged in his affidavit that he had been engaged in more than one investigation involving the troubled highway department. "I was assigned to a number of separate investigations into allegations of criminal conduct by individual contractors, subcontractors and suppliers, and current and former highway department employees," he wrote.

Scarentino's claims about a supposed cover-up drew noteworthy support.

William Elliot, who until July 1990 was Stratton's chief investigator at the highway department, testified that he resigned after he became convinced that Stratton was promoting a cover-up with the knowledge and approval of Governor Carruthers and U.S. Attorney William Lutz.

Elliot testified that alleged wrongdoing in the highway department could be between $200 million and $600 million during the previous three years alone. Governor Carruthers said earlier that a task force he appointed concluded problems involved only $250,000 during the previous five years and that little, if any, of it involved criminal acts.

He and Stratton both insisted there was no cover-up.

As part of their work, investigators with the Federal Highway Administration alleged Lonsberry helped steer department contracts to a company partly owned by an influential state lawmaker close to Governor Carruthers. Federal investigators had a string of other allegations. Among them, they said the highway department neglected its own regulations and secured property by trespass and through coercion; that department employees routinely accepted gifts and gratuities from contractors and failed to report possible bribery attempts; at least one major paint supplier for ten years purportedly misrepresented its products through false certifications, product substitution or false labeling; another company supposedly provided substandard sign materials without having to take cuts in payments.

I reported on the allegations in June 1990 after independently securing a copy of a 54-page report compiled by federal investigators.

Governor Carruthers fumed after reading the story. He criticized the report as poorly prepared and, probably, overreaching. He said much of it could be classified as little more than a compendium of highway department gossip. "This thing was stolen and put out to the public." He complained.

In truth, I obtained a copy of the report from a confidential source who supplied it voluntarily.

Some of what was alleged in the federal report was mentioned as early as mid-1988 in reports of the Governor's Organized Crime Prevention Commission.

Federal officials, as part of their June 1990 report, asked that Stratton and Lutz respond with possible prosecutorial decisions in 60 days.

Stratton promptly asserted that he would not be rushed in his own work by disclosure of the federal investigators' report. He then set out on a concerted effort to learn who "leaked" the report.

The highway department scandal became a substantial issue in the 1990 gubernatorial campaign. Democrat Bruce King, who was seeking election to his third term as governor, said Stratton appeared obsessed with trying to silence his critics and their accusations of a cover-up.

Republican Frank Bond said he would make the highway department's troubles a priority. "I'm simply not going to leave any rock unturned in getting to the problem at the highway department. The truth of the matter is it's got to stop," he said.

Democrat Tom Udall, competing in 1990 to succeed Stratton as attorney general, accused Stratton of failing to address allegations aggressively enough and called for appointment of a special prosecutor.

William Elliot, the former state investigator who once worked for Stratton, formally asked that a grand jury invite him to present information he feared the jury might not otherwise hear as part of the investigation into alleged widespread fraud.

A special prosecutor? Stratton had given the impression that he'd rather walk away from politics than appoint a special prosecutor. He insisted his investigation had turned up nothing at the highway department worth prosecuting. Finally three months before he was to leave office and under increasing pressure, he appointed Albuquerque lawyer Chris Key to serve as an independent special prosecutor. Stratton made the move two days after state District Judge Steve Herrera lifted a gag order on Elliot who accused Stratton of a cover-up.

Udall succeeded Stratton as attorney general in January 1991 and Key promptly suggested that Udall appoint as many as three more special prosecutors to work on other related cases. Key said he had reviewed all major allegations and could not dismiss any of them as frivolous. "There's a lot of wrong at the highway department. The real issue is which of the allegations are criminal and which are something else," Key said.

Key had secured indictments against two men in one case and said at

Tom Udall (right), attorney general from 1991–1998, said problems at the state Highway Department during the 1980s and early 1990s could constitute one of the state's biggest cases of corruption ever. In the end, though, Udall said he found nothing criminal.

least eight other cases seemingly were worthy of criminal prosecution.

Udall soon afterwards appointed Albuquerque attorney Jack Love as a special prosecutor.

But by early summer 1991 Stratton's and Udall's authority to appoint special prosecutors to pursue highway department wrongdoing was challenged in court by an attorney for one of the defendants in the investigation. State District Judge W.C. "Woody" Smith in Albuquerque directed that two grand juries empanneled as part of the investigation be sent home at least temporarily.

Smith's directive was challenged and in July 1991 the state Supreme Court ruled the attorney general was not authorized by law to appoint a special prosecutor for the investigation; the responsibility belonged to district attorneys.

Investigations by state and federal agents spread over four years were effectively killed. Udall came to be convinced that little of what ranking highway officials had alleged in sworn statements involved criminal acts. And, he said, evidence of cover-ups had yet to be found.

Not everyone agreed, including some who put their careers on the line while making statements under oath to expose wrongdoing. Some in the highway department insisted that if just one or two people in the right places had been indicted, others would have fallen like dominoes.

Paying to Dance and Work

Attorney General Tom Udall became involved in another high-profile case just as the highway department investigations were being put aside.

Robert Vigil of San Miguel County came out of nowhere in the 1990 Democratic primary to win the race for state auditor against Al Romero, who previously held the post from 1983–1986. Vigil was unopposed in the general election.

Less than a year after taking office in January 1991, Vigil found himself accused of extortion and other wrongdoing.

He set out in October 1991 to raise campaign money the old-fashioned way: He went after contributions from people who relied on him for contract work. It was the kind of fund-raising practice in place long before Vigil got into politics.

Vigil's re-election committee mailed letters to certified public accountants around New Mexico, asking them to sell books of $50 tickets to a dance to commemorate Vigil's October 26th birthday. Money raised would offset "ongoing financial demands," Vigil's backers said. Vigil's planned re-election bid in 1994 came to mind.

Santa Fé certified public accountant Donald Daymon was sent a book of 20 birthday dance tickets. Independent accountants like Daymon do about 95 percent of the work performed under the name of the State Auditor's Office. Working under contract, they in effect are the auditors who annually check the books of government agencies.

The State Auditor's Office with its relatively small staff oversees such work.

Daymon's firm in 1989 got $564,000 worth of projects from the State Auditor's Office. It received more than $400,000 in 1991.

In political circles, if you're handed a book of 20 fund-raising tickets, you're usually expected to sell them all or buy what you can't sell. That's the expectation even if you don't make half a million dollars from government business every year.

Even before the birthday dance tickets, Daymon was given 40 $50-tickets for a fund-raiser that was organized soon after the 1990 primary to help pay off Vigil's expenses from the just-completed campaign.

"I guess he figured that was my quota," Daymon told me.

Daymon said he sold what he could but in the end, he and one of his partners each wound up buying $800 worth of tickets.

Daymon screamed foul when he was given the second round of dance tickets in September 1991. He promptly returned all the tickets along with a two-paragraph letter in which he accused Vigil of abusing the power of his office.

"Extortion," he called it.

"This isn't an election year. The only motivation I can see now is that he wants to build a campaign kitty so high that nobody would run against him," Daymon said. "I know I may not do another dime's worth of government work but this guy's bad news. I refuse to participate in anything that means this guy might serve two terms."

Vigil acknowledged he might see things as Daymon did if he were in his shoes. But promptly added that it's the way political fund-raising always had been run in New Mexico.

Udall pledged to investigate.

Vigil was questioned by AG investigators and waited anxiously for findings. When none came in four months, he cried foul.

"They had been investigating kickbacks and bribes and this kind of stuff," Vigil told me ... "They've asked me the same questions a hundred different ways."

Meanwhile, said Vigil, the AG's office refused to provide his agency with legal advice on other matters. "These people at the attorney general's office just aren't doing their jobs," he said.

Udall ran a protracted investigation but never filed charges against Vigil.

Vigil frequently danced with controversy but was elected to another four-year term as auditor in 1994 nonetheless. Then he was elected state treasurer in 2002. That's when his real troubles began.

Early in Vigil's term as treasurer, federal investigators began looking into accusations of criminal acts involving both Vigil and his predecessor, Democrat Michael Montoya. Both men eventually were indicted on charges of taking thousands of dollars in kickbacks from financial advisers seeking state business.

Vigil, just before his indictment, resigned as treasurer in October 2005 rather than face what appeared to be certain impeachment. The state Legislature had decided to hold a special extraordinary session to begin impeachment proceedings.

Vigil was convicted of one count of attempted extortion and was sentenced to three years in prison.

Montoya in 2005 pleaded guilty to federal racketeering and was sentenced to 40 months in prison.

When Whistleblowers are Targeted

Whistleblower protection surfaced periodically as an important element of government ethics reform. Whistleblowers in government were largely behind investigations into wrongdoing at the state highway department in the 1980s and 1990s, and some who stepped forward with accusations took hits for their roles.

But if problems at the mammoth highway department drew widespread attention, a little-known state agency was positioned to go on with business as usual in 1989 when it fired one of its longtime employees who thought it was time to end a system that was skewed against consumers.

Taos resident Maurilio Durán, 58 at the time, was fired by the state Manufactured Housing Division after he criticized what he said was his agency's inaction on consumer complaints about poorly built manufactured housing. Durán was the only inspector assigned to tend to consumer issues in nine northern counties. He said people were being forced to live with major structural problems in their homes because of inaction by the state.

Durán said he lost his $18,000 a year job after he testified in 1987 in a Tucumcari courtroom on behalf of a mobile home buyer and against his own employers. Durán had argued that the new mobile home of a Tucumcari truck driver was in such sorry condition that the sale should be revoked. Durán's superiors wanted him to drop the consumer's complaints.

Stanley Frost, then a state district judge in Tucumcari and later a state Supreme Court justice, toured the home as part of a two-day trial and agreed with Durán.

Durán said he also was being punished for telling me in August 1989 that the state Manufactured Housing Division routinely disregarded consumer complaints against certain large manufacturers and dealers who reportedly had won favor with some in the state agency.

One of Durán's supervisors said he was fired because he was unreliable and incompetent. But Leonard Scott, chairman of the division's supervisory board, said Durán was one of the agency's best inspectors.

Durán's personnel records showed that for ten years Durán responded aggressively to consumer complaints about leaky roofs, crooked floors or torn carpets in mobile homes that for many buyers represented lifelong dreams. "People work all their lives to save enough money to buy their own house. You can imagine how they feel when they end up with something that starts falling apart before their eyes," he said.

Consumers who struggled to pay their bills, just like him, needed a voice, he said.

Longtime New Mexico Senate leader, Manny Aragón of Albuquerque, was the champion of the underprivileged until he was charged with lining his pockets with huge sums of public funds.

Democratic state Representative Max Coll of Santa Fé called Durán's termination "atrocious."

"I think it's atrocious that anybody would be fired for reporting somebody who is breaking the law," Coll said. "They're supposed to be a regulatory agency. When they stop being a regulatory agency, it's a dereliction of duty that is required by state law. If the agency chooses who they are going to regulate and who they're not, we don't need them."

Durán filed a lawsuit and after months of denials the state Manufactured Housing Division reached a financial settlement with its fired inspector. Each side pledged as part of the agreement not to disclose the amount of the settlement.

"It will be a comfortable start," Durán told me. "It will help me pay my lawyer, get me out of debt and get a fresh start."

Champion of the Poor Tumbles

Representative Max Coll was among state legislators who reliably called for protection of whistleblowers. So, too, was Senator Manny Aragón, an Albuquerque Democrat who for decades wielded extraordinary influence in the Legislature.

Aragón, himself, was snared by corruption charges in 2007. He and others were charged in connection with a scheme running from 1999 through 2004 to skim millions of dollars from construction of the Metropolitan Court Building in Albuquerque.

Aragón first professed innocence then in 2008 pleaded guilty to fraud and was sentenced to 67 months in prison. He also was fined $750,000 and was ordered to pay nearly $650,000 in restitution.

For three decades Aragón stood as the state Legislature's most-vocal and reliable advocate for the poor and disenfranchised. His huge theft of public funds for personal use belied the image he cultivated over 30 years. In time he likely justified his criminal conduct while stewing over what he considered to be a humiliating defeat when he was challenged for the coveted Senate President Pro Tempore post in 2001 and lost. Aragón held the position since 1988 and was embittered by his defeat.

Aragón's corruption case was one of the state's biggest scandals and in 2012 spurred legislation to increase penalties for corrupt conduct of public officials.

Loud calls for such reform began with the much-publicized cases of former state treasurers Robert Vigil and Michael Montoya.

The 2012 law, which cleared both the House and Senate without a single negative vote, could require public officials convicted of corruption-related crimes to repay their legislative salaries and forfeit substantial state pension benefits.

Other laws passed since the early 1990s clamped down on when legislators could solicit campaign donations and required more-detailed reporting about political contributions.

The central reform measure of 1993 drew this comment from its sponsor, Senator Joe Fidel, a Grants Democrat. "The main thrust of the bill is disclosure, and disclosure and a lot more disclosure,"

But throughout legislative debate over government ethics reform during the past several decades, lawmakers invariably asserted that ethics legislation is complex and difficult to write. While covering all the bases of propriety, for example, it's important not to deny anyone the right to contribute to the political candidate of his/her choice, some have argued.

The 1992 Legislature supposedly was poised to address major ethics reform proposals. Republicans pressed for it. But Senator Tom Rutherford, an Albuquerque Democrat, argued that newly reported information about deepening poverty in New Mexico all but required lawmakers to spend their time during the short 30-day session, not on government ethics, but on trying to help the exploding number of needy New Mexicans. He scolded Republicans and others who didn't agree.

"To require the Legislature to spend time on something that can't possibly be accomplished in this session at the expense of people who are going to lose their diapers and their medication for lack of funding is the cheapest kind of political grandstanding," Rutherford said.

"You cannot comprehensively succeed in setting new standards and proscribing new conduct for state officials in a legislative session like this when the real problem facing this state is what to do with the increasing number of helpless people."

Politics, wherever practiced, probably have never been free of questionable, even indictable, conduct. New Mexico certainly has been no stranger to old-time politics. For years while I worked as a government reporter I heard of a governor who purportedly paid a ranking administrator to stay home because he stirred too much havoc with other employees. The practice reportedly went on for months until the no-show administrator was eligible for retirement.

I heard the story from, among other sources, a relative of someone who supposedly carried paychecks to the administrator's home.

From the Roybal Files...
The Santa Fe New Mexican, Columns, August 26, 1990; December 16, 1990
Cracking Down on Questions; Allegations Making Many Mad

Some administrators at the troubled state Highway and Transportation Department are taking steps, at least with me, to change how inquiries about their work are handled. They've asked that I submit all questions in writing and then wait for responses.

Written questions assure that they keep track of all inquiries and that each one gets an adequate response, says the department's chief lawyer, Art Waskey. He said there are a lot of people asking questions of the department, which over the past year has had to cope with state and federal agents investigating a string of allegations about possible widespread criminal activity.

Some of the most-serious allegations have come in sworn statements from one of the department's highest-ranking administrators, Engineering Design Division Director Robert Ringer.

I've tried not to overburden highway department employees with requests. For each eight or ten tips I've gotten about the department over the past year, I've probably made no more than one inquiry to agency administrators. By sorting through information, it's generally easier to get responses to allegations that wind up having more substance than others.

Some department administrators are clamping down anyway. Floyd Romero, the department's Disadvantaged Business Program manager, was cautioned last week in my presence not to stray during an interview from a prepared list of questions I submitted several days earlier. He didn't stray but he did respond to a few follow-up questions directly related to those on the prepared list instead of forcing me to go back to my office, type up the new questions and submit them later.

Romero knew he merely was carrying out one of a public official's principal responsibilities: being accountable to the public for how its money is spent.

Attorney General Hal Stratton for some time has been hearing allegations of corruption in the huge highway department, which has an annual budget of $450 million. Some who have complained now think Stratton is sitting on their allegations.

Stratton denies it but that doesn't quiet his detractors.

One highway department employee wrote to Stratton in October 1988 to complain that he had been reassigned because he turned away two road grader salesman who wanted him to change specifications on what the department had ordered.

"I told them that the specs were developed by a committee of the department and that I would not change them on my own," he told Stratton.

He said his superiors told him his "perception of the specifications" was wrong.

"I understand that we are both charged with the duty to protect the public trust and to conduct our actions in a manner that will serve the best interests of that public, not those of special interest groups," he told Stratton.

The man's call for an investigation was supported in a strongly worded letter from the New Mexico Board of Registration for Professional Engineers and Surveyors.

The highway department employee, in a note written later to a Santa Fé legislator, expressed dismay that nothing seemed to have been done about his complaint.

Governor-elect Bruce King, after naming Joe Anaya of Stanley to the state Highway Commission last week, said he's a longtime admirer of the retired highway department employee who hails from King's hometown.

"I knew he could help me out so I asked him if he needed a job or if he wanted something with prestige," King said. "He told me he was really enjoying retirement so he'd take something with prestige."

16
THE TREACHEROUS TRAIL OF DWI

If another, oh, thirty heartbeats had separated 17-year-old Kevin Martínez from the vehicle of a drunken Chamisal man that warm night in September 1994, the Dixon teenager likely would be well into a productive career by now and carefully tending to teens of his own.

Another thirty heartbeats and Martínez would have been able to pull into his parents' home an hour before his ten p.m. curfew.

But it wasn't to be.

It was a Sunday night. Martínez and 29-year-old Rodney Arellano were traveling in different directions on State Road 75. Martínez had just dropped off his girlfriend after the two watched a movie in Española and was half a mile from the comfort of his bedroom when his compact car was slammed into by Arellano's oncoming vehicle.

Arellano reportedly had a blood-alcohol level that was more than twice the state's legal limit.

"I know he shouldn't drink like that and drive," the man's wife told the *Rio Grande SUN*. "He feels bad about what happened, but I don't think he intentionally did it," she said of the fatal wreck.

That's what is terribly sad about drunken driving: So many things happen that people, while sober, never would want to occur.

Arellano in time turned himself in.

Martínez's mother, Marsha, said she didn't have to be convinced that her son's killer wasn't out to inflict death and anguish on a night that ended one life and turned others upside down.

"Nobody means to do something like that," said the mother who lost her only child. "I don't think anybody goes out there and intentionally tries to kill someone. But that doesn't excuse (anyone) from what they did."

Alcohol and car wrecks sadly are woven through too much of New Mexico's wondrous fabric. Small crosses and other memorials can be found alongside many New Mexico roadways to mark sites where motorists or their companions met untimely ends. They're called *descansos*.

Many are simple wooden markers. Some are more ornate. They're staked on the ground, nailed onto trees and hung on fences.

The stretch of State Road 76 that runs east from Española through Chimayó and toward Truchas has more than its share of *descansos*. It has more than its share of vehicular accidents. Due largely to speeding or alcohol/drug consumption, the two lane road long has been one of New Mexico's deadliest.

As mentioned in an earlier chapter, my *Tia* Bertha lost her life while still a teen on that road one Christmas Eve, making it my first indirect experience with the scourge of DWI.

I drove that road with my son and daughter multiple times a week when they were kids. *Descansos* were occasional topics of our conversations. New additions, in particular, drew our attention.

There was no way for me to know for sure, of course, but I'd tell my kids that probably more than half of the *descansos* we came upon marked sites of crashes due to drunk driving. And something close to half of those likely symbolized deaths not of drunk drivers but of passengers in autos driven by drunk drivers. Then there were those unfortunate souls, like Keven Martínez, who had no reason to suspect that their lives were at risk because of decisions made by others coming their way and possessing a reckless disregard for life.

My message to Pablo and Carla: Be smart about your own conduct, pick your friends carefully, and watch out for the other guy.

One of those "other guys" thoughtlessly thrust himself into my life and those of my children when they were young enough to still be riding special car seats. We were approaching Santa Fé from the north on U.S. 84-285 as we headed home. A crazed driver sped past us, weaving wildly from lane to lane as a moderate flow of traffic climbed up Tesuque Hill. I didn't see him again until his vehicle spun out of control in northbound lanes at the intersection of St. Francis Drive and Agua Fría Street.

The next thing I knew, he slammed into my children and me broadside, spinning our new vehicle around until a metal light pole abruptly stopped us.

Nobody was maimed or killed in that mid-1980s crash. But the young driver, who went on to become a successful artist in Santa Fé, never will know just how much injury he inflicted on our family that night.

A decade later, a top aide to Governor Bruce King was arrested in Albuquerque and charged with DWI. Richard Maestas, assigned to work on corrections-related issues, responded by doing what would have been expected from any of King's political appointees: he resigned his post. "The message is not written on any memo, but it has been clear from the start—

that is that working in the governor's office is like working in a fish bowl, and there is no such thing as personal conduct that is irrelevant to the job," said King spokesman John McKean.

"The governor has a little chat with everyone who is hired in this office ... He makes it clear that public service is a privilege, and public service in the governor's office is a higher privilege, and it's something that can be withdrawn."

The Albuquerque policeman who arrested Maestas that November night in 1991 said the retired Santa Fé postmaster had a blood-alcohol level of 0.18 percent, exceeding what was then the legal limit of 0.10 percent.

The governor and his wife, Alice, did not drink and did not serve alcoholic beverages at functions of which they were sole sponsors.

There was no state government rule that applied to drunken driving by New Mexico's 18,000 classified employees. Exempt employees, like Maestas, worked at the discretion of their superiors.

Stephen Veals, director of community relations at Piñon Hills Hospital in Santa Fé, said every effort should be made to get drunk drivers off the road. But added that because alcoholism is a disease, an employee at the hospital would get "every opportunity" to enter rehabilitative treatment and still remain employed.

Some of New Mexico's high-profile officials working outside the governor's office said Maestas probably should not have felt pressed to leave his $27,400 job with King.

Santa Fé Mayor Sam Pick said he would not force any of his employees to resign after a DWI arrest. "We want them to get counseling, and if we need to, we provide it at our expense," he said.

Ari Fleischer, press secretary to Republican U.S. Senator Pete Domenici, said dismissal would not be automatic. "It would be considered ... Counseling is something the senator would encourage for the employee."

Democratic U.S. Senator Jeff Bingaman said he would consider circumstances of each case before making a decision affecting employment.

Democratic U.S. Representative Bill Richardson said through spokesman Stu Nagurka that counseling would be encouraged after the first DWI arrest, dismissal "would be in order" after a second arrest.

One year later, discussions and attitudes about DWI would begin to be turned upside down for many in New Mexico. Gordon House, 33 of Thoreau, was arrested for DWI after driving his pickup the wrong way on Interstate 40 near Albuquerque on December 24, 1992, slamming into an Oldsmobile carrying a family of five. The mother, Melanie Cravens, and her three daughters, ages five, seven and nine, were killed.

The family was driving to Albuquerque's west side to get an elevated view of Christmas lights in the city.

House, married and the father of two children, was alone in his truck while driving east on the westbound lane at speeds reportedly exceeding 85 miles per hour. House's blood-alcholo level, tested when he arrived at an Albuquerque hospital, was said to be 0.18 or nearly twice the legal limit.

The wreck drew publicity statewide then nationally. So, too, did the 1994 trial that led to House's DWI conviction. More publicity and emotions were stirred that same year by two trials in Taos where prosecutors sought to get House convicted of multiple vehicular homicide charges. Both trials, which together lasted five weeks, ended in hung juries.

A third trail on the same charges was scheduled in Doña Ana County. There House was convicted of the vehicular homicide charges in May 1995.

Publicity of the case and emotions associated with it didn't end there. The Doña Ana convictions were appealed and in 1997 the state Court of Appeals reversed verdicts of the jury trial.

The following year the state Supreme Court reversed the Court of Appeals and upheld the convictions.

A Supreme Court record referred to media attention that followed the case throughout as "frenetic."

One month before the deadly House crash, New Mexico Attorney General Tom Udall appeared before a state legislative committee to repeat his previous calls for reform of drunk driving laws.

Truth be told, people pressing for substantially tougher DWI laws in New Mexico had been outnumbered for years. The fingers on one hand might have sufficed when it came to counting New Mexico families that had not contributed to drunken driving on state roads. It was never a great source of pride but it was true, nonetheless.

Further, luck more than abstinence or moderation had to be credited by so many who escaped death, injury or citation. That included me in my youth. Except for occasional bursts of pressure, zero tolerance for DWI hadn't been pushed very hard prior to the House-Cravens crash because so many in New Mexico were concerned about where such a push might lead. New Mexicans have big families. New laws that might require extended jail time, large fines or confiscation of vehicles could bring enforcers right up to a family's door.

"Just about everybody has friends or relatives who get into trouble because of alcohol," said Santa Fean Richard CdeBaca, a career state policeman who retired in 1983 after a brief tenure as chief.

Many of the state's politicians recognized all that. Too, more than a few of them had long enjoyed financial support from the powerful liquor lobby, which was in no hurry to curb alcohol consumption.

There also had been increasing efforts to recognize alcoholism not merely as a vice but as a disease that must be figured into any considerations of punishment.

If there had been a steady drum beat against DWI over the years, it had come from the state's news media. Consider this no-holds-barred passage from the pre-World War II *Santa Fe New Mexican*:

"Six months in the penitentiary for a drunken automobile driver who ran down a car and injured several people; and he will spend the six months there unless turned loose by 'a politically minded governor or a weak-kneed parole board,' quoth the vigorous and outspoken District Judge Mike Otero, who is occasionally available when not disqualified by his eminent district attorney or some of the beneficiaries of the rotten Hannett-Vogel law firm to strike a blow for law and order. The carnage of the automobile is bad enough when drivers are sober; and the drunken driver is a menace which must be exterminated."

Udall seemingly drew strength from the House-Cravens crash. He redoubled efforts to secure stricter drunken driving laws and he attracted new, spirited allies in the fight. Nadine Milford, mother of the deceased Melanie Cravens, became an unstopple force as she worked with Udall and others.

It took years, but eventually changes to state laws included lowering of the legal blood-alcohol level from .10 to .08; DWI penalties were increased to include more jail time for offenders; some repeat offenders would be adjudicated as felons, their acts no longer considered to be misdemeanors; vehicles could be impounded or permanantly taken; ignition inter-lock devices were required in offenders' vehicles; and drive-up liquor windows were closed statewide.

Measured approaches were scorned by some during early stages of the reform movement. "Why are we still going to be dragging our heels. I just think we need to throw the book at them," said state Representative Jerry Alwin, an Albuquerque Republican.

Not all joined reformers in their optimism as stricter laws were passed. Former State Police Chief Richard CdeBaca, said decades after his retirement that he was pleased to see the Legislature act on reforms. But his enthusiasm was restrained.

Indeed, a 2002 government report found that nearly half of all fatal crashes in New Mexico still involved alcohol.

"Every time there is a multiple fatal accident caused by a drunk driver, we hear the public outrage that we need more stringent laws," CdeBaca told me for his biography, *Chief of Police, The Career of Richard CdeBaca During Extraordinary Times in New Mexico 1956–1994.*

"But alcoholism, being an addiction, is not going to stop with the bigger fines, harsher jail sentences and confiscation of cars. The alcoholic has to stop drinking and not get behind the wheel of a car, period. Ignition inter-locks, electronic ankle bracelets, designated drivers, suggested DWI license plates, pink hats and all the other absurd stuff have not worked effectively."

"We read about individuals who have been arrested numerous times, some as many as 20 or more, and they are still driving."

Stricter laws hadn't scared drunk drivers off to roads of another state, to be sure. Still, although alcohol was involved in nearly 50 percent of New Mexico's fatal crashes in 2002, records reflected a drop in the state's DWI crashes following adoption of new laws. Alcohol-related crashes dropped 31 percent from 2002–2008, and the state dropped substantially in national rankings of alcohol-related deaths on roadways in 2009, according to a report by Anne Constable in *The Santa Fe New Mexican.*

CdeBaca was correct when he talked about the unsettling number of drunk drivers who continue to fall through the cracks of DWI reform legislation. People still pass out in their cars in the middle of the day in the middle of freeways and interstates. Too many do not pass out and keep on driving. An overburdened court system and crowded jails cannot handle all the offenders sent their way.

Sadly, far too many parents still stand at their doors, waiting for children who will never arrive even though they were 30 heartbeats or so away from putting the day's perils behind them.

From the Roybal Files...
The Santa Fe New Mexican, Column, July 4, 2004
DWI Question: Political Sign of the Times

It was more than a decade ago and I had just finished interviewing a candidate for the state House of Representatives as a reporter for *The Santa Fe New Mexican* when I came upon the paper's associate publisher in the hallway.

She wanted to know how the interview went.

"Did you ask if he's ever been arrested for DWI?" she wanted to know.

I hadn't but I didn't feel particularly bad about it. I had no cause to ask whether the candidate had been arrested for drunken driving, I felt, any more than I had reason to ask if he had tossed a rock through his neighbor's window on his way out of the driveway that morning.

How times have changed.

It is now routine to ask candidates for public office about DWIs. *The Santa Fe New Mexican's* associate publisher was telling me years ago that she wanted it to start becoming a routine even back then.

Driving drunk is very serious business these days. People killed by drunken drivers a decade ago were just as dead as those killed today, to be sure. It's just that more of us have come to be far less tolerant of highway deaths brought on by drunken driving.

Politicians and DWIs, well, we'd prefer that they don't mix.

Because we're all innocent until proven guilty, though, reporters have learned to alter their questions. Increasingly, politicians are asked if they've ever been convicted of DWI, not merely arrested.

Now, that lets a lot of folks off the hook. We've come to learn largely through news reports of an inordinately large number of people who are arrested for DWI but never end up having to face a judge. The judicial system's inability to get people who are arrested for DWI into court on time often leads to charges being dropped.

More than a few people running for public office have likely been able to say honestly that they've never been convicted of drunken driving, even though they have been guilty of driving drunk, maybe even arrested for it.

I think reporters' questions probably have to be modified even beyond the point of distinguishing between arrests and actual convictions. If we're going to confront people in the public eye on this topic, I think we need to ask if they've ever driven drunk, period.

Forget about arrests, convictions and blood-alcohol content. Mr. Candidate, have you ever driven in a condition that a reasonable person would describe as being drunk? Three beers in an hour usually gets a person beyond the legal limit. Have you, Mr. Candidate, ever had that much to drink—or more—and then gotten behind a wheel and onto a road that innocent people rely upon to get them through their daily lives?

Many of us, whether we've run for public office or not, would have to respond affirmatively to that question. Many of us, I hope, have recognized the error of our ways and never will make such reckless mistakes again.

But back to the politicians. If the question that I propose were asked, reporters not only would stand to learn whether the person had driven drunk—which is the real information we're trying to get at no matter how the questions is posed. But we'd also likely learn whether the person before us speaks the truth in difficult situations.

Every politician has his or her detractors. If any of them has been known to drink and drive, and denies it publicly, someone else will likely step forward with more information, and someone after that, too.

Even if conclusive proof were lacking, it's the kind of mess any politician would want to avoid. Better to fess up at the beginning and proclaim it to be conduct never to be repeated.

I mean, why not get to the heart of the matter? If we don't want our politicians to drive drunk, why not ask them if they do, press them to respond and then let opinions fall where they may?

17
Love and Despair Around New Mexico's Young

The blue van from the funeral home pulled slowly out of the man's driveway on a frigid early morning in January 1997. It turned onto the state road in rural Medanales, heading toward the freezing Río Chama just ahead and the cold confines of an Española mortuary beyond.

As the van moved away but still in view of the family home, it passed a school bus traveling in the opposite direction en route to collecting kids for their daily exposure to lessons of their public classrooms.

Inside the Medanales family home, a tiny girl named Della had just died in her bed. She was in the hands of those she loved, surrounded by her stuffed animals and colorful Christmas lights still strung along her headboard.

She woke up around 5:30 a.m., just long enough to signal to others in the home that she was ready to bid farewell.

Della never rode a school bus, not a big, noisy yellow bus like the one that rolled into Medanales on the day of her passing to pluck waiting youths out of remarkably frosty weather.

Born 16 years earlier, Della never spoke a word. She never took a step. She probably never grew to four feet tall and likely weighed little more than 30 pounds when she died.

She would have been overwhelmed in a big school bus.

The appeal of school buses, to be sure, wears thin on youths before long. But it is a rare kid in rural parts who hasn't waited wide-eyed for the day when he or she can take the big steps up beyond narrow folding doors of a yellow bus, look the driver in the eye then make the quick turn to face the sea of benches and the rectangular space from which so many stories—true and false—have been spun.

Della never had the chance to get lost in such dreams. She was born sick, very sick, and never got well. Nobody who knew her ever thought she would. If she surprised anyone, it was with her will to embrace life for so long.

When pneumonia delivered death, it also deposited grief, but not tragedy. Tragedy is what envelops homes where children's lives are cut short by violence imposed by others or in homes where children are taken without ever having experienced a true, lasting love—if they experienced any love at all

I watched a very touching, heartfelt expression of a father's love as Della was driven away from her family's arms.

Della's father stood in a cold wind a step or two away while the stilled body of his second-born child, draped by a green blanket, was carefully loaded onto the mortuary van.

Its rear double doors closed, the van pulled out along the driveway that winds around the side of the house before merging onto the state road that tracks along much of the perimeter of the family's property.

Della's father walked silently behind the van for a while before parting from the driveway and cutting a straight line through a few inches of fresh snow blanketing the ground. He made his way alone to the perimeter fence that runs parallel to the roadway and waited for what he knew would be one of his most-painful images ever.

He had just reached the fence when the van passed alongside the school bus and approached him from his left on the opposite side of the fence. He walked until he ran out of yard, trailing the van through the snow as if yearning to tear his hand through the wire barrier to run his fingers through his daughter's thin hair one last time before she left the comfort of her home behind.

The mortuary van moved slowly away from the grieving father and his property beyond a dip in the road

Tim Roybal and daughter, Della, were part of a family team that helped secure improvements in care for the disabled.

and through a string of cottonwoods that line the riverbank beyond.

Death moved quietly down the road. Its impact had never been so profound for Della's father, my brother, Tim.

Kids bring life to fathers like little else so the pain can be brutal when the children depart too soon. These next few pages will tell a little about how the lives of children and youths affected times in New Mexico and how times in New Mexico affected those young lives during the last millennium and in the one that followed.

Young daughters, of course, don't always come to know of the love that embraced Della Roybal's difficult life in Medanales. Two girls abandoned on the railroad tracks near Los Cerrillos in southern Santa Fé County, decades before Della was born surely thought they might never experience such love. Their story was recorded by Victoria D. de Sánchez and later shared with me by her son Leveo V. Sánchez for his 2015 biography, *Nerve of a Patriot*.

"One day a physician who knew Grandmother sent her a message saying that he had witnessed a Black lady putting her two children on the railroad track so that they would be killed by a train," wrote Victoria. "He rescued the children and took them to his office in Los Cerrillos. He then wrote Grandmother to ask if she would come and get them."

Leveo Sánchez's great grandmother, Josefa Davis, was a prominent and influential resident of nearby Galisteo. She kept and raised the older girl, Bluebell. The younger half-sister was taken in by another family member. Bluebell and Josefa Davis grew very close. As Josefa suffered from blindness and increasing frailty, it was Bluebell who tended faithfully to her. "Bluebell was like a part of our family. She was very loyal to my great-grandmother," Leveo told me.

One kid's very brief entry into my own life was worthy of note, and it's been attached to my memory ever since because of what it told about people's expectations big and small.

This young boy was well on his way to learning the importance of keeping at least some expectations in check as he spirited himself across my path at Santa Fé's Nava Elementary School one afternoon in the early 1990s.

The boy of nine or ten had a beaming face and a basketball that he dribbled at his side. He raced down the sidewalk in my direction as I approached the school gym to watch my daughter's co-ed team from upriver shoot some hoops against the hosting Nava squad.

"I get to play today ..." the boy shouted at me as he moved toward the gym door, which I held open for him while smiling broadly.

"Way to go!" I shot back immediately, interrupting the boy to share in his enthusiasm even though I knew he must be part of the home team against which my daughter's squad from Pojoaque would be matched that day.

The boy was too excited to be thrown off by a stranger's interruption and he finished his sentence after skipping only a beat or two.

"I get to play today ... if somebody gets hurt!" he said, running past me and into the wave of children's screams that blew out of the gym and through the open door.

Of course. Suddenly, it became clear. I didn't have to worry much about this kid shutting down my daughter's play inside the lane or dashing past her repeatedly to score in double figures by game's end.

Oh, he wore a team jersey, but the holes for the arms drooped down to his waist. He had cutoff pants, not shiny uniform trunks. His dribble was good enough, all right. But chances were this kid would rarely get beyond the sidelines on the gym floor that day.

I knew his position well. I, too, had worn ill-fitting, faded jerseys that grade school coaches gladly would have tossed in the trash had it not been for the bench warmers they had to carry in the name of community goodwill.

The boy streaking his way into the Nava Elementary gym didn't appear at all disheartened by his prospects, which clearly he understood.

His chances were slim. But he had chances, nonetheless, and that was good enough for him.

Chances slip away, though, and hopes dim with time for far too many in New Mexico. Historically, more than a quarter of New Mexico's children sadly have come to learn to keep their expectations in check.

A report from New Mexico Kids Count greeted the state into the 2018 New Year with dismal statistics. The numbers were compared to those reported the previous year. And the previous year was not good. More of the state's children lived in poverty in 2017; more went without health insurance and more teens and children lived in single-parent households, reported *New Mexican* staffer Robert Nott.

Sorry conditions have long caught the attention of the state's politicians and government leaders, even if none of them has been able to find the fix. Democrat Paul Bardacke and Republican Frank Bond lamented during their 1990 gubernatorial primary campaigns that nearly a third of all students who enroll in New Mexico's public schools eventually dropped out.

I offered in a column that even the best of safety nets can't save everyone, but if almost one in three fail the educational system, then the system must be failing.

Rhetoric and effort were not lacking. Efforts simply never gained much traction. Democrat Jerry Apodaca while governor from 1975–1978 reorganized the Department of Education to give public schools a greater voice at the governor's table and help ensure that they were never far from top-level attention.

Democrat Toney Anaya, who as governor from 1983–1986, spent much of his time trying to secure from taxpayers and the Legislature new, larger sums of money for public education.

Republican Garrey Carruthers, who succeeded Anaya as governor, told how sound schools would drive economic growth.

Democrat Bruce King, while campaigning in 1989 for his third term as governor, apparently felt Carruthers wasn't getting much accomplished. He essentially applied different words to Carruthers' assertions and pledged that quality education would be "the first step" to improved long-term economic development. Public schools and higher education "must become the highest priority of our next governor," King said.

Successive candidates while trying to win entry into the governor's office promised their own formulas for invigorating New Mexico's public schools. Yet, 40 years after his father left the office, Democrat Jeff Apodaca lamented during his own campaign for governor in 2018 that in key areas, performance of the state's public schools ranked 50th—dead last—in the country.

Big names and big money undoubtedly impacted some young lives along the way. The National Science Foundation in 1993 announced it would provide up to ten million dollars to help place more New Mexico minority students in science and engineering careers. The project would be in addition to a ten million grant the foundation previously awarded to New Mexico to make systemic changes in school math and science programs.

All of it struck at areas that begged for attention. What continued to cry for attention even louder, though, were conditions that left far too many students in positions where they couldn't care less about new science and math programs. They're the ones who stack dropout numbers. Then there are all those who stay in school but are "lost" nonetheless.

A young man I met late in the 1980s named Juby Benavídez was one who as a youth likely would not have been excited by new science and math programs in school. Juby watched me shoot pictures one day in the tiny community of Las Tablas, just north of El Rito. At first, he had the look of a guy with little use for a newspaperman swinging through to mind other people's business.

But Juby, to my surprise, promptly offered to help. In his view, at least, Las Tablas was his town, and he wanted to make sure this visitor

Juby Benavides of Las Tablas north of Española found purpose as a community sentry.

got what he needed. He let me know that if I took his picture before I left, he would consider himself paid in full. I asked him to return to the spot outside a package liquor store where I first noticed him, and then I snapped away.

I thought I had seen the last of Juby until he strolled into *The Santa Fe New Mexican* newsroom a couple of weeks later, asking if I had an extra copy of the photograph I'd taken of him.

Clearly, the man's enthusiasm could be stirred. But I couldn't help thinking that this guy who had staked out what seemed like a semi-permananet spot for himself outside a package liquor store in a tiny backroads village hadn't gotten much attention over the years.

Juby Benavídez, while driving his car down one of those backroads a couple of years after our visit was struck from behind and killed by a logging truck.

New Mexico has more than its share of people who feel disengaged from systems that supposedly exist for their benefit but don't quite manage to reach their targets.

"Our (public school) system thinks its okay for one third of our kids to fail so long as the others make it," Pedro Atencio, an adiministrator with the State Department of Education, told me in 1994.

In truth, accurate reporting likely would show dropout rates of 50 to 60 percent in parts of New Mexico, he said.

"I don't think it has anything to do with difficulty of the work as students progress. It has more to do with motivation and self-esteem," he said. "We set up the highest standards and then reward only those who meet them. I think kids see through that because they know some kids have more than others to deal with in life. There's less and less correlation between what we parents see as success in high school and what kids think success really is."

Motivation and self-esteem without question are central elements in how young lives develop. They are elements that must drive educational systems, home environments—and even grade school basketball teams—if chances for success are to remain alive.

Ah, but competing powers have raised their ugly heads more and more over the years, tearing at motivation and self-esteem, ripping them apart; at times never giving them a chance to make their existence known. Child neglect, abuse and other malignant signs of grossly dysfunctional families have created a landscape where young criminals, not mere delinquents, demand attention.

"Through the years we've seen problems ... with the way society has changed and what has happened to our youth," said Albuquerque Democrat Raymond Sánchez, who in 1993 was serving as speaker of the New Mexico House of Representatives.

Changes have led to youths committing more murders and other violent crimes, Sánchez said. Changes were rooted at least as much in changing compositions of families as in changing family values, he said.

Alice King, wife of three-term Democratic Governor Bruce King, made a name for herself in New Mexico as an untiring advocate for children. She was an enthusiastic defender of kids who bumped into trouble in the 1970s and 1980s. But as time went on, well, she wondered if some youths—whom she still wanted to help—might do better with a little less coddling.

Alice King in the early 1980s was chairwoman of a committee that helped review the state statute that determined how the legal system treated youthful offenders. A new Children's Code was adopted as state law, and Alice King's reputation as an aggressive advocate for children and youth became as much a part of the New Mexico landscape as the massive plains that extend east from her family's ranch in Stanley.

For Alice King, it seemed as if no child was a throwaway. Opportunities to turn a young life around were not to be quickly abandoned.

Throughout the first decade and more of her advocacy, she stood firmly opposed to publicly releasing names of first-time youthful offenders.

First-time offenders should not be publicly branded as troublemakers, possibly making it harder for them to get back in line, she argued.

But time has a way of reshaping opinions.

Alice King and her husband, the governor, had become concerned by the early 1990s that many youthful offenders were taking their misconduct much too lightly, King spokesman John McKean told me in September 1993. Some need to feel more accountable for their wrongdoing, he said.

The Kings read the papers just like anybody else, he added, and it sure looked like violent crimes by teens were increasing to troublesome levels.

"When youngsters are convicted of rather serious crimes they tend not to take those convictions very seriously," McKean said. "Mrs. King still has a problem with publication of names of youngsters who are accused of relatively non-violent crimes. She no longer feels it's practical to withhold the names of older children who are accused of violent offenses."

"It's a growing recognition that older teens are committing many of the violent crimes in this state and around the country."

The serious re-evaluation of how young violent offenders were to be treated unfolded even as the Kings in 1992 successfully pressed for creation of a new Department of Children, Youth and Families. Two years earlier, Bruce King pledged throughout his campaign for a third term to open such an agency. King and his wife argued at every opportunity that if so-called front-end social needs—such as early child education and pre-natal care—are tended to then more-expensive back-end problems—such as welfare dependency and imprisonment—could be curtailed.

The governor and his wife were determined to make the new agency succeed even amid austere times.

The department of about 750 employees was formed by pulling away parts of other state agencies that deal with children and family needs. Those bureaus and divisions took their budgets with them, but the King's new department still didn't have money for grand initiatives.

It would all work out, the governor asserted. His confidence was bolstered by an old tale passed along within the King family for generations. The governor shared it with me.

"My father used to tell me a story of a man going through the country. He would ask people if they could show him how to make soup with a nail. They all said, 'no.' So then the man asked for a pot and some water and he pulled out a nail and put it in the pot. He started stirring it around in the water and it all began to boil. He stirred some more and then said, 'Boy, we sure would have a better stew if you only had a few 'taters.' So the people brought him some potatoes and then he said it would be even better with carrots, and he kept on that way until he had a real good stew."

So it would go for the new Department of Children, Youth and Families, King insisted. Once started, it would fill in later to better address needs of a changing state, he said.

"I think it will be beneficial to one and all," he said.

Oh, it had become hard to miss the changes in our state that had escalated for quite some time. Those changes were largely what prompted the Capitol's review of how it treated youthful offenders in the 1980s, during King's second gubernatorial term, only to require another hard look a decade later.

As *The Santa Fe New Mexican's* editorial page editor in 1982, I wrote an editorial following an incredible arrest of several Santa Fé teens that April at a time of night when they all should have been home in bed. Incredible information gave rise to the editorial.

City policeman LeRoy Lucero recovered a cache of weapons from a car in which two 16-year-olds, a 15-year-old and a 13-year-old were riding en route to the city landfill for a fight against rivals. The car reportedly was loaded with, among other weapons, a nine m.m. automatic pistol; a .45-caliber pistol with extra clips of ammunition; a fully loaded .38 caliber pistol; a 30:30 rifle; a three-foot-long nail-studded club; three steel swords; and four Chinese martial arts swords.

One might have thought somebody's mother had been slowly tortured to death by a band of despicable aliens and the fate of the entire city rested on revenge.

A little more than ten years later I wondered in a column if cold-hearted aliens from a planet where respect and affection died eons earlier might have been responsible for an especially gruesome murder eight miles north of Española. A 44-year-old man apparently had been killed by a blow to the head, his corpse then chopped to pieces, probably with an axe, and left near a woodpile alongside the family's chicken coop.

No, it wasn't an alien, I wrote after the suspected killer was identified. It was somebody whom we might have brushed up against at the grocery store or at the filling station earlier in the week; somebody who shared our space in a beautiful region of northern New Mexico but, clearly, not our feelings for one another.

Those feelings had eroded over years for reasons big and small. Margaret Kegel, an accomplished Santa Fé attorney who went on to become a hearing officer for the region's children's court cases, told how evidence of the erosion could be witnessed in everyday occurrences.

It might have been described as our communities' loss of innocence.

Kegel came upon a carload of teens racing down Cerrillos Road one day and couldn't help but recall her own childhood, a time when so much seemed rooted in Santa Fé's small-town character.

The teens observed by Kegel displayed no interest in maintaining the pace established by others driving that day on the city's busiest thoroughfare. They switched lanes repeatedly before coming upon a group of slow-moving autos bunched together across each lane of the road.

The teens wound up directly behind a car driven by an elderly lady who was driving slowest of all. Waiting momentarily for an adjacent lane to clear, the teen-age driver maneuvered his car around the elderly driver before speeding past her while his companions aimed obscene gestures and epithets in the lady's direction.

"I never could have gotten away with that when I was in high school," said Kegel, daughter of a former district attorney, Walter Kegel. "If I had tried, people in at least two or three other cars on the street would have recognized me and would have phoned home to report me even before I got there. When I got home, it wouldn't have been pleasant."

It wasn't her family's notoriety that had Margaret Kegel feeling like she had to watch her conduct as a kid. "It was the same for anyone. Everybody knew everybody," she told me.

If only innocence were all that had been claimed by changing times. Anger and violence were injecting themselves far too often into people's lives. What better evidence of that than a man's butchered body left to rot alongside his family's chicken coop? Eventually, police said the victim of that hate-filled murder north of Española was brutalized by his own son. The 20-year-old son was arrested after reportedly confessing to police while describing his own young life as dim and filled with abuse.

Santa Fean Joe Castellano, a former district attorney who was serving as a state district judge at the time, said an increasing number of people were growing up with anger and hatred following abusive childhoods.

"You just can't miss all the anger, hatred and violence in some people," Castellano said.

He told of a case over which he had recently presided and which likely would never be erased from his mind.

"It was a case where the father and mother were involved with drugs and alcohol," Castellano said. "For a prolonged period of time the father would order the kids to stand at attention around his bed and watch while he had sex with his wife. The children, all boys, were seven, nine and eleven years old. When the biggest boy was old enough to get an erection, the father ordered him to take a turn on the bed. The mother responded later by saying she didn't even enjoy it."

"The eleven-year-old boy will undergo years and years of therapy.

The question is: Can he overcome what has happened to him? It likely will be easier for the younger children since their exposure was more limited."

Castellano said people dragged into situations where life is so demeaned often are the ones who wind up filling New Mexico's prisons. "We're losing so many children who have been sexually abused or emotionally abused," he said.

Addressing the root causes for often-unspeakable violence among youths would best be left to someone else, Santa Fé Undersheriff Ray Sisneros told me in 1993. He loaned his voice, instead, to those wanting young people to face greater consequences for their actions.

"Before, kids were afraid to get in trouble. Now, the thing among kids is to ask what's the worst that can happen if they get caught: Get sent to Springer (boys school) for two years? Big deal!"

"I think if kids are old enough to know the difference between right and wrong and they do wrong, why shouldn't the world know about it? Hiding things has caused a lot of the trouble that we see now. Kids have probably been overprotected."

Root causes of trouble no doubt were all over the map. And in some cases, trouble of the 1990s looked an awful lot like trouble of a decade earlier. Remember the four Santa Fé teens caught in the early 1980s with an arsenal of weapons en route to a fight at the city landfill? An Albuquerque couple feared trouble in May 1995 when they discovered an armful of weapons missing from their home.

The couple's 16-year-old son reportedly left to his Northeast Heights high school that morning toting three rifles, three handguns, a shotgun and what police initially described as "a couple thousand rounds of ammunition."

Police found the teen holed up in a drainage tunnel, apparently intending to retaliate against classmates who beat him earlier.

We had reached the point where some kids were too well armed to look for fights. Fights among youths while I grew up in the 1950s and 1960s often ended simply with ice packs over tender bruises and stern talks from parents at home about the need to hang around with the right people. Fights didn't lead to shoot outs or funerals.

In time, though, fights increasingly led to purchases of new shirts or dress suits bought by family members who knew the clothing was not long for the light of day and that heavy hours ahead would be marked by pastors' homilies about innocence lost and troublesome times.

So many families have gone to great lengths to avoid such times. Fabián Chávez, a respected carpenter in and around the state Capitol during the 1930s and 1940s, was driven to his wit's end by one of his eleven children. Fabián Chávez Jr. was a self-described free spirit. "It got me into trouble more than once," he said.

He was no stranger to spankings and other firm discipline at home. Discipline was reinforced by nuns at the red-brick Roman Catholic school just a few blocks from the Chávez home. It was, that is, when the boy was in school. It was not uncommon for him to skip school for an entire week.

But nothing worked to the satisfaction of the wayward boy's parents or to that of the nuns.

The Chávez family was well connected politically and one day the elder Fábian reluctantly decided it was time to put his connections to work. He no longer was inclined to allow his son to simply outgrow his streak of independence that had him straying so far from what was accepted at home.

Father and son one day in the mid-1930s walked from their eastside home past large vegetable gardens and beyond the little river that bisects Santa Fé. They crossed the Plaza and approached the county courthouse on Grant Street just south of the First Presbyterian Church. Young Fabián was uncertain about where his father was leading him at such a determined pace.

He recalled the walk for me decades later for his 2008 biography, *Taking on Giants, Fabián Chávez Jr. and New Mexico Politics*:

"We walked into the courthouse and went directly to see the district attorney, David Chávez Jr., who was a friend of my father's and the brother of Dennis Chávez, who had just begun serving as a U.S. senator. My dad had good connections. He knew both the district attorney and the judge, Miguel Otero. Dad was known as *don* Fabián and he was a highly respected gentleman.

"Dad must have talked to the DA ahead of time because my father got right into the discussion as soon as we arrived. He told the district attorney that he just didn't want me getting into deep trouble or getting hurt in any way. I guess, in his eyes, I was sort of incorrigible. I knew he was worried that I was going to stray into something serious.

"The DA asked my father in Spanish, 'Are you sure that you want to put the boy in Springer?'"

Judge Otero later asked the same question.

"My dad's response both times was, 'Yes, he has to learn.' He said he had lectured and whipped me before and it hadn't done any good."

Springer is a small community on the rolling prairie on the western edge of the Great Plains about 125 miles northeast of Santa Fé. It also was home to a reform school by the same name. Even in the mid-1930s, the name of Springer had its connotations, particularly among wayward boys and their families. Not quite a detention center back then, mere mention of the name struck fear in boys across New Mexico. Imaginitive minds regarded Springer as a sort of farm club for places like Alcatraz, Leavenworth and Sing Sing.

"Once the decision was made (to send me out), things went smoothly," said Fabián Chávez Jr. "They walked me down to the sheriff's office and arrangements were made to drive me to Springer."

The Springer Boys School, even after adoption of a revised Children's Code in the early 1990s, was still used to house certain youths for a maximum of two years. But the new law of more than 300 pages allowed older teens charged with first-degree murder to be tried directly in adult court. Teens tried in juvenile court could still be sentenced as adults for numerous other felonies. The law also allowed for intervention when families appeared to be breaking down so as to avoid court involvement.

Judges, district attorneys, psychologists, medical doctors, public defenders, law enforcement officers and state government experts participated in crafting the new law. House Speaker Sánchez sponsored the original legislation that led to changes. The bill passed the House by a vote of 68-1.

"I think this bill in its present form sends a very strong message to parents: You better start looking after your families," Sánchez said.

Alice King began her advocacy for children and youths at a time when troubled New Mexico kids, with relatively few exceptions, were best described as delinquents, not criminals. But even as youths turned harder and she recognized the need for less coddling, she remained an inspiration for those who wondered what more could be done to keep young New Mexicans off paths of self-destruction and away from the hopelessness, the anger that can maim and kill indiscriminately like a plague.

Perhaps, it was too much to expect. Well after Alice King's passing in 2008 so much seemed to continue to spin out of control despite revisions to state laws, attempts at public school reform and annual reports that consistently reminded New Mexicans that we bring up the rear on a lot of the life issues that matter.

Is it our failure to keep expectations in check that has kept so many of us reaching, always reaching to obliterate those paths of self-destruction and hopelessness that await the most vulnerable?

Maybe, but it doesn't seem like our reversal of fortunes rests in the innocence displayed by a young boy wearing half a uniform and dribbling contently into a school gym ever ready to play—if somebody gets hurt.

For those who need reminders that disruptive times, dismaying times don't only befall New Mexico, there is the all-too-common emergence of incidents that go by names like Columbine, Sandy Hook, Parkland and Santa Fé, Texas.

From the Roybal Files...
The Santa Fe New Mexican, Column, June 18, 1993
It's the Children, Not the Dads, Who Really Make Father's Day

Father's Day shouldn't be forgotten, so I'm writing about the occasion in this column two days early.

No, this is not a last-minute plug for Hallmark Cards. Call it just a line or two inspired by a photograph of what might be the most-dazzling string of dancing girls ever assembled.

Maybe it's just a father's pride showing through as he looks yet again at the photo and admires the unfettered display of affection and sense of accomplishment among Pojoaque third-graders who had just given their all for parents at a school program.

A father's pride: That's the whole point. The man who leans back on his lounger and waits for adulation on Father's Day is missing an opportunity to appreciate what put him in that overstuffed chair in the first place.

Father's Day, after all, should be to appreciate the kids.

It's something Hallmark has missed. The card company makes a killing with sappy cards that strain to express children's love for the fathers. But with enough advertising, the company could add to its fortune with cards for fathers to tell their children how life without them might be spent waiting for symphonies that never come instead of enjoying school programs staged in buildings that still smell of the bread, green beans and meat loaf served on plastic trays to chattering grade-schoolers earlier in the day.

Children's presents for Father's Day are wrapped but presents of the unwrapped variety actually come year-round. I got a great one from my nine-year-old daughter, Carla, on a warm July evening at home last year.

My son, Pablo, and a friend of his had pitched a tent outside to take advantage of a breeze that was blowing through the huge cottonwood in our front yard. It was a night the two boys had staked out for themselves so Carla was left inside inquiring gently about chances for something special of her own.

I offered her the foldaway couch bed in the living room, which the kids customarily used only on adventurous days framed around late-night television.

This night, the moments before bed were devoted to the games of a little girl. (I can say that in these days of super sensitivity because this little girl who sparkles on the dance floor is just as adept on the basketball court and in the classroom).

Who among all her friends and cousins, she inquired as I sat at her side, is the tallest? The fastest? The smartest? The nicest? And, yes, the cutest?

She set one ground rule going in: I could not pick her in any of my responses.

As hard as it was for a proud father, I stuck to the rule, biting my tongue on those occasions when I thought I would stray.

The game done, Carla freed herself of any and all restrictions while expressing softly her appreciation for her father and his time.

I tucked her small body into the large bed and kissed her on the forehead after stroking her golden brown bangs backward in a single, well-pacticed motion.

As I walked away into the darkness, Carla's voice promptly caught up: "I save all your kisses, Dad," she said. "I still have the first kiss you ever gave me."

The challenge, I suspect is to nurture such affection so that it still might be expressed at, say, 16 or 25. Perhaps it's easy for a father to reflect on the wonders of his children when they are still small. The challenge might be to keep the fond reflections flowing after independence and defiance begin touching young lives.

The challenge, without question, is met by many all around us. Bruce

Dancing girls of Pablo Roybal Elementary School in Pojoaque gave color to life during the 1990s.

King will point proudly to an unprecedented fourth term as governor should he win re-election in 1994. If he loses, he still can look fondly upon two grown sons who excel in both business and politics.

Senator Jeff Bingaman occasionally is beyond reach of reporters because of time he has committed to his 13-year-old son and the boy's mounting skills on the basketball court.

Senator Pete Domenci has raised eight children, pouring some of his most-heartfelt attention into congressional business that addresses needs of the mentally ill, a problem one of his own daughters has lived with for more than 20 years.

Father's Days are driven by young men embraking onto business or politics and younger girls in dancing clothes who need not worry yet about where their own skills and promising paths might lead. The biggest cheat amid it all might be the father who allows himself only one day out of every 365 to appreciate it.

From the Roybal Files...
The Santa Fe New Mexican, Column, February 20, 1994
It's Time to Lead, Not Manage

It's Sunday so your kids ought to be reasonably well rested from their latest week in school. I wish I were only talking about weariness that comes from battling armies of numbers and legions of historical accounts.

Increasingly, youths in our public schools are having to struggle to avoid violence that no responsible parent would dream of allowing at home.

Just during the past two weeks, a student at Capshaw Junior High School was arrested after hurling a good-sized rock at a girl who was trying to walk away from hecklers.

A student at Alameda Junior High had Valentine's Day roses that were sent to her by her father stolen by rivals, then crumpled on the floor in front of her locker while she was away.

On Thursday, a seventh-grader at DeVargas Junior High was attacked by several other students and stabbed badly enough to be treated at a hospital.

A day later, a student at Alameda Junior High apparently was stabbed during a school dance.

In Albuquerque, attempts to curb school violence have led to battles about how high girls can brush their hair and how low boys can drop the waists of their trousers.

Dress codes can't hurt. But resolution of our schools' problems with violence don't hang on the droop of a kid's pants.

Such wrangling, I suspect, is little more than a frustrated attempt by school officials grasping to impose order among the hundreds of students they supervise. It's superficial. Or, at best, it's a first step in what has to be a more-spirited effort to engage kids in something other than rebellion.

But to light inspirational fires under students, such flames must first be ignited under many, many more of the people who run our schools.

Merely hearing them express alarm after trouble occurs already has grown old.

In the schools, as in government, people seemingly have concluded that if they merely manage, they don't have to lead.

I don't know what kind of manager perennial presidential candidate Jesse Jackson is. But he's undeniably one of the most-inspiring people ever to address a gym full of kids.

He's done it in New Mexico and around the country.

He's moved youths to the edge of their seats. He's gotten them to spring to their feet. He's inspired them to burst into song and shout with confidence, "I AM somebody!" He's left many in tears before walking off their campuses—and out of their lives.

I rode in a bus with Jackson a few years ago after one such performance at what was then a troubled Río Grande High School in Albuquerque. Jackson's face glowed with pride in his own inspirational skills as he moved on to another stop.

Problem is, hopscotchng into school gyms every few years during political campaigns isn't much help. If anything, it merely teases kids with inspiration before sending them back to the dull corners of monotony.

This isn't rocket science, folks. It's basic. And Jesse Jackson isn't the only one who can make it work.

Unless somebody in New Mexico assumes enough of a leadership role to shake our educational system into providing full, daily doses of motivation—to students and educators, alike—we're going to have hallways full of people who are convinced the only way to make their marks on the community is by wearing droopy trousers.

Meanwhile, parents will grow increasingly wary about sending their children to school. And with good cause.

From the Roybal Files...
Albuquerque Journal, Column, July 4, 2006
All N.M. Kids Deserve Opportunity

As we commemorate the anniversary of our great country's independence, yet another report tells of the painful disparity in the lives of citizens in this land of hope and promise.

Equality, of course, is among the greatest of our promises. We promised not equality of income or stature, but equality of rights and opportunity.

Our founding fathers must have known how difficult it would be to meet expectations created by their soaring words because they, themselves, stopped well short of providing what they envisioned.

It has been left to later generations to move our country forward toward that more-perfect union. The condition of its children, perhaps as much as anything, tells each generetaion how it is doing.

The Annie E. Casey Foundation, in its latest Kids County report, shows clearly that there are immense disparities in the quality of life of children across our country; it suggests strongly that for so many infants leaving hospitals where they were born for the surroundings that will become their homes, equal opportunity is not in the air as they draw their first breaths. For far too many, it never will be.

Rich or poor, we need look no further than New Mexico to view disparities. In the latest Kids Count report from Baltimore, our state ranked 48th among 50 in key areas that measure a child's quality of life. It's gotten to where many of us can guess the two states—the only two—that fared worse: Mississippi and Louisiana.

The number of New Mexico children living in poverty (based on 2003–2004 data) increased from the last annual report. Thirty-three percent of our state's children under age six live below the federal poverty level, compared to 21 percent nationally. Most of New Mexico's poor children live in homes where at least one parent works.

An author of the Kids Count report says there are no quick fixes. "When you have a lot of poverty, you have a lot of bad outcomes," said William O'Hare.

Some of those "bad outcomes" actually undermine efforts to improve child welfare. Let's look at just one.

It's no secret that people's opportunities tend to increase along with their level of education. And as more is learned about how our public schools can be improved, parental involvement is seen as a critical element. But parental involvement is less—very often, substantially less—in poor families.

Hopelessness and indifference are frequently to blame, without doubt. So are the lack of time and access. It's hard for a parent to get to school during designated hours while working two jobs. It's hard for a parent to get to school while tending to children at home and while the family's only car has been used to get another member of the household to work.

"Poverty is the strongest and most-persistent threat to high student achievement," concludes the latest report from The Rural School and Community Trust in Arlington, Virginia.

Existing poverty will continue to be a drag on efforts to reduce poverty in the future in what has become one of the most-common of vicious cycles. Those efforts are further restrained when people of influence balk at systemic changes that are needed to break the nasty cycles.

In all walks of life 230 years after our nation's birth, we can't simply sing the praises of equal opportunity. We must acknowledge that in so many ways, we are still the paternal force that in not-so-distant decades tried using schools to "cleanse" Native Americans of their language and culture so that their chances of "success" might be enhanced.

Alongside Native Americans, Latinos recognize their mounting presence in New Mexico, where already they comprise 45 percent of the population. Yet, they see that their representation is far less than that in many circles where they could make a difference. At our state's flagship university, only 85 of the 830 faculty members are Latino.

Preaching success is not enough. If we are to battle poverty effectively, it is imperative that we create opportunities for more to model success and nurture its many forms; to break through persistent barriers among populations that have concluded through generations that sustained progress is beyond their reach.

Centuries after Jefferson, our collective pursuit of happiness is often confined to established paths. Cries of objections resonate from within self-satisfied institutions when initiatives would take us onto roads less traveled.

Those cries should be as loud when we allow so many of our tired ways to fuel complacency and convince us that vastly better lives will come soon enough to those who really want them—no matter the odds that are stacked against them.

18

The King Who Would be Governor

Calling Bruce King a politician would be like calling the magnificent cottonwood forest that lines most of New Mexico's Río Grande a stand of trees. King was governor of our state for 12 years, far longer than anybody else. He served as governor in the 1970s, 1980s and 1990s. And he was a successful leader of the state House of Representatives as well as a popular Santa Fé county commissioner before that.

His biography couldn't stop there, though, because he also was one heck of a humorist; perhaps as good as any who has called New Mexico home.

He didn't always mean to be funny. Offering cover for King one day, House Speaker Raymond Sánchez explained that what was in the governor's heart didn't always make it through his mouth in tact.

King was no stranger to malapropisms, to be sure. His most familiar was the one he told a state legislator about a controversial bill that King said he feared could "open a box of Pandoras" if approved.

But the lifelong cowboy from the Estancia Valley on the edge of the Great Plains also had a natural manner that prompted smiles and a love for telling stories drenched in subtle humor.

Wacky. Simple, detractors called him.

Well, if he was simple, he was simple like a fox, Democratic stalwart Eric Serna said of his longtime mentor.

And King had some help when it came to being cunning. Ed Delgado, a radio personality, former Democratic state legislator from Santa Fé and one-time ad man for King, enjoyed telling stories. He particularly enjoyed stories that showcased the prairie wit of King, his old pal the cowman.

One of Delgado's favorites was rooted in King's first term as governor from 1971–1974. It begins with Delgado recalling repeated attempts to get King to sit down for lunch or dinner at the rather posh Palace Restaurant, a popular hangout of local politicians just off the Plaza. King preferred a less-glitzy chain restaurant.

Bruce King was never short of quips while campaigning.

Said Delgado: "Bruce would always say, 'Let's just go down to Mr. Steak.'

"One day we were walking out of Mr. Steak and Bruce stopped to talk to the cashier about a little metal sign that was hanging on the wall. The sign said the restaurant served only Colorado prime beef.

"Bruce told the guy, 'We've got beef here in New Mexico and why don't you serve New Mexico beef?'

"The guy said it just isn't as good as Colorado beef. So Bruce said, 'Well, I'm Bruce King. I'm governor of New Mexico and I raise cattle. I say New Mexico beef is just as good as any other beef.'

"When we got outside the door, Bruce poked me with his elbow a few times and said, 'I guess we told him, didn't we Ed?'"

Delgado was given credit, even though he hadn't said a word. King was like that with his friends.

Along with his fondness for the story, Delgado had a good reason for telling it to me when he did. King was in the midst of his 1990 primary race for governor. I gave the story a little space in our paper, including the fact that managers of Mr. Steak removed their boast about Colorado beef soon after being lectured by King. Delgado, no doubt, figured the cute story would get King some good ink.

Indeed, King called Delgado the next day to thank him for the favorable publicity. Delgado's well-honed sense of timing as a storyteller, politician and ad man once again served King well.

The Prison Riot and Endless Handshakes

King relied on his growing ranks of friends and other New Mexicans who felt comfortable moving along the middle of New Mexico's political road to claim his first term as governor in 1970 by beating Republican Pete Domenici of Albuquerque. King narrowly defeated Republican Joe Skeen of Picacho in 1978 to secure a second term.

Environmentalists soon concluded they might have a friend in the moderate Democrat. King created the state Environmental Improvement Division in his first year as governor as the state took steps to improve protection of its air and water. King in time also organized attempts to improve planning of works coming out of his administration and to bring increased order to the system governing thousands of state government employees.

Pleased as King might have been, his detractors had more than enough to criticize.

Paul Bardacke, a former state attorney general, was among three

Democrats competing against King in the 1990 gubernatorial primary. Bardacke didn't waste time while going after one of the darkest stains on King's record: the 1980 state prison riot in which crazed inmates killed 33 other convicts, butchering many of them, during 36 hours of hell.

A grand jury assigned to evaluate conditions in 1978 told how the prison ten miles south of Santa Fé was designed to hold 850 inmates but was consistently 50 percent over capacity. Other grand juries during the late 1970s were filled with harsh findings and recommendations that governors and state legislators approve large, new appropriations for the Corrections Department to address overcrowding and grossly inadequate staffing numbers.

Two governors and five legislatures spent more than $20 million on renovations during the ten years prior to the riot, *The Santa Fe New Mexican* reported. A multi-million dollar renovation was underway when the riot blew. Work, however, was far less than what was required, according to dire reports coming out of the prison.

Years of negligence, misfeasance, corruption and systemic abuse of a far-reaching snitch system among inmates filled many in the prison with hate and anger. In December 1979, reform-minded inmate Dwight Duran wrote to Governor King and said "terrible consequences" were coming soon because of the state's refusal to make necessary prison improvements.

A grand jury report dated January 18, 1980, urged immediate attention.

Paroled just before the riot, Duran told King "the prison's going to blow."

It did on February 2, 1980, becoming one of the nation's worst prison riots ever.

Bardacke criticized King for supposedly contributing to conditions that led to the uprising as well as for his decision to delay police intervention until after so many were killed.

And when talk turned to the future, Bardacke took King on early for saying that he wanted to promote good education, more jobs and happier families without ever offering much about how he would do it. So King and his people went to work and later began running ads that told of 74 specific points on how he would address his main issues.

Bardacke then scoffed that King was offering everything to everyone.

"He's kind of hard to please," said King.

King also found state Republican Party Chairman John Lattauzio to be rather difficult that year. Lattauzio distributed a letter to hundreds of New Mexicans in which he leveled several personal attacks against King. King was unqualified to be governor partly because of the comic gaffes that could come out of his mouth at inopportune times, in inopportune places, Lattauzio said.

It was all pretty difficult to take for the two-term former governor, who said he was not too unlike Will Rogers.

Said King: "I never met a person I didn't like—but if this guy keeps on, I might develop (something against him)."

King dispatched Bardacke and other competitors in the 1990 primary, collecting 52 percent of the votes to Bardacke's 38 percent. Tony Scarborough and Bob Gold split remaining votes. King took his winnings to do battle with Lattauzio and GOP gubernatorial nominee Frank Bond.

King's foxy—if old-time style—was visible late in that year's general election campaign. The Santa Fe New Mexico Oil and Gas Association was in the midst of its annual meeting in Santa Fé's Eldorado Hotel. King and Bond were invited to address the group.

While more than 200 association members waited in their seats, director and forum moderator Darwin Van de Graff called King to the speaker's table at the front of the large room. He wanted to flip a coin to see whether King or Bond would speak first. No sign of King despite the call. All waited for a while but eventually Bond called the coin toss and lost.

King was still out in the hallway talking to people but was on his way in, Santa Fé attorney and occasional King surrogate, John Pound, offered somewhat sheepishly.

King was well known for not leaving a hand unshaken wherever he came upon people. Few would get away without being asked about their families, their homes or their jobs—often all three.

"How many people are in the hallway?" Van de Graff asked impatiently.

"Three, so it'll be about ten minutes," Pound quipped, drawing a nervous laugh from the group seated in the room.

When King finally entered, Van de Graff commented, "We've heard you like to make a late entrance to get more attention, but this is ridiculous."

When informed that he had won the coin toss, King nodded politely and said he would let Bond go first.

No Stranger to Sunrises

Successful political campaigning doesn't come easily. It involves cramped schedules, hard work and long hours. Having just won the governor's race in the 1990 Democratic primary, King took only a couple of hours off before starting in on the general election race against Bond. He knew he would come upon plenty of familiar faces.

"I don't think there's anybody in the state who knows more people by their first names," said Kay Marr, a former King speechwriter who also served him as secretary of the Department of Finance and Administration.

As a life-long and successful rancher, King was no stranger to sunrises. He was up and going by dawn the day after the 1990 primary. He got two hours sleep that night and was out in the lobby of his Albuquerque hotel pumping hands and passing out literature to the doorman and desk clerk at 5:30 in the morning.

He left to visit with reporters at television and newspaper offices then departed for Santa Fé where he attended two funerals, then dropped in to chat with *The Santa Fe New Mexican's* recently appointed associate publisher and to wish her well.

The general election campaign had him in Roswell with just weeks to go before voting. As usual, King sought to secure as much contact with electors as possible during a hectic day.

A hurried campaign visit to a senior citizen's center was one of several scheduled stops that day and required King to temporarily leave a reception sponsored by a Roswell city councilor at her home. He apologetically left the house, promising to return in half an hour.

He said later, "I got to the center and sat down with this group of elderly ladies. They were just as sweet as can be, like my mom at that stage of her life. We were talking and they insisted, of course, that I stay and eat so the meal started with the salad, which was a cube of Jello over a leaf of lettuce with nuts sprinkled on top.

"I knew I had to get back to the city councilor's reception, and so I was looking for a way to leave the (senior) center and still preserve a little respect. I poked at the Jello and said, 'Well, I guess I better finish my dessert so I can get going.' One of the ladies lifted her head and said, 'Dessert? Did we already eat?'"

King didn't always come upon admirers, of course. Early in the 1990 general election campaign one group took him to task for an earlier decision that went against its interests. His response there was one he turned to more than once as the campaign progressed.

"Well, if you don't like me, you can still vote for Casey," King suggested, referring to running mate, Belen car dealer Casey Luna. A vote for Luna, of course, was a vote for King since the governor and lieutenant governor ran as a team.

King, ever the cheerleader for New Mexico, liked to say the state had

Bruce King visits with children in southern New Mexico during a campaign stop while angling for votes of the children's parents.

plenty of good minds to pursue progress. No need to hire people from far and wide. "We'll get the best people we can find in New Mexico and see how we can turn things around," he said as he looked forward to his third term as governor.

A third term? The first two terms were nothing to crow about, said one-time Republican stalwart, John Irick. "He's brought in every political hack of the last 30 years he could lay his hands on and given them a job," he said of King.

King always balked at attempts by others to paint him as a villain. He had pretty good rags-to-riches stories and shared them occasionally when times allowed. They were stories about his family's difficult early years when his parents left the Texas plains in 1918 and settled in New Mexico's Estancia Valley. King's parents traded a Model-T Ford for a 160-acre homestead where the family lived for a time in a tarpaper dugout. The Kings by 1990 had a reported worth of five million dollars. The family came to own a butane company and held more than 400,000 acres, including leased public lands.

Those early years were etched in King's mind, but he said with a broad, toothy smile that he knew when it was time to stop talking about the family's struggles.

Bruce King talks with this book's author while campaigning for a third term as governor.

"One day the kids started telling me, 'Boy, aren't you glad you live with us now, Dad?'"

At the sprawling family ranch, Alice King was as much a partner to the long-serving governor as she was around the Capitol. Bruce didn't hesitate to give her credit no matter what her role even when he had to employ his skills as a shrewd politician to spin a story in his favor when it might otherwise have worked against him.

So it was with this one: The Kings were walking outdoors at their ranch one day amid livestock, machinery and tools when a large rattlesnake suddenly appeared at their side. Husband and wife both were shaken but it was Alice who promptly reached for a shovel and separated the reptile's head from its body. Bruce jumped away to escape any threat.

"I was too fast for that dern snake," he told me through his familiar grin.

Alice, Bruce would tell electors on the campaign trail, added value to every vote that came his way. Voters get two Kings for the price of one, he'd assert over and again. And he joked during the 1990 campaign that there was another good reason for him to frequently ask his longtime partner to follow him to microphones on the campaign trail.

"I always have Alice say a few words. That way she won't tell me later what I forgot."

At just about every campaign stop, King asserted that he earned a reputation for being prudent and efficient as state government's chief executive. "If it aint broke, don't fix it," he was fond of saying during his first two terms as governor.

As he campaigned for a third term in 1990, he seemingly concluded that he wanted to be associated with something else just as direct but perhaps a little more inspiring. He and Alice wanted everyone in New Mexico to feel important; needed and wanted, he said.

Some dismissed it as corny. King didn't flinch.

"Some people think that because you mingle with the workers and treat them as equals that you don't know what you're doing," he told me.

It was all vintage King, supporters insisted.

"You can be at the Waldorf Astoria and, by golly, if Bruce King sees you, he's going to go over and shake your hand," said longtime Democratic state Representative Nick Salazar of Ohkay Owingeh Pueblo.

Salazar said he and his son Earl were eating one day at the Mayflower Hotel in Washington, DC, where King happened to be attending a meeting with business leaders and other government officials. "He was in there with a whole bunch of real important people, but he got up and shook our hands just like if we were at home."

A Third Win and One Diploma on the Wall

King, at 66, won a third four-year term as governor in the 1990 general election. The win was unprecedented and it wasn't even close. King claimed 52 percent of the vote, Bond 45 percent.

One Albuquerque television station declared less than an hour after the polls closed at seven p.m. that King defeated Bond. Well before eight p.m., a *mariachi* band began playing for festive King supporters assembled at the Ramada Classic Hotel.

The boyish-looking 47-year-old Bond had insisted that King's tired ways left New Mexico in old political ruts. It left the state poor of money and poor of spirit, he said, adding that New Mexicans had to resolve not to be poor anymore.

But in the end, it was King's positive tone, his warm embrace of the state and its people that supporters said persuaded voters to support a man who might be New Mexico's best example of a down-home populist.

"A lot of people in New Mexico still consider him to be a very special politician," said King's adept spokesman, John McKean.

King rose to prominence with only one diploma posted on his wall, that of a tiny high school in Stanley. He enrolled at the University of New Mexico but left without a degree.

After toiling for years in the state Legislature, he tried but failed to win his party's gubernatorial nomination in 1966, losing to T.E. "Gene" Lusk of Carlsbad. He sought the nomination again in 1968 but lost to Fabián Chávez Jr. of Santa Fé.

King, however, wasn't to be denied the aura of a special politician. He secured the Democratic nomination for governor in 1970 then comfortably won his first term over Domenici, 51-46 percent. He won his second term in a tight general election race eight years later against Skeen, 50-49 percent.

Domenici and Skeen both were elected to Congress following their losses in gubernatorial races, and for years seemed invinceable, Domenici in the Senate and Skeen in the House of Representatives.

King's third election to a four-year term in 1990 assured him special status. Republican Edwin Mechem won four gubernatorial races spread over the 1950s and 1960s. But Mechem's terms each were two years long, and he left his final term a month early to serve briefly in the U.S. Senate so his time of service was just short of eight years.

King's victory margin in the 1990 governor's race was the largest since 1964. His presence in the race was intimidating from the start. Bill Sego, a prominent Republican who ran unsuccessfully for governor in 1982, considered getting into the 1990 race but stayed out because a poll he commissioned showed King would be tough to beat. Democrat U.S. Representative Bill Richardson clearly yearned to enter that year's Democratic primary but in the end stayed out because, he said, his wife asked him to—but also after his own poll showed that he, too, could lose to King.

The Goodwill Begins to Fade

Moving into their third term, neither King nor wife, Alice, hid their intent to secure a fourth in 1994. But the goodwill they took with them into the Capitol for their third soon began to fade.

With good reason, the state's environmentalists were some of King's strongest supporters, even in his race against Bond, who was a former member of the Sierra Club. "King was a principal architect in the creation of the state's environmental protection system and a sponsor of its key air and water laws and endangered species protection," Sierra Club officials Jay Sorenson and Stephen Verchinski wrote in the endorsement of King in 1990.

Arguably, King might have done more to promote environmental protection than any of New Mexico's other governors of the period. Among his most-notable accomplishment was creation of the state Environmental Improvement Division in 1971. King promised during the 1990 campaign to elevate the agency to a cabinet-level deparment and he did.

He found himself walking a tightrope, though, a month into his third term when it came time to name a head for the new department. King already had riled environmentalists with his reappointment of Anita Lockwood as secretary of the Energy, Minerals and Natural Resources Department. Environmentalists accused her of favoring business development over conservation and of disregarding criticism.

Those same environmentalists submitted two names they wanted King to consider as secretaries for the new Environmental Improvement Department. They thought King had agreed to pick one of the two after meeting with him to discuss the appointment. But King later informed them that he was considering elevating Ray Powell Jr. from the governor's staff to become the EID head. Powell's father was King's longtime friend who was serving as state Democratic Party chairman at King's behest.

Judith Espinosa, a 42-year-old lawyer, former state Transportation Department secretary and one of the two names submitted to King by environmentalists, eventually got the appointment but not before seeds of discontent were planted.

Opponents during the 1990 campaign described King as a man who couldn't say no when people came calling with requests. But during his first five months in office following that campaign, King had drawn a lot of attention for saying no—and he did it when it involved some of his closest friends.

King said no to higher taxes that would have allowed teachers and government workers to get more than minimal pay raises in 1991.

He said no to labor unions who tried to get too much while pressing for a collective bargaining law.

He said no to House and Senate Democratic leaders who wanted to convert the chief clerks of their chambers from part-time to full-time positions and to hire staffs for offices that would be open year-round.

King was criticized during his previous two terms for appearing to give a state job to almost anyone who sold one of his campaign raffle tickets. Early in his third term he was accused of not caring enough for loyal Democrats while structuring his administration.

Representative Luciano "Lucky" Varela, a Santa Fé Democrat, was among those who thought King could have done better for his political party while filling the hundreds of state jobs available to the governor.

King also took heat during the April 1990 meeting of the state Democratic Central Committee in Albuquerque. Taos County Democratic Chairman Frank "Skit" Trujillo and others said Hispanics were locked out of key decision-making processes. Trujillo specifically blamed state Democratic Chairman Ray Powell. Because of King's long, close association with Powell, King was implicated in the criticisms.

And it wasn't the first time that King was accused of inadequately acknowledging contributions of Hispanics to his successful campaigns. During one of King's earlier terms as governor, Hispanic legislators from Albuquerque grew upset about the shortage of people from the Duke City's South Valley in King's administration.

"I've appointed several of our friends from the South Valley. Problem is, as soon as they get their jobs, they move up to the Heights," King fired back in his defense and only half in jest.

In May 1991, just five months into his third term, King met in his office for a few minutes with former Santa Fé Mayor Art Trujillo to address issues that Trujillo said threatened King and the state Democratic Party. Trujillo had claimed two high-profile political victories over King and there was tension between the two men.

Trujillo had been New Mexico's Democrtic national committee member since he beat King for the post in 1983, leaving King bitter.

Then after having moved from Santa Fé to Albuquerque, Trujillo was elected Bernalillo County Democratic chairman at the party's April 1991 meeting, defeating a candidate King publicly supported.

Trujillo said he wanted to meet with King in May to "work out all the differences we've had."

"We're going to put the past behind us. We're going to run the show together," he said.

King over the years had come to learn that people often are quick to want a share of power and authority, but Trujillo's public muscle flexing did not sit well with the governor. And within just two years it would become so painfully apparent to many just how averse King was to people injecting themselves into what he considered to be his show.

But before that jolt, King seemingly was unable to pull himself away from having to address sniping and discontent from multiple quarters.

In May 1991, King signed an executive order, giving unqualified support for the New Mexico Human Rights Act but left unaddressed an issue that had grown increasingly sensitive when talk turned to the anti-discrimination law.

Homosexuals believed they should be mentioned specifically in the

Human Rights Act and anything resembling King's executive order that dealt with unlawful discrimination in the work place.

Several Democratic legislators, led by senators Tom Rutherford of Albuquerque and Carlos Cisneros of Questa, tried but failed during the 1991 legislative session to amend the Human Rights Act to specifically protect homosexuals.

Toney Anaya, Democratic governor from 1983–1986, issued an executive order doing precisely that but the order did not have the effect of law and expired when Governor Anaya left office.

King spokesman John McKean said the current governor stood squarely against unlawful discrimination despite the restraint in his executive order. "The governor didn't try to anticipate every possible situation where discrimination might be alleged," McKean said.

Governor King, himself, picked up on that point later. "I didn't single out us farmers and ranchers either so I didn't single out anybody," he said.

He said politicians must approach some issues delicately—even when there's no question about where they stand—so some people who see things differently aren't upset.

"If you get too far out, then you separate yourself from the far right, for lack of a better term. You don't need that. You can be supportive of all the people," he said.

King long had seen himself as a pragmatist, a centrist who was willing to veer just enough from the middle stripe to keep a solid majority of the citizenry satisfied, if not completely happy.

King didn't move nearly enough to please homosexuals and others who thought homosexuals should have clearly expressed protections in the Human Rights Act. In their minds, King wasn't at all supportive.

Problems followed King into the second year of his third term. The governor, while delivering his annual state-of-the-state address in January 1992, imposed a hiring freeze on government as part of his attempt to stretch revenues even at a time when demand for services was increasing.

What about a tax increase to pay for the state's mounting needs in education, health care and other areas? he was asked.

"The thing is, I've never come upon lines of people asking me to raise their taxes," he told me.

It tracked with King's long-held conviction that it was senseless to try to lead people where they don't want to go.

King pledged to veto any measure passed by the Legislature that called for raising taxes to expand what was projected to be a $2.1 billion budget in the ensuing fiscal year.

King predicted his administration would save seven million dollars through his freeze on hiring within the 17,000-plus classified employee work pool, sharp restrictions on out-of-state travel and limits on discretionary spending, including professional service contracts.

"I realize these are forceful measures that won't be popular in all quarters, but I'm firmly determined that we tightly manage the state's public money," he said.

He called for understanding from state workers and school employees who were asked to forego pay increases.

"There is no one in New Mexico who more than myself holds in high esteem and appreciation the very hard and good work of the thousands of our very fine public employees in state government and our public school and higher education teachers, professors and employees," King said. "I believe I have demonstrated that time and time again over my 35 years of association with state government."

Representatives of the two major teacher unions in New Mexico were not at all pleased and they made their feelings known among their members and others who called for fortifying education.

"I wish we had more to give," King said.

It was a rocky 1992 legislative session for King. And even amid the palpable discontent, an undercurrent of uneasiness was building among the faithful and the not-so-faithful.

Detractors said King looked tired and bored with the job that he had held for nine years.

Alice King, even as she talked about pursuing a fourth Bruce King administration, told me in an in-depth interview in November 1991 that she, at 61, could not rule out running for governor, herself, one day. She was flattered, she said, knowing that some people were talking about it.

It sounded at least a little as if groundwork was being laid for election of New Mexico's first woman governor in the not-too-distant future. Alice King was in as good a position as anyone to claim the milestone. Born on a dairy farm in Moriarty, Alice initially dreamed simply of finding a rancher with whom to spend her life. She found one when she was 17 in Stanley, barely more than a stone's throw to the north along State Road 41. He was a fellow with a toothy grin, an irregular gait and a future in politics that nobody could have predicted. Were Alice to be elected governor one day, it simply would have added to the landscape of surprises molded by the small-town rancher and his wife.

Two Kings for the price of one, the governor promised repeatedly on the 1990 campaign trail. Having helped secure a third King term, Alice didn't actually sit in the governor's office because she didn't need to. King and his staff at the time were temporarily housed in the old PERA Building while the Capitol underwent renovation. Alice King had her own office and it was quite impressive, larger than the office held by Chief of Staff James Lewis and only slightly smaller than the one occupied by the governor.

Not all talk about Alice becoming New Mexico's first governor some day was flattering.

"Bruce absolutely has gone to sleep at the head table," said one of the state's leading Republicans who asked for anonymity while speaking of the 67-year-old governor in November 1991. "He's slipping and we're beginning to see that maybe he can't handle it. I think the Kings are aware of it and I think that's why we're hearing about Alice."

Similar thoughts had begun circulating among capitol reporters.

It was a cheap shot by a nameless accuser, fumed Democratic Party Chairman Ray Powell. "I would honestly say that Bruce is every bit as effective as I remember him in his previous two terms," Powell said. "As a matter of fact, he gets more done now with less effort because of his experience and his good cabinet."

Republicans weren't willing to let the image of an uninspired governor fade away, however. "I've heard that Alice is picking up the slack for Bruce, giving speeches in place of him, and even when he's present," said Frank Bond.

Alice King insisted that if she were to run for governor, it would be after 1994 when her husband planned to secure an unprecedented fourth four-year term.

The thought of what might easily be seen as a never-ending King dynasty sparked at least a little discomfort.

No matter. In August 1992, King officially kicked off his campaign for a fourth term. Already, 169 New Mexicans reportedly had joined what was called King's Gold Boot Club for donors of $1,000 or more.

Jamie Koch, a longtime King confidant and operative, was the campaign's finance chairman.

Polls Confirm Suspicions

The re-election fund-raiser came on the heels of a statewide public opinion poll that showed King would trail U.S. Representative Bill Richardson by two points in a race pitting the two men in the 1994 Democratic primary for governor.

The poll, which I was first to obtain, was done by respected Research and Polling Inc. of Albuquerque but the company, when approached, refused to disclose to me or anyone who commissioned the survey. Both Richardson and King denied paying for it. Republicans didn't claim ownership, either.

Richardson, who has served in the Congress since 1983, didn't deny interest in the 1994 governor's race. But he said a poll so early, along with its secretive origins, could foment unnecessary divisions among state Democrats.

King grew uncharacteristically irate when I repeatedly refused to disclose who gave me the poll results. He was fit to be tied.

King apparently hadn't expected serious oppostion in the 1994 Democratic primary. He anticipated a general election challenge from the likes of Republican Garrey Carruthers, who King succeeded as governor in 1991. Suddenly, out of the blue, there was Bill Richardson moving with King stride for stride, according to the Albuquerque polling company.

King spokesman John McKean correctly noted that the poll essentially reflected a virtual tie because of its six percent margin of error. Being down by two meant nothing, he insisted.

Still, it wasn't good news for King. Twenty-three percent of poll respondents said they were uncommitted. King supporters had boasted how 1990 polls showed as many as 99 percent of New Mexicans knew King. A politician with that kind of name ID has to smile until he's told nearly a quarter of all those who know of him don't know if they would vote for him in a two-man race.

"When all is said and done," I wrote in a column, "if a candidate tells you he'd rather be trailing in a poll by two percentage points than leading by two percentage points, vote for the other candidate."

King won big in 1990 but with more than two years before he would face re-election, he seemingly was slipping in the voters' esteem.

Although King did not know who commissioned the poll, it didn't keep him from speculating. King was as subtle as the subtlest of politicians. But if one listened carefully as the governor talked of the poll's results, it was clear he thought Richardson—or someone tied to Richardson—paid for the survey.

King twice alluded to Richardson during an outburst of two or three minutes as he positioned his substantial frame directly in front me. The first came while referring to the poll's conclusion that Richardson would beat King 67 to 21 percent in northeastern New Mexico, a region Richardson had worked hard while representing it in Congress during the previous ten years.

"He had better not take a shot at me if he thinks he's going to take San Juan County 67 percent to 21 percent," King told me. "I don't think anyone's going to beat me in San Juan County. No one ever has."

The governor alluded to Richardson a second time, subtly, oh, so subtly, while speaking of how Richardson's total score in the poll had him running no better than a dead heat with King.

"I'm not going to have bad polls when I do them. We're the ones who are going to be paying for those polls," King said, suggesting poll questions can be structured to collect desired results."

McKean only a few months earlier mused about how people really had to know King to recognize when he was angry. There was absolutely no mistaking his anger when King turned to profanity while insisting, unsuccessfully, that I tell him who slipped me a copy of the poll. In the process, he angrily asserted again that some polls aren't worth spit.

As King began collecting $1,000 contributions for his Gold Boot Club in 1992, there was major discomfort among the state's American Indians and they no longer were in a giving mood. Indian leaders across the state had begun moving on plans for widespread video gambling on tribal lands. Such gambling already had begun and King, a Baptist, was adamantly opposed to it. He wrapped his opposition around the fact that the state Legislature had yet to approve video gambling on non-Indian lands.

"Indians should be entitled to everything we do in the state. We haven't been allowed to do video gaming, so they shouldn't either," King said.

He grew irate when the state liquor industry disclosed it would propose that the 1993 Legislature authorize up to 23,000 video gaming machines around New Mexico. King pledged to veto any such bill.

He redoubled his opposition and by May 1993, Indian leaders needed little coaxing to express their discontent. King was scorned and even mocked by people who traditionally had been his political allies when 40 Indian leaders met to express unity for multiple tribal causes.

The message came across plain and clear: King was in hot water with many of New Mexico's Navajos, Apaches and Pueblo Indians. Video gambling was only one of multiple issues discussed but it was one of those radiating the most heat.

Mescalero Apache President Wendell Chino said King had "reneged" on promises. "We're here to address Governor Bruce King's insensitivity and hypocrisy," Chino said.

About 104,000 Indians lived in New Mexico in 1993. The All-Indian Pueblo Council estimated that 75 percent of registered Indian voters went to the polls and voted for King in the 1990 gubernatorial election.

Hoping to redirect at least some attention away from video gambling, King offered to appoint a task force to further study conditions that saw oil and gas production on tribal lands facing dual taxation by Indians and the state.

"I, as a tribal leader, am getting fed up with another task force," said Lloyd Tortalita, first lieutenant governor of Acoma Pueblo.

Santa Clara Governor Walter Dasheno, who was appointed by King to the state Indian Affairs Commission, said Indians often get "tokenism" instead of meaningful help from state government.

Jicarilla Apache President Leonard Atole said King had been generous with smiles and handshakes but not in meeting economic development needs of Indians.

"He is not going to be our next governor ... if he doesn't improve on his report card." Atole said.

Indian representatives had just prepared a so-called report card that found King to be "failing" in the issues of sovereignty, accessibility and leadership. He scored "excellent" in making promises and "poor" in keeping promises.

Ernie Lovato, former Santo Domingo Pueblo governor and previously a vocal King supporter, said Indians continued to be neglected. "We need to give a message: no more free Indian votes," he said.

King continued to insist as 1993 drew to an end that Indians had opened gaming parlors illegally. Video gaming was a demon in King's eyes and he took comfort in polls that showed most New Mexicans supported a statewide lottery but were far less enthusiastic about video gaming. Prevailing supposition about those poll results was that people more directly associated video gaming with organized crime and other unsavory elements than they did a lottery.

King's popularity without question wasn't wearing well, and not just among Indians. All motorists had reason to grouse. King approved a six-cent gasoline tax included in a measure passed by the 1993 Legislature after administration economists undershot their revenue projections by $160 million for the ensuing fiscal year.

And there was mounting discontent among high-profile Democratic officials. It seemed to focus on King's reluctance to say no while meeting with petitioners face-to-face, only to reject their requests later when decision time arrived.

"I don't like this idea of having to do things twice just because he doesn't always make himself clear from the start," said Santa Fé state Representative Luciano "Lucky" Varela. "It's wasted time and effort on our part."

House Majority Whip Ben Luján of Nambé was upset with King's veto of legislation that would have eased soaring property tax burdens on long-time Santa Fé residents. Río Arriba Democratic *patrón*, state Senator Emilio Naranjo, was offended that King did not come to his defense when state party lawyer Ray Schowers publicly called Naranjo an "S.O.B." and "a terrible, self-serving person."

Jamie Koch, King's finance chairman, predicted peace would come. "At this stage, I'm sure there are people who haven't gotten everything they wanted. But we're ready to do everything needed to get re-elected," Koch said.

Die-hard supporters remained in reasonably good supply. By May 1993, King had more than $300,000 in pledged campaign contributions and more than $200,000 of it was already in the bank, a substantial amount for that period.

Well financed or not, King in the summer of 1993 managed to reawaken anxiety among some of the state's most-vocal environmentalists. Jim Baca, a favorite of those environmentalists, had resigned as state land commissioner to accept a federal appointment as director of the U.S. Bureau of Land Management. King named his longtime friend and supporter, Ray Powell Jr., to succeed Baca.

Neither Powell nor his father, the state Democratic Party chairman, had the confidence of vocal environmentalists.

The state Land Office is charged with managing resources that generate large sums for the state annually. It also is relied upon to balance expectations of people with widely conflicting interests on issues like oil and mineral extraction, livestock grazing and environmental protection.

What if Ray Powell Jr. while at the land office turned out to reflect the same rancher-friendly positions of the governor? King was asked at the news conference where he announced Powell's appointment.

"That wouldn't be all bad. I'd do the job myself if I had the time," said King.

Alice King laughed with approval from her chair a few feet away from the governor. King, in acknowledgement, nodded his head while glancing in her direction as if the two had anticipated the question.

How much, King was asked, was he willing to court and win anew the support of hard-charging environmentalists who previously signaled they would not be enthusiastic about Powell's selection?

"We don't like to see anybody drop off the side but sometimes you can't do anything about it," King said, signaling he would not be pushed off his middle-of-the-road approach to governing.

There was at least a hint of overconfidence reflected in words coming from the governor, Koch and others in King's camp. There was, anyway, until another public opinion survey delivered disheartening news in July

1993. The poll of Albuquerque residents done by *The Albuquerque Tribune* and KRQE-TV found 58 percent of those questioned did not want King to seek a fourth term; 27 percent did. One-third of those who wanted to see King in the 1994 race wanted him to lose.

King through a spokesman sought to minimize the significance of the poll, telling how it only involved Albuquerque and included Democrats and Republicans alike. Spokesman John McKean told how King needed only Democrats in the 1994 primary.

Still, Republicans would get to vote in that year's general election and unless King won there, he'd have to face moving back to his ranch in Stanley sooner than planned. And the governor's team couldn't downplay Duke City opinions too much because Albuquerque by far remained the state's largest city.

CASEY STEPS TO THE PLATE

From all appearances, King was in serious trouble and conditions were about to get much worse with news I broke on a hot summer day in June 1993. Lieutenant Governor Casey Luna, elected to his first statewide office as King's running mate in 1990, told me he had grown to feel so underused and disrespected that he could not rule out running against King in the 1994 gubernatorial primary.

Luna, recognized statewide as a hard-driving Belen businessman, walked into the lieutenant governor's office saying he wouldn't want a job that didn't keep him busy. On that note, he promptly jumped on the Democratic-controlled Legislature, accusing lawmakers of being too slow while addressing state needs. "We've just been skipping a lot of rope and not doing much work," he said.

Luna said repeatedly while campaigning for lieutenant governor that New Mexicans would not be disappointed by the King-Luna team. Just more than two years after the team's election, Luna said of King: "I don't know how to put it. I'm very, very loyal to the governor ... I just think (he) needs all the help he can get. I feel very sorry for him many, many times because he is getting an awful lot of backlash that he really doesn't deserve ... I like to use my time constructively and I do think the governor needs a lot of help ... I think sometimes the advice the governor gets is not the most-constructive advice."

Luna stressed that his preference was to remain on King's team but not if he was going to be kept locked away from participation.

King fumed.

Within months, Luna was preparing to challenge King in the June

1994 Democratic primary. "I think the office deserves better than it's got," Luna said, abandoning some of the restraint of earlier comments. "I don't want to waste my time. I don't want to just sit in an office."

It was one of the most-rebellious acts in New Mexico Democratic Party politics in years. But Luna, owner of a Ford dealership in Belen, was hardly the rebel.

He was a self-made millionaire with big hands and thick wrists who got his first job washing dishes at the age of 12. He became a master of household chores early out of necessity while his mother sometimes held down four jobs at once to support Luna and five siblings.

"I remember I used to get so mad because when I was making tortillas, I couldn't make them round," he told me soon after being elected lieutenant governor.

Oh, Luna could get mad, all right. It's just that his decision to bolt from King surprised some because Luna made it to the top as a small businessman by holding firmly to the precepts of team effort, loyalty and hard work.

Luna's decision to challenge King naturally led to some changes within the Capitol. King used to enjoy getting out of the state periodically as governor. He was gone at least 58 days in 1993, leaving Luna to serve as acting governor without much to do.

Suddenly King decided to avoid leaving Luna in charge whenever possible. Two assumptions jumped to mind: King was concerned Luna would do something as acting governor to make himself look good; or, he would do something to make King look bad.

King spokesman John McKean wove both possibilities into one delicate statement. "You normally expect that the lieutenant governor is on your team and will carry out your instructions while you're gone. But if the lieutenant governor is running against you, I don't know that you can make the same assumption."

Elected governor three times, King had been unable to part company with his lieutenant governors on good terms.

Roberto Mondragón, who was King's lieutenant governor for his first two terms, differed openly with King. King occasionally was known to question Mondragón's judgment. "Well, you know, Roberto has his own way of doing things," King told me once of his lieutenant governor.

Mondragón was left smarting angrily from what King told me after Mondragón accused the millionaire King of using his post as governor to make himself richer.

"I guess Bob is a little bit unhappy that life hasn't treated him well," King said.

Mondragón and others aiming rhetorical fire at King were spurred further in their attacks as 1993 drew to a close. King and his family had engaged in a controversial and increasingly publicized land swap with the federal Bureau of Land Management. In the swap, the Kings gave the BLM 17,000 acres near the El Malpais National Monument south of Grants in return for 700 acres in the lucrative Santa Fé real estate market. Professional appraisals, said the parties, showed that they each traded property worth $1.7 million.

But others said the prime land obtained by the Kings adjacent to the expensive Las Campanas development was worth as much as seven million with a potential for far greater value once developed.

The deal was finalized in 1992 but controversy surrounding it grew with time. The whole thing smacked of a remarkable sweetheart deal that King was able to secure through his political connections.

It was bad news for King, even among supporters.

Mondragón pounced, cracking a smile while telling of King's assertion that both parties in the trade got a fair deal. Although pronounced "Mal-pay" in English, *Malpaís* in Spanish means bad land. And the property the Kings got rid of along the lava-covered landscape south of Grants was baaaad land, Mondragón said with a chuckle.

Former Press Aide Jim Baca Adds to Surprises

When it came to public opinion, King seemed to be all but on the ropes when leading New Mexico environmentalists began encouraging Jim Baca to join the 1994 Democratic gubernatorial primary. By then, Luna had submitted 1,260 pages of nominating petitions, more than the 959 pages submitted by King.

"It was more than 13,000 signatures, and we got almost every one of them in six days," Luna said.

King wasn't intimidated and reportedly expressed relief about his parting with Luna. "I'm glad to be rid of him," he supposedly told the *Las Cruces Sun-News*.

King later denied making the comment but *Sun-News* editor Harold Cousland stood by his paper's story.

Baca years earlier had served as King's press secretary before being elected state land commissioner twice and then winning appointment in 1993 as federal BLM director. But Baca didn't last long in Washington. He was forced out as BLM chief after taking stands environmentalists across the country enthusiastically embraced, including proposed revisions to livestock grazing rules on public lands managed by the BLM. Environmentalists were happy; ranchers weren't.

Baca commissioned a poll to see how he would do in New Mexico's 1994 gubernatorial primary. He planned to use poll results and early indications about financial support before deciding whether to enter the governor's race.

It would be a late start for Baca. Luna knew that if he and Baca were both in the race to split anti-King votes, the governor could well stay at the Stanley ranch with his cattle and put off campaigning until the general election.

Luna and Baca met four months before the scheduled June primary. "I just flat out told him, 'You can't win, Jim,'" Luna said later.

Baca got in anyway. He was short on funds and behind King and Luna in public opinion polls. Still, he hoped to position himself as ready, reasonable and pure while King and Luna slugged it out.

Slug it out they did. Luna said he felt like a material witness to a crime while watching King's third gubernatorial term unfold. King's latest term had been a fraud on New Mexico, he asserted.

Luna aimed such barbs at King almost non-stop while ensuring that many voters would reject a fourth term for the governor. Luna's oft-aired television ads about the Kings' controversial land swap with the BLM tore at the governor's cherished image as a good old boy simply looking out for interests of the average voter.

Meanwhile, the schism between King and environmentalists remained. The Conservation Voters Alliance and the Sierra Club endorsed Jim Baca in the primary race. "I can say the environmental community feels betrayed (by King)," said Sally Rodgers, an executive board member with the Conservation Voters Alliance.

Indians in the state, too, remained sour on King. King had not backed away from his assertion that Pueblo Indians along the Río Grande were running video gaming parlors illegally.

No matter. A large, modern electronic sign along busy U.S. 84-285 in Tesuque boldly flashed messages like "Play Video Gaming. WIN CASH". It was a sort of thumb to the eye of Governor King.

A little north at Pojoaque Pueblo, Indians had begun construction of a casino intended to accommodate the rising popularity of video gambling.

King continued to refer to New Mexico's Indians as his good friends but his assertion belied an unmistakeable turn in the political mood. It didn't help when King's spokesman insisted publicly that if it weren't for the stark poverty of Navajos in northwestern New Mexico, the state wouldn't rank so low in many of the social conditions that define quality of life.

Press Secretary John McKean promptly apologized for remarks but the damage was done.

In truth King, himself, had argued that statisticians who merely put numbers on paper often overlook the big picture. Statisticians can fail to account for extraordinary conditions in isolated areas. Conditions on Indian reservations, particularly on isolated Navajo lands, drag down numbers that otherwise would reflect decent conditions in the state, he said.

"The first thing we need to do is figure out who's doing the figuring," he told me, referring to those who often are anchored in offices while preparing statistical reports about conditions far afield.

King eventually won the June 1994 primary but he emerged as a seriously wounded candidate. Luna narrowly missed upsetting King, collecting 36.4 percent of the vote to King's 38.8 percent. Baca received 24.7 percent.

Sixty-one percent of the voting Democrats cast ballots for someone other than King. And more than half of the people eligible to vote were so disinterested that they didn't bother going to the polls.

It was all rather insane, implied Democratic Party Chairman Ray Powell. Still, the most-repeated criticism of King was not insane at all. His calls for staying the course failed to inspire enthusiasm among those who wanted more comprehensive, long-term planning for a state that seemed mired in the muck of poverty.

Charges of elitism also were directed at King's entourage.

STUNNED BY "GARY WHO?"

Unease—even turmoil—within the Democratic Party wasn't helped when King took his first steps into the general election campaign with a peculiar embrace of his newly elected runningmate, Albuquerque attorney Patricia Madrid. Madrid would be a good "helper," particularly to his wife, Alice, said King.

"I didn't cringe at all. But I told (King) it's a good thing he has a lieutenant governor candidate who has a good sense of humor," Madrid told me.

Madrid would be anything but the submissive second fiddle one might conclude King wanted in the lieutenant governor's office. Democrats tried to brand King and Madrid as "Team New Mexico," but Madrid herself said it all felt like "a Chinese marriage because the electorate arranged it." King didn't pick her and she didn't pick King.

In fact, there was bad blood between Madrid and Ray Powell, state Democratic Party chairman and King confidant. Madrid years earlier publicly accused Powell of working against her while she tried unsuccessfully to win the party's 1990 nomination for attorney general.

Problems mounted for King when Roberto Mondragón broke with Democrats to accept the Green Party's nomination to run for governor in the November 1994 general election. Mondragón knew victory would be a long shot. But if the liberal-minded Greens drew five, ten, 15 percent of the vote in November, almost all of them would be pulled away from King. It left Democratic leaders quivering because two-way general elections for governor in New Mexico historically were determined by less than five percent of the vote.

Republicans surprisingly nominated millionaire entrepreneur Gary Johnson, a 41-year-old political novice, as their gubernatorial candidate.

Johnson talked about the need for low taxes and low crime rates. And government, well, government needed to be downsized, he said.

He quickly caught fire as Democrats battled to overcome their disenchantment with themselves. Johnson took an early lead in public opinion polls and held on to leads going into Election Day.

Lieutenant governor candidates who didn't feel isolated in general election campaigns likely could be counted on one hand. But given King's troublesome history with his lieutenant governors, Madrid grew increasingly anxious as the November election approached.

She had moved beyond her initial diplomatic response to King's assertion that she would be a good "helper," particularly to his wife. "I probably will not work on any projects with Mrs. King because they are not my particular interests," Madrid said.

During the campaign, Madrid essentially was scooted off to court Hispanic voters. "I've been disconnected with the governor," Madrid told me in mid-October. She wasn't out on the campaign trail at the time. She was in her Albuquerque law office. "I haven't been out on many major political occasions. I've just been running my own tough little campaign up north. I think it's unintentional. But I think it's important that I become more visible."

Madrid said she had expected to be used on more television commercials, appealing not only to disaffected Hispanics but to women, including those eager to see a woman elected lieutenant governor at long last.

"I'm not really making those decisions," she said of campaign strategy.

Some public opinion polls showed the King ticket trailing Johnson and running mate, Walter Bradley, by five to seven points at the time. Johnson said his own poll had him up by 11 points.

As for Luna, well, King's organization was still trying to secure his endorsement even while Madrid expressed frustrations. Attempts to win Luna over had even reached into the White House. A last-minute surge for King was needed and Democrats were desperate so they approached U.S. President Bill Clinton.

President Clinton was in Albuquerque October 17 and in a meeting with Luna in the city's convention center tried to invoke party discipline. But President Clinton failed to secure Luna's endorsement for King.

And when the president and U.S. Representative Bill Richardson suggested that Luna risked dangerously dividing the New Mexico Democratic Party, Luna refused to sit silently, telling of misguided party leadership.

Johnson beat King a few days later, collecting 50 percent of the vote to King's 40 percent. Mondragón received the remaining ten percent, leaving him to be accused by some Democrats as the spoiler.

It wasn't the ending that the 70-year-old King had in mind for his 40 years in New Mexico government. Having served as governor for 12 of the previous 23 years, King was going home again.

New Mexicans had heard, mostly in jest, how King's two brothers, Sam and Don, were only too glad to have Bruce occupied in Santa Fé as governor for years at a time. It left them to run the family cattle business largely as they saw fit.

King and I had our rough patches. The roughest was at that $1,000-per-plate fund-raiser early in his 1994 re-election bid when I first refused to tell him who commissioned the public opinion poll that showed him in a very tight race with Bill Richardson. He stood toe to toe with me then lost control. He shouted and cursed and threatened to become a lot tougher to get along with.

He got over it and to the end continued to call me his good friend.

Carla's Dad Had a Tiny Cubicle

Bruce King and I had a chance meeting during the noon hour one day in Santa Fé's Furr's Cafeteria near the Capitol. My young daughter, Carla, liked Furr's. Our dishes of food before us, Carla and I sat alone in a padded booth near the cash register. Suddenly King's unmistakeable cowboy twang could be heard behind us as the governor made his way down the aisle to pay his bill, shaking hands with other patrons along the way.

King reached our booth and already had thrust his substantial right hand in my direction before realizing it was me in the booth. I introduced the governor to Carla, and he made himself comfortable for the next several minutes while hunching over our table.

It became evident how King planned to use his time during the chance encounter. Unbeknownst to him, I had my own plans.

Dominating the conversation, King generously went about telling Carla that he thought very highly of me. I was a hard worker and a good reporter, he said.

My own plan was to get the governor to focus his attention on Carla and her promising future, to talk about the importance of young people preparing themselves to become leaders in their own time. Who better than the governor to praise a grade-schooler's accomplishments and encourage her into even greater works?

"Governor, we're having lunch here today because I'm really proud of Carla's work both at home and at school," I said, hoping to open the door for King to follow.

King nodded in Carla's direction then promptly returned to trying to make her feel good about her Dad. As soon as he finished his next comment about our long relationship, I jumped in with more praise for Carla, again hoping that the governor would pick up where I left off.

But my plan wasn't working. The back and forth between King's intentions and mine went on for another minute or so. Finally, before I could finish my latest remarks about Carla's dutiful approach to her responsibilities, King interrupted, placed his hand on my shoulder and said, "I'm sure all of that's true, and we're all very proud of you, Carla, but what I'm trying to say, Dave, is that you're a pretty good guy yourself and Carla ought to be very proud of you, too."

There were enough smiles to go around.

Carla, I felt, could draw more than one lesson from the brief visit with the governor who had no equal.

A day or two before leaving the governor's office for the last time, King and wife, Alice, walked unannounced into *The Santa Fe New Mexican's* news room to say farewell to anyone who was around. My blue cubicle was one of the first that they came upon. I happened to be in the news room that day instead of at my desk at the Capitol. With managing editor Rob Dean at their side, the governor and his wife both expressed surprise at the size of my cubicle, which was probably less than four-feet-by-four-feet square, the smallest in the room.

I had worked from one of the building's largest cubicles for a while until a new, young reporter walked in for her first day on the job. A year out of college, she, too, was a Roybal though we are unrelated. I tried to get her hired at the paper soon after her graduation from the University of New

Mexico, confident of her abilities and still working to create a more-diverse news staff.

The Santa Fe New Mexican didn't hire her that first year. Dejected, she left her résumé and I encouraged her to come back in a year or so if she hadn't heard from one of the editors by then. Together, we would try again, I pledged.

She made that second visit and secured the reporting job that she prepared herself for at considerable expense. More than a little timid, she walked in for her first day and was directed to the building's smallest cubicle, where she promptly began unpacking her supplies. The cubicle was so small it would have been an insult to anyone and almost certainly demoralizing to someone arriving for her career's first job.

I didn't like what I saw and I showed my displeasure by openly asking the lady to unpack instead at my cubicle. I would take my own supplies and files out and move into the tinier space. Much of my time was spent at the Capitol or on the streets anyway, I told her.

The folks in charge couldn't escape noticing or hearing later of my displeasure.

I was in that small cubicle when the governor and his wife stopped to visit. Alternately, they expressed dismay that I had injected myself into the workings of their administration, their election campaigns and much of state government from such a tiny post. They expected something rather substantial, they said.

I was in the naughty box, I told them only half jokingly, knowing that over the years at least some my superiors didn't always appreciate that the aggressive approach I took with me on my rounds outside the building customarily followed me back inside where the paper's business unfolded.

I remained in the tiny cubicle until I resigned from the paper two years later.

Among mourners in the Capitol Rotunda in December 2008 for the wake of Alice King, I stood mostly at the outer edges of the crowd, observing both the grief associated with death and the joy that inevitably comes from having known such a substantial person.

In the end, I moved into the long line of King friends, associates and supporters to express condolences to the family seated in a row of chairs. The line moved slowly. I saw the former governor stand a few times but mostly he sat, shook hands and offered his familiar knodding of the head.

When my turn came, King kindly rose to his feet as we grasped hands. We quietly exchanged a few words then, not surprisingly, he offered a brief story. It was true to the former governor's reputation, complete with a long sentence, subtle humor and, of course, admiration of his partner of 61 years. He poked me more than once with an elbow as he talked. That, too, was characteristic of his one-on-one visits.

"Alice worked with me from the very beginning," he said. "She was a great partner. I remember going out to that first (Santa Fé) County convention and Alice told me, 'Don't let them talk you into running for anything,' and after a long night I came back home as a candidate for the county commission, and she said, 'You let them talk you into running, didn't you,' and I said, 'Yeah, but they assured me we were going to lose.'"

He butted his head against mine as if for a final farewell.

As I was to recall later, it was the last time I saw King before his passing in November 2009, less than a year after he interred his wife.

From the Roybal Files...
The Santa Fe New Mexican, Column, August 4, 1991
King and Fans Join Together To Do the Wave

I tore a page out of Gov. Bruce King's book the other day, the page that says: When in doubt, wave broadly and smile.

I waved and wished the governor a good morning from my seat in the bleachers of the old gymnasium at the Santa Fé Indian School, where King was addressing a seminar of state and tribal government leaders.

It was either wave or sit quietly, looking bewildered as King wound down an impromptu introduction of some of the folks seated before him. He had singled out state Supreme Court Justice Richard Ransom, state Rep. John Underwood, D-Ruidoso, state Highway Department Secretary Louis Medrano, Sandoval County Commission Chairman Joe Lang, former Santa Fé District Attorney Walter Kegel and several others.

All, of course, were introduced in the standard King fashion as "my good friend..."

Near the end, the governor paused briefly, then said, "I started to introduce David Roybal as my good friend, but I don't want to confuse anyone."

Another pause.

"There's David Roybal in the back."

As he had with the previous introductions, King led the polite applause.

Friend or not I was confused, no matter that the governor didn't intend to stir confusion.

King is the man who pitches himself as the reincarnation of Will Rogers. Never met a person he didn't like—even occasionally combative state Republican Party chairmen—King says repeatedly.

During the 1990 gubernatorial campaign, King introduced me to a couple of ranchers in Roswell, and as he turned around to chat with them privately, he said, still referring to me, "Oh, yeah, he's a good friend of mine."

Some editors have been known to show the door to any reporter so described by a politician. Our editors simply have gotten to know Bruce King.

King has suggested periodically over his long political career that perhaps I have been particularly hard on him. Still, nothing says reporters can't be the governor's friends, King spokesman John McKean told me in a brief phone conversation after I returned from the Indian school gym.

"But sometimes, singling out a friend from the press among non-press people can be risky," he acknowledged.

As I hung up the phone at my desk, I found myself smiling and waving broadly for the second time that day. I wasn't motioning to anyone except, maybe, the image of a rascally old politician.

From the Roybal Files...
The Santa Fe New Mexican, Column, December 21, 1993
Will Land Swap Become King's Waterloo?

Democrat Bruce King might be the least pretentious governor we've had.

He's probably pumped more hands and slapped more backs than any ten other New Mexico politicians combined.

He's liked by many who have never even voted for him.

Amid his popularity, it's been no secret that King is a rich man. Depending on how many cattle were on the ranch in Stanley on any given day, family operations were worth around five million dollars, King said while on the verge of winning his third gubernatorial term in 1990.

But people generally have not begrudged King his wealth. Despite his riches, he's been regarded as a sort of Everyman in New Mexico. If he's got a lot more money than the rest of us, he must have worked for it, ran the common line of thought.

And even if he's rich, he hasn't turned up his nose on those who aren't.

Much of the public's good will, though, appears to be in jeopardy. The reason: King's controversial and increasingly publicized land swap with the federal Bureau of Land Management.

The swap saw King give the BLM 17,000 acres near the El Malpais

National Monument south of Grants in return for 700 acres in the lucrative Santa Fé real estate market. Citing professional appraisals, the parties agree they each gave up property worth $1.7 million.

But others say the land obtained by King adjacent to the expensive Las Campanas development is worth as much as seven million as it sits with a potential for far-greater value if developed.

The trade was finalized a year ago but the controversy refuses to go away. There's little wonder why. The whole thing to many smacks of a remarkable sweetheart deal, the very sort of thing that has tainted countless other politicians but which King has been able to avoid while fostering his image as a folksy political grandfather to be trusted with your final dime.

King vigorously tries to squelch notions of high-level favoritism in the swap. He insists the trade is fair and argues that any benefit he might gain should be chalked up to coincidence and good fortune.

As the governor tells it, the BLM approached him with the trade offer years ago and asserts he never was terribly excited by it, remaining somewhat of a reluctant participant.

Nonetheless, the swap was allowed to avoid time-consuming public appeals in the federal bureaucracy. Had it run through customary procedures, the deal almost surely still would be waiting final action.

Critics of the swap suggest the deal was placed on the fast track so it could be finalized before Manuel Luján Jr. of New Mexico left his post as secretary of the U.S. Department of Interior under which the BLM is administered.

King and his spokesman, John McKean, point to the obvious while scoffing at the accusation. Luján is a Republican and was part of the administration forced out of Washington last January by the Democrats who King campaigned for aggressively, McKean said.

And, he said, even though King and Luján are New Mexico political contemporaries, they're mere "acquaintances."

McKean is straining.

Lujan was much-criticized as Interior secretary and said five years ago when he retired from Congress that he yearned to return to New Mexico to pursue a less-demanding lifestyle. Bets are he wouldn't have accepted another four years in the president's Cabinet even if Republicans had maintained control of the federal administration.

McKean implies that if King had been interested in getting a special favor from Washington, he would have waited until the Democrats were in charge. That, of course, would have triggered greater suspicions of favoritism.

And if King and Luján are mere acquaintances, then Timmy and

Lassie were no more than another kid and his pet.

Luján, throughout the time he represented northern New Mexico in Congress, was a role model to Hispanic youths of the region. I said as much to King and Luján's brother, former state Republican Chairman Edward Luján, while the two chatted in the governor's office during a ceremonial bill signing earlier this year.

King quickly agreed and offered that one of his own role models was Luján's father, who was a popular Santa Fé mayor during the 1940s.

None of it by itself comes even close to proving that a chummy conspiracy gave rise to King's land swap with the BLM.

And even if King cannot restore his image as New Mexico's trusty political grandfather, nothing says he can't favorably position himself on other controversial issues between now and his 1994 re-election bid to recover ground he seemingly has lost with the state's voters.

But without question, the BLM land swap is the one issue on the political landscape that most threatens to deny King his much-coveted fourth term as governor.

The thought that the issue could blow sky high, as much as anything, has a handful of prominent Democrats unwilling to rule out challenging King in 1994.

19
They All Had Plans, Yet Here We Are

Gary Johnson: "Governor No"

Gubernatorial candidates campaigned throughout New Mexico in 2018, acting as if they had plans that other political office holders had never imagined or talked about. Voters had heard it all, yet the state of two million residents remained mired at or near the end of just about everything that measured quality of life in the United States.

Oh, New Mexico wasn't poor like Kolkata is poor. It was important to stress that, counseled my old friend, A. Samuel Adelo, a retired oil company PR man who I recruited to merge his frugal Pecos upbringing with his Notre Dame education to write a Spanish column for *The Santa Fe New Mexican* beginning in 1980.

Republican Gary Johnson from the start in 1994 bucked the trend of New Mexico politicians. Perhaps not since peanut farmer John Burroughs in the 1950s, had anyone put forth such a meager plan for improving the state's historic conditions.

Veteran television news anchor, Dick Knipfing, while talking of Republican candidates well into the 1994 GOP primary referred to Johnson as "that other guy." He couldn't immediately think of Johnson's name and didn't seem terribly embarrassed. Few knew of the 41-year-old political neophyte with a huge construction company in Albuquerque until he started running quirky TV ads to introduce himself. He ran them early and often.

I all but wrote Johnson off in a column that ran just days before he won the Republican nomination. I asked what if Johnson turned out to be like David Cargo, who shocked the Republican establishment in 1966 by claiming the gubernatorial nomination after most of the state's GOP leaders lined up behind former Albuquerque legislator Cliff Hawley?

Those chances seem to be dying, I wrote, with appearances like the one Johnson recently had made in Las Cruces. While there, Johnson admitted he knew nothing about some of the biggest issues the region struggled with for years.

But Johnson wasn't rattled. In time, as he moved through the general election campaign, he showed he didn't rattle easily, or at least he didn't stay rattled beyond the initial moments of discomfort. Young, handsome and athletic, Johnson looked like he might have spent his entire adult life modeling for athletics catalogues. But the self-made millionaire asserted he was no stranger to hard, dirty work.

"I used to walk through restaurants to take toilets out of (restrooms) to rout out the sewer," Johnson told me in an interview.

He was very much in touch with the state's mainstream, he insisted. And, he offered, minorities constituted more than half of the work force at Big J Enterprises, the Albuquerque construction company that he launched 20 years earlier as a one-man operation.

Probably 60 percent of Big J's workers were minorities, mostly Hispanics, and they weren't just in lower-level positions, he said.

I dared to ask Johnson to name three or four of his company's minority supervisors. He drew a near total blank.

He named one Hispanic man, fell silent, then said, "I can't name any supervisors at all right now. Let me think."

Another pause.

"I'm sorry," he said. "I just can't. I've got a real block. I don't know that I could name three employees of any kind now."

"You have to understand, over the last year, I've been removed from my business to run the campaign."

I phoned Johnson's business manager at Big J. The total number of minorities at the company was well below the 60 percent estimated by Johnson. It turned out that 39 percent of the 470 full-time employees were either women or minorities.

Johnson talked to his spokeswoman, Diane Kinderwater, about his interview with me. Kinderwater told me later that Johnson confessed he likely could not have named his own children at the time.

Johnson wasn't particularly interested in learning names—or even hearing them at all—during a casual campaign stop that took an unexpected turn on him. Cargo, the former governor, told me of being invited to breakfast midway through the general election campaign. The invitation came from Manuel Luján Jr., the unassuming GOP official who represented Albuquerque and northern New Mexico in Congress for 20 years before serving as U.S. Interior secretary from 1989–1992.

"Manuel asked me to be at Herbs and Roses, the restaurant in the Marriott Hotel up in the Heights, at seven fifteen," Cargo told me. "It's a pretty ritzy, high-priced joint. You can't even talk to the kitchen help there."

"Why would I want to go there?" Cargo asked Luján. "I couldn't figure it out. Then I realized it was because Gary Johnson was going to be around."

Cargo said he suggested García's restaurant on Central downtown as an alternate meeting site.

"We walked in and, heck, Manuel knows everybody down there," Cargo said. "I had shaken hands with everybody in the place after a while and Manuel talked to at least half of them. We told Gary he ought to get up and talk to people but he didn't seem interested. He said nobody there was likely to vote for him anyway."

It wasn't the traditional way to court votes in New Mexico. Still, Johnson ended up getting all the votes he needed—far more than what he needed to deny Democrat Bruce King an unprecedented fourth four-year term as governor. Johnson collected 50 percent of the 1994 general election votes compared to King's 40 percent. Green Party candidate Roberto Mondragon got the remaining ten percent.

Johnson trounced one of New Mexico's legendary Democratic politicians. Four years later, he beat another Democratic Party A-lister, the young former Albuquerque mayor, Martin Chávez. The vote total in 1998: Johnson, 55 percent; Chávez, 45 percent.

As governor, Johnson pressed unsuccessfully for widespread use of public school vouchers and legalization of cannabis. He also took every opportunity to slow the growth of state government and to minimize the role of government in people's lives.

To that end, he used his veto authority 200-plus times during his first year in office. Before he was done as governor, he set a national record for his number of vetoes. House Democratic Whip Ben Luján dubbed Johnson "the veto *vato*."

The swath of vetoes indiscriminately killed proposals of Democrats and Republicans alike. Among legislative proposals that had funding requests reduced or rejected were those for public school health programs, health care for the elderly and disabled and community cancer patient support.

"He cut the money for cancer kids; he cut money for other legitimate programs," said Senate Republican Whip L. Skip Vernon of Albuquerque. Vernon was not entirely joking when he said he might challenge Johnson, the wiry tri-athlete, to a benefit boxing match. Money raised, said Vernon, a still-solid former college football player, could be used to restore funding vetoed by Johnson.

One could sense Vernon's desire to take a few swings.

Along with his vetoes, Johnson likely will be most remembered for his support of gambling ventures on Indian lands. Millions of dollars gleaned from gambling casinos gave Indians new political clout. Johnson benefited from it throughout his time as governor.

I was with New Mexico Indian leaders in Albuquerque as part of a PR contract with the state Office of Indian Affairs when longtime Mescalero Apache President Wendell Chino died in November 1998. Chino, whom I came to know well, was not at the meeting. Within minutes Johnson's office called Indian Affairs Director Regis Pecos at the Albuquerque conference and asked that he quickly write a few sentences that the governor could issue to the news media as a tribute to Chino. Pecos in turn asked me to write the tribute. I did and what I assembled was attributed to Johnson in the following hours and days.

Johnson ran for U.S. president as the Libertarian candidate in 2012 and again in 2016. He failed to generate enough support to be included in national television debates.

Manuel Luján Jr. Tracked Constituents

Manuel Luján Jr., a kind and unassuming Republican from Albuquerque, represented northern New Mexico in the U.S. Congress for 20 years beginning in 1969 and rarely allowed himself to stray from what his constituents wanted—at least the constituents who communicated with him.

Luján defeated Democratic incumbent Tom Morris to claim the seat that reached to the Colorado border.

Scientific polling had yet to inject itself into daily lives of politicians, so Luján as a congressman regularly mailed questionnaires to constituents to measure their opinions. Luján told me he relied on the informal surveys "quite a little bit" while determining positions he took on issues.

A survey from the summer of 1982 offered Luján these insights: By a 3-to-1 margin, constituents favored reducing social programs. They favored cuts in foreign aid by ten to 1, and only 51 percent supported cuts in national defense. Three-fourths of the respondents said they had been adversely affected by President Ronald Reagan's economic program, but by a 4-to-1 margin, they said they thought the program should be given a little more time to work.

Anyone who knew Luján realized he would not stray from the conservative philosophical message reflected in results of that survey—at least not until another survey might show that he should.

If Luján isn't remembered for anything else, I wrote in a July 1982

New Mexican editorial, he'll be remembered for the frequency with which he polled his constituency.

But there was room to question the accuracy of his surveys. About 150,000 copies of his summer 1982 questionnaire were mailed; only 40,000 were returned. Survey after survey, Luján could be hearing from the same group of people who over the years had grown to identify with the Republican congressman. Many of the 110,000 who didn't respond to the survey might have concluded that Luján didn't represent their interests and that their views wouldn't get much attention in his office.

The self-effacing Luján had something less than a thundering presence in Congress. He spent much of his time not as a principal sponsor of major legislation but helping with basic constituent services, such as applying for government services, tracking down lost benefit checks, securing federal community grants or helping families stay in touch with members serving in the military.

He was one of New Mexico's most-popular Republicans. Still, he drew a surprisingly well-supported challenge in 1980 from 31-year-old Democrat Bill Richardson, who moved to New Mexico two years earlier.

Luján defeated Richardson, 51 percent to 49 percent, in what was the nation's closest congressional race in 1980.

Population growth and reapportionment gave New Mexico a third congressional district in the U.S. House of Representatives before the 1982 election. Redistricting left Luján ensconced in a district that consisted largely of the Albuquerque metropolitan area. From there, he continued winning two-year terms until he gave up his post at the end of 1988.

Newly elected U.S. President George H.W. Bush promptly appointed Luján Interior Department secretary. Luján was eager to return to New Mexico so President Bush, himself, had to persuade Luján to serve in the new administration.

The Washington news media considered Luján to be prone to gaffes in part, at least, because the Cabinet secretary took ownership of his mistakes in a city where blame tends to be pushed onto others. Luján, for example, gave wrong information to a reporter while discussing royalty payments from mineral rights. Told later of his error, Luján apologized and said frankly, "I didn't know what I was talking about."

Luján served as Interior secretary through the end of President Bush's term in December 1992.

"Lonesome Dave" in the Hinterlands

Republican Governor David Cargo, if it weren't for other obligations of his office, might have spent all day every day talking to people working in their gardens or struggling with repairs under the hoods of battered, old pickups.

The folksy Cargo, in office from 1967–1970, charmed people in Mora, Cañones, Anton Chico, Dixon and multiple other outlying communities. Just as importantly, he was charmed and inspired by them.

When talk turned to Mora, for example, Cargo beamed as he spoke of the community that embraced him as governor, mostly because of his work to help residents there minimize strains inflicted by muddy winter roads and other nagging symbols of hard times.

"That county's so poor, but those are my folks up there," he told me in 2004. He was at the state Capitol, trying to get $200,000 from the Legislature for a new library in Mora. He was instrumental in getting the original library opened in 1990 and donated most of the books to get it started. They were largely his books. Cargo till his death in 2013 at the age of 84 claimed that he read a book a day.

But the little library in Mora had recently been closed when I ran into Cargo in 2004. Approximately 6,000 books along with equipment were moved to temporary quarters across the road that runs through town. "The old library had mold, it had pigeon droppings and a lot of things had gone wrong," he told me.

Cargo, a lawyer, was paying rent for the storage along with the librarian's salary, at least temporarily, until a new library could be built.

The original David F. Cargo Library was across a popular bar along State Road 518, a two-lane road that bisects the community of stunning mountain scenery, spirited local politics and hard-pressed economic conditions on the eastern slopes of the Sangre de Cristos.

The bar was run for more than half a century by Tommy "Tío" Casados. Casados was shot in the head and killed at the age of 75 in November 1996. Politics and homespun conversations had drawn Casados and Governor Cargo close. The former governor posted $1,500 of his own money as a reward for information leading to an arrest.

Only a few years earlier, Casados had called Cargo at his Albuquerque home to share a story that had just unfolded and involved them both.

It seems a man from Taos to the north walked into the bar one day and didn't have much good to say about anything.

"He had already been drinking, I guess," Cargo said. "He sat down and just started taking off on everything. Tommy told me all about it."

Soon the visitor took to drinking beer and shooting pool with some of the locals. Nothing about the small town seemed good enough for him. He knocked one thing after another. Still, the pool playing continued mostly uninterrupted until the disgruntled visitor aimed his barbs at the tiny library across the road.

"Tommy said the next thing he knew he saw this pool stick coming down on the guy who wound up being laid out on the floor," Cargo said.

The library was off limits when it came to criticism of the impoverished community, or at least it was in the story that Cargo recounted for me.

Actually, he said Casados wasn't the only one to phone him about the fight.

"The guy who got hit called me first," Cargo said. "He called me and said it was all my fault. I can't remember his name but he said he was from Taos and that he got his arm broken by one of my thugs out in Mora.

"I told him I didn't know what he was talking about. He admitted he had criticized the library, said it was small and that it didn't even have a decent sign on it. That's about the time he got hit."

Cargo, himself, for at least a brief period was considered to be a physical threat by no one less than his own lieutenant governor, E. Lee Francis. Francis had just cast a tie-breaking vote on a controversial liquor reform bill and Cargo called him on the carpet for voting against the governor's wishes.

Former state policeman, Richard CdeBaca, told me of the blow up for his 2013 biography, *Chief of Police*.

"One morning before the Senate convened, I got paged to report to Lieutenant Governor E. Lee Francis' office. He was livid and told me that he wanted to get a restraining order on Governor Cargo. When I asked him why he wanted to do that, he told me with a straight face, 'Because the son-of-a-bitch threatened me and I don't appreciate it.'"

Francis so feared Cargo at the time that he demanded full State Police security around the clock.

"I got after Lee," Cargo told me later. "Lee could get a little temperamental but generally speaking, I got along pretty well with him."

Cargo and former Democratic Lieutenant Governor Roberto Mondragón in 2004 helped lead efforts to build a library in tiny Anton Chico northwest of Santa Rosa on the prairie near the Guadalupe and San Miguel County line. It was a grass-roots, community effort spear-headed by Cargo, reported the *Santa Rosa News*.

Cargo and Mondragón, who was lieutenant governor two times under Bruce King, often were like-minded mavericks. Cargo was known for bucking the Republican establishment, courting Democrats and going off on his own whenever he was so inclined. He embraced the moniker,

"Lonesome Dave," while making the rounds through forgotten communities. He secured temporary fixes to old-time problems but if there were long-term solutions to those problems, they waited to work their magic long after Cargo left the scene.

Bill Richardson: "Fighter" for New Mexico, the U.S., the World (?)

Bill Richardson, a former congressional aide to U.S. Senator Hubert H. Humphrey of Minnesota and others, moved to New Mexico from Washington, DC, in 1978 when he was in his late 20s. He came in search of a U.S. congressional seat to claim as his own, detractors said.

Those detractors said Richardson, already well-versed in government and politics, anticipated New Mexico gaining a new congressional district in the early 1980s because of population growth and reapportionment.

But first Richardson would challenge Republican congressman Manuel Luján Jr. in 1980 for the northern New Mexico district seat that Luján held since 1969. Richardson had no real expectation of winning, planning simply to introduce himself to voters and begin building a network of supporters in the region that would constitute most of the new congressional district to be contested in 1982.

Born in Pasadena, California, to a Mexican mother and Anglo father, Richardson as a youth attended a private school in Mexico City for seven years but grew up largely in Boston. The years of experience he gained later as a congressional aide in Washington gave him the footing he planned to use in his own career as a mover and shaker.

Once in New Mexico, Richardson presented himself as a Hispanic, and he said the "root" of Hispanic people is the same no matter their origins. "I feel I have an attachment to that community," he told me.

He spent substantial sums on television and radio ads in which he addressed voters in Spanish during the 1980 campaign against Luján. Yes, he was new, he said, but that meant he was free of ties to political bosses.

Richardson lost to Luján, 51 percent to 49 percent, but began building a reputation as a tireless campaigner. He boasted of campaigning 12 to 14 hours seven days a week while Luján supposedly "was doing nothing."

Richardson opted against a recount of election results. "I had prepared myself to lose. All I wanted was to lose respectably so that my political prospects were not foreclosed," he said.

Going into the 1982 Democratic primary campaign, the 33-year-old Richardson knew his principal rival for the new northern congressional district would be Roberto Mondragón, who was in the final year of his second term as lieutenant governor. Mondragón, while finishing his first term as lieutenant governor, ran unsuccessfully for Congress in 1974, losing to Luján 58.6 percent to 39.7 percent.

"I think Bob is good. But he's had his chance. I haven't had my chance," Richardson told me. "I have my ideas and I'd like the people to give me a chance to test them ... I'm not attached to the status quo. Roberto is the status quo."

The Democratic primary race figured to be close between Richardson and Mondragón. Richardson considered an endorsement by *The Santa Fe New Mexican* to be critical. But *The Santa Fe New Mexican's* editorial board was evenly split. Mondragón was known and appealing in multiple ways. Questions about Richardson lingered after his first meeting with the board. So, as the paper's editorial page editor, I called him in for a second meeting and then a third. He walked into that third, hastily called meeting with water still dripping from his thick black hair as if he had hurriedly stepped into and out of his shower before dashing to the paper's downtown office on East Marcy Street.

Unbeknownst to Richardson, I was on his side but I came across as the aggressor in those meetings, asking most of the questions that others raised in our private deliberations. If Richardson hedged, I pressed. I wanted doubts addressed.

But the editorial board's tie vote did not change after Richardson left that third meeting, not immediately. The city editor finally changed his vote. He wasn't entirely won over by Richardson but he thought that the paper should not duck out on an endorsement in what had been a very high-profile race.

"Bill Richardson is one of the most-impressive candidates to move along New Mexico campaign trails in years," I wrote in the endorsement editorial. "He is filled with energy and enthusiasm. He is extremely well-acquainted with many of the needs and problems of northern New Mexico. And beyond identifying needs, he has advanced some aggressive proposals for addressing them. He is studied and articulate."

"No other candidate in the Democratic race for the 3rd Congressional District has kept pace with Richardson in any of this. His knowledge and drive, in fact, could help him stand out from the mass of men and women who make up the House of Representatives and give New Mexico much more than a third body in Congress' lower chamber."

Richardson beat Mondragón, 36 percent to 30 percent. Remaining votes were split between George Pérez and Tom Udall.

Mondragón was to remain as one of New Mexico's most-promising politicians never to have served in Congress.

Richardson said he wanted to stand out for his constituent service. On that front, he wanted to outdo even Manuel Luján Jr., he said. But Richardson had no intention of stopping at the U.S. House of Representatives. He wanted to be U.S. president, he told me early in his career. There would be stops along the way, he figured, each of them very desirable: New Mexico governor, U.S. secretary of state, vice president.

Richardson soon pitched himself as "The Fighter for the North," alluding to the new northern New Mexico congressional district he had just claimed as his own. But even as he hoped the moniker would ingratiate him to the regionally minded voters dominated by Hispanics and Indians of the new congressional district, Richardson was never able to completely free himself of a troublesome perception among some voters.

He acknowledged to me as he began the political career that would be grounded in New Mexico that some people likely would always consider him a carpetbagger. (I would learn later of the lasting anger that could be aroused in Richardson by references to anything that hinted of his migratory nature of the time.)

"Is it a disadvantage that I'm not a native? Yes. But what can I do? I can't be born again," he told me.

He began seriously contemplating a run for governor in 1990 and then again in 1994. He considered it critical to his political future to serve as governor because he needed to make a record for himself as an administrator, not merely a congressman. The governor's office would allow him to do that.

Richardson in 1989 was still contemplating what would have been his first race for governor when a five-inch segment of a column I wrote in April of that year got him hopping mad. "Richardson moves home into suitcase", read the headline. "Carpetbagger" was nowhere to be found in the headline or the column itself. But it must have been what Richardson read when he looked at the piece because he stopped talking to me directly for more than a year. And he must have directed his spokesman, Stu Nagurka, to pay little attention to my phone calls because Nagurka suddenly became largely unresponsive.

The column told how Richardson had just sold his house in Tesuque and that he was building a new one just a few miles closer to town off Hyde Park Road. "The commute to Tesuque was too much," Nagurka told me for the column. "It would take additional time and it just wasn't worth it."

I wrote in that column: "Richardson, you might recall, is the Democrat who prides himself on traveling to all corners of his large northern congressional district at least once between elections. That's a lot of traveling for a man who wants to avoid the few miles from Santa Fé to Tesuque."

Construction of Richardson's new home was expected to be completed that summer. "Until then, Richardson will tuck his boots under beds of different hotel rooms around the district," I wrote.

Hoyt Clifton, director of the state's Bureau of Elections, told me the U.S. Constitution required only that Richardson, to represent New Mexico in Congress, be a state resident.

"Richardson says he's a resident of both the district and the state even though he doesn't have a house at the moment," I wrote.

Richardson took heat in and around New Mexico for being on the road so much. Much of the criticism was for trips around the United States and abroad that he logged at a pace few others in the U.S. House could match. A congressional watchdog group monitoring the term that ended in 1989 ranked Richardson fifth on a list of House members who took trips paid for by business interests.

Many of the trips were needed to promote his college scholarship fund, he offered, in defense against assertions that such trips generally were little more than lobbyist-funded vacations.

Richardson again pondered a race for governor in 1994 before bowing to incumbent Bruce King and what would be his ill-fated attempt to win a fourth gubernatorial term.

Richardson in 1996 won election to his eighth two-year term in Congress before resigning in February 1997 to accept President Bill Clinton's appointment as U.S. ambassador to the United Nations. It was a high-profile post but still wouldn't get Richardson the administrative experience he so desired.

That would come with his next appointment. President Clinton in July 1998 asked Richardson to serve as U.S. Energy secretary, a Cabinet-level post with a huge bureaucracy and a potential for frequent high-profile national publicity.

Richardson was no stranger to high-profile publicity, having stepped into international hotspots and meeting with the likes of Cuba's Fidel Castro and Iraq's Saddam Hussein. Richardson joked that he might easily become known as our nation's undersecretary of thugs.

Clinton and his vice president, Al Gore, seemingly had plans for Richardson. Richardson and Gore were close. Gore was preparing to run for the presidency in 2000. Richardson had developed enough of a profile to be considered as Gore's running mate. His reputation as a tireless worker and successful fund-raiser along with his Hispanic background added to his appeal in a nation with a growing Hispanic presence.

I resigned from *The Santa Fe New Mexican* in 1996 and started a one-man government affairs and public relations company. Richardson approached me in 1998, asking that I add to what was then a two-person speech writing staff at the Energy Department. I was flown to Washington to be familiarized with agency employees and, presumably, to be impressed by the extraordinary setting of world power.

I was, without question, impressed. But I had two young children at home and a move to Washington would not work at the time. So I wrote speeches for the U.S. Energy secretary from my home office. I was supplied via email and other internet avenues with all the information I needed to craft speeches to be delivered in Washington, New York, Utah, Cancun, Russia and other stops.

My days routinely began at six a.m. to account for the two-hour time difference between Washington and New Mexico. They customarily extended to midnight and beyond.

As one of the nation's highest-ranking Hispanic officials, Richardson drew frequent invitations to address Hispanic groups. Most, if not all, of those assignments came my way. I even got one or two calls from the White House to contribute to speeches being crafted for the president or vice president.

My general mandate from Richardson: Stress at every opportunity the importance of expanding educational and employment opportunities not only for minorities but for women, too. Richardson took important steps within his agency to practice what he preached, and I was to call attention to those steps.

These comments that I wrote early on made their way into several prepared remarks: "By the year 2005, Latinos will be this country's largest minority group. In fifty years, we will comprise one quarter of the U.S. population. Let's create conditions today that will ensure that by the year 2050, Latinos account for one-quarter of all U.S. business owners, a quarter of its bankers, scientists, doctors, college presidents, mayors, governors and Cabinet secretaries."

Solidifying the Clinton administration record was the central mission, of course. But if there also was hope of laying groundwork for a Gore-Richardson campaign in 2000, those hopes were crushed by word of security breaches within the Energy Department and the accompanying Wen Ho Lee controversy that severely tarnished Richardson's standing.

Wen Ho Lee was a Los Álamos National Laboratory employee whom Richardson reportedly speculated might have given U.S. nuclear secrets to the Chinese government. Lee was cleared but the protracted mess left Richardson looking like too much of a liability to be placed on a national ticket.

Connecticut Senator Joseph Lieberman was picked to run with Gore in 2000. The ticket was narrowly defeated by Republicans George W. Bush and Richard Cheney.

Richardson successfully ran for New Mexico governor in 2002, trouncing Republican John Sánchez by 17 percentage points. Richardson took office in January 2003 as the only Hispanic governor in the United States.

He won a second gubernatorial term in 2006, defeating Republican John Dendahl, 68 percent to 32 percent, securing the highest percentage of votes in any gubernatorial election in New Mexico history.

And, again, it was all part of a bigger plan. Richardson still dreamed of being U.S. president. He not only wanted to win his races for governor; he wanted to win them big. He spent extraordinary amounts of money in each race: $7.3 million combined in his 2002 primary and general election campaigns; followed by collections exceeding $13 million in 2006.

(Gary Johnson spent $2.8 million to win re-election in 1998. Richardson's expenditures in 2002 were well more than double the combined amounts spent by Johnson and Democratic challenger Martin Chávez in 1998.)

And Richardson wasn't simply stroking his ego. He knew that if he overwhelmed his rivals in gubernatorial races, those records would be referred to over and again when he stepped into the arena of presidential politics.

He stepped into that arena for the 2008 Democratic campaign but he didn't stay long. Barack Obama, Hillary Clinton and John Edwards dominated the race that picked up steam beginning in 2007. Richardson was out by early January 2008.

Richardson ran a steady fourth through the end of 2007. That wouldn't lead to a popping of champagne corks. It had some speculating that Richardson, after seeing his chances dwindle, had turned to positioning himself to be the party's vice presidential candidate.

February 5, 2008, loomed large. That's when Democrats in New Mexico and 22 other states would cast their votes. Richardson might have wanted to give New Mexicans the extraordinary opportunity to vote for one of their own but increasingly it appeared as if Richardson might be embarrassed when votes from his home state were counted.

He collected just two percent of Iowa's delegates as 2007 turned to 2008. Signs pointed to a similar fate in New Hampshire as voting there approached. Obama was gaining momentum. It looked like he, Clinton and Edwards each could have respectable finishes in New Mexico. Richardson might have to struggle to claim even the slimmest of victories at home and defeat at home was no longer out of the question.

New Mexico isn't Bill's for the taking, I wrote in an *Albuquerque Journal* column that ran January 8, 2008. New Hampshire could give Obama a lock, wrote columnist David Broder that same day. Richardson withdrew his candidacy two days later.

"I don't think that man (Richardson) is qualified to be president," New Mexico political strongman, Emilio Naranjo, told me just a week earlier. Richardson was stung to see the remarks in print.

Richardson would have to console himself with the fact that he distinguished himself as the first New Mexican and the nation's first Hispanic to have made a serious run for the U.S. presidency.

Perhaps. But perhaps more than that could still develop.

Obama won the 2008 Democratic primary. Richardon, who endorsed Obama after a controversial break from the Clintons, was later vetted as a possible Obama running mate but he and others lost the nod to Delaware Senator Joseph Biden.

The November general election went to Obama and Biden. Richardson's name floated as a possible secretary of state in the new administration but it was Hillary Clinton who got the appointment. Obama on December 3, 2008, announced he selected Richardson to be secretary of Commerce. But Richardson withdrew just a month later amid a federal grand jury investigation into pay-to-play allegations tied to his work as New Mexico governor.

Was Richardson scandal-prone? I asked in a December 9, 2008, *Albuquerque Journal* column. Only a few years earlier a ranking Democratic U.S. senator accused Richardson of showing "extreme contempt" for the Senate after having been confirmed for two previous presidential appointments. Senator Robert Byrd, claiming that Richardson was not forthright with senators while addressing security breaches at the Energy Department, publicly advised Richardson never to step into the Senate again in pursuit of its blessings.

Grand jury charges connected to the pay-to-play investigation were never filed against Richardson, who waited for the probe to play out while he finished his second term as New Mexico governor. He boasted excessively about his work as governor while campaigning for president. In truth, when pressed to get beyond his talking points, his record wasn't as impressive as he thought.

Tim Russert of NBC's "Meet the Press" pushed beyond those talking points and Richardson did not fare well. Richardson insisted the state was making progress when Russert told how New Mexico, during Richardson's fifth year as governor, ranked near the bottom in areas like violent crime, teen dropouts, residents without health insurance and people living below the poverty line.

When Richardson finished as governor in 2010, he could take comfort knowing that he had been busier than most who had gone before him yet had to accept that he hadn't solved the state's ills. Such an accomplishment, in all likelihood, would require successive governors working together.

Richardson arrived onto New Mexico's political scene in the early 1980s, claiming incorrectly that he had been the principal foreign policy aide to U.S. Sen. Hubert Humphrey, not merely one of several aides. A star college baseball player, he claimed he had been drafted to play for the Kansas City Royals. He wasn't.

Decades later, even while being asked to join the U.S. presidential administration of Barack Obama, Richardson was holding to his assertion logged in the *Guinness World Records* that he had broken Theodore Roosevelt's 1907 record for handshaking.

Richardson asserted that he shook 13,392 hands in eight hours in 2002 while campaigning for governor. A Richardson constituent, Los Alamos scientist Glen Graves, had long thought that someone should look harder at that claim. Graves calculated that Richardson would have had to shake a hand every 2.17 seconds to accomplish the fete.

"It would have required a (steadily moving) line six miles long," said Graves, who called me to share his calculations. And, said Graves, Richardson could not have taken breaks—big or small—during those eight hours.

Problem is, Richardson said he shattered Roosevelt's record while shaking hands at the New Mexico State Fair then at a tailgating party miles away.

Reading remarks prepared for him, Obama mentioned Richardson's claim to the hand-shaking record while introducing Richardson on national television as the nominee for Commerce secretary. Obama immediately looked away from the text and flashed an incredulous look before teasing that he would look into the assertion.

Richardson finished his second term as New Mexico governor in 2010 and returned to work in the private sector. He could honestly present himself as one of New Mexico's most-accomplished politicians even though coveted service as U.S. secretary of state and American president escaped him.

Domenici Brought Home the "Pork"

Republican Pete Domenici during six terms in the U.S. Senate became a bright star for his party in Washington but his biggest contribution to New Mexico was the role he played in ensuring that large sums of federal dollars continued flowing to the state in good times and bad.

Domenici in 1973 succeeded Democrat Clinton P. Anderson in the Senate and picked up where Anderson left off when it came to protecting federal installations—and their substantial budgets—in New Mexico.

Domenici of Albuquerque served through 2008 and was largely responsible during that period for protecting budgets of four U.S. military bases and two national laboratories in New Mexico.

When Domenici retired from office because of failing health, New Mexico was near the top five among states in terms of its ratio of federal employees to the total population. No state was more dependent on federal spending.

Even when political tempermant turned against so-called pork in favor of attempts to balance the ever-growing federal budget, Domenici made sure he brought home the bacon.

And much of what he brought home fed the nation's substantial military muscle. When the Persian Gulf War broke out in January 1991, Domenici said other nations had seen a United States not seen for some time. "They have sure seen some guts. And they have seen some pretty good excellence put together in terms of America's capabilities," he told me. He predicted death or capture of Iraqi President Saddam Hussein.

More Americans, he said, were recognizing that the United States, as a world leader, must take on "onerous tasks" periodically.

Domenici for years was recognized as New Mexico's most-popular politician. "Saint Pete," he was often called.

But nobody should get carried away with the reputation, said a fellow Republican. Domenici benefited from distance and the buffers that go with it, asserted former Governor David Cargo. "You send Domenici to Washington and he's a statesman. If he were in Santa Fé, he'd be a bum in three months," Cargo told me.

Domenici disclosed in 1989 that he wanted to be elected to a fourth term the following year. "As New Mexico's most-popular politician, he probably could achieve that even if he spent the next 18 months fishing in Texas," I wrote in a column for *The Santa Fe New Mexican*.

Democrat Bill Richardson took plenty of heat as a publicity hound throughout his time in politics but Domenici might have worked his press office just as hard. The intensity was described for me by one of the senator's aides.

And then there was the physical evidence. Domenici's office dispatched to *The Santa Fe New Mexican* nearly 30 news releases in a single month with well more than a year to go before the 1990 election.

Domenici's people got so caught up in publicity that they issued a news release trumpeting a decision by the Federal Aviation Administration to grant $209,000 for improvements to the small Las Vegas, New Mexico, airport. The FAA had taken no such action. *The Las Vegas Optic* gave top billing to a story that told of the error.

There were red faces within the Domenici crowd, but the news releases kept coming.

Domenici in 1988 had a close brush with the U.S. vice presidency. George H.W. Bush had just been nominated and was deliberating whether to pick Domenici or two-term Indiana senator, Dan Quayle, as his running mate.

Quayle, 41 at the time, was picked over the 56-year-old Domenici.

"I don't think there's any question that in my case, every serious adviser to the president in the waning 48 hours recommended me," Domenici said four years later, still unable to conceal his disappointment.

It wasn't experience or qualifications, or even New Mexico's lack of electoral muscle, that got in his way, said Domenici. It was a question of generations; Bush wanted to balance his ticket with a younger man.

So said the senator. But 25 years after an inexperienced Quayle joined the Bush ticket, extraordinary news shook New Mexico voters and many in Washington's political circles. Domenici in 2013 revealed that in 1978 he had fathered a son with the then-24-year-old daughter of former Nevada senator Paul Laxalt.

Domenici learned news of the affair was about to be made public.

New Mexico's senior senator was married and had eight children.

"I deeply regret this and am very sorry for my behavior," said Domenici, who offered that he had remained silent about his extramarital affair at the request of the boy's mother.

As part of the vetting process, it long has been customary for people to be asked if they have any skeletons in their closet before being nominated to high-profile positions in government. If Bush asked the question of Domenici in 1988, a candid response would have knocked Domenici out of consideration as a running mate.

Domenici died in September 2017 at the age of 85.

Gentleman Jeff Bingaman

If Democrat Jeff Bingaman were to be accused of anything during his decades as a U.S. senator, it would have had little to do with a hot temper.

"Republican Colin McMillan, who has been around New Mexico politics for decades, can now make a substantial new entry to his list of accomplishments: He has gotten Gentleman Jeff Bingaman mad. Few can make that claim," I wrote in an August 1994 *New Mexican* column.

"Like some people hoard money, Bingaman seemingly stashes away emotions, as if certain the day will come when he really needs them ... The soft-spoken Democrat must have filled reservoirs with laughter and shrieks suppressed before they ever saw the light of day."

Bingaman, an Eagle Scout by age fifteen, got hot under the collar after McMillan, a former Republican state legislator, dared to accuse Bingaman of being a career politician and of hiring out-of-state investigators to dig up dirt on McMillan.

Bingaman by 1994 had served four years as state attorney general, twelve as a U.S. senator and was asking for election to a third Senate term.

He didn't respond directly to McMillan. Instead, he approved a campaign ad that did. "As a career politician of twenty-five years, McMillan has been rejected time and time again for statewide office," a narrator said on Bingaman's behalf.

That was tough talk—very tough talk—for Bingaman. And it got tougher.

McMillan often has had to settle for appointed posts, read a statement from Bingaman's office, because voters statewide have refused to accept McMillan's "narrow agenda."

Who could have known that Bingaman or anyone in his office had such a vocabulary?

Bingaman, in his first race for the Senate in 1982 defeated moon-walking astronaut Harrison Schmitt. Schmitt, the Republican incumbent, upset Democrat Joseph M. Montoya six years earlier.

Montoya in 1976 repeatedly made light of Schmitt's accomplishments as an astronaut and it hurt him. Far more delicately, Bingaman asked voters during his campaign against Schmitt: "What on Earth has he done for you lately?"

Republicans accused Bingaman during the 1982 campaign of failing to meet his responsibility in the wake of the state's brutal 1980 prison riot in which 33 inmates were killed by other convicts. Bingaman was assigned by the state legislature to investigate causes of the uprising and to report his findings.

"Bingaman did his job well and continues to press for changes which his investigation showed are needed," I wrote in an October 1982 *New Mexican* editorial endorsing Bingaman in that year's U.S. Senate race.

"The fact is, Bingaman has scored for New Mexicans throughout his term as attorney general. He hasn't been flashy, but he has been sound, honest and even-handed," the editorial read.

During five terms in the Senate that ended in 2012, Bingaman developed a pro-environment record, working to reduce greenhouse gas emissions and develop green technology. He supported affirmative action and voted against a constitutional ban of gay marriages. He also helped ensure that New Mexico's share of federal funds remained high.

I followed Bingaman into a Valencia County political rally as he campaigned for re-election in 1988. Valencia County voters liked their politicians cut from the old molds, politicians like their own Tibo Chávez, lieutenant governor from 1951–1954. It wasn't long before I bumped into Chávez at the rally.

Chávez liked to press the flesh and tell stories as he worked a crowd. At the time he was author of two books about life in New Mexico. As he visited with people, he was prone to ask about moms and dads back home. If armed with necessary information, he would trace a family name for generations before excusing himself and moving on to someone else in the crowd.

He quickly began giving me his standard let's-talk-about-your-life treatment when our paths crossed at the rally. He learned soon that he was talking to a reporter but unlike other politicians who might have promptly excused themselves or used the opportunity to talk about their many accomplishments—real and imagined—Chávez stuck to what had long served him well.

"I work up at the courthouse," said Chávez, serving then as a state district judge in Belen. "Come visit me. I'll buy you lunch."

He was warm and engaging even though he knew I wouldn't write a word about him that day. I was at the rally covering Bingaman and was able to stray only because the first-term senator was moving stiffly through the crowd offering little more than polite, soft handshakes.

"Doin' as best I can," Bingman would reply more often than not whenever anyone had the senator's attention long enough to politely ask how he was doing.

Toney Anaya Championed Rights, Progress Without Ever Finding His Groove

Toney Anaya was propelled into the governor's office in 1983 and it was neither low-profile, gentlemanly behavior nor old-time politics that got him there.

Anaya was state attorney general from 1975–1978, immediately preceding Jeff Bingaman in the office. Anaya might have been New Mexico's most-aggressive attorney general ever. He undoubtedly was one of the state's most-popular AGs despite possessing something less than a genial personality.

"Anaya made the attorney general's office mean something to the people of New Mexico," I wrote in a May 26, 1982, *New Mexican* editorial endorsing Anaya in that year's gubernatorial primary. "The office had been a small operation that caught the attention of few persons besides politicians who were willing to trade off obscurity in a state office building for a title, some influence and a steady paycheck.

"Anaya transformed the office into an active and visible defender of public interests, focusing on consumer-related issues and a vigorous attack against crime and corruption in government."

Four years after leaving the AG's office, Anaya took the same hard-charging, independent approach with him into the governor's office. Told early on that some who contributed money to his campaign likely would expect jobs or favors in return, Anaya publicly offered to give money back to anyone who felt so entitled.

One might have expected a positive response from the public but it was mixed at best. Arrogance is what some saw in the new governor's position. Perceptions of arrogance would follow Anaya throughout his term as governor.

Anaya was certain that messaging was his central problem; support would come if only more people understood him and his many, many missions.

Anaya not only was a man in a hurry. He seemingly was in a hurry to improve anything and everything under New Mexico's blue sky. Arguably, it kept him from seeing the kind of success he dreamed of in some areas

"I think the governor felt at the time I joined him that his message wasn't getting across," said Bob Gold, a veteran radio man and government lobbyist whom Anaya hired as his third communications director while still settling into space provided for governors on the Capitol's Fourth Floor. "I'm not sure I served him well. It sounds like it's easy to do, but when you're working for such a busy person and you have so many parts of a story to tell, it can become rather difficult."

Anaya pressed hard to get more money into public education. He wanted economic development to move beyond tired approaches and into new, high-tech initiatives to be rooted in well-funded research up and down the Río Grande corridor. He pressured New Mexico's financial institutions to invest more money in the state, particularly with small businesses looking to expand as well as with those just getting started. Women and minorities were grossly underrepresented in board rooms of private businesses, university faculties and administrations and in the better-paying jobs of national laboratories and other federal installations in New Mexico. Anaya made it clear he was tired of the excuses and explanations used to prop up those long-standing conditions.

Through executive order, he insisted on equal rights and opportunities for gay men and lesbians in state government. (The legislature was not inclined to guarantee such rights in state law.)

Anaya pressed for international human rights, rapid rail transit, water conservation and environmental protection all while working to keep New Mexico financially afloat amid a national recession and repercussions of a massive tax cut approved by the state legislature just prior to Anaya taking office.

Late in his term, Anaya through executive order made New Mexico the nation's first sanctuary state for refugees from Central America.

"I think his supporters and critics alike feel he probably should have taken on only three or four principal changes over the four-year term instead of trying to do so much in one year," Gold told me.

I succeeded Gold in the efforts to sharpen the governor's message and focus his energies, becoming Anaya's fourth communications director during his first 18 months in office.

Just prior to that, I had worked for a year as a reporter, mostly at the Capitol, with Albuquerque's NBC-TV affiliate. I went to KOB after leaving *The Santa Fe New Mexican* as editorial page editor at the end of 1982. The television work at KOB offered new learning experiences but my pay there, even after being increased twice, was not enough to support my young family. I expressed my situation multiple times to news room executives who in turn expressed their own limitations, the last time being at a meeting over lunch with anchor Dick Knipfing at the Albuquerque Country Club.

Leaving KOB, I promptly landed work at the state Corrections Department, where I worked as an executive aide to Secretary Michael Francke within Anaya's administration.

Six months later, the governor and I visited in the Capitol about his desire to make yet another change in his communications office. Honored by his offer, I accepted the job as communications director/press secretary but within weeks told my wife, Kay, that Anaya in time likely would need to find someone to succeed me.

Anaya had grown increasingly disturbed about information being leaked from his offices, and he wanted me to help him address what he considered to be a serious problem. He openly discussed with me issues and strategies driving his ambitious agenda but restricted what I was able to share with others around me. It limited the amount of work I could delegate.

Anaya placed considerable confidence in my judgment and advice but, clearly, it was for me to defer when differences in our approaches arose. I would address his concerns about leaks and otherwise do my best at the post but I didn't see how I could stay at it for much more than a year. My intent was to help Anaya solidify his footing during my time at his side.

There was much to do. Calls for Anaya's impeachment already were circulating within the Capitol, orchestrated largely by longtime eastside Republican Senator Billy McKibben. Anaya was not one to back away from a fight so he was easily drawn into toxic verbal exchanges with McKibben and others. It was like red meat for some in the news media. The controversy all but stopped Anaya's initiatives in their tracks.

Anaya's detractors would have had a hard time making a case for misfeasance or malfeasance in office. Calls for impeachment were grounded largely on claims that Anaya exceeded his authority while skirting the Legislature. They were further fueled by federal investigations initiated by then-U.S. Attorney Bill Lutz. Anaya said Lutz, a Republican, sought to incriminate him in 13 investigations centered on supposed payoffs and political corruption. Most of the investigations were done by the FBI at Lutz's request, Anaya said.

The investigations, said Anaya, began after he criticized the Reagan administration during a trip to Mexico. "I got word soon after I returned that the administration was out to get me."

Anaya repeatedly denied wrongdoing. "Absolutely nothing ever came from investigations against me because there was no wrongdoing for Lutz to find," he said.

Lutz in time denied engaging in politically motivated investigations even though he had nothing to show from his efforts.

Back when calls for impeachment swirled around Anaya, the governor reluctantly accepted my strategy for getting beyond the controversy. Anaya's contact with the news media was sharply curtailed for weeks, and his daily schedules were arranged to keep him away from the fray. If McKibben and cohorts were happy to wrestle in the mud, they would be left to wrestle with themselves.

Anaya didn't like it but the storm eventually passed. "David Roybal was single-most responsible for saving the governor from impeachment," Bob Gold said later.

McKibben came to recognize he had allowed his early disgust with Anaya to go unchecked. Micro-managing might have been Anaya's most serious fault, he suggested. "I think Governor Anaya had an inordinate amount of courage, and I think that translated into him wanting to have a hand in everything that took place," he said.

As Anaya prepared to leave office in 1986, Republican Garrey Carruthers positioned himself to succeed him. Carruthers throughout the campaign expressed support for capital punishment. Anaya opposed it and was accused of protesting Carruthers' stance by commuting the death sentences of all five men on New Mexico's death row following Carruthers' election in November.

In truth, Anaya made that decision even before Carruthers began his campaign. Anaya was prepared to commute the five death sentences midway through his term. He collected support for such a move in private meetings with the Catholic archbishop and other religious leaders. Others, too, encouraged him to act on his decision, including most of his executive staff.

Anaya was not yet one to turn to scientific public opinion surveys, even on a major issue like this. Chief of Staff Robert McNeill said he wasn't aware of Anaya commissioning any such surveys as governor.

The governor had my full support on his decision to commute the five death sentences, but not on the timing. Probably everything else that he still hoped to accomplish would be sacrificed by the commutation of sentences at mid-term, I told him; he would be emaciated politically, the backlash would be so intense within the legislature as well as in the general public.

From the start, Anaya knew he would appear cowardly if he waited to act until he walked out of the Capitol on December 31st.

Agreed. So, I suggested, why not act when he still had a month or two left in office? He would be seen even by his critics as someone who was willing to stand and take the heat for his convictions. That, I said, accurately reflected his character.

And so it went. The commutations came just before Thanksgiving.

I excused myself from Anaya's administration in August 1985 after 11 months but not without a long conversation with Anaya's assertive administrative assistant, gate-keeper Shirley Scarafiotti. Scarafiotti earlier had expressed displeasure that the governor hired me on a day when she was away from her office. I hadn't, after all, knocked on a single door or contributed a dime to his election campaign.

But Scarafiotti and I came to respect one another. She called me at home upon learning that I turned in my notice to resign. There were many reasons to stay, she argued, including the relationship that Anaya and I had developed. Plus, she said, there was the possibility that the U.S. Attorney Lutz and others might wrongly conclude that I was leaving because investigations into Anaya's conduct were about to find dirt.

Indeed, I learned later that U.S. Senator Pete Domenici, who recommended to President Ronald Reagan that Lutz be appointed U.S. attorney, made at least one phone call within his circle to advance such a supposition.

Anaya called me "a class act" in a letter that I carried with me out the door. "You set the bench mark that must be met for professionalism, preparation and follow-through," he wrote.

Anaya would have one more communications director before leaving office. If Anaya had been one of New Mexico's most-popular attorneys general, his term as governor ended with some of the lowest public approval ratings known to be recorded.

More than a decade after he left the governor's office, Anaya called me at home to ask that I join him in his latest efforts. Governor Bill Richardson had appointed Anaya chairman of the New Mexico Highlands University board of regents. Anaya said he asked university President Sharon Caballero to consider me among others who might be brought in as interim director of university relations. Anaya's phone call was followed by one from Caballero, who inquired about my interest.

"We need help with some heavy lifting," Anaya told me after acknowledging sympathetically that my daily roundtrip commute would be 200 miles.

I liked the job far more than I anticipated so I tolerated the 200-mile commute longer than I planned, leaving Highlands after a little more than a year.

Anaya served out his appointment at the university and moved on to work with Richardson in other capacities.

In 2014, without admitting guilt Anaya settled a civil case brought by the Security Exchange Commission. Anaya was accused of concealing from investors prior violations of law by two high-level officials at a water resource company he once ran, according to Reuters. Anaya agreed to a five-year ban from penny stock offerings.

Time put distance between Anaya and his political dreams. While governor, Anaya considered himself worthy of consideration for service as U.S. attorney general. There also was a nice sound to the title, first Hispanic U.S. president.

Jerry Apodaca and the Image He Couldn't Shake

Jerry Apodaca of Las Cruces in 1974 became the first Hispanic elected governor in New Mexico since 1918. He didn't spend a lot of time talking about his Hispanic roots, not like Toney Anaya, who followed him into the governor's office nine years later.

Apodaca moved through his four-year term as New Mexico's chief executive, determined to be known as the state's "education governor." It was a label that several other governors of the period and in different states sought to have affixed to their legacies.

Apodaca brought added focus and dollars to the state's education efforts while reorganizing state government to create a cabinet system that included 12 departments. He proposed a comprehensive plan for educational excellence from kindergarten through graduate school and recommended pay increases for faculty and other university employees.

He pressed for increased access to student loans, expanded post-secondary vocational programs and capital improvements at college and university campuses.

Apodaca also fought entrenched powers within state government to modernize a very troubled Corrections Department that suffered from an inadequate and neglected system for classifying inmates, from years of prison overcrowding and corrupt administrators. They were problems that festered during and after Apodaca's term as governor and were underlying causes of the brutal 1980 riot at the old Penitentiary of New Mexico south of Santa Fé.

But so many of Apodaca's good intentions were overshadowed by some of the people who claimed him as a friend as well as by the high-profile personality that he liked to cultivate at least occasionally.

Apodaca's name came up in an FBI wiretap of alleged organized crime figures. His name was mentioned alongside those of people like Irving "Slick" Shapiro and Jimmy "The Weasel" Fratianno.

It meant nothing, insisted Apodaca. A lot of people like to drop his name when they think it might benefit or otherwise satisfy them, he said. There are those, he said, who like others to think they know people in high places.

As for problems possibly caused by his own personality, Apodaca said simply, "I don't live a modest kind of life."

But he stressed that he didn't need shady characters to help him in his ambitious pursuits.

Apodaca made the remarks while meeting with *The Santa Fe New Mexican*'s editorial board in January 1981 while contemplating a run for the U.S. Senate. He made similar remarks while meeting with Albuquerque journalists in April. It was as if Apodaca wanted to assure journalists that he was not crooked and that he did not seek to associate with those who were.

Bottom line, he suggested: No one has produced evidence that he had acted criminally.

Despite his efforts, Apodaca's path was not cleared. Fighting for his political life, he alleged in April 1982 that the *Albuquerque Journal* was out to ruin him politically and otherwise. Apodaca by then had entered the Democratic primary for U.S. Senate. His primary opponent was outgoing New Mexico Attorney General Jeff Bingaman. Waiting for one of them in November's general election was Republican incumbent Harrison Schmitt.

Apodaca called for a grand jury investigation, alleging that an investigator for the *Albuquerque Journal* and other persons conspired to violate state laws and his civil rights by supposedly inducing people to give perjured testimony linking him to organized crime.

Through much of Apodaca's gubernatorial term, it appeared as if Apodaca and then-Attorney General Toney Anaya, both Democrats, entered government merely to fight with each other while trying to advance their political careers. It wasn't always civil.

"For the kind of conversations I've had with the governor in the past, it was extremely free of profane language, although there were a few four-letter words," Attorney General Anaya told the Associated Press in 1977.

Anaya referred to a phone call he took from Apodaca hours earlier after a consultant working for Anaya publicly called Apodaca an "errand boy" for a top state Democratic Party official whom Anaya was prosecuting for alleged bribery.

Apodaca's occasional foul language and bursts of temper without question worked against the governor's repeated attempts to disassociate himself from what he acknowledged to be "shady characters."

Some of Apodaca's outbursts became public. Others did not.

One-time lawmaker, Fabián Chávez Jr., served informally as an intermediary between Apodaca and Anaya. Chávez told me of one meeting he witnessed between Apodaca and Anaya when the governor supposedly was consumed with anger after he felt Anaya betrayed a pledge to stay quiet about an issue that the two men recently discussed.

Apodaca, according to Chávez, threatened to cut off two of Anaya's body parts and stuff them down his throat.

During his time as governor, for sure, Apodaca had little use or respect for Anaya.

Apodaca at one point said Anaya acted as if he alone had a lock on propriety.

The two men eventually patched things up. Anaya while governor appointed Apodaca to the University of New Mexico Board of Regents, citing Apodaca's previous contributions to education.

The two also worked together in 1990 to help organize the shortlived National Institute of Former Governors.

Apodaca, amid his successes, suffered repeated body blows that would have left many down and out. He lost his 1982 Senate race against Bingaman. But ten years later he refused to rule out another bid for the Senate or the governor's office. He wouldn't have been without supporters.

"This man ought to be running for president," state Senator Mary Jane García said of Apodaca in 1992.

UDALL FINALLY SNAGS A POST AND DIGS IN

For a while in 1995, it looked as if Democratic Attorney General Tom Udall and Republican Governor Gary Johnson were determined to reprise the contentious relationship that once tore at Toney Anaya and Jerry Apodaca.

Among duties, the attorney general is to serve as the state's chief law enforcement officer and principal legal adviser to the governor.

Johnson seemingly thought that meant Udall was supposed to stand with him through thick and thin like a loyal dog. Udall figured it was for him to give Johnson his best legal advice then stand back if the governor disregarded his counsel.

Udall did that more than once when fellow Democrat Bruce King was governor. Udall opined that King was authorized to sign carefully constructed gambling compacts with American Indians. King, who was opposed to gambling, disagreed. He took a good chunk of state money to pay former Democratic Attorney General Paul Bardacke to argue his case.

Johnson soon followed King as governor and signed gambling compacts with the Indians as he promised he would. But Udall opined that those compacts were not carefully constructed and refused to defend Johnson in a lawsuit filed by gambling opponents.

In a separate matter, Udall refused to defend Johnson's decision to restrict publicly funded abortions. In fact, he joined a lawsuit intended to block Johnson's policy, calling it discriminatory against poor women.

Johnson said Udall's office budget should be cut. If the attorney general couldn't be relied upon for support, Johnson argued, then he should give up a chunk of his budget so the governor could pay private lawyers to defend him.

Differences between Udall and Johnson were rooted in more than just conflicting opinions about law. Udall hadn't said so publicly but he would have liked to challenge Johnson in his bid for re-election in 1998.

Udall moved to New Mexico from Arizona with political service very much on his mind. He is the son of Stewart Udall, who served as U.S. Interior Department secretary from 1961–1969; the nephew of long-time U.S. Representative Mo Udall.

Tom Udall in 1982 ran for New Mexico's newly created third Congressional District but finished a distant fourth in a four-man race in the Democratic primary that was won by Bill Richardson.

Udall ran again for Congress in 1988 as the Democratic nominee to succeed Republican incumbent, Manuel Luján Jr., in the state's 1st Congressional District. He narrowly lost to Republican Steve Schiff.

Udall was elected state attorney general in 1990 and served two terms through 1998.

That year he ran again for the state's third Congressional District seat, defeating Republican incumbent, Bill Redmond. It took him three campaigns in two different districts for Udall to finally get into the House of Representatives. He served there until he won election to the U.S. Senate in 2008, succeeding retiring Republican incumbent, Pete Domenici.

He has built a reputation as an aggressive advocate for environmental protection, Indian rights and civil rights.

GARREY CARRUTHERS HITS STRIDE A LITTLE LATE

Republican Garrey Carruthers might have hit his stride as a public official when he became president of his alma mater, New Mexico State University, in 2013. That was 13 years after he finished his term as governor.

He secured the NMSU presidency on a 3-2 vote of the board of regents. He was pushed out by the regents in 2018. They said they had become discouraged by enrollment numbers and fundraising results. But the true motivation behind Carruthers' ouster likely was rooted in his public statements that went against Republican Governor Susana Martínez's reliance on sparse budgets for higher education.

Carruthers pared costs at NMSU and worked to make it easier for students to graduate in four years.

But he also carried baggage with him, having served as assistant U.S. Interior Department secretary under the controversial James Watt. Carruthers also raised eyebrows in multiple quarters when he said there was no scientific consensus on climate change. "I don't know. I'm an economist. I don't do global warming," he said in 2013.

As governor from 1987–1990, Carruthers came to refer to Santa Fé as "The Company Town." The company in the government capital was politics, as Carruthers saw it. And he didn't particularly care for it.

He'd hop into his 1967 Mustang and ride off into other communities every chance he got. He tended to favor those with golf courses nearby.

Carruthers wasn't New Mexico's first governor to embrace a laissez-faire approach to leadership from the Capitol. But it's unlikely that anyone had put such a happy face on it. Well-coiffed, smartly dressed and with a broad, toothy smile, Carruthers considered himself to be one of New Mexico's great salesmen and hoped to be regarded as a friendly New Mexican.

"In a kidding way I say there, if not for me, goes the greatest hustler in the world," Carruthers told me in 2008 while referring to Fabián Chávez Jr., a former state legislator and longtime New Mexico promoter.

Energy, charm and skill are what Carruthers had in mind when he mentioned "hustler."

During just a few weeks in the spring of 1989, Carruthers traveled to Washington, DC, Taiwan and Chihuahua, all in the name of promoting economic development. Carruthers, while campaigning for governor, promised to make economic development his top priority. But economic growth in New Mexico remained anemic. New Mexico was one of 13 states that scored no better than C's and D's in an economic report of the period issued by the Corporation for Enterprise Development.

Prospects of New Mexicans weren't helped by the Carruthers administration's bothersome tendency to hire help from out of state, fumed Roman Maés, then a Democratic state senator from Santa Fé.

Some Republicans weren't happy either. Donald Martínez, then-chairman of Republicans in Río Arriba County, grew frustrated when he couldn't get a meeting with Carruthers to discuss unemployment in northern New Mexico, much of which suffered from unemployment rates between ten and thirty percent.

Martínez said he tried for weeks to get an appointment with Carruthers. "I haven't heard anything, not one single word. We haven't been able to get the governor to discuss our needs," he said.

If Carruthers yearned for a reputation as a hustler, his yearnings were set back when he said publicly during one of his trips out of state that some of New Mexico's smaller rural communities might simply have to fade away rather than expect development that would sustain them.

Former Republican Governor David Cargo commented about Carruthers' approach to his responsibilities as his four-year term was in its final months. "Carruthers has been in Santa Fé for maybe fifteen months,

Former New Mexico governors Jack Campbell, David Cargo, Bruce King, Garrey Carruthers and Toney Anaya all wanted to invigorate New Mexico. (Photograph by LeRoy N. Sánchez)

Former governors David Cargo, Jerry Apodaca and Bruce King share stories at a Santa Fé gathering.

not four years. His biggest danger is being hit by a golf ball," Cargo said of Carruthers' frequent trips out of state, more than a few of them giving him time to sharpen his golf skills.

"He has avoided criticism by totally avoiding controversy, and we're all still hoping he takes a serious interest in government before he leaves office," Cargo said.

A Withdrawn Susana Martínez

Susana Martínez, who ended two four-year terms in 2018, might have been New Mexico's least-engaged governor in decades.

The state's gross domestic product grew by an average of 0.6 percent annually from 2010–2017, according to the Bureau of Economic Analysis.

Economies in neighboring Arizona and Colorado were growing. Texas was booming, said Lonna Atkeson, a political science professor at the University of New Mexico.

"How long can you stay in a recession?" Atkeson asked, alluding to New Mexico.

From the Roybal Files...
Albuquerque Journal, Column, June 12, 2007
Richardson Needs to Leave New Mexico Out of It

A good-humored Texan comes to mind when I think of all the people who likely aren't terribly impressed when Bill Richardson repeatedly, often clumsily, prefaces responses to questions on the U.S. presidential campaign trail with boasts about what he has accomplished as New Mexico governor. More on the Texan later.

Being governor of New Mexico rounds out Richardson's résumé that is impressive enough to command attention anywhere. Richardson might have the best résumé taken into a presidential race, at least in modern times, colorful Democratic guru James Carville remarked on national television weeks ago.

Richardson wanted to be elected governor here, as I mentioned in an earlier column, in large part to round out his résumé en route to a presidential race. He's talked openly of wanting to be president since at least the 1980s.

A stint as governor would give Richardson administrative experience, something he wasn't getting while serving as one of our representatives in Congress. Turns out his appointments as U.N. ambassador and then energy secretary late in the Clinton administration gave him a boost even before he became New Mexico governor. No one can accuse him now of never having administered a major operation from the top down.

Being governor of the 47th state certainly doesn't hurt Richardson in his bid to become president. But, remember, many of our fellow U.S. citizens still don't recognize the Land of Enchantment as part of the Union. You don't have to watch street-side interviews of late-night TV to learn of Americans who think New Mexico's capital is Mexico City, Tijuana or Madrid.

!Ay Chihuahua!

That gets me back to the man in Texas with whom I engaged in a brief conversation a few months ago. My wife and I had just walked up to a Customs counter at Houston's international airport. We were returning from a trip to Mexico with a daughter and son-in-law who had just walked away from the same counter after having their papers inspected.

It took the agent only a moment to read that my wife and I were returning to New Mexico. "Isn't that something?" he said. "I just finished checking another couple who's flying home to New Mexico. Two couples back to back! I guess that means there's pretty much no one in New Mexico until you people return."

The smile on the agent's face was more friendly than snide so I played along. "Yeah," I said, "we were lucky enough to get folks from Arizona to come in and feed the goats while we were gone."

The agent grinned, nodded his head and waved us along to hunt for our next line. He knew we were U.S. citizens, all right. He just didn't seem to think that as New Mexicans, we bump into many other people—citizens or otherwise—unless perhaps we stray occasionally into Texas.

Being governor of New Mexico, clearly, doesn't carry much weight in some circles. We might be proud of Big Bill for trying to make a serious run for the White House. But in such a race, New Mexico is a small fish in our nation's huge pond. Dodging reporters' questions to talk about what he's done for New Mexico hurts him for more reasons than one. Among them: His record is not as impressive as his résumé once you get beyond the talking points.

Host Tim Russert of "Meet the Press" pried beyond the résumé and into the record last month. Richardson insisted we're making progress when Russert told how our state, during Richardson's fifth year as governor, ranks near the bottom in areas like violent crime, teen dropouts, residents without health insurance and people living below the poverty line.

When Richardson claims to be turning the ship around, he's talking about New Mexico, not New York, California, Texas or Ohio. Voters—and the news media—aren't as impressed as he'd like them to be.

20
New Mexicans and Our Neighbors to the South

As travelers in central Mexico approach the gritty city of Compostela, Nayarit, near the Pacific Coast, a huge outcropping of rock screams for attention from a hill towering above the narrow two-lane road. The hill north of Puerto Vallarta and south of Tepic commonly is called *El Cerro del Ermitaño*.

According to legend, an old hermit who got tired of city life took to calling that rock-faced hill his home. There, he roamed in solitude for years until a growing number of men in Tepic and Compostela unceremoniously began taking their wives to *el cerro* and leaving them there.

Despite years of romancing—and unrelenting efforts—some of these households remained childless.

Legend says that men around *el cerro* grew impatient with their wives and lovers who bore them no children. Year after year, these frustrated *Mexicanos* took the women to the foot of *el cerro*, leaving them there to keep one another company.

The men did not know of the hermit.

Before long, not only was *el cerro* populated with women, the joyful sounds of children could be heard throughout the hill.

In the legend, *los hombres Mexicanos* were too confident to consider that they, themselves, might be responsible for lovemaking that failed to produce children. Surely, it was the women who were to blame so they were sentenced by their men to spend the rest of their lives at *el cerro*.

I don't know if the legend ends by saying that the women—and the hermit—lived happily ever after. That outcome apparently is left to imaginations.

El cerro, as it had for thousands of years, rose over the landscape in 1540 when Francisco Coronado left from that region to explore La Nueva México in the northern regions of New Spain. Coronado arrived in Mexico from Salamanca, Spain, only a few years earlier and served briefly as governor of Nueva Galicia, as the region came to be named.

Part of that region, Compostela was founded by Spanish Basque, Cristóbal de Oñate. Don Cristóbal was father of Juan de Oñate, who nearly fifty years after Coronado cut his own trail into New Mexico and in 1598 became its first governor.

Compostela, Nueva Galicia: The names applied within Mexico reflect Spanish origins of the region's early explorers. The state of Galicia in northwestern Spain was home to both the Roybal and Vigil families before some members left for the New World. Santiago de Compostela is the capital of Galicia state in Spain.

Research yet to be completed suggests that ancestors on my grandfather José Albino Roybal's maternal side can be traced to times of Coronado and the founding of Nueva Galicia

I felt an inexplicable pull to Nueva Galicia my first time through in 2007 despite knowing little of its history.

My wife, Marlene, and I were taken to visit a vocational school for teenagers in the seaside village of La Peñita de Jaltemba south of Compostela and found a campus with 500 students and only 15 IBM computers for students and staff alike.

Upon our return to New Mexico, we embarked on what became a complicated—but successful—project to get more than 220 used computers into Nayarit. Help was secured from the Santa Fé Public Schools, the Rodey Law Firm in Albuquerque, the *Albuquerque Journal*, Jerry Pacheco of International Business Accelerator in Santa Teresa and Mesilla Valley Trucking.

The Bay of Jaltemba annually welcomes New Mexicans and hundreds of others to Nayarit, Mexico.

More than 220 used computers donated in New Mexico make their way to Nayarit in 2008.

Albuquerque orthodontist Charles W. Kenney read of my push to get used computers and offered to buy a new computer for the effort. Ray Camp, a 90-year-old retired businessman in Las Cruces, said he had a home computer that still worked well and offered it for the Mexican students.

Computers were distributed not only within the school at La Peñita but to Conalep system schools through much of Nueva Galicia.

It wouldn't be a New Mexico story, I suppose, if so many New Mexicans hadn't become involved.

The often-frustrating project born of neighborly intentions promptly drew expressions of appreciation, no matter that the shine from most of the donated computers was long gone. "For so long, we have had nothing. Now, at least, we have hope," said one resident of the region where an estimated 30 to 40 percent of young men eventually try to cross the international border hundreds of miles away to improve their lives.

The school in La Peñita invited me back to be the *padrino* of its graduating class of 2008. After continued contacts with *Licenciado* Ángel Orosco Villegas, then the director of the Conalep school in La Peñita, he offered: "David Roybal is a person in Mexico who is always looking for ways to strengthen education in support of those most in need ... working for the benefit of youths who struggle to improve their lives."

It was through the computer project that my family came to meet

Children like these kindergarten students in La Peñita de Jaltemba benefit annually from activities organized by Santa Feans Roque García and Mona Cavalli (positioned in rear of classroom) who are part-time residents of Nayarit.

Manuel Rodríguez, a middle-aged builder in La Peñita whose life of hardships truly is one for the storybooks.

In 2014, I published *MANUEL Of The Americas, Historia de Fuertes Amores*, to tell of the Rodríguez family that had experienced extraordinary hardships, intense love and undying devotion. It's a story about life when just about everything except the will to survive has been stripped away.

Manuel from the age of six helped his father farm a small piece of land high in the *sierra* above their home. Water was diverted from an arroyo at a distance to feed a large ditch that Manuel's father and two others dug to irrigate the garden. To their surprise, huge fresh-water shrimp came with the muddy water as it flowed out of the arroyo.

Spreading his hands apart by ten or 12 inches Manuel said in Spanish, "They were big animals. You wouldn't believe how many."

Manuel and his father would collect them in buckets and take them into the village where they were quickly sold. "We always took the biggest ones to my mother," Manuel said.

Manuel, meanwhile, found himself hopelessly stuck in public school. His very first teacher was unable to guide Manuel into grasping some of her most-basic lessons. Arithmetic was his biggest obstacle.

"I was having so much trouble with the numbers at school that I was afraid I wouldn't get into second grade," Manuel told me. "I came up with the idea to invite my teacher and another teacher to come with me to the ditch that my father built in the hills and join me in catching shrimp. I was hoping that after we did that, they would pass me to the second grade."

Was it an attempt at bribery at such an early age?

"No, no," said Manuel. "All I wanted was for them to see that I knew about ditch building and that I was very good at catching shrimp. I wanted them to see that even though I was having trouble in school, I was good at something and that I had a future."

The teachers accepted the invitation and each went home with some of the oversized shellfish. Manuel was promoted to the second grade but found himself once again in the tutelage of the strict, wiry woman who shepherded him through the first. Manuel, still struggling with classwork, especially arithmetic, dropped out of school at mid-year and never returned.

Manuel learned numbers on his own as a young teen while working as a *peón* at various construction sites near his family's rented two-room home of wooden slats and dirt floor.

It was a time when his mother was carrying her tenth child, gravely ill late in the pregnancy. She died during childbirth; her baby boy delivered dead. Manuel's father, once so attentive to his family's needs, lost himself in drink. Manuel found himself responsible for tending to the entire family: the father and eight siblings plus himself.

Two years after his mother's death, Manuel fell in love with a woman, a *veracruzana* recently arrived in La Peñita, whom he wanted to bear his own children. Manuel took Elena Pérez as his wife after a four-month courtship. Elena suddenly found herself in the company of not only a husband but a large, impoverished family looking to her and Manuel for support.

Still wondering how she could possibly adjust to it all, Elena soon became aware of a new responsibility. She was pregnant. Her life had been turned upside down during the previous year and suddenly she was preparing to bring her first child into that hard, uncertain world.

"At that time, I think people looked at us as the poorest family in La Peñita," Manuel said.

He concluded there was no way he could support everyone with what he earned in Mexico so he reluctantly looked toward the United States nearly 800 miles away. Elena, tending to their four-month-old baby plus many of Manuel's siblings and his father, was incredulous.

"I told her my plan was to send money back to her every week. She got very sad. I asked her if she wanted me to give her money so that she and our baby could go back to Veracruz to be with her parents."

No matter how overwhelmed, Elena would not leave La Peñita. "I made myself strong," she told me. "I told Manuel, 'Here is where you left me. Here is where I will be.'"

Manuel left for California's San Joaquin Valley where he picked grapes and other produce on large farms in cool weather of early mornings and in the heat of afternoons. He was given additional responsibilities at his last stop. "We were paid one dollar for every box of grapes that we cut," he said. "I would earn forty-five or fifty-five dollars every day cutting grapes and then another forty-five or fifty-five dollars to collect the grapes from the other workers."

Manuel returned to La Peñita after eight months in California. He

Elena Rodríguez of Nayarit shares a tender moment with Rebecca Roybal of New Mexico.

made enough money to begin building a home and start the kind of life he dreamed of. That dream included opening his own small construction company, where he had his wife and, eventually, his children helping.

Then a dream of our own struck wife Marlene and me after cultivating friendships with the Rodríguezes and others of the region, including Canadians and U.S. citizens living parttime in homes built by Manuel. "We've worked hard all our lives. Why can't we build a small home of our own here, for the winters?" Marlene asked me.

So Manuel and his crew of industrious young men went to work. The clean angles and strong, uniform construction belied Manuel's struggles with arithmetic as a child.

Generations earlier, Marlene's ancestors and mine became a part of Mexico's history as they arrived from Spain and made their way north toward the Río Grande, some undoubtedly moving past *El Cerro del Ermitaño*. Incredibly, I could feel the pull of that history. Suddenly, beginning with an unexpected project of securing and sharing computers, our families' stories in Mexico were in the process of getting a new chapter. As Manuel approached 50, the hard work that enveloped most in his family every day seemed intended to keep dreaded hardships away more than to secure luxuries that never truly appeared to be within grasp anyway.

The basics of life have a way of shaping days in Mexico. I came upon evidence of that reality while observing a late afternoon unfold on a hillside in Rincón de Guayabitos near La Peñita. The intensity of summer had taken hold along the region. Days were hot and humid. Red brick walls of a house going up on a slope overlooking the blue Pacific were nearing their designated height after months of construction.

The sun had begun sinking behind hills late in the day when a couple of laborers still at the work site turned their attention away from collecting and rinsing tools to a burst of aerial activity that unfolded behind them. Inexplicably, one of the laborers took a few steps to pick up a small stone off the packed ground. He flung the stone with no pretense of playfulness then reached for another stone then another. The second worker promptly joined the first in flinging stones. They were aiming at perhaps a dozen swallows that seemingly had begun their search for a place to roost for the night.

These were Manuel Rodríguez's workers and they were doing more than attempting to break up the unexpected assembly of small birds. They were trying to scare them away, far away. I soon learned why.

The disastrous world economic crisis that began in 2008 was draining this already-economically challenged nation. People were hurting. Money was tight. Jobs were scarce and there were no signs that things would get better—not for a while. People who had work were glad for it and understandably were prone to feel threatened by anything that might separate them from their jobs.

"People say that swallows looking to nest on the houses are a sign that the rainy season is almost to begin," one of Manuel's workers told me. "It's too early for the swallows to be doing this."

A few more stones were flung before cleanup at the job site was completed and the workers began their treks home, leaving the swallows to nest where they chose.

The rainy season along La Peñita does not entirely stop construction jobs in their tracks. But heavy rains can slow work, particularly in early stages, and that can force temporary reductions in work crews. It's what Manuel's two laborers at the Guayabitos job site dreaded as they worked beneath the swallows.

Manuel and his family by that time had pulled themselves out of a prolonged period of extraordinarily hard conditions. But they still struggled. Manuel dealt with it all at times with humor while telling family members of the many skills he developed during his lifetime. His skills were rooted not only in experience but in intelligence, he said. "If I had stayed five more minutes inside my mother, I wouldn't be here with the rest of you. I would be over in NASA, working as an astronaut. I was almost born a scientist," he joked.

If only delaying birth by five minutes truly could ensure success, staggering bouts of financial distress might be avoided altogether; dangerous treks across borders need not be contemplated; swallows of folklore would draw no stones.

This book's author interviewed dozens of Mexicans, like Genaro Rodríguez, en route to publishing *MANUEL of the Americas, Historia de Fuertes Amores* in 2014.

From the Roybal Files...
The Santa Fe New Mexican, column, April 28, 1996
Little girl's grit alters perspective

On a school day alongside waves of the Pacific Ocean in central Mexico a girl of about 12 worked at a wooden table peddling brightly painted ceramics while her mother sold lace cloth at her own table several yards away.

Still wet after a long walk on the beach, I approached the girl's table and inquired in Spanish about the cost of an intricately painted turtle that was about the size of my hand.

"Fifty *pesos*," the girl replied in Spanish, the language to be used throughout our brief visit.

At an exchange rate of just more then seven *pesos* per one U.S. dollar, the price quoted came down to about seven bucks American.

"And for that one," I asked, pointing to a slightly larger piece that incorporated faces of the sun and moon.

"Fifty *pesos*," she said again, glancing toward her mother as if to get approval to engage in what she anticipated was about to unfold.

She anticipated correctly.

"What's your name?" I asked.

"Carolina," she said, bowing her head just slightly.

The game was on. It was more fundamental for her than for me. I was, after all, on vacation with a little money to spend. She was out to make money to help keep her family afloat.

"It's a pretty name," I said. "How much for both?"

Carolina was barely as young as my own daughter. I jostled with her, in fact, as I do regularly with my daughter. Carolina, it immediately became clear, had been taught to hold her own.

She looked again at her mother then said, "Eighty-five *pesos*. It's a good deal for both."

"I don't know. I'm liable to get them home and nobody will like them," I said.

"How can they not like them?" she asked. "Look, it's good work. Eighty *pesos*," she offered.

I kicked the sand once or twice. "Seventy *pesos*," I countered.

Carolina was dismayed.

"No, no," she said. "That's barely more than what we pay for them."

In concealed jest, I turned to a new tact.

"We're friends," I said. "Friends treat each other well in situations like this."

"We're not friends!" Carolina shot back.

"Sure we are," I replied, reaching into the pockets of my shorts for several large pebbles I plucked off the beach earlier in the day. "Look, I have the three prettiest rocks that rolled onto the beach today. I was going to take them home and sell them for ten *pesos* each. Thirty *pesos*. But if you take all three, I'll let you have them for fifteen *pesos*. That's half price—and it's because we're friends."

"What am I going to do with rocks?" Carolina inquired in disbelief.

I paused for a second or two while looking around us and then up toward the blue sky. "Why, you can throw them at the pelicans," I said. "You can throw them up at the pelicans so they don't get your table dirty."

I cracked a small smile. Carolina smiled back broadly as if to acknowledge that the game was up and probably to signal relief that this *Americano* apparently was not really as crazy as he first appeared to be.

I gave her 85 *pesos*, wished her a good day and walked away with two ceramic pieces that today add a little more character to my old adobe house about 1,500 miles north from where Carolina and I engaged in a little business.

On those frequent occasions when I'm resting far afield, I seek out people like Carolina. Merely looking at her and imagining her limited prospects could have been disheartening. Getting to know her, even just a little, was inspiring. I suspect there always will be people like her, out sharpening skills that will get them through life, no matter that they ought to be in school.

Carolina likely will never own a home full of worldly possessions. She almost certainly never will rise to a position from which she can put a stop to the corruption that rips at parts of her country and fuels rampant poverty. That will have to come some day from people in Mexico who consider leadership to mean more than merely getting to stand at the front of the line.

That, to some degree, is a problem faced by all countries, I suppose.

21
Back Home in Cundiyó

The small real estate ad in a 1988 copy of *The Santa Fe New Mexican* told of a small house in Cundiyó, ideal for artists or writers. With a large spruce tree standing tall like a sentry in the yard just off State Road 503, the property was near two mountain streams that merged before flowing into Santa Cruz Lake, read the ad.

To me, it didn't sound like an ideal hangout for artists or writers. It sounded like my grandparents' old adobe home, the home where my mother and her thirteen siblings took life along with their first steps into a world of simple joys and trying times.

The four-room home had been sold out of the family and a few years later was back on the market. It didn't stay on the market long. I moved my own young family into the home that was built years before New Mexico acquired statehood and was instrumental in shaping the lives of so many, including mine.

Oh, to be sure, there would be plenty of writing and artwork in the home after I purchased it. I tended to the writing. My wife, Marlene, and daughters, Carla and Rebecca, tended to the art. Son, Pablo, contributed with music, much of it his own.

While cultivating our interests and skills, we were able to dip into an old, lingering culture that encourages thoughtful examination—and appreciation—of some of the most-basic elements of life, many of which tend to be doused and forgotten even in the most culturally sensitive cities.

I was able to visit, learn and laugh with my *Tía* Rebecca and *Tío* Emiliano during their final years of life. My neighbor, Félix, was the colorful character who, with a shovel at his side, spoke incredulously about how others came to advise against killing snakes and drove in vehicles from city stop to city stop with dogs on their laps.

I mined many stories from my new surroundings, which of course weren't new at all.

In time I doubled the size of Grandpa Pedro Vigil's home, most of the work done with my own hands. I preserved an old ceiling board on which my grandfather wrote in pencil: 11-15-1907. Then I added a ceiling board of my own to record the passage of time as well as the presence of new family members. Grandchildren Sofía, José Martín, Seth and Brianna became the fifth generation to bring new adaptations of life into the old home with squeaky hardwood floors.

Dial telephones were unheard of while Grandpa Pedro lay the adobes for his home in the early 1900s. He was a stoic man but even he might have smiled to learn that his simple home one day would receive phone calls from the White House. Phones in his home would be used to connect to the internet through which speeches written inside the adobe walls would be dispatched to a member of the president's cabinet in Washington, DC, for delivery in distant parts of the world.

Books written inside Grandpa Pedro's old home would be distributed from Peru to Spain.

In 1988, in so many ways, I came back home to Cundiyó. Truchas, the treasured community of my father's childhood, is just a few miles up the hill. Spirits of the two old villages have never left my side.

The Cundiyó home built before statehood by Pedro Vigil was expanded in time to welcome elders and children of the Vigil-Roybal family as well as many others.

Four generations of an extended family assembled at the author's Cundiyó home in 2017 to welcome the group's latest member, José Martín Córdova.

Sofía Córdova enjoys the garden of her grandparents' Cundiyó home.

José Martín Córdova rides Grandpa David.

Bibliography and Newspaper Articles

Books:

Bishop, Greg. *Project Beta, The Story of Paul Bennewitz, National Security, and the Creation of a Modern UFO Myth*. New York, New York: Pocket Books, 2005.

Cargo, David Francis. *Lonesome Dave, The Story of New Mexico Governor David Francis Cargo*. Santa Fé, New Mexico: Sunstone Press, 2010.

Ebright, Malcolm. *Land Grants & Lawsuits in Northern New Mexico*. Albuquerque, New Mexico: University of New Mexico Press, 1994.

King, Bruce, as told to Charles Poling. *Cowboy in the Roundhouse, A Political Life*. Santa Fé, New Mexico: Sunstone Press, 1998.

Koch, Jamie. *New Mexico Political History, 1967–2015: Conversations With Those Directly Involved*. Santa Fé, New Mexico: Sunstone Press, 2018.

Madrid, Arturo. *In The Country Of Empty Crosses, The Story of a Hispano-Protestant Family in Catholic New Mexico*. San Antonio, Texas: Trinity University Press, 2012.

Márquez, Rubén Sálaz. *New Mexico, A Brief Multi-History*. Albuquerque, New Mexico: Cosmic House, 1999.

McWilliams, Carey. *North From Mexico, The Spanish-Speaking People of the United States*. New York, New York: Greenwood Press Publishers, 1968.

Poling-Kempes, Lesley. *Valley of Shining Stone, The Story of Abiquiu*. Tucson, Arizona: The University of Arizona Press, 1997.

Roybal, David. *Chief of Police, The Career of Richard CdeBaca During Extraordinary Times in New Mexico 1956–1994*. Santa Fé, New Mexico: Sunstone Press, 2013.

Roybal, David. *MANUEL of the Americas, Historia de Fuertes Amores*. Santa Fé, New Mexico: David Roybal Communications, 2014.

Roybal, David. *Nerve of a Patriot, Global Trails of Leveo V. Sánchez*. Santa Fé, New Mexico: David Roybal Communications, 2015.

Roybal, David. *Taking on Giants, Fabián Chávez Jr. and New Mexico Politics*. Albuquerque, New Mexico: University of New Mexico Press, 2008.

Sánchez, Victoria D. de. *In The Footsteps of An Educator, The Memoirs of Victoria D. de Sánchez*. Alexandria. Virginia: 1989.

Swastika yearbook. Compiled by *Swastika* Yearbook staff. Las Cruces, New Mexico: New Mexico State University, 1972.

Trujillo-Oviedo, Patricia. *Images of America, Chimayó*. Charleston, South Carolina: Arcadia Publishing, 2012.

Newspapers:

Roybal, David. "Northern New Mexico Lifestyle Story Shared." *The Santa Fe New Mexican*, December 1978.

Roybal, David. "Cracking Down on Questions," "Allegations Making Many Mad." *The Santa Fe New Mexican*, August 26, 1990; December 6, 1990.

Roybal, David. "King and Fans Join Together To Do the Wave." *The Santa Fe New Mexican*, August 4, 1991.

Roybal, David. "It's the Children, Not the Dads, Who Really Make Father's Day." *The Santa Fe New Mexican*, July 18, 1993.

Roybal, David. "No Candidate Will Declare as 'Pick's Boy'." *The Santa Fe New Mexican*, October 31, 1993.

Roybal, David. "Angry Outbursts Might Cost Jaramillo Election, And More." *The Santa Fe New Mexican*, November 19, 1993.

Roybal, David. "Will Land Swap Become King's Waterloo?" *The Santa Fe New Mexican*, December 21, 1993.

Roybal, David. "It's Time to Lead, Not Manage." *The Santa Fe New Mexican*, February 20, 1994.

Roybal, David. "David Roybal Column." *The Santa Fe New Mexican*, June 12, 1994.

Roybal, David. "Memory Falls into Ghostly Seasonal Trap." *The Santa Fe New Mexican*, October 31, 1995.

Roybal, David. "Little Girl's Grit Alters Perspective." *The Santa Fe New Mexican*, April 28, 1996.

Roybal, David. "Time Has its Own Pace in Villages of Northern New Mexico." *The Santa Fe New Mexican*, December 23, 2002.

Roybal, David. "A Ghost Story for Halloween." *The Santa Fe New Mexican*, October 19, 2003.

Roybal, David. "DWI Question: Political Sign of the Times." *The Santa Fe New Mexican*, July 4, 2004.

Roybal, David. "Fancy Names, Fancy Prices Not For Me." *The Santa Fe New Mexican*, August 19, 2004.

Roybal, David. "All New Mexico Kids Deserve Opportunity." *Albuquerque Journal*, July 4, 2006.

Roybal, David. "Painful War Souvenir Trumps Unreturned Salute." *Albuquerque Journal*, April 17, 2007.

Roybal, David. "Richardson Needs to Leave New Mexico Out of It." *Albuquerque Journal*, June 12, 2007.

Roybal, David. "Alberto Gonzales' Failures Are His Own." *Albuquerque Journal*, September 2, 2007.

Roybal, David. "My Climate Change Theory Croaked – Or Not." *Albuquerque Journal*, September 9, 2008.

www.ingramcontent.com/pod-product-compliance
Lightning Source LLC
Chambersburg PA
CBHW020217170426
43201CB00007B/244